Beyond Control

BEYOND CONTROL
*Drug Prohibition, Gun Regulation,
and the Search for Sensible Alternatives*

JACOB SULLUM

Essex, Connecticut

Prometheus Books
An imprint of The Globe Pequot Publishing Group, Inc.
64 South Main Street
Essex, CT 06426
www.globepequot.com

Distributed by NATIONAL BOOK NETWORK

Copyright © 2025 by Jacob Sullum

All rights reserved. No part of this book may be reproduced in any form or by any electronic or mechanical means, including information storage and retrieval systems, without written permission from the publisher, except by a reviewer who may quote passages in a review.

British Library Cataloguing in Publication Information available

Library of Congress Cataloging-in-Publication Data available
ISBN 978-1-4930-8466-1 (cloth : alk. paper)
ISBN 978-1-4930-8467-8 (electronic)

∞™ The paper used in this publication meets the minimum requirements of American National Standard for Information Sciences—Permanence of Paper for Printed Library Materials, ANSI/NISO Z39.48-1992.

*To Francine, Meira, and Avital,
who no longer keep me company during the day
or fall asleep to my bedtime stories at night
but still like a good argument*

Contents

Introduction: The Twin Crusades 1

Chapter 1: The Racist Roots of Drug Laws 21
Chapter 2: The Racist Roots of Gun Laws 53
Chapter 3: The Drug War in Black and White 77
Chapter 4: Gun Control in Black and White 101
Chapter 5: Drugs, Guns, and the Constitution 127
Chapter 6: Drug-Related Violence. 159
Chapter 7: The False Promise of Gun Control. 185
Chapter 8: Hope for Help 213

Acknowledgments 243
Notes 245
Index 289

Introduction

The Twin Crusades

"Unjust, Cruel, and Even Irrational"

Weldon Angelos grew up in a musical family. His father, a Greek immigrant, aspired to be a country singer, while relatives on his mother's side were jazz and country musicians. Angelos's tastes were somewhat different: By his early twenties, he had gotten a start as a rap producer.[1]

Angelos had collaborated with well-known hip-hop artists, including Snoop Dogg. He had his own label in Salt Lake City, Extravagant Records. To supplement his income and help support his two young children, Angelos also sold marijuana, which is how he ended up with a 55-year federal prison sentence at the age of 25.[2]

That jaw-dropping punishment, demanded by a statute aimed at armed drug dealers, starkly illustrates how drug and gun laws interact to produce results that make a mockery of justice. In vainly striving to control inanimate objects they associate with disorder and violence, legislators create penalties that send human beings to prison for years, decades, or sometimes the rest of their lives.

Angelos was not exactly a cannabis kingpin. His 2003 arrest, which stemmed from an investigation by a joint state and federal task force, was based on three eight-ounce sales to a childhood acquaintance who had become a police informant. "I really didn't want to deal with this guy, because he was one of those people that no one really wanted to be around," Angelos recalls. But "he was bugging me and bugging me, and so I really just did it kind of to shut him up."[3] The proceeds totaled about

$1,000. When police searched Angelos's apartment, they found $18,000 in cash and two bags containing about three pounds of marijuana.

The cops also found three semi-automatic pistols—two in a safe and one in a locked briefcase—that Angelos, who had applied for a concealed carry permit, says he kept because he "needed something to protect my family." When he was growing up, he explains, "we lived in a rough neighborhood," and his father, who "had an affinity for firearms" and used to take him target shooting, "always said it's important to keep a gun around."[4] But because of those guns, Angelos was convicted on three counts of possessing a firearm "during and in relation to" or "in furtherance of" drug trafficking. The first such offense carried a five-year mandatory minimum sentence, which rose to 25 years for each subsequent offense, with all sentences to be served consecutively.[5]

"I really didn't believe that this was even a possibility," says Angelos, who initially was not familiar with federal mandatory minimums. "I thought I was just being threatened because they were hoping that arresting me and putting pressure on me would lead to the arrest of famous rap artists. And when that didn't happen, they threw the book at me."[6]

Angelos turned down a proposed plea deal that involved a 15-year sentence for one count of selling marijuana and the associated gun charge. He thought "15 years for $300 worth of marijuana as a first-time offender" was grossly disproportionate. He had "just signed a major record deal, had two young boys," and thought "this would ruin my life."[7] Prosecutors seemed determined to do that one way or another. After Angelos rejected their offer, they obtained an indictment that included a litany of 20 charges with combined potential mandatory minimums of 105 years—a vivid example of the prosecutorial power that helps explain why 97 percent of federal criminal convictions are based on guilty pleas.[8]

"I was facing a hundred years," Angelos recalls, "but in my mind, you know, this is America. There's a judge that can intervene. I just felt that something would change. I was in denial." He "didn't start realizing" the full gravity of the situation until the trial. "My attorney tried explaining it to me, but I was really ignorant because I'd never been in the system," he says. "And once I was convicted, then it sunk in, like, OK, this is real; this does happen in America. My attorney looked at me and said 'that's

55 years' when I got convicted on those three charges. That's the point when I realized, OK, this is serious: I'm going to prison for 55 years."[9]

A jury convicted Angelos on 13 counts in addition to the gun charges. Paul Cassell, the federal judge who sentenced Angelos in 2004, tried his best to minimize the prison term, giving him just one day for those other charges. But Cassell was legally bound to impose the 55-year mandatory minimum, which he called "unjust, cruel, and even irrational." He noted that it was "far in excess of the sentence imposed for such serious crimes as aircraft hijacking, second-degree murder, espionage, kidnapping, aggravated assault, and rape." He urged then-President George W. Bush to "commute Mr. Angelos' sentence to something that is more in accord with just and rational punishment."[10]

Just and rational punishment has never been a hallmark of the twin crusades against drugs and guns. These long-running policies both aim to promote safety, and they are often rationalized by the rhetoric of saving children and protecting public health. Drug control and gun control are symbolically potent. But there is little evidence that either has had a positive impact and much evidence that they have caused serious harm. Both criminalize conduct that violates no one's rights, leading to unjust arrests, harsh prison terms, and the erosion of civil liberties, especially the right to armed self-defense and protections against unreasonable searches and seizures.

The burdens imposed by these two public safety strategies reinforce each other, since gun possession increases penalties for drug offenses and drug offenses disqualify people from legally possessing guns. Those burdens fall disproportionately on people of modest means and members of racial and ethnic minorities—a fact that progressives frequently decry in connection with the war on drugs but tend to overlook when the disparities arise from enforcement of gun laws. And while progressives often note the racist roots of drug prohibition, they are less apt to recognize that gun control has a similarly sinister history. There is a corresponding disconnect among conservatives, who tend to be skeptical of gun control but are much more inclined to support drug prohibition.

"Many citizens who enthusiastically favor criminal laws to punish illicit drug users vehemently oppose criminal laws to punish gun possession," the philosopher Douglas Husak notes. "The converse is true as well. Many commentators who are critical of criminal laws against drug users believe the state should do more to punish gun owners."[11]

Maj Toure, a libertarian who founded the group Black Guns Matter in 2016, frequently challenges fellow Second Amendment advocates to rethink their support for the war on drugs, which he argues is inconsistent with conservative principles. Meanwhile, he says, his "friends on the left" argue that "we need more gun control," to which he replies: "So you support racist policies that unnecessarily target black and brown people?"[12]

Those two camps, this book aims to show, have more in common than they generally recognize. The concerns that animate critics of drug prohibition and critics of gun control are fundamentally similar: Both complain that the government is overstepping its proper bounds by treating people as criminals for no good reason. In doing so, they say, the government violates fundamental rights based on arbitrary legal distinctions. Progressives ask why people should go to jail simply because they consume psychoactive substances that politicians do not like. Conservatives ask the same question about people who own firearms that politicians do not like or who possess guns without meeting burdensome regulatory requirements. Some conservatives have even begun to question the justice and constitutionality of punishing gun owners who belong to broadly defined categories of "prohibited persons."

The striking historical and contemporary parallels between drug control and gun control show that both sets of skeptics are right. Recognizing that commonality can help us begin to discuss alternatives and ultimately replace unjust and ineffective strategies with policies and programs that might actually work. That means focusing on harms rather than drugs and guns themselves, understanding how current policies magnify those harms, and pursuing strategies that are more carefully tailored to the problems that politicians say they are trying to address.

Those politicians are not always consistent on these issues, as illustrated by the evolving positions of the two major-party candidates who faced off in the 2020 presidential election. Over the years, Joe Biden and Donald Trump contradicted themselves as well as each other when they discussed what the government should do about drugs and guns. Biden transformed from a zealous drug warrior into a reformer, while Trump went from advocating legalization to promising aggressive enforcement of prohibition, even while criticizing Biden's legislative record as excessively punitive. And although the two men were seemingly far apart on gun control by 2020, they had previously expressed strikingly similar views.

That history illustrates two points that are worth keeping in mind as we explore the parallels between drug control and gun control. First, people do change their minds about these issues, whether because of political expedience, emerging evidence, or a combination of the two. Second, even the bitterest adversaries can agree that both drug laws and gun laws are problematic in at least some ways.

"A Big Mistake"

For decades, Biden was one of the most vociferous drug warriors in Congress. During most of his 36 years as a Delaware senator, he was eager to show that Democrats could be even tougher on drugs than Republicans. His legislative legacy includes the top anti-drug hits of the 1980s and 1990s.[13]

Biden played a leading role in establishing the mandatory minimum sentences that sent drug offenders to prison for years or decades based on nothing more than the weight of the substances they possessed, sold, or helped distribute. His enthusiasm for ever-harsher punishment included a federal sentencing scheme that treated smoked cocaine as if it were 100 times worse than the snorted kind and prescribed a minimum five-year sentence for possessing as little as five grams of crack—less than the weight of two sugar packets.[14]

"We have to hold every drug user accountable," Biden declared in 1989, "because if there were no drug users, there would be no appetite for drugs, and there would be no market for them."[15] He bragged about putting more cops on the street and subsidizing prison construction.[16] Just a few years before he entered the 2020 presidential race, he was still publicly proud of the incarceration-expanding Violent Crime Control and Law Enforcement Act—or, as he preferred to call it, "the 1994 Biden Crime Bill."[17]

During his 2020 presidential campaign, Biden presented himself as a reformer who had seen the error of his old punitive instincts. He conceded that the scientifically baseless penal distinction between crack and cocaine powder, which resulted in glaring racial disparities, was "a big mistake."[18] He switched from pushing mandatory minimums to advocating their elimination. He promised to "decriminalize the use of cannabis," "automatically expunge all prior cannabis use convictions," and "leave decisions regarding legalization for recreational use up to the states." He said he would "broadly use his clemency power" to commute the sentences of nonviolent drug offenders and specifically said anyone who had been convicted of marijuana offenses "should be let out of jail."[19]

Fifteen months after taking office, Biden took a first step toward delivering on his promise to ameliorate the damage done by the draconian drug policies he had long supported. He shortened the sentences of 75 nonviolent drug offenders, the first in a series of commutations that ultimately totaled more than 4,000, far exceeding the previous record set by Barack Obama.[20]

In October 2022, Biden announced a mass pardon for people convicted of simple marijuana possession under federal law.[21] Those marijuana pardons covered thousands of Americans. But because they excluded people who had been convicted of growing or distributing marijuana, they did not free any prisoners.[22] Although Biden claimed he was "expunging thousands of convictions," that was not true: Federal pardons do not entail expungement of criminal records, which would require new legislation.[23] And despite his promise not to interfere with state laws allowing medical or recreational use of marijuana, Biden continued to support federal prohibition, unlike nearly every candidate he had beaten for the 2020 Democratic nomination—including Kamala Harris, who began supporting marijuana legalization in 2018 and later became Biden's vice president before replacing him as their party's 2024 presidential candidate.[24]

The same day he announced the marijuana pardons, Biden directed Attorney General Merrick Garland and the Department of Health and Human Services (HHS) to review marijuana's classification under the Controlled Substances Act.[25] Since 1970, marijuana had been listed in

Schedule I, a category supposedly reserved for drugs with a high potential for abuse and no accepted medical use—drugs so dangerous that they cannot be used safely even under a doctor's supervision. Biden noted that "we classify marijuana at the same level as heroin" and treat it as "more serious than fentanyl," which he said "makes no sense."[26]

In August 2023, HHS said marijuana should be moved to Schedule III, which includes prescription drugs such as ketamine, Tylenol with codeine, and anabolic steroids.[27] The Justice Department accepted that recommendation in May 2024, when it proposed a rule to that effect.[28] The shift conceded that marijuana's Schedule I status was scientifically unsupportable, as critics had argued for half a century.[29] But its practical implications were limited.

Moving cannabis to Schedule III would facilitate medical research by eliminating regulatory requirements that are specific to Schedule I.[30] It also would allow state-licensed marijuana suppliers to deduct standard business expenses on their federal income tax returns, eliminating a crushing financial burden that makes it hard to turn a profit, let alone invest in expansion.[31] But those businesses would remain criminal enterprises under federal law, which makes it hard for them to obtain financial services and exposes them to the risk of prosecution and civil forfeiture.[32] While an annually renewed spending rider shielded medical marijuana suppliers from those threats, prosecutorial discretion was the only protection for businesses serving the recreational market.[33] Rescheduling marijuana would not even make it legally available as a prescription medicine, which would require regulatory approval of specific cannabis-based products.[34]

Despite Biden's avowed concern about the barriers to education, housing, and employment that people with marijuana records face, neither his pardons nor marijuana's pending reclassification eliminated those collateral consequences. Nor did they address the legal disabilities triggered by marijuana convictions, cannabis consumption, or participation in the cannabis industry, such as the loss of Second Amendment rights under gun laws and ineligibility for admission, legal residence, and citizenship under immigration law.[35]

The steps that Biden touted as "marijuana reform," in short, left federal pot prohibition essentially untouched, which is how he wanted it. By 2024, 38 states had legalized medical marijuana, and 24 of them, accounting for most of the U.S. population, also allowed recreational use.[36] More than two-thirds of Americans, including nearly nine out 10 Democrats and more than five out of 10 Republicans, favored legalization.[37] But Biden, unlike Harris, continued to resist the idea.

More generally, Biden continued to parrot hoary rhetoric that suggested the main problem with the war on drugs was that it had not been waged aggressively enough. He promised to "beat the opioid epidemic" by "stop[ping] the flow of illicit drugs" and "working with state and local law enforcement to go after the traffickers."[38]

For more than a century, politicians had been making the same promise, claiming they could stop Americans from consuming forbidden intoxicants by interdicting the supply and prosecuting traffickers. And for more than a century, they had failed to deliver on that promise, not for lack of trying but because the economics of prohibition doom all such efforts.

"You Have to Legalize Drugs"

Donald Trump acknowledged that reality in 1990, when he was famous as a billionaire New York developer rather than a politician. Trump called the war on drugs "a joke" and recommended legalization instead. "We're losing badly the war on drugs," he said during a speech in Miami. "You have to legalize drugs to win that war. You have to take the profit away from these drug czars." In an interview after the speech, Trump said he hoped "people will start to realize that this is the only answer; there is no other answer."[39]

By "drug czars," Trump meant traffickers, not the appointees charged with running the U.S. Office of National Drug Control Policy, which a Biden-backed law had created two years before.[40] In conceding that the war on drugs was unwinnable, Trump was at odds with Biden and nearly every other prominent politician.

As a Republican presidential candidate 25 years later, Trump implausibly claimed his 1990 remarks did not count as an endorsement of legalization. "I said it's something that should be studied and maybe should continue to be studied," he said. "But it's not something I'd be willing to do right now."[41] On marijuana legalization specifically, Trump's position in 2016 was essentially the same as Hillary Clinton's.[42] Although he was not keen on the policy, which he claimed had led to "some big problems" in Colorado, he said, "I really believe we should leave it up to the states."[43]

By 2024, Trump was endorsing the legalization of recreational marijuana in Florida, his state of residence. "Someone should not be a criminal in Florida" for possessing marijuana "when this is legal in so many other States," he said.[44] Trump also said he supported marijuana rescheduling and cannabis banking reform.[45]

Regarding the war on drugs more generally, Trump doubled down on the usual approach. "I'm gonna create borders," he said in a 2016 campaign video. "No drugs are coming in. We're gonna build a wall. You know what I'm talking about. You have confidence in me. Believe me, I will solve the problem."[46]

During his first term as president, Trump never managed to build that wall, let alone stop drugs from "coming in." After he was elected to a second term in 2024, he blamed Mexico and Canada for that failure, threatening to impose punitive tariffs on them "until such time as Drugs, in particular Fentanyl, and all Illegal Aliens stop this Invasion of our Country!"[47]

Trump's tough anti-drug stance did not stop him from commuting more than 60 drug sentences during his first term, starting with Alice Marie Johnson, a first-time offender who had received a life sentence for participating in a Memphis cocaine trafficking operation.[48] "You have many people like Mrs. Johnson," Trump told Fox News in 2018. "There are people in jail for really long terms." The solution, he added, had to go beyond clemency. "There has to be a reform, because it's very unfair right now," he said. "It's very unfair to African Americans. It's very unfair to everybody."[49]

True to his word, Trump supported the FIRST STEP Act, a package of criminal justice reforms that he signed into law at the end of 2018. Among other things, that law retroactively applied the reduced crack penalties that Congress had approved in 2010, shortened sentences for repeat drug offenders, expanded "good time" credits for federal prisoners, barred the stacking of multiple firearm charges in a single drug case (the practice that generated Weldon Angelos's 55-year sentence), and widened the "safety valve" that allows low-level, nonviolent offenders to avoid mandatory minimums.[50]

In backing the FIRST STEP Act, Trump was taking the advice of his son-in-law Jared Kushner, who argued that the president could attract support from African Americans and white moderates by taking a stand against the excesses of the war on drugs.[51] Toward that end, Trump highlighted Johnson's case during his 2019 State of the Union address, in a 2020 Super Bowl ad, and at the 2020 Republican National Convention, where Johnson gave a grateful speech.[52] During the 2020 campaign, Trump attacked Biden from the left on drug policy, faulting him for pushing harsh laws that had disproportionately hurt black people.[53] Trump's campaign picked up that theme again in 2024 before Biden was replaced by Harris, saying, "We must not forget that it was Joe Biden who was a key figure in passing the 1994 Crime Bill, which disproportionately harmed Black communities through harsh sentencing laws and increased incarceration rates."[54]

After he lost the 2020 election, Trump complained that he did not get the political benefit he expected from supporting drug policy reform. "Did it for African Americans," he told a *New York Times* reporter in 2022. "Nobody else could have gotten it done. Got zero credit."[55]

Notwithstanding that bitter experience, Trump granted "a full and unconditional pardon" to Silk Road founder Ross Ulbricht on the second day of his second term. Trump noted that Ulbricht, who at that point had served 11 years in federal prison, "was given two life sentences, plus 40 years," for creating a website that connected drug buyers with drug sellers, a punishment that the president described as "ridiculous."[56]

Trump's stance on drug penalties seemed to contradict his long-standing tough-on-crime instincts. Even as he decried "very unfair" drug sentences, he expressed admiration for brutal drug warriors like Philippine President Rodrigo Duterte, who likened himself to Adolf Hitler while urging the murder of drug users.[57] Trump bragged about his "great relationship" with Duterte, who he said had done an "unbelievable job on the drug problem."[58] Consistent with that take, Trump periodically endorsed the death penalty for drug offenders—a recommendation he reiterated during his 2024 campaign, saying he would urge Congress to "ensure that drug smugglers and traffickers can receive the Death Penalty."[59]

During a 2023 interview with Trump, Fox News anchor Bret Baier pointed out that someone like Johnson would have been "killed under your plan." Trump was flummoxed. "No, no, no," he said. "It would depend on the severity," he added. He also noted that the death penalty he imagined would not apply retroactively to Johnson herself and suggested that, had it been the law at the time, it would have deterred her from getting involved in drug dealing.[60]

"I Generally Oppose Gun Control"

While Biden and Trump had similar views on drug policy by 2020, Biden was notably more inclined to support gun control. But here, too, both men's views had evolved.

As a senator in 1985, Biden voted for the Firearm Owners' Protection Act, which was backed by the National Rifle Association (NRA). That law, which passed both houses of Congress by overwhelming margins, included several provisions that were welcomed by gun rights supporters, along with new firearm restrictions.

The law allowed interstate sales of rifles and shotguns, provided the transfers were completed in person and complied with state law; restricted enforcement of federal gun laws; tightened the definition of gun dealers who were required to obtain federal licenses; eliminated paperwork requirements for ammunition sales; and allowed people to travel with unloaded firearms through jurisdictions with strict gun laws, as long as they complied with the law at their destination. At the same time, the law banned the sale of newly produced machine guns to civilians and added to the categories of people who are not allowed to possess firearms.[61]

"I believe the compromises that are now a part of this bill have resulted in a balanced piece of legislation that protects the rights of private gun owners while not infringing on law enforcement's ability to deal with those who misuse guns or violate laws," Biden said in July 1985. "During my twelve and a half years as a member of this body, I have never believed that additional gun control or federal registration of guns would reduce crime. I am convinced that a criminal who wants a firearm can get one through illegal, nontraceable, unregistered sources, with or without gun control."[62]

When he was preparing for his 2020 presidential run, Biden did not want to talk about the Firearm Owners' Protection Act, even though it was supported by many of his fellow Democrats at the time. "Cherry-picking an out-of-context quote from 1986 doesn't even begin to address Joe Biden's unparalleled record on gun safety," Biden campaign spokesman Bill Russo insisted. Russo bragged that Biden "led the way to pass the Brady Bill in 1993, establishing the background check system that has kept guns out of the hands of millions of dangerous individuals," and "authored the bill banning weapons of war—assault weapons and high-capacity magazines—for a decade."[63]

The first law that Russo mentioned, the Brady Handgun Violence Prevention Act of 1993, made the disqualifications imposed by previous legislation enforceable through background checks that it required federally licensed firearm dealers to conduct before completing sales. The second law, the "assault weapon" ban that Congress approved in 1994, was actually introduced by Senator Dianne Feinstein (D–Calif.), but it was folded into the "Biden Crime Bill."[64]

After the "assault weapon" ban expired in 2004, Feinstein repeatedly introduced new, supposedly improved versions. Biden passionately supported that effort, which was a central component of the gun control agenda he outlined during his 2020 campaign. He also supported expanded background checks for gun buyers, a crackdown on homemade guns, and "red flag" laws, which disarm people deemed a danger to themselves or others.[65] The party platform on which Harris ran for president in 2024 likewise endorsed all those policies.[66]

Trump traveled the gun control road in the opposite direction. In his 2000 book *The America We Deserve*, he staked out a middle ground between "the extremes" of the two major political parties. "Democrats want to confiscate all guns, which is a dumb idea because only the law-abiding citizens would turn in their guns and the bad guys would be the only ones left armed," he wrote. "The Republicans walk the NRA line and refuse even limited restrictions." By contrast, he said, "I generally oppose gun control, but I support the ban on assault weapons and I also support a slightly longer waiting period to purchase a gun."[67]

By 2011, when Trump toyed with the idea of seeking the Republican presidential nomination, he was flatly declaring that "I am against gun control."[68] Two years later, he described himself as "a very strong person on the Second Amendment."[69] He staked out a similar position during his 2016 race. In his 2015 book *Great Again*, Trump emphasized the Second Amendment's importance as a safeguard against tyranny and criminal aggression.[70] In interviews, he called himself "a big Second Amendment person," in contrast with then-President Barack Obama, "a non–Second Amendment person." Asked whether he supported new gun laws to prevent mass shootings, Trump replied, "The gun laws have nothing to do with this. This isn't guns. This is about, really, mental illness."[71]

Were there "any circumstances" in which Trump would favor "limiting gun sales of any kind in America?" a moderator asked during a 2016 debate. Trump's response was unqualified: "No."[72]

In reality, Trump did support some forms of gun control, including red flag laws and a ban on firearm possession by people on "no fly" lists.[73] As president, he went so far as to say that police should "take the gun first" and "go through due process second" when they think someone is dangerous.[74] He also spoke favorably of requiring background checks for all gun transfers, raising the minimum age for buying long guns, and banning "assault weapons."[75]

None of those comments translated into policy changes. But Trump did instruct federal regulators to unilaterally ban bump stocks, rifle accessories that facilitate rapid firing, by reinterpreting the legal definition of machine guns. Even supporters of a legislative ban thought that move was legally dubious.[76] The U.S. Supreme Court agreed in 2024, when it ruled that the bump stock ban exceeded regulators' statutory authority.[77]

BIPARTISAN INCONSISTENCIES

Trump, whose party affiliation flipped around from 1987 to 2012, was not a conventional conservative.[78] For a while after the 2017 mass shooting in Las Vegas, it seemed he had reverted to the gun control position he took in 2000, and it was hard to tell what he actually thought. But historically, conservatives generally have taken a dim view of gun control while enthusiastically embracing the war on drugs.

Addressing the NRA's national members banquet in 1983, President Ronald Reagan hailed the defeat of a 1982 California ballot initiative that would have required registration of handguns. Had it passed, he said, police would have been "so busy arresting handgun owners that they would be unable to protect the people against criminals." He acknowledged the "nasty truth" that "those who seek to inflict harm are not fazed by gun control laws" and called for "reform" of "firearms laws which needlessly interfere with the rights of legitimate gun owners."[79]

In the same speech, Reagan touted his determination to "cripple the drug pushers" through mandatory minimum sentences, "firm and speedy application of penalties," and abolition of federal parole. And although he said "we will never disarm any American who seeks to protect his or her family from fear and harm," that was plainly not true, since the drug laws he was keen to enforce underlie a policy that denies millions of Americans the right to armed self-defense even when they have no history of violence.[80]

Reagan saw no contradiction between those two positions, and the same was true of many Republican politicians decades later. Legislators who received high grades from the NRA, signifying opposition to gun control, were often enthusiastic about drug control. Senator Tom Cotton (R–Ark.), for example, promised he would "always defend our Second Amendment rights in Congress" and received a 92 percent position rating from the NRA when he ran for reelection to the Senate in 2020.[81] During the debate over the Trump-backed FIRST STEP Act, Cotton distinguished himself as one of the most gung-ho drug warriors in Washington, opposing even modest sentencing reforms.[82]

Among members of Congress, Senator Mitt Romney (R–Utah) was by far the top beneficiary of campaign spending by the NRA or allied groups and individuals, which totaled more than $13 million in his presidential and Senate races as of October 2023.[83] Romney opposed Utah's 2018 medical marijuana initiative and said the broader legalization movement "reflects the passion and zeal of those members of the pleasure-seeking generation that never grew up."[84] Asked whether "a change in strategy" was appropriate in light of the deadly violence associated with Mexico's crackdown on drug traffickers, he blamed drug users rather than prohibition, saying "they are contributing to the deaths of people around the world."[85]

Right-leaning defenders of the Second Amendment see gun control as misguided, misdirected, and harmful to innocent bystanders. They decry overreaching criminal laws, overzealous enforcement, and invasions of privacy when they are aimed at restricting access to firearms. But gun rights advocates are notably less exercised by similar abuses in the prosecution of the war on drugs.

A mirror image of these attitudes is common across the political aisle. The contrast between Biden's second thoughts about the war on drugs and his continued enthusiasm for restrictions on firearms, like the contrast between Harris's determination to ban "assault weapons" and her support for legalizing marijuana, reflects a broader contradiction. Left-leaning critics of the crusade for a "drug-free society" argue that it is worse than futile, hurting innocent people in pursuit of an impossible goal. But their concerns about ineffectiveness, overcriminalization, police abuse, and mass incarceration tend to melt away when the target is the guns that drug dealers carry rather than the substances they sell.

Consider Senator Cory Booker (D–N.J.), who rebuked Biden for his drug policy record during a 2019 Democratic presidential debate. "There are people right now in prison for life for drug offenses because you stood up and used that 'tough on crime' phony rhetoric that got a lot of people elected but destroyed communities like mine," Booker noted.[86] When it came to drugs, Booker recognized the danger of that approach. But when it came to guns, he favored a panoply of new restrictions that would expand the excuses for imprisoning people—especially black people from communities like his.[87]

Unsurprisingly, the positions of politicians like Cotton, Romney, and Booker are broadly consistent with the views of Republicans and Democrats generally. Republicans are much less inclined to support drug policy reform than Democrats. According to a 2024 Gallup survey, 53 percent of Republicans thought marijuana should be legal, compared to 85 percent of Democrats.[88] In a 2021 survey commissioned by the Drug Policy

Alliance and the American Civil Liberties Union, just 40 percent of Republicans favored "eliminating criminal penalties for drug possession," compared to 85 percent of Democrats.[89] Partisan differences on gun control are even starker: While 88 percent of Democrats favored stricter regulation in a 2023 Gallup poll, just 26 percent of Republicans did.[90]

Given Americans' tendency to self-segregate along political and cultural lines, those partisan differences are reflected in stark legal differences from state to state. In Texas, for example, possessing two ounces or less of marijuana is a Class B misdemeanor, punishable by up to six months in jail and a fine up to $2,000. People who grow marijuana, even for their own use, face felony charges for any amount greater than four ounces.[91] In California, which legalized recreational marijuana use in 2016, public possession of an ounce or less is no offense at all, provided the pot possessor is 21 or older. It is also legal for adults to grow up to six plants and keep the produce at home.[92]

When it comes to gun policy, the pattern is reversed. In Texas, any legal gun owner who is 21 or older may carry a handgun in public for self-defense.[93] In California, public possession of a loaded handgun is legal only with a government-issued permit, which for many years was very difficult to obtain because applicants had to demonstrate "good cause." After a 2022 Supreme Court ruling forced California legislators to eliminate that requirement, they made permits easier to obtain but much harder to use, banning guns from a wide range of "sensitive places."[94] California also imposes many other gun restrictions that Texas does not, including a waiting period for purchases, registration of firearms, a prohibition of private sales, a ban on "assault weapons," and a restriction on magazine capacity.[95]

I have no illusions that anti-gun progressives and anti-drug conservatives will suddenly join hands once they realize that the public safety policies they endorse have the same drawbacks as the ones they resist. But I do hope that exploring the parallels between drug control and gun control will replace certitude with doubt and mutual disdain with some measure of sympathy. Recognizing that noble motives are no guarantee of happy outcomes in either area clarifies the stakes and invites a potentially productive conversation about better-targeted policies that would do more good while causing less harm.

Introduction

Outline of the Book

Chapter 1 traces the racist roots of drug restrictions in the United States, showing that such legislation was driven largely by animosity toward out-groups that political elites viewed as threatening. Opium, cocaine, and cannabis were all ingredients in patent medicines that were available without a prescription in the nineteenth and early twentieth centuries. White, middle-class Americans commonly consumed these drugs for many years before deciding they posed a threat that demanded tight legal restrictions or total prohibition. While racism was by no means the only reason for that shift, it often figured prominently in prohibitionist rhetoric, which portrayed opium smoking as a noxious Chinese habit that was spreading to the white majority; drew a similar link between marijuana and Mexicans, who supposedly became violent and uncontrollable under the weed's influence; and warned that "cocaine-crazed negroes" were wreaking havoc in the South.

Chapter 2 shows that racial prejudice likewise played a central role in early gun control laws, which were driven largely by fear of slave uprisings. Living in a society where white supremacist violence was at first institutionalized and later tolerated, if not abetted, by government officials, African Americans understood the value of the right to arms. Widely admired black leaders ranging from Frederick Douglass to Martin Luther King Jr. embraced the right to armed self-defense as a crucial safeguard against racist aggression.

Just as African Americans widely recognized the potentially lifesaving value of firearms, white supremacists understood the threat that armed black people posed to the existing social order. "There is little doubt that the earliest gun controls in the United States were blatantly racist and elitist in their intent," sociologist William Tonso noted in 1985.[96] "The historical record provides compelling evidence that racism underlies gun control laws—and not in any subtle way," gun policy historian Clayton Cramer agreed a decade later. "Throughout much of American history, gun control was openly stated as a method for keeping blacks and Hispanics 'in their place,' and to quiet the racial fears of whites."[97]

Chapter 3 shows that drug prohibition's racially skewed effects continued long after the bigotry expressed by many of its early supporters was no longer politically or socially acceptable. Black Americans are much more likely than white Americans to be arrested, prosecuted, and incarcerated for drug offenses. That gap cannot be explained by racial differences in rates of drug consumption or drug dealing. And even when policies are advertised as helping black communities, as with the federal crack penalties enacted in the 1980s, their costs fall mostly on those same communities. It is therefore not surprising that progressives commonly describe drug policy reform as a "racial justice" issue.

Chapter 4 shows that gun control, even when divorced from an explicitly racist agenda, also disproportionately burdens African Americans. Gun restrictions tend to be especially severe in high-crime jurisdictions where the need for armed self-defense is most acute, and those jurisdictions include cities with large black populations. Attempts to enforce those restrictions, including "stop and frisk" programs and prosecutions for illegal gun possession, generally do not distinguish between dangerous criminals and otherwise law-abiding people trying to protect themselves from those criminals.

Even when they have no history of violence, black people are especially likely to have criminal records that disqualify them from owning guns, and they are especially likely to be prosecuted for violating that rule. Someone convicted of a nonviolent drug felony, for example, is not allowed to possess a gun for self-defense even decades later. Given the racial skew in drug prosecutions, that person is disproportionately likely to be black. African Americans are also overrepresented among drug defendants who receive additional punishment because they own guns, even if they never use them to threaten or harm anyone.

Chapter 5 considers the constitutional implications of drug and gun laws, which would be deeply troubling even if those laws affected all racial and ethnic groups equally. National regulation of drugs and guns required a broad conception of congressional authority that was at odds with the principle of enumerated powers and our federalist system of government. Enforcement of drug and gun laws, whether at the federal or state level, raised numerous other constitutional issues, which generally have been resolved in favor of broader government power, wider police discretion, expanding encroachments on privacy, and less individual freedom. One notable exception to that general trend in recent years has been the Supreme Court's Second Amendment rulings, which overturned several long-standing gun restrictions and cast doubt on the constitutionality of many others.

Chapter 6 highlights additional costs imposed by the war on drugs, starting with the frequently horrifying violence it invites by authorizing police to invade people's homes in search of substances that politicians have deemed intolerable. Like alcohol prohibition, the war on drugs also feeds violence by creating a black market where that is the primary way to resolve disputes, fosters official corruption, and makes intoxicant use more dangerous, magnifying the harms it is supposed to prevent.

Chapter 7 scrutinizes the logic of what politicians like to call "common-sense gun safety legislation." The effectiveness of gun control is hotly contested. But legal, political, and practical realities severely limit what it can reasonably be expected to accomplish, and decades of research have produced little evidence that popular prescriptions such as "assault weapon" bans, "universal background checks," and red flag laws work as advertised. Gun policies, which tend to impose broad restrictions in the hope of reaching a small subset of concern, often seem ill-designed to alleviate the problems they aim to address.

Chapter 8 closes the book by outlining alternatives to the twin crusades against drugs and guns, based on the seemingly modest but ultimately radical concept of "harm reduction." As applied to drugs, harm reduction rejects a black-and-white choice between abstinence and addiction, recognizing that different patterns of use entail different levels and kinds of risk. It accepts that people will continue to seek altered states of consciousness, as humans always have, and strives to minimize the negative consequences. Crucially, it acknowledges that efforts to prevent substance abuse also can cause harm, and it seeks to minimize both kinds.[98]

As applied to guns, harm reduction likewise requires distinguishing between beneficial and harmful uses of these tools. About one-third of American adults collectively own something like half a billion firearms, only a tiny percentage of which are used to commit crimes or suicide (which accounts for most deaths involving firearms).[99] Law-abiding gun owners use firearms for hunting, target shooting, and self-defense.

The question is how to accommodate those lawful uses while striving to reduce homicides and suicides. The answer lies in policies and programs that focus on those problems instead of trying to limit the general availability of firearms.

Nowadays there is no shortage of critics who argue that the war on drugs is a failure on its own terms and complain that it promotes police abuse, undermines civil liberties, and unjustly punishes people for conduct that is not inherently criminal, which they say is especially troubling because the targets are disproportionately black. Critics of gun control make the same basic points. But these two groups of critics tend to divide along partisan and ideological lines, which blinds them to the common ground they share. This book aims to survey that territory.

Chapter One

The Racist Roots of Drug Laws

"Immediate and Rigid Legislation"
Around 2 a.m. on Monday, December 6, 1875, "a posse of police" led by Captain William Douglass descended upon 609 Dupont Street in San Francisco. The cops arrested Fannie Whitmore, Cora Martinez, James Dennison, and Charles Anderson, along with "two Chinamen who kept the place."[1]

That place, *The San Francisco Examiner* explained, was an "opium den," and this was the first raid conducted under an ordinance that the city's Board of Supervisors had enacted on November 15. The ordinance decreed that "no person shall, in the city and county of San Francisco, keep or maintain, or become an inmate of, or visit, or shall in any way contribute to the support of any place, house, or room, where opium is smoked, or where persons assemble for the purpose of smoking opium, or inhaling the fumes of opium."[2]

The supervisors made that crime a misdemeanor punishable by a fine of $50 to $500—something like 3 to 30 percent of a California clerk's annual salary at the time.[3] Violators also could be jailed for 10 days to six months.

The four patrons and two proprietors nabbed by Douglass and his crew were convicted the same day and paid the minimum fine, so you could say they got off lightly.[4] Then again, the experience of being hauled off to court for conduct that had been perfectly legal a few weeks before must have been jarring. And the sweeping scope of the city's ban, which on its face reached not only commercial establishments but also any private residence "where opium is smoked," was pretty startling too.

San Francisco's ordinance applied only to opium smoking, not to oral consumption of the same drug, which had long been widely available in over-the-counter patent medicines, or even to injections of morphine, an opium derivative. That was not an oversight. The law was designed to target a habit associated with a despised minority—a habit that alarmed police, politicians, and the press precisely because it was associated with a despised minority.

That habit, the Board of Supervisors worried, was spreading to the European-American majority. As the board's Health and Police Committee explained, "opium-smoking establishments kept by the Chinese" were serving "white men and women." These places were "patronized not only by the vicious and the depraved, but are nightly resorted to by young men and women of respectable parentage and by young men engaged in respectable business avocations."[5]

The committee was aghast that "habitués of these infamous resorts inhale the fumes from the opium pipes until a state of stupefaction is produced." And "unless this most dangerous species of dissipation can be stopped in its inception," it warned, "there is great danger that it will become one of the prevalent vices of the city." These "infamous resorts" were "an unmitigated evil," demanding "immediate and rigid legislation."

That "rigid legislation" was the nation's first anti-drug law, if you don't count the legally contentious alcohol bans that 13 states enacted in the mid-nineteenth century, most of which did not last long.[6] It presaged many other laws, some much more draconian, that aimed to stamp out politically disfavored methods of intoxication. And it established a pattern that would be repeated with cocaine and marijuana, which likewise inspired fear at least partly because they were perceived as drugs favored by threatening out-groups.

"The most passionate support for legal prohibition of narcotics has been associated with fear of a given drug's effect on a specific minority," David F. Musto concludes in his classic 1973 drug policy history. "Certain drugs were dreaded because they seemed to undermine essential social restrictions which kept these groups under control."[7]

Scholars such as law professor George Fisher have challenged Musto's gloss, arguing that the main motivation for early anti-drug laws was anxiety about intoxicant use by white Americans, especially young people. Fisher argues, for example, that opium den bans generally were enforced in a way that suggests the authorities did not much care whether Chinese residents smoked opium, provided they kept the habit to themselves.[8] But there is some overlap between Musto's take and Fisher's, since prohibitionists seemed to view opium and other drugs as vectors of contamination that could transmit the debauchery, dissipation, and degradation they saw as characteristic of certain minorities.

That pattern illustrates the point that the distinctions drawn by drug laws are inherently arbitrary, driven by historically contingent factors rather than science or logic. Since all psychoactive substances can be abused, understanding why politicians decide to ban only some of them requires understanding the context in which they make those decisions.

"THE WORST CLASS OF PEOPLE"

Testifying before the California Senate's Special Committee on Chinese Immigration the year after Captain Douglass's raid, another San Francisco police officer, George W. Duffield, averred that "ninety-nine Chinamen out of one hundred smoke opium" and "every house" had an opium den. Duffield described Chinese immigrants as "the worst class of people on the face of the earth."[9]

In a report submitted to the committee on behalf of the San Francisco Police Department, another officer, James R. Rogers, echoed the concerns that had driven the Board of Supervisors to action. "This habit had formerly been practiced by the Chinese almost exclusively, every Chinese house being provided with the drug, together with all the implements for using the article," he said. But in recent years, "not less than eight places have been started, furnished with opium pipes, beds for sleeping off the fumes, etc." Although "these latter places were conducted by Chinamen," they were "patronized by both white men and white women, who visited these dens at all hours of the day and night."[10]

This was a common and persistent complaint. A decade after Rogers's testimony, state Senator John Lenahan (D–San Francisco) warned that

Chinese residents of his city, "all" of whom seemed to "indulge in the vice," were "diligent in the induction of others into the accursed habit." Opium dens were "everywhere," he said, and "we are assured that white men, women, boys and girls are continually made victims of the deadly drug."[11]

Wasn't San Francisco's ban supposed to put an end to that? Despite the 1875 ordinance, Rogers reported in May 1876, "the practice, deeply rooted, still continues." And "in enforcing the law with regard to this matter," he said, police "have found white women and Chinamen side by side under the effects of this drug—a humiliating sight to any one who has anything left of manhood." That comment reflected anxieties about opium-fostered race mixing, including the fear that Chinese men were using the drug to seduce or sexually enslave white women.[12]

In 1873, for example, *The New York Times* reported that "a large number of white girls residing in [Chinatown] are rapidly becoming addicted" to opium smoking. "They live with the Chinese when they can find no other home," the paper said, since "they are always welcome at the firesides of those to whom they sell their souls for the sustenance of their bodies." The author described a "squalidly dressed white girl" at a Chinese "club-house" who was "lying upon a bed, apparently stupid from the opium fumes that filled the rooms." Asked about her, "the man who conducted the writer" replied, "Oh, hard time in New York; young girl hungry. Plenty come here. Chinamen always something to eat, and he like young white girl. He! he!" The guide said this "with a horrible leer," the reporter noted.[13]

"Within the walls of an opium den all fiends are equal," *The San Francisco Examiner* complained in 1889. "Colored men and white women lie about the floors, inhaling the fumes of the drug until, stupefied, they fall into the opium-smokers' sleep. The majority of loose women who ply their trade on the streets in the southern section of the city have been brought to their degraded condition by the use of opium, or by association with users of it."[14] Five years later, the *Examiner* was appalled at "the horrible condition of the opium-depravity" in Salt Lake City, as illustrated by a raid in which "two white women were found lying on the floor completely under the influence of the drug, and almost in a nude state."[15]

In his 1890 book *How the Other Half Lives*, muckraking journalist Jacob Riis described a house in "the Chinese quarter" of New York City inhabited by "women, all white, girls hardly yet grown to womanhood, worshipping nothing save the pipe that has enslaved them body and soul." Riis was disturbed by their equanimity: "Of the depth of their fall no one is more thoroughly aware than these girls themselves; no one is less concerned about it. The calmness with which they discuss it, while insisting illogically upon the fiction of a marriage that deceives no one, is disheartening."[16]

The American Federation of Labor (AFL), making the case against Chinese immigration in 1902, described "little girls no older than 12" who "were found in Chinese laundries under the influence of opium." Through "some wily method," the AFL said, "they have been induced by the Chinese to use the drug," and "what other crimes were committed in those dark and fetid places when these little innocent victims of the Chinamen's wiles were under the influence of the drug are almost too horrible to imagine."[17]

While Riis reported that "scrupulous neatness" was "the distinguishing mark of Chinatown," the California Senate's immigration committee said the opposite was true in San Francisco, describing Chinese homes as "filthy in the extreme." If it weren't for "the healthfulness of our climate," the committee theorized, "our city populations would have long since been decimated by pestilence from these causes."[18]

A member of the committee, Senator Edward J. Lewis (D–Colusa), elaborated on his disgust at life in Chinatown. "We went into places so filthy and dirty that I cannot see how these people live there," he reported. "The fumes of opium, mingled with the odor arising from filth and dirt, made rather a sickening feeling creep over us." Since "the whole Chinese quarter is miserably filthy," he added, "the passage of an ordinance removing them from the city, as a nuisance, would be justifiable."[19]

As politicians like Lewis saw it, the opium problem was inextricably intertwined with the Chinese problem. If the government could not forcibly remove these "filthy" foreigners, as Lewis seemed to prefer, it could at least make life as difficult as possible for them. As former California congressman (and future governor) James Budd put it at an 1885 anti-Chinese meeting in Stockton, it was "the duty" of local authorities to make conditions so "devilishly uncomfortable" that the Chinese would be "glad to leave."[20]

Legislators certainly tried. San Francisco's ban on opium dens, which cities like Stockton imitated, was just one facet of a broad, long-running legal campaign against Chinese immigrants. In addition to attempts at outright bans on Chinese immigration into California, that campaign included special taxes, discriminatory regulations, and restrictions on the right to hunt, fish, own land, vote, and testify in court.[21]

These measures were prompted by large-scale Chinese immigration to the United States, which began during the California Gold Rush in the 1850s. The immigrants were overwhelmingly men, many of whom worked in California's mines and, later, on the transcontinental railroad. Between 1860 and 1880, the Chinese-American population rose from about 35,000 to more than 100,000. That was still less than 1 percent of the total U.S. population, but the vast majority of the immigrants settled in California, where they accounted for 9 percent of the population and perhaps a quarter of workers. Many white Californians were alarmed by this alien presence.[22]

"A Human Tidal Wave"

From the beginning, the influx of Chinese immigrants aroused resentment and hostility, including attacks on Chinese miners by native prospectors.[23] In 1850, the California legislature imposed a $20 monthly tax (about a fifth of an unskilled laborer's earnings) on foreign miners, which was later reduced but also amended so that it applied only to Chinese immigrants.[24] Eight years later, the legislature approved "An Act to Prevent the Further Immigration of Chinese or Mongolians to This State," which the California Supreme Court deemed unconstitutional in an unpublished decision.[25]

The court also rejected an 1862 law imposing a special monthly tax on residents from China who were not already subject to the miner's tax. Legislators were explicit about their goals, calling the bill "An Act to Protect Free White Labor Against Competition With Chinese Coolie Labor, and to Discourage the Immigration of the Chinese Into the State of California." As the justices saw it, those legislators were trying to exercise powers that the U.S. Constitution assigned to the federal government: the imposition of import duties and regulation of commerce with foreign nations.[26]

Economic developments stoked the anti-Chinese sentiment reflected in such laws. The Gold Rush was over by the end of the 1850s, and the Pacific Railroad was completed in 1869. The "Long Depression" of the 1870s added to anxieties about economic competition from Chinese immigrants while simultaneously driving them toward trades and small businesses previously dominated by white Californians.[27]

The complaints about Chinese competition, which were amplified by labor unions, the Workingmen's Party (founded in 1877), and middle-class businessmen, turned virtues—thrift and a strong work ethic—into vices. Anti-Chinese agitators groused that the immigrants were willing to work hard for less pay because they kept their living expenses low, subsisting on meager diets and tolerating the crowded conditions decried by state legislators. Although that complaint was hard to reconcile with the portrayal of Chinese residents as indolent opium addicts, nativists were unfazed by the inconsistency.

On a Sunday in April 1876, the *San Francisco Chronicle* filled its front page with an article about the "Chinese Problem" that weaved together these contradictory themes. "Celestials," it said, were prone to opium smoking, gambling, prostitution, and "other vices." But they were also hardworking and entrepreneurial, creating "a human tidal wave" of "disastrous competition" for "our miners, mechanics, and even tradesmen." They had opened laundries, cigar shops, "small ware" stores, and vegetable stands. These "peculiar people" had "quaint and curious" customs, and they were experts at "economizing space," combining "ingenuity and industry" with "the vices and abominations of the Chinese character." They had no "higher ambition than that of hoarding money."[28]

The *Chronicle* devoted a section of the article to "the opium dens of San Francisco," which it said "probably number several hundred." In contrast with the claims of cops like Duffield and politicians like Lenahan, the paper allowed that "the practice of opium-smoking among the

Chinese" was "perhaps not universal" but said it nevertheless "prevails to an alarming extent."

The article, which described opium's subjective effects as "delicious and entrancing," also cast doubt on the distinction that the city's Board of Supervisors had drawn between modes of consumption. "The use of opium in this form does not appear to produce the baneful results arising from eating the drug," it said. "Nor is there any danger of fatal result, as from overdosing with morphine." In fact, the paper said, "opium-smoking may be regarded as simply a new—perhaps an improved—form of drunkenness." Unlike alcohol consumption, the *Chronicle* reported, opium smoking "develops no fighting [or] destructive impulses," and it is "a slower system of poisoning than the use of alcoholic stimulants."

Despite those qualifications, the *Chronicle*'s dismay at this possibly "improved" form of intoxication was unmistakable. The opium dens "patronized by the lower classes defy description," the paper reported, but gave it a go anyway: "Imagine a room less than fifteen feet square, with a ceiling about eight feet high. In this room on the four sides are arranged three tiers of bunks, the heads against the walls. Here opium-smoking accommodations are furnished for forty persons. The only method of ventilation is through the door, and this is often closed and fastened. The fumes of burning opium, the stench and impurities arising from this huddled nest of human beings, and the suffocating properties of the atmosphere, ought certainly to kill any decent human being in an hour, but it seems to have only a pickling effect on the Chinaman."

The implication that Chinese immigrants were *not* decent human beings was spelled out in the same paragraph. "If anything were needed to complete the degradation of the Mongolian race," the *Chronicle* said, "the besotting effects of this pernicious practice furnishes [*sic*] the 'lower deep' beyond which moral and physical debasement cannot possibly go." Worse, that practice had attracted "American men and women," who "not infrequently are found in a state of complete insensibility" after "pulling away together at the pipe."

The *Chronicle* saw opium smoking as emblematic of a broader problem: Chinese immigrants were unassimilable. While "the emigrants to our shores from every other quarter of the globe in time become naturalized citizens," the paper complained, "a Chinaman never takes the slightest interest in anything pertaining to the public good or the national sentiment."[29]

"SMOKING OPIUM IS NOT OUR VICE"

What was to be done? Rather incongruously given its scathing criticism of supposedly inherent Chinese depravity, the *Chronicle* cautioned against "intemperate language" and "threatening conduct," which might lead to "violence" that would discredit the anti-Chinese movement. This was a realistic concern in light of the violence California already had witnessed, including an 1871 Los Angeles riot in which hundreds of men looted Chinatown and murdered 19 residents.[30]

"We must so conduct this moral crusade against further emigration of these hordes that the whole world will approve and applaud," the *Chronicle* said. "The mechanics and laboring men of California and the Pacific coast cannot afford to admit squarely that the only question involved in this movement is one of competition and of dollars and cents. There is a moral and social aspect to the matter more important than any other."

The "moral crusade" championed by the *Chronicle* soon inspired the Chinese Exclusion Act of 1882, the first federal law to ban immigration based on national origin. The law, which applied to "skilled and unskilled laborers," notionally made exceptions for certain categories of visitors, but permission was difficult to obtain. Congress also made Chinese immigrants already living in the United States ineligible for citizenship and required them to obtain reentry permits when they traveled abroad.[31] Such policies were applauded by the "anti-Chinese leagues" that began to proliferate across the West in the late nineteenth century.[32]

Other anti-Chinese measures of this era were neutral on their face but clearly aimed at a specific ethnic group. San Francisco, for example, set a minimum space requirement of 500 cubic feet per resident for private dwellings (thereby forbidding common living conditions in Chinatown), restricted the hours of theater performances (targeting Chinese opera), and required licenses for laundries in wooden but not brick structures—licenses that Chinese laundry owners somehow were never able to obtain.[33] That last ordinance passed muster with the California Supreme

Court, which saw it as a valid exercise of the city's police power. But the U.S. Supreme Court later unanimously ruled that the law's discriminatory enforcement violated the Fourteenth Amendment's guarantee of equal protection.[34]

San Francisco's ban on opium dens fell into the same category as the housing, theater, and laundry regulations. It was a law ostensibly motivated by public health and safety concerns that in practice targeted unwelcome foreigners. Western cities and states followed San Francisco's example, which provoked additional court challenges.

In 1886, a federal judge in Oregon upheld a Chinese man's conviction under a state law banning the sale of opium for nonmedical use. "Smoking opium is not our vice," U.S. District Judge Matthew Deady wrote, "and therefore it may be that this legislation proceeds more from a desire to vex and annoy the 'Heathen Chinee' in this respect, than to protect the people from the evil habit. But the motives of legislators cannot be the subject of judicial investigation for the purpose of affecting the validity of their acts."[35]

The following year, by contrast, the California Supreme Court blocked enforcement of a Stockton ordinance that made it a crime for two or more people to gather for the purpose of smoking opium. In the majority opinion, Justice Jackson Temple remarked on the law's intrusiveness.

"To prohibit vice is not ordinarily considered within the police power of the state," Temple wrote. "A crime is a trespass upon some right, public or private. The object of the police power is to protect rights from the assaults of others, not to banish sin from the world or to make men moral. . . . Such legislation is very rare in this country. There seems to be an instinctive and universal feeling that this is a dangerous province to enter upon, and that through such laws individual liberty might be very much abridged." Concurring Justice Van Paterson likewise argued that "every man has the right to eat, drink, and smoke what he pleases in his own house without police interference."[36]

The court nevertheless conceded that the secondary effects of personal habits such as opium smoking "may justify the [state] legislature in declaring these vices to be crimes." But it concluded that local governments lacked such authority under California's constitution.

State legislators would soon do what the California Supreme Court said cities could not. Six years before the justices nixed Stockton's opium ordinance, California already had made it a misdemeanor to maintain "any place" where opium is "sold or given away to be smoked at such place." The state criminalized all nonmedical opium sales in 1907 and made possession illegal in 1909, the same year that Congress banned the importation of opium for smoking.[37]

"Half-Baked Legislation"

Aside from import taxes, the Smoking Opium Exclusion Act of 1909 was the first federal law aimed at preventing deliberate consumption of a psychoactive substance in the United States. Like the San Francisco ordinance that inaugurated the anti-opium campaign, it targeted a habit that was seen as alien to American culture. While it prohibited importation of "smoking opium or opium prepared for smoking," it expressly allowed importation of opium "for medicinal purposes."[38]

That exception covered the traditional American use of opium and its derivatives, which consumers could buy over the counter during the nineteenth and early twentieth centuries. Patent medicines, which were promoted as remedies for a wide range of symptoms and illnesses, often included ingredients that today can be legally obtained only by prescription. Brands containing opium or morphine included Perry Davis' Painkiller, Mrs. Winslow's Soothing Syrup, and Ayer's Cherry Pectoral.[39] The prevalence of opiates in legal products sold "for medicinal purposes" was reflected in a law that Congress approved three years before it took up the Smoking Opium Exclusion Act. The Pure Food and Drug Act of 1906 required that patent medicines "bear a statement on the label" indicating the "quantity or proportion" of 10 specified drugs, including opium, morphine, heroin, cannabis, cocaine, and alcohol.[40]

That same year, Congress passed a law that required a prescription for opiate and cocaine sales in the District of Columbia, which was part of a trend that began at the state level in the late nineteenth century.[41] But the Pure Food and Drug Act, which was aimed at providing information to consumers and preventing the sale of "adulterated or misbranded or poisonous" products, did not require a doctor's prescription to purchase remedies containing the listed drugs. Nor did that law address the sale of opium itself. The Smoking Opium Exclusion Act aimed to fill that gap.

The bill's supporters said its passage was urgent in light of the International Opium Commission that was then meeting in Shanghai. The U.S. government, which was flexing its influence by taking a leading role in international drug control, had instigated the conference and was keen to demonstrate its seriousness by enacting federal legislation. During the congressional debate over the bill in January 1909, Senator Henry Cabot Lodge (R–Mass.) emphasized that the State Department "is extremely anxious that this legislation shall be passed as soon as possible."[42]

Members of Congress took heed. The Senate approved the bill that very day, and the House of Representatives followed suit less than a week later. Although legislators were united in viewing opium smoking as an evil that should be stamped out if possible, there was some disagreement about the effectiveness and constitutionality of the proposed law. But even the objections made it clear which drug users Congress had in mind.

"Smoking opium is manufactured abroad, exclusively in China," Rep. Sereno E. Payne (R–N.Y.) said. Although "there is a process by which it can be manufactured in this country from medicinal opium," he added, "Chinamen desire opium prepared for smoking in their own country." Still, "rather than not have it at all they would take that prepared in this country, undoubtedly."[43]

Given that prospect, Payne was skeptical that the law would have much impact on opium smoking: "Opium will still come in to be used for other purposes, and there is nothing in the bill, there can be nothing in any effective law passed by Congress, to prevent any person in the United States preparing opium for smoking or using it as smoking material from the opium brought in for other purposes. It cannot be done. We would have practically the same consumption of opium for smoking as we have now."

Rep. Joseph H. Gaines (R–W.Va.), who called the bill "a piece of half-baked legislation," took a similar view. "Because of the conservatism of the Chinese people," he said, "they so much prefer to have their opium prepared in China that the high rate of duty has not stimulated the manufacture of opium in this country; but it is a notorious fact, known of all men, that those who are addicted to the opium habit will secure the drug in some form, even though not the preferred form, if they are prevented from getting it in the form in which it is preferred." Instead of "protecting the morals of the country," Gaines thought, the import ban would "stimulate the manufacture and preparation of opium for smoking in this country."[44]

Payne eventually came around. After conferring with the secretary of state, he said he was "very cheerfully for this bill," having been persuaded that it would "tend in some manner to make it more difficult and therefore to suppress in part the use of smoking opium." But Gaines, while emphasizing that he was "yielding to no man . . . in my hostility to the practice of opium smoking and in my hostility to the drug habit generally," remained opposed.[45]

"It takes plenary power to stamp out such a habit—if it can be suppressed at all—the full police power," Gaines said. "Our federal government does not have it." Although he suggested that "a prohibitive internal-revenue tax on the transportation of opium for smoking" might make the import ban more effective, he still was not sanguine about the prospects of eradicating the habit through legislation.

"This is a matter that the civilized nations of the world have been considering for a century," Gaines noted. "It must occur to every man that if a thing which is so desirable to be done as stamping out the smoking of opium could be done by a simple law prohibiting the importation of opium, that remedy would have been thought out and applied long ago."

With a few exceptions, legislators were unfazed by the constitutional and practical objections to the bill. "It is a righteous measure," declared Rep. James Mann (R–Ill.). He thought the law, aimed at a drug favored by foreigners whom Congress had already deemed unfit for citizenship, was plainly "in the interest of humanity" and "one great step forward again in the civilization of the world."[46]

As advocates of stricter drug laws saw it, that "great step" left much work to do. Activists like Hamilton Wright, a pathologist who chaired the U.S. delegation to the 1909 opium conference in Shanghai, pushed Congress to expand its restrictions on opium and other drugs. In a 1910 report to Congress, Wright invoked the fear of miscegenation, which had played a role in agitation for local and state legislation against opium smoking. "One of the most unfortunate phases of the habit of opium smoking in this country," he said, "is the large number of women who have become involved and were living as common-law wives of or cohabiting with Chinese in the Chinatowns of our various cities."[47]

The efforts of Wright and like-minded reformers culminated in the Harrison Narcotics Tax Act of 1914, which aimed to curtail nonmedical use of opiates. The law taxed the drugs and regulated their distribution, allowing a doctor to dispense them only "in the course of his professional practice" and allowing sales to consumers only if they had "a written prescription."[48] The Harrison Act also covered cocaine, which followed a trajectory similar to opium's in the public discourse about drugs.

"Cocaine-Crazed Negroes"

Cocaine, like opium, was once a common ingredient in products that Americans could legally buy without a doctor's note. Coca leaf had a long history as a stimulant and medicine, going back thousands of years in South America, and its active ingredient was first isolated in 1860.[49] Within a few years, cocaine was showing up in patent medicines such as Peruvian Syrup and Cocaine Toothache Drops.[50] As its name indicates, the original version of Coca-Cola, introduced in 1886, included coca leaf extract. So did Vin Mariani, the "popular French tonic wine," which was first marketed a bit earlier and won endorsements from celebrities such as Pope Leo XIII, Thomas Edison, Emile Zola, and Sarah Bernhardt. Sigmund Freud extolled the benefits of snorted cocaine powder as a medicine and conversational lubricant.[51]

Initially, there was nothing inherently disreputable about consuming cocaine for medical or recreational purposes—which were often hard to distinguish, since even beverages such as Coca-Cola and Vin Mariani were marketed as health tonics. But the public impression of the drug took a turn by the early twentieth century, at least partly because of its purported effects on black people. That shift bears more than a passing resemblance to opium's transformation from a widely used remedy into an intolerable Chinese menace to public health and morals. "Just as opium was associated with the Chinese in the drive to outlaw it," Lester

Grinspoon and James B. Bakalar note in their 1976 study of cocaine's social evolution, "so cocaine was associated with blacks."[52]

In February 1914, *The New York Times* ran an article under the headline "Negro Cocaine 'Fiends' Are a New Southern Menace." The subhead warned that "murder and insanity" were "increasing among lower class blacks because they have taken to 'sniffing' since deprived of whisky by prohibition"—a reference to the alcohol restrictions imposed by several Southern states.[53]

The author, Edward Huntington Williams, was a physician who published some two dozen books over the course of his career, covering subjects such as liquor legislation, opiate addiction, and the history of science. Although "stories of cocaine orgies and 'sniffing parties,' followed by wholesale murders," might "seem like lurid journalism of the yellowest variety," Williams said, such rumors had a basis in fact, and "there is no escaping the conviction that drug taking has become a race menace in certain regions south of the [Mason-Dixon] line."

That menace, Williams claimed, stemmed from the pharmacological effects of cocaine, which "make the 'fiend' a peculiarly dangerous criminal." Those effects, he said, included "hallucinations and delusions," "increased courage," and "homicidal tendencies." They also allegedly included "a temporary immunity to shock—a resistance to the 'knock down' effects of fatal wounds," such that "bullets fired into vital parts, that would drop a sane man in his tracks, fail to check the 'fiend'—fail to stop his rush or weaken his attack." To illustrate that point, Williams repeated a story told by Asheville, North Carolina, Police Chief John Lyerly.

The story involved a "hitherto inoffensive negro" who was "running amuck" in a "cocaine frenzy." The man tried to stab a storekeeper and then began beating "various members of his own household." When a responding officer, accompanied by Lyerly, tried to arrest the assailant, "the crazed negro drew a long knife, grappled with the officer, and slashed him viciously across the shoulder." Deciding that deadly force was required, Lyerly "drew his revolver, placed the muzzle over the negro's heart, and fired." But "the shot did not even stagger the man," and "a second shot that pierced the arm and entered the chest had just as little effect."

That experience, Williams said, persuaded Lyerly to replace his revolver with "one of heavier calibre." According to Williams, "many other officers in the South, who appreciate the increased vitality of the cocaine-crazed negroes, have made a similar exchange for guns of greater shocking power for the express purpose of combating the 'fiend' when he runs amuck."

As if that were not scary enough, Williams also reported that cocaine improved the "marksmanship" of those "lower class blacks." He thought "the record of the 'cocaine nigger' near Asheville, who dropped five men dead in their tracks, using only one cartridge for each, offers evidence that is sufficiently convincing."

Williams's warning appeared 10 months before Congress approved the Harrison Act. Cocaine's inclusion in the law was driven largely by rising concerns about the drug's addictive potential. But "when respectable people decided that cocaine was a dangerous drug," Grinspoon and Bakalar note, "they were inclined to concentrate on what used to be called the dangerous classes—the poor, especially blacks."[54] And the threat that "respectable people" perceived was magnified by the belief that cocaine made "the dangerous classes" even more dangerous.

Williams was far from alone in worrying about "cocaine-crazed negroes." A 1900 *New Orleans Times Democrat* article warned that "a pint" of a cocaine-laced drink would turn "a stupid, good natured negro into a howling maniac." In a 1905 *New York Tribune* article, Colonel C.J. Watson of Georgia reported that "many of the horrible crimes committed in the Southern States by the colored people can be traced directly to the cocaine habit." The same year that Williams's article appeared in *The New York Times*, the *Medical Record* published a piece in which the doctor similarly claimed that "a large proportion of the wholesale killings in the South during recent years have been the direct result of cocaine, and frequently the perpetrators of these crimes have been hitherto inoffensive, law abiding negroes." Also in 1914, Christopher Koch, vice president of Pennsylvania's pharmacy board, averred that "most attacks upon white women of the South are the direct result of a cocaine-crazed negro brain."[55]

Hamilton Wright took up the same theme while lobbying Congress to enact anti-drug legislation that went beyond the ban on importing opium for smoking. In his 1910 report to the U.S. Senate, Wright averred that "the use of cocaine by the negroes of the South is one of the most elusive and troublesome questions which confront the enforcement of the law in most of the Southern States." He described cocaine as a "creator of criminals and unusual forms of violence," a "potent incentive in driving the humbler negroes all over the country to abnormal crimes."[56]

By 1915, the year after Congress took Wright's advice, Ernest K. Coulter, the New York lawyer and journalist who founded the organization that became Big Brothers of America, was describing this menace as a widely recognized phenomenon. "As you probably know," he wrote in an essay published by the New England Watch and Ward Society, "the cocaine habit has made fearful havoc in certain districts of the South—especially among the negroes." He alluded to "atrocious assaults" committed by "unfortunate black victims" of cocaine's use as a labor stimulant.[57]

David Musto notes that "the fear of the cocainized black coincided with the peak of lynchings, legal segregation, and voting laws"—"all designed to remove political and social power from him." He suggests that "fear of cocaine might have contributed to the dread that the black would rise above 'his place.'" The evidence, he says, "does not suggest that cocaine caused a crime wave but rather that anticipation of black rebellion inspired white alarm."[58]

In the two decades preceding the Harrison Act, historian Catherine Carstairs notes, "numerous journals, newspapers, and books from both the North and the South" claimed that "growing numbers of black men and some poor whites used cocaine and that black use of cocaine posed a significant threat to the security of whites. News and medical reports frequently depicted black men on cocaine as frenzied, manic, homicidal, lascivious, excitable, criminal, and immoral. They were accused of raping white women, and killing white men. Both southern segregationists and northern doctors urged the government to take strong measures against this dangerous new drug."[59]

Those appeals, Carstairs argues, encouraged states to require prescriptions for cocaine, which nine had done by 1900. Although George Fisher finds that evidence of a racial motivation for the first five such laws, all enacted in the North, is "wholly lacking," he concedes that it seems to have played a role in the South, where "reports of cocaine-driven crime among African Americans emerged" around the turn of the century.[60]

Every state had banned nonmedical use of cocaine by 1915, the year that the Harrison Act took effect.[61] That law did not cover marijuana, which was the target of local and state legislation beginning in the 1910s but would not be regulated at the federal level until 1937.

"A Lust for Human Blood"

Like opium and cocaine, cannabis was a drug that white, middle-class Americans used for many years before deciding it posed a danger that demanded prohibition. Cannabis was first listed in the *U.S. Pharmacopeia* in 1850, and during the nineteenth century Americans could buy it in the form of elixirs like Piso's Cure, Kohler's One-Night Cough Cure, and Dr. H. James Cannabis Indica. Such products were sold as treatments for a wide range of maladies, including coughs, colds, corns, cholera, and consumption.[62] As with opium, the difference between oral medical use and recreational smoking seemed to influence changing perceptions of the drug, and so did its association with outsiders perceived as strange, inferior, and threatening—in this case, immigrants from Mexico.

Mexican immigration to the United States increased substantially early in the twentieth century, when the U.S. Census count of Mexican-born residents rose from a bit more than 100,000 in 1900 to nearly half a million in 1920.[63] Immigrants brought marijuana smoking with them, and the habit caused enough alarm that in June 1915 the Texas border city of El Paso prohibited all distribution and possession of the drug, which until then had been available from local retailers or by mail without a prescription. The city council cited "a great public emergency" created by marijuana's "injury to public health and public morals."[64]

By that point, seven states, starting with Massachusetts in 1911, had restricted cannabis sales to authorized medical use.[65] But El Paso's ordinance was unusual because it imposed a comprehensive marijuana ban, with no exception for people with prescriptions.

A sensational story that the *El Paso Times* and the *El Paso Herald* covered on their front pages in January 1913 sheds light on the concerns that motivated the ban. "Juarez was thrown into a panic yesterday afternoon when an unidentified Mexican ran amuck, killing one policeman, wounding another and cutting two horses before he was knocked unconscious and arrested," the *Times* reported from Juárez, just across the Rio Grande from El Paso. According to police, the man, who also chased a visiting El Paso couple while crying "Death to Protestants" (per the *Times*) or "*vamos*" (per the *Herald*), was "a victim of 'marihuana,' the 'Mexican opium,' and had been smoking the drug all day." The *Herald* described marijuana as "that native Mexican herb which causes the smoker to crave murder," creating "hallucinations which frequently result in violent crimes."[66]

A year later, the *El Paso Herald* confirmed that marijuana madness had crossed the border. Under the headline "Policeman Lassoes a Drug Crazed Mexican," the newspaper reported that the arrestee had run "through the glass front doors" of stores on South El Paso Street, then led two mounted officers on a chase, outrunning the horses for three blocks. "Blood was flowing from the cuts he sustained as the result of jumping through the glass doors," the *Herald* said, and "a quantity of marihuana was taken from him at the police station."[67]

An article published in the same newspaper that May reminded readers that marijuana users were a danger to others as well as themselves. Under the headline "Poisonous Weeds of Mexico Cause Death," the paper averred that "violent insanity follows use of marihuana." While the story acknowledged medical use of cannabis, in the form of a tincture used to treat rheumatism, it declared that "people who become addicted to smoking marihuana finally lose their minds and never recover." It described "a Mexican in Veracruz who had smoked a marihuana cigarette" before killing a police officer and wounding three other people. "Six policemen were needed to disarm him and take him to the police station, where he had to be put into a straight jacket," the *Herald* reported. "Such occurrences are frequent."[68]

So frequent, apparently, that they led El Paso County Chief Deputy Sheriff Stanley Good to take up the cause of marijuana prohibition. "The most atrocious crimes which have come under the notice of the local police and sheriff's departments have been attributed to mari juana [*sic*] fiends," the *El Paso Times* reported in May 1915, noting that Good was urging a ban and planned to "take the matter up" with the city council.

"One under its influence is devoid of fear and as reckless of consequences or results. There are instances where the drug crazed victim has been placed in jail, but in many cases officers have been compelled to slay the fiend in order to save their own lives."[69]

The next day, the *El Paso Herald* quoted Good directly, amplifying the need for a ban. "The use of marihuana, particularly in this section of the country, is increasing at an alarming extent and demands regulatory measures similar to those enforced against the importation of cocaine and other harmful drugs," Good declared. Although "the effects of the drug upon users are not generally known to the public," he said, "the most noticeable effect is the fearlessness and bravado that users assume under its influence." That effect, Good reported, was a threat to public safety. "A large percentage of the crimes committed are by men saturated with the drug," he said. "Most Mexicans in this section are addicted to the habit, and it is a growing habit among Americans."[70]

Good evidently got a quick response. The very next day, El Paso City Attorney Joseph M. Nealon said he was drafting an ordinance aimed at preventing the use of marijuana as an intoxicant.[71] The city council enacted that law a few weeks later as an emergency measure in light of "the dangerous and powerful properties of the drug and the increasing sale of it in the city."[72] It prohibited possession as well as distribution of marijuana, prescribing fines up to $200 (more than $6,000 in current dollars) for violators. Although Nealon had suggested the ordinance would allow medical use of cannabis by prescription, the ordinance drew no such distinction.[73]

The *El Paso Times*, which said "the drug is considered the most deadly of any known," credited the law's passage to Good's lobbying. "Marihuana is known to create in the users a lust for human blood," the newspaper reported. "The most atrocious murders committed in El Paso have been attributed to marijuana fiends."[74]

"A Handy Excuse"

How much of an impact did such concerns have on the debate about marijuana policy? The answer depends partly on where and when the debate was happening.

By 1918, 10 states had passed laws aimed at curbing nonmedical cannabis consumption. Upon examining local press coverage, George Fisher finds little or no evidence that "fear of pot-crazed Mexicans" played a significant role in "the nation's first six anticannabis states," where he says the main motivation was "fear of cannabis use among White people" and "especially White youth."[75] And as the historian Isaac Campos has shown, the themes of anti-cannabis agitation in the United States—in particular, the claim that the drug caused murderous madness—mirrored anxieties that had long been expressed in Mexico, which banned cultivation and distribution of marijuana by regulatory edict in 1920.[76]

When Campos looked at stories published in American newspapers from 1910 through 1919, he found that articles referring to *marihuana* or variations thereof—the Spanish name—were much more likely to portray the drug in a negative light than articles referring to *hashish*, an older term that was often used interchangeably with *cannabis*, the name that physicians preferred. While Campos thinks that difference "surely reflects in part the influence of Mexican discourses" about marijuana, it may also reflect Americans' readiness to believe that violence was a common side effect of cannabis consumption when they viewed it as Mexican habit.[77]

Like Campos and Fisher, the historian Adam Rathge argues that the role of racism in marijuana prohibition is commonly overstated. He emphasizes that concerns about the hazards of cannabis as an oral medicine predated the emergence of recreational smoking linked to Mexico. "Marijuana prohibition in the United States was not a swift or sudden byproduct of racism and xenophobia toward Mexican immigrants," Rathge writes. Rather, it was "the culmination of broad evolutions in public health and drug regulation coupled with a sustained concern about the potential dangers of cannabis use dating to the mid-nineteenth century."[78]

Dale Gieringer's account of what happened in California, one of earliest states to target cannabis, is consistent with that gloss. According to Gieringer, Henry J. Finger, the California Board of Pharmacy member who spearheaded California's first marijuana law, thought it was only logical that California should regulate cannabis along with opiates and cocaine, for which prescriptions had been required since 1907.[79]

Finger did not mention Mexicans when he broached the subject of cannabis regulation in a July 1911 letter to Hamilton Wright, a fellow delegate to an opium conference in The Hague the following year. Finger instead expressed concern about "a large influx of Hindoos" into California. He described this group, which actually consisted mainly of Sikhs from Punjab, as "a very undesirable lot" who had "started quite a demand for cannabis indica" and were "initiating our whites into this habit."[80]

That October, the *Los Angeles Times* did mention Mexicans in a story about potential cannabis legislation. "In view of the increasing use of marihuano [*sic*] or loco weed as an intoxicant among a large class of Mexican laborers," the paper reported, "F.C. Boden, inspector of the State Board of Pharmacy, yesterday formulated an appeal to the State authorities asking that the drug be included in the list of prohibited narcotics." The board's lobbying also inspired an article that appeared the following month in *The Washington Post*, which said "the Mexican Marihuano," which "destroys body, soul and mind," had been "brought into California by the Mexican laborers, who are greatly addicted to it."[81] A month later, an *Oakland Tribune* story about the pharmacy board's push for cannabis restrictions likewise reported that "much of the drug is brought into California by Mexican laborers, among whom it works havoc."[82]

Consistent with those concerns, the law that California legislators ultimately approved in 1913 mentioned "loco-weed" as well as "preparations of hemp." Gieringer suggests "the new menace was incorporated by simply adding 'loco-weed' to the text." Despite the references to foreigners, he argues, California's cannabis law is best understood as one manifestation of the Progressive impulse to regulate potentially dangerous products. "It appears that cannabis-using Hindoos and Mexicans were merely a handy excuse for the [pharmacy] board to work its will," he writes.[83] But the picture looks different in at least some of the states that acted later.

"THE LOCO WEED THAT MEXICANS SMOKE"

In Texas, state action against marijuana lagged behind local bans. Yet the fears expressed at both stages were similar.

When El Paso banned marijuana in 1915, state legislators in Austin did not perceive a problem as urgent as the one that politicians in that city thought demanded immediate action. But in 1919 the state legislature approved a general narcotics law that prohibited the transfer of opiates, cocaine, chloral hydrate, and cannabis "except on prescription." Notably, that law specified that the covered products included "any preparation known and sold under the Spanish name of 'MARIHUANA.'"[84] Four years later, state legislators banned possession of "adulterated" or "misbranded" drugs with "the intent to sell." Those categories were defined to include any drug that was not properly formulated and labeled for medical use.[85] And in 1931, the Texas legislature made possessing any amount of marijuana, except by prescription, a felony punishable by up to five years in prison.[86]

When the first state law took effect, the *Austin American-Statesman* described marijuana as "a favorite of Mexicans" that produces "a very delightful effect of seeing beautiful visions of angels and other wonderful things."[87] But an article published a few months earlier in the same newspaper, which reported that marijuana "has become widespread in Texas and surrounding States," offered a decidedly more alarming take. It quoted an internal revenue officer who warned that the drug's "worst effect comes when the homicidal instinct is aroused." He averred that "many persons run amuck after smoking marihuana, and these are dangerous, as their one idea seems to be to kill someone."[88]

The year that Texas banned possession of marijuana with intent to sell, *The Austin American* reported an incident in which "a Mexican" who was "crazed by marihuana . . . ran amuck" on a train from Monterey to Matamoros, "stabbing five persons."[89] A couple of months later, the paper described the drug as a menace that "some of the cities in Texas have combatted" but treated it as relatively new to Austin. It highlighted a local "marihuana den" that "will rival the famous opium dens of Chinatown in San Francisco." Noting that "marihuana is used by Mexicans and others," the paper again warned that "some smokers become crazed and in the height of its influence commit murder, and other crime." Unfortunately, it said, "there is no state law against the use of the weed."[90]

Around the time that state legislators finally rectified that situation, the *American-Statesman*, which called cannabis "the loco weed that Mexicans smoke," warned that it is "extremely intoxicating"—so intoxicating that "a young Mexican boy" who was "hopped up on marijuana" when police arrested him was still high five days later.[91] The year after Texas banned marijuana possession, the same paper hailed the state's "battle against the ever-increasing and insidious use" of the "Mexican narcotic weed." With "the increased emigration of Mexicans to the United States" in recent years, it explained, "the growing and use of marihuana" had "greatly increased," prompting local and state crackdowns. The article alluded to marijuana's alleged criminogenic properties, saying legislators took notice after "defense attorneys began claiming their clients charged with murder and other law infractions were 'marihuana-crazed'" when they committed their offenses.[92]

In New Mexico, as in Texas, marijuana prohibition began at the local level. Albuquerque, for example, banned the sale of marijuana in 1917.[93] The main reason cited was the use of marijuana by soldiers, and local press coverage suggests why that phenomenon was viewed with alarm.[94]

That year, the *Albuquerque Morning Journal*, in a story about the 59-day jail sentence imposed on a local man, Enrique Martinez, for growing marijuana, described the plant as "a deadly weed, which is akin to Indian hemp." Once "the habit is formed," the paper reported, "it soon ends in death." Martinez's crime was discovered when police came upon "a Mexican boy about 17 years old" who "had gone 'loco'" and was "raving like a maniac" after smoking the "powerful narcotic."[95]

Two months later, another Albuquerque newspaper, *The Evening Herald*, described marijuana as "a habit-forming drug familiar to Mexicans on both sides of the border." Although marijuana, "known to scientists as Indian cannabis," had medical uses "in small doses," the newspaper said, "in large doses it is an active poison." When smoked, the *Herald* asserted, the plant caused "utter recklessness," as illustrated by the story of "a little Mexican sub-lieutenant named Acosta" who, under the influence of a marijuana-induced delusion that he could singlehandedly capture Washington, D.C., fired at U.S. border guards near El Paso, who "killed him before he got across the line." That incident, the paper said, was "a fair sample of the way marihuana is apt to affect an out-and-out addict."[96]

Six years after Albuquerque banned marijuana sales, the state legislature followed suit.[97] While the measure itself attracted little press attention locally, contemporaneous newspaper stories suggest that concerns about cannabis-caused violence were still salient. "The Mexicans mix the dried leaves with tobacco and smoke them in cigarettes," the *Albuquerque Journal* reported in 1922. "The effect is inflammatory stimulation. The marihuana excites the nerves, deadens fear, turns a coward into a swashbuckler, accentuates evil propensities."[98]

A story in the same newspaper the following year, describing "a record haul of marihuana" seized from a woman named Refugia Avila, was more explicit. "According to both the police and sheriff's office," the *Journal* reported, "the smoking of these cigarettes has been responsible for many of the worst fights and most murderous attacks of recent years. They say that after one has smoked two or three of these cigarettes he is crazed and after half a dozen, and often less, runs 'amok' . . . bent on the destruction of everything in his path."[99]

The story was similar in Arizona, where Phoenix banned the cultivation, distribution, and possession of marijuana in 1917. The *Arizona Republican* reported that marijuana "has long been used by many Mexicans, not only in Phoenix, but wherever Mexicans have been found" and that "many of the arrests of Mexicans made by the police are for causes arising out of the use of the weed."[100] When Williams, Arizona, enacted its own marijuana ban 11 years later, local legislators said the drug, which was "becoming prevalent among a certain class" of the town's residents, "tends to cause insanity and render the user thereof a menace to the public peace and safety."[101]

As in Texas and New Mexico, the state legislature was slow to act. In 1921 Arizona Governor Thomas E. Campbell vetoed a bill that would have banned cultivation and distribution of marijuana, objecting that it did not allow for medical use.[102] The state legislature finally banned marijuana in 1931, when it approved a narcotics law that made possession and sale of the weed a felony.[103]

During the period when editorialists, police officials, and civic groups were agitating for state prohibition, coverage of marijuana by Arizona newspapers featured several familiar themes. The plant, which the *Arizona Daily Star* in 1917 described as "the insidious drug of Mexico, a little of which will make a jackrabbit fight like a rattlesnake," was strongly associated with Mexicans, who were typically described as its users, growers, and peddlers.[104] Marijuana was said to cause insanity, imbue its users with extraordinary courage and strength, and inspire heinous crimes. In the 1910s and 1920s, the Arizona press repeatedly highlighted the purported connection between marijuana and shocking acts of violence by Mexicans, in the United States as well as their native country.[105] Arizona newspapers also warned the public about marijuana's general potential to facilitate deadly violence, as in a 1931 *Tucson Daily Citizen* article headlined "Murder Drug That Gives Gunmen Courage to Kill," which described it as a "dope plant" that was "smuggled from Mexico."[106]

"Superhuman Strength"

Supporters of marijuana bans in the Southwest said the drug gave its users extraordinary courage and superhuman strength while inspiring homicidal rage—a decidedly dangerous combination. These purported effects were strikingly similar to the ones that cocaine alarmists like Edward Huntington Williams had attributed to that drug and strikingly at odds with marijuana's later reputation as a "dropout drug" that rendered its users docile and indolent.[107]

In a 1917 report on marijuana in Texas, Reginald F. Smith, assistant to the head of the U.S. Department of Agriculture's Bureau of Chemistry, amplified the claims about marijuana's role in violent crime. Smith's report included several letters in that vein from members of El Paso's police department. Captain L.L. Hall averred that regular marijuana users "become very violent," "seem to have no fear," and "will attack an officer even if a gun is drawn." He said marijuana imbues its users with "abnormal strength," such that "it will take several men to handle one man." Another El Paso police captain, J.E. Stowe, reported that marijuana inspires "a lust for blood," makes its users "insensible to pain," and gives them "almost superhuman strength when detained or hindered from doing what ever they are attempting to do." El Paso Police Chief B.J. Zabriskie likewise remarked on "the strength that a human has when under the influence and the confidence he has regardless of the class of trouble."[108]

Smith, who described El Paso as "a hot-bed of 'Marihuana fiends'" that probably "became infected" via "old Mexican soldiers" in Juárez, thanked Stanley Good for his assistance in assessing the drug's impact. Smith did not merely quote the police claims; he unreservedly endorsed them, emphasizing "the danger to which peaceful citizens are subjected by coming in contact with 'Marihuana fiends.'" When marijuana "is smoked," he said, it "is not only injurious to the health of the smoker but often causes him to commit heinous crimes, thereby rendering himself a source of danger to the community where he holds forth."[109]

In light of these problems, Hall and Zabriskie both urged federal action against marijuana. So did Smith, who recommended that Congress amend the Harrison Act to include cannabis and that states ban nonmedical use.[110]

The Texans who were beating the drum against cannabis made it clear that they viewed marijuana smoking as an alien habit imported from Mexico, and press accounts often described marijuana-fortified criminals as Mexicans. But like Good, who worried that marijuana smoking was "a growing habit among Americans," Smith noted that "the sale of the drug is not confined to Mexicans," since "American soldiers, negroes, prostitutes, pimps, and a criminal class of whites in general are numbered among the users of this weed."[111]

This fear of a foreign drug habit spreading to native-born Americans recapitulated a central theme of nineteenth-century agitation against opium smoking. It showed up in early efforts to ban marijuana and resurfaced as Harry J. Anslinger, who ran the Federal Bureau of Narcotics (FBN) from 1930 to 1962, encouraged states to enact "a uniform law to prohibit the growing of marijuana plants."[112]

A 1933 *New York Times* story said marijuana use "constitutes an ever recurring problem where there are Mexicans or Spanish-Americans of the lower classes."[113] A 1934 *Times* report from Denver said "the consumption of marijuana appears to be proceeding virtually unchecked in

Colorado and other Western States with a large Spanish-American population." While "the drug is particularly popular with Latin Americans," the paper reported, "its use is rapidly spreading to include all classes."[114]

The New York Times attributed "most crimes of violence" in the West to marijuana, echoing the claims that played a conspicuous part in El Paso's ban and in Smith's USDA report. Anslinger, who kept a file of grisly crimes he attributed to marijuana, likewise maintained that such violence was common. "Prolonged use of Marihuana frequently develops a delirious rage which sometimes leads to high crimes, such as assault and murder," the FBN asserted in a 1936 pamphlet. "Hence Marihuana has been called the 'killer drug.' . . . Marihuana sometimes gives man the lust to kill, unreasonably and without motive. Many cases of assault, rape, robbery and murder are traced to the use of Marihuana."[115]

In 1932, by contrast, the FBN had minimized the threat posed by marijuana, saying newspaper coverage "tends to magnify the extent of the evil." Anslinger initially urged state legislation rather than a federal solution, partly based on constitutional concerns. But he later said he felt pressure from "sheriffs and local police departments" in the Southwest and West who were worried about "Mexicans" they "claimed got loaded on the stuff and caused a lot of trouble—stabbing, assaults, and so on." By his account, those concerns helped persuade him to support a federal ban.[116]

In his 1937 *American Magazine* essay "Marijuana: Assassin of Youth," which noted that Congress was considering "a bill to give the federal government control over marijuana," Anslinger described the havoc he attributed to the drug. "How many murders, suicides, robberies, criminal assaults, holdups, burglaries, and deeds of maniacal insanity it causes each year, especially among the young, can only be conjectured," he wrote. "Addicts may often develop a delirious rage during which they are temporarily and violently insane. . . . This insanity may take the form of a desire for self-destruction or a persecution complex to be satisfied only by the commission of some heinous crime."[117]

While Anslinger emphasized the threat to young people, he noted the Mexican connection. The "cigarettes" he blamed for a girl's suicide "may have been sold by a hot tamale vendor," he said. He also described "a hot-tamale salesman" in Birmingham, Alabama, who for years had been "peddling marijuana cigarettes to students of a downtown high school." More generally, he noted that marijuana "came in from Mexico" and "swept across the country with incredible speed."[118] In a 1937 statement to the House Ways and Means Committee urging approval of a federal ban, the FBN likewise said "Mexican peddlers" had introduced marijuana cigarettes "about 10 years ago," after which the habit "spread like wildfire," bringing with it "crime in its most vicious aspects."[119]

The FBN was not shy about playing up marijuana's connection to minority groups. The bureau circulated an oft-repeated estimate that "50 percent of the violent crimes committed in districts occupied by Mexicans, Turks, Filipinos, Greeks, Spaniards, Latin-Americans and Negroes may be traced to the use of Marihuana."[120] During congressional testimony in 1937, Anslinger presented a letter from Floyd K. Baskette, a Colorado newspaper editor, that described "a sex-mad degenerate, named Lee Fernandez," who had "brutally attacked a young Alamosa girl" while "under the influence of marihuana." Baskette added: "I wish I could show you what a small marijuana cigaret can do to one of our degenerate Spanish-speaking residents. That's why our problem is so great; the greatest percentage of our population is composed of Spanish-speaking persons, most of whom are low mentally, because of social and racial conditions."[121]

Testifying before a Senate subcommittee in July 1937, Anslinger offered a letter from "the prosecutor at a place in New Jersey" that described a supposedly marijuana-induced murder "of a particularly brutal character" in which "one colored young man killed another, literally smashing his face and head to a pulp." Anslinger displayed the photograph enclosed with the letter, which caused some confusion. "Was there then in this case a blood or skin disease caused by marihuana?" Senator James J. Davis (R–Pa.) asked. Anslinger corrected him: "No. This is a photograph of the murdered man, Senator. It shows the fury of the murderer."[122]

Echoing the campaign against opium, fears of race mixing figured in Anslinger's concern about marijuana. He kept a file of stories that reflected his anxieties about drug-facilitated miscegenation. One such item described "colored students at the Univ. of Minn." who were "partying with female students (white) smoking and getting their sympathy with stories of racial oppression." The "result," it said, was "pregnancy."[123]

A race-baiting *New York Times* story about the rape and murder of a Chicago nursing student, published a few weeks after President Franklin Roosevelt signed the Marihuana Tax Act into law, combined the specter of miscegenation with warnings about drug-induced violence. "Police pointed out that many of the other killings and attacks on women in hotels and hospitals have been done by Negroes," the *Times* reported. "Many youths on the South Side are smoking marijuana, the police said, and the effects of the illegal weed have incited them to attack white women."[124]

"MEXICAN PEDDLERS"

As Fisher sees it, the youth-in-peril message epitomized by Anslinger's "1937 anticannabis screed" in *The American Magazine* was far more important in achieving national prohibition than his "private" or "low-profile" expressions of bigotry. Although Anslinger's "racial attitudes" may have "fed the ferocity of his assault on marijuana," Fisher argues, such sentiments, no matter how widely shared, were not the main reason that assault succeeded. Anslinger understood that "the most potent weapon against the drug trade was the fear among White voters and lawmakers that their own youth would fall prey," Fisher says, and "he exploited that fear with devastating effect."[125]

That fear, however, cannot be neatly separated from the fear of foreign contagion. The year before the Texas legislature approved the state's 1931 marijuana ban, the *American-Statesman* ran a story under the headline "Mexican Held for Selling Dope to School Children."[126] Several similar stories about Mexicans, explicitly identified as such, who were caught peddling marijuana to teenagers appeared the year after the ban took effect.[127] Arizona newspapers also noted the arrests of Mexicans charged with selling marijuana to "children" and "young boys."[128]

Concerned citizens in California were beginning to draw the same connection. "Marijuana, perhaps now the most insidious of our narcotics, is a direct by-product of unrestricted Mexican immigration," a Sacramento resident complained in a 1935 letter to *The New York Times*. "Mexican peddlers have been caught distributing sample marijuana cigarettes to school children."[129] A statement by two New Orleans officials that Anslinger submitted when he testified in favor of the Marihuana Tax Act likewise combined the two themes, saying "the Mexicans" in Colorado "make [marijuana] into cigarettes, which they sell at two for 25 cents, mostly to white school students."[130]

The connection between marijuana and Mexicans came up several times when the House Ways and Means Committee considered the Marihuana Tax Act in April and May 1937.[131] By contrast, no one explicitly mentioned Mexicans when the bill was discussed on the floor of the House that June. Rep. Frank Buck (D–Calif.), a member of the Ways and Means Committee, said "the worst thing" about the marijuana trade was that "it is being peddled by itinerant dealers and peddlers throughout the country and sold to our high-school students, starting the young out as drug addicts." Another committee member, Rep. Daniel Reed (R–N.Y.), agreed that "the most alarming aspect of this illicit traffic is the sale of marihuana cigarettes to the boys and girls, especially those of high-school age."[132]

Although we cannot say for sure which "peddlers" Buck and Reed had in mind, the FBN and local officials in New Orleans had described them as Mexican in statements submitted to the Ways and Means Committee. Summarizing the testimony considered by the committee for their colleagues, the two congressmen also mentioned the purported connection between marijuana and violent crime. "Hardened criminals use the drug to steel themselves for their operations," Buck said. "The use of the drug leads to insanity and crime," Reed added. To "illustrate the effects of this deadly drug," he described several horrifying murders that Anslinger had attributed to marijuana, which Reed suggested accounted for something like half of all homicides.[133]

By this time, the link between Mexicans and marijuana was firmly established in the minds of journalists and presumably in the minds of their readers as well. It seems likely that the Mexican nexus made Americans more receptive to Anslinger's warnings about underage use and marijuana-inspired violence. "Even those who might have been motivated mainly by the identity of the drug's users were unlikely to simply say, 'We have to ban this because Mexicans use it,'" Campos notes. Instead, "they made arguments about what *happened* when Mexicans or anyone else used it."[134] While it would be an exaggeration to say that cannabis prohibition was motivated mainly by a desire to oppress Mexicans, it seems clear that "racial attitudes," sometimes reflected in overtly racist rhetoric, influenced discussions about how the government should respond to the "killer drug."

As we'll see in the next chapter, the role of racism in America's early gun laws was, if anything, even clearer. But while the association of opium, cocaine, and marijuana with minority groups played a role in discrediting those drugs, helping to pave the way to prohibition, the dynamic in the context of firearm regulation was quite different. Instead of pushing general restrictions on guns, legislators enacted laws that aimed to maintain white supremacy by disarming African Americans.

Chapter Two

The Racist Roots of Gun Laws

"A Good Revolver"

Frederick Douglass, who was born into slavery in either 1817 (his estimate) or 1818 (the date historians later calculated), emancipated himself in 1838 by traveling from Baltimore to Philadelphia on trains and boats, posing as a sailor. But for years, even after he became a celebrated abolitionist and wide-traveling orator, Douglass had to worry about the very real possibility that he would be kidnapped and returned to slavery—a threat that was not resolved until British supporters raised the money to pay off Thomas Auld, the man who claimed Douglass as his property, in 1846.[1]

Given that experience, Douglass's take on the Fugitive Slave Act of 1850 was not surprising. That law, which Congress passed as part of a compromise aimed at preserving the Union, charged federal officials with helping slaveholders recover "fugitives from service or labor," required the assistance of "all good citizens," and criminalized interference with that process. "The True Remedy for the Fugitive Slave Bill," Douglass remarked in 1854, "is a good revolver, a steady hand, and a determination to shoot down any man attempting to kidnap. Let every colored man make up his mind to this, and live by it, and if needs be, die by it. This will put an end to kidnapping and to slaveholding, too. We blush to our very soul when we are told that a negro is so mean and cowardly that he prefers to live under the slave-driver's whip—to the loss of life for liberty. Oh! that we had a little more of the manly indifference to death, which characterized the Heroes of the American Revolution."[2]

When Douglass wrote those words, Dred Scott was still attempting his own escape from slavery, an odyssey that involved litigation in state and federal courts rather than a clandestine journey north. Scott's lawyers argued that the man who purported to own him, U.S. Army surgeon John Emerson, had surrendered any such claim by taking him to postings in Illinois and Wisconsin Territory. Those jurisdictions, where Scott had lived for a total of four years, prohibited slavery. Scott's legal campaign began with state lawsuits that he and his wife, Harriet, filed in Missouri the same year that Douglass's friends bought his freedom from Auld. It culminated in an infamous decision that the U.S. Supreme Court delivered 11 years later—a ruling that alluded to white fears of the armed self-defense that Douglass recommended.[3]

One of the issues raised by *Dred Scott v. Sandford* was whether the plaintiff qualified as a U.S. citizen, as required for standing in federal courts. In the majority opinion he read to a packed courtroom at the U.S. Capitol on March 6, 1857, Chief Justice Roger Taney vigorously rejected that proposition.

The Framers, Taney said, viewed black people as "an inferior class of beings who had been subjugated by the dominant race, and, whether emancipated or not, yet remained subject to their authority." Those "beings" therefore "had no rights or privileges but such as those who held the power and the Government might choose to grant them." According to the consensus when the Constitution was written and ratified, Taney averred, a black man "had no rights which the white man was bound to respect."[4]

As Taney saw it, it was manifestly absurd to believe that "the large slaveholding States" would have consented to a constitution that treated African Americans as citizens, which would entitle them to the "privileges and immunities" guaranteed by Article IV, Section 2. That status, the chief justice noted, would give "persons of the negro race" the right to travel freely between states, to "go where they pleased at every hour of the day or night without molestation," to exercise "the full liberty of speech," to "hold public meetings upon political affairs," and to "keep and carry arms wherever they went."

Taney, a Marylander who had freed his own inherited slaves but believed the federal government had no business interfering with what former Vice President John C. Calhoun had called "the peculiar institution," was determined to protect the prerogatives of Southern property holders, including their supposed right to own other human beings. He took it for granted that the "privileges and immunities" of citizens included a right to arms, on par with basic rights like freedom of movement and freedom of speech. But he also took it for granted that the very idea of black people with the right to "keep and carry arms wherever they went" would have alarmed the Southerners who approved the Constitution.

That premise was supported by a long history of colonial and state laws that explicitly aimed to disarm black people, often including notionally free individuals as well as slaves. In fact, the fear to which Taney alluded was the main driving force behind early gun laws, which Southern legislators saw as a bulwark of white supremacy and a vital precaution against the terrifying threat of slave uprisings. After the Civil War, that tradition continued—overtly at first and then in a subtler form.[5]

The post-war constitutional amendments aimed to make Taney's nightmare come true. The Thirteenth Amendment, ratified in 1865, abolished slavery, while the Fourteenth Amendment, ratified in 1868, clarified that "all persons born or naturalized in the United States and subject to the jurisdiction thereof" were entitled to "the privileges or immunities of citizens" and "the equal protection of the laws." Yet from Reconstruction through the Jim Crow era, firearm regulations remained a tool to maintain the social order by keeping black people in their place. They supplemented the racist terrorism that served the same end, leaving African Americans defenseless against violence that public officials either tolerated or assisted.

In this context, of course, black people were especially keen to exercise the fundamental right of self-preservation, without which any other rights were of little use. From slavery through the civil rights movement of the 1940s, 1950s, and 1960s, white supremacist violence fostered a robust tradition of armed self-defense in African-American communities. Black leaders such as Douglass, Ida B. Wells, W.E.B. Du Bois,

T.R.M. Howard, Roy Wilkins, and Martin Luther King Jr. embraced that tradition.[6]

The clash between racial oppression via gun regulation and armed resistance by the targets of those laws suggests the life-or-death stakes that can be obscured by the dry details of firearm legislation. It also shows that gun control, like drug control, historically was motivated largely by the desire to control people whom legislators viewed as "an inferior class of beings."

"Negroes Insurrections"

The population of Virginia, England's first American colony, had grown to roughly 44,000, including about 3,000 African slaves, by 1680, the year that the Virginia Assembly approved "an act for preventing Negroes Insurrections."[7] Citing "the frequent meeting of considerable numbers of Negroe slaves under pretence of feasts and burialls," which was "judged of dangerous consequence," legislators decreed that "it shall not be lawfull for any Negroe or other slave to carry or arme himselfe with any club, staffe, gunn, sword, or any other weapon of defence or offence."[8]

The same law also forbade a slave to "depart from his masters ground without a certificate from his master," which was to be issued only "upon perticuler and necessary operations." A slave who violated the latter rule would be punished by "twenty lashes on his bare back well layd on." The penalty for "any negroe or other slave" who "shall presume to lift up his hand in opposition against any christian" was 30 lashes. The law authorized deadly force against a slave who "shall absent himself from his masters service" and resist recapture.

Beginning in the seventeenth century, in other words, legislation that restricted access to firearms was intertwined with legislation aimed at preventing resistance to slavery. That pattern continued through the eighteenth century and into the nineteenth.

Although Kentucky's 1792 Constitution declared that "the right of the citizens to bear arms in defense of themselves and the State shall not be questioned," a law enacted the same year said "no negro, mulatto, or Indian, whatsoever, shall keep or carry any gun." The only exceptions within those groups: A "house-keeper" was allowed to have "one gun" at home, and "all negroes, mulattoes and Indians, bond or free, living at any frontier plantation, may be permitted to keep and use guns ... by license of a justice of the peace."[9]

During the antebellum period, Southern gun control laws commonly applied to free black people as well as slaves. In fact, the legal rules were often looser for the latter than for the former, who were perceived as posing a double threat: as examples of freedom that might inspire discontent among slaves and as potential accomplices to the resulting rebellions. "More often than not," law professors Robert Cottrol and Raymond Diamond note, "slave state statutes restricting black access to firearms were aimed primarily at free blacks, as opposed to slaves, perhaps because the vigilant master was presumed capable of denying arms to all but the most trustworthy slaves, and would give proper supervision to the latter."[10]

In Florida, an 1825 law simultaneously expanded permission for slaves to use firearms and authorized white patrols to "enter into all negro houses and suspected places," "search for arms and other offensive and improper weapons," and "seize and take away all such arms, weapons, and ammunition." Six years later, Florida, which at times had allowed free black people to own firearms if they were able to obtain a government license, eliminated that possibility. After 1852, Mississippi likewise had an outright ban that applied to all black people, enslaved or not. As of 1860, Maryland decreed that "no slave shall carry any gun" without his master's permission, while "no free negro shall be suffered to keep or carry a firelock of any kind, any military weapon, or any powder or lead" without a license.[11]

The fears that inspired such laws were periodically renewed by actual or incipient slave rebellions. Most dramatically, the Haitian Revolution, which began in 1791 and ended in 1804 with the former French colony's independence, illustrated what could happen if slaveholders let down their guard.[12] Closer to home, Gabriel Prosser, an enslaved Virginia blacksmith, was hanged in 1800 along with 34 alleged collaborators in connection with "the first large-scale insurrection plot the South had known up to that time." Inspired by the ideals of the American and French revolutions, Prosser and his fellow rebels reportedly planned to burn Richmond and take Governor James Monroe hostage.[13]

Hundreds of slaves from plantations near New Orleans joined an 1811 revolt that aimed to take the city but did not survive its first battle with a white militia, which was followed by grisly reprisals in which the heads of decapitated slaves were displayed as a warning to others who might be inclined to rebel.[14] Denmark Vesey, a free black carpenter who helped found Charleston's African Methodist Episcopal Church, was executed in 1822 for planning a mass revolt of South Carolina slaves.[15] Other incidents—including the 1831 rebellion led by enslaved preacher Nat Turner that killed about 60 white men, women, and children in Southampton County, Virginia, and radical abolitionist John Brown's 1859 raid on the federal armory in Harpers Ferry, also in Virginia—underlined the threat that slaveholders sought to mitigate through gun control.[16]

The year after Nat Turner's rebellion, Virginia enacted a law that said "no free negro or mulatto shall be suffered to keep or carry any firelock of any kind, any military weapon, or any powder or lead."[17] The following year, Tennessee revised its constitutional guarantee of the right to arms, restricting it to "free white men."[18] Arkansas and Florida took the same approach when they drafted their original constitutions later that decade.[19]

An 1833 Georgia law made it illegal for "any free person of colour in this state" to "own, use, or carry fire arms of any description whatever." In 1848, the Georgia Supreme Court noted that "free persons of color have never been recognized here as citizens" and therefore "are not entitled to bear arms, vote for members of the legislature, or to hold any civil office." Delaware likewise forbade "free negroes and free mulattoes to have, own, keep, or possess any gun [or] pistol," except when they had obtained a license from a justice of the peace based on special circumstances. In an 1856 case involving a state liquor ban, the Delaware Court of General Sessions cited "the prohibition of free negroes to own or have in possession fire arms or warlike instruments" as an example of laws authorized by the state's "police power."[20]

Under North Carolina's constitution, "the people" had "a right to bear arms for the defense of the state." In 1843, when the North Carolina Supreme Court upheld a ban on "going armed with unusual or dangerous weapons, to the terror of the people," it noted that the law left "the citizen" with the "perfect liberty to carry his gun" for "any lawful purpose." North Carolina nevertheless made it illegal for "any free negro, mulatto, or free person of color" to carry a gun without a court-issued license. The North Carolina Supreme Court upheld that law in 1844, noting that "the free people of color cannot be considered as citizens" and, in any event, could legally carry guns if they were able to obtain a license issued "in the exercise of a sound discretion."[21]

"AT THE MERCY OF OTHERS"

After the Civil War, slave codes were replaced with "black codes," which aimed to maintain white supremacy by imposing employment arrangements that resembled slavery and otherwise restricting the rights of supposedly emancipated African Americans, including the right to arms. In 1865, Mississippi decreed that "no freedman, free negro or mulatto" was allowed to "keep or carry fire-arms of any kind" unless he was "in the military service of the United States government" or held a license granted by the local "board of police." Other Southern states, including Alabama, Florida, Louisiana, Maryland, and South Carolina, enacted similar laws.[22]

These edicts inspired appeals for federal protection. In a message to Congress, a November 1865 convention of black leaders in South Carolina asked, "inasmuch as the Constitution of the United States explicitly declares that the right to keep and bear arms shall not be infringed—and the Constitution is the Supreme law of the land—that the late efforts the Legislature of this State to pass an act to deprive us [of] arms be forbidden, as a plain violation of the Constitution." During Reconstruction, Congress frequently heard complaints that white militiamen, police officers, and the Ku Klux Klan, with or without explicit legal authority, were forcibly and systematically disarming African Americans, including Union veterans who had bought their rifles from the federal government after completing their service.[23]

In response to the deprivation of freedmen's rights by the black codes and other forms of oppression, Congress enacted several pieces of legislation, including the Freedmen's Bureau Act of 1866, which applied to the former Confederate states, and the Civil Rights Act of 1866, which broadly declared that "all persons born in the United States and not subject to any foreign power, excluding Indians not taxed," were U.S. citizens without regard to "race and color" or "any previous condition of slavery or involuntary servitude." Among other things, the Freedmen's Bureau Act, which Congress passed over President Andrew Johnson's veto after an earlier version failed to attract the requisite two-thirds majorities, guaranteed freedmen "full and equal benefit of all laws and proceedings for the security of person and estate, including the constitutional right of bearing arms." The Civil Rights Act likewise promised "full and equal benefit of all laws and proceedings for the security of person and property."[24]

Although the Civil Rights Act did not specifically mention the right to arms, the debate surrounding its passage indicates that it was understood to guarantee that right, which was a conspicuous concern of the law's supporters.[25] The debate over the Fourteenth Amendment, which reflected the central principle of the Civil Rights Act, likewise indicates that it was meant to make the Bill of Rights, including the Second Amendment, binding on the states. That was the view expressed by Rep. John Bingham (R–Ohio), the main author of the Fourteenth Amendment's first section, and Senator Jacob Howard (R–Mich.), who introduced the Fourteenth Amendment in the Senate, and it went uncontradicted even by the amendment's opponents.[26]

"To a man," Second Amendment scholar Stephen P. Halbrook notes, "the same two-thirds-plus members of Congress who voted for the proposed Fourteenth Amendment [in 1866] also voted for the proposition contained in both Freedmen's Bureau bills that the constitutional right to bear arms is included in the rights of personal liberty and personal security. No other guarantee in the Bill of Rights was the subject of this official approval by the same Congress that passed the Fourteenth Amendment."[27]

It is no mystery why supporters of civil rights legislation and the Fourteenth Amendment were concerned about attempts to disarm black residents of the Southern states. "Have colored persons the right to own and carry firearms?" the *Loyal Georgian*, a black newspaper published in Augusta, asked in 1866. The answer: "You are not only free but citizens of the United States and as such entitled to the same privileges granted to other citizens by the Constitution."[28]

The next paragraph, which was lifted directly from a Freedmen's Bureau circular, noted that the Second Amendment "gives the people the right to bear arms" and "states that this right shall not be infringed." While "any person, black or white, may be disarmed if convicted of making an improper or dangerous use of weapons," it said, "no military or civil officer has the right or authority to disarm any class of people, thereby placing them at the mercy of others. All men, without distinction of color, have the right to keep and bear arms to defend their homes, families or themselves."

The necessity of that right in the face of white supremacist aggression was repeatedly underlined in accounts collected by Congress. In 1871, Rep. Horace Maynard (R–Tenn.) described what happened when Klansmen attacked the home of an elderly black man. The homeowner, "under these circumstances of menace and terror, from his humble 'castle of defense,' fired and killed one of the party and drove off the rest," Maynard reported. "The man killed was found to be a constable of the district, and one of the others was the sheriff of the county." The homeowner was prosecuted and acquitted.[29]

According to an 1872 congressional report, Halbrook notes, "a single black man" in North Carolina "successfully defended his house with firearms from a dozen Klansmen." A black Georgia man testified that, after "Klansmen broke into his house and shot him three times," he "returned fire and shot one of the Klansmen, causing the whole group to flee."[30]

An 1874 editorial in the *New Orleans Republican* emphasized the importance of the right to arms. "The colored people and their white Republican friends desire very much to live and remain at peace with their neighbors and fellow-citizens," the paper said. "But when they see negroes lynched upon bare suspicion of larceny of old silverware, and their relentless white persecutors acquitted when cruel murders are proved against them, they are regularly forced to price a few shotguns.... If it be generally known that in each negro cabin in the country there is a lively weapon of defense, there will not be such a constant recurrence of homicides as have disgraced the annals of this State for many years. We expect these shotguns to prove famous peacemakers."[31]

"That Protection Which the Law Refuses to Give"

The homicides to which the *New Orleans Republican* referred included an 1873 massacre in Colfax, Louisiana, that grew out of a dispute over the 1872 elections. Hundreds of black militiamen occupied the courthouse in Colfax, where they were joined by local residents seeking protection after an armed group of white men murdered a black man in front of his family. About 150 Klansmen and Confederate veterans responded by setting fire to the building and shooting people as they fled. They also summarily executed 34 black prisoners. In total, more than 100 black people were killed.[32]

A federal trial of several men allegedly involved in the massacre ended with a hung jury in 1874. After a second trial, which concluded just before the *New Orleans Republican* decried "cruel murders" by white supremacists, the jury acquitted all the defendants of homicide and acquitted five of all other charges as well. William J. Cruikshank and two other defendants were convicted on 16 counts of conspiring "to prevent the peaceable assemblage of the negroes," of trying to prevent them from voting and "bearing arms," and of "generally taking away their rights."[33]

The U.S. Supreme Court overturned those convictions in 1876. In *United States v. Cruikshank*, the court ruled that the statute on which the charges were based, the Enforcement Act of 1870, exceeded the federal government's constitutional powers to the extent that it authorized prosecution of private parties rather than public officials. While the Fourteenth Amendment "prohibits a State from depriving any person of life, liberty, or property without due process of law" and "from denying to any person within its jurisdiction the equal protection of the laws," the majority said, it "adds nothing to the rights of one citizen as against another." Those rights, it said, "are left under the protection of the states."[34]

Cruikshank is sometimes described as rejecting the proposition that the Fourteenth Amendment made the Bill of Rights binding on the states, as its framers intended and as the Supreme Court eventually concluded. But the court did not discuss that issue in *Cruikshank* and had no need to do so in a case that did not allege state violation of constitutional rights. The First Amendment, it noted, "prohibits Congress from abridging 'the right of the people to assemble and to petition the government for a redress of grievances.'" And under the Second Amendment, it said, the right to bear arms "shall not be infringed by Congress" (although that provision actually is phrased more broadly than the First Amendment, with no mention of Congress specifically). The court did not address the question of whether the Fourteenth Amendment required states to respect those rights.

In any event, the promise of state "protection" from crimes like the Colfax massacre, lynching, and other acts of racist aggression was cold comfort at a time when black people plainly could not rely on that protection, even to vindicate their rights after the fact. That problem only became worse with the end of Reconstruction and the beginning of the Jim Crow era. By the late nineteenth century, local and state officials in Southern states were routinely turning a blind eye to such violence or actively participating in it.

That reality was reflected in the work of Ida B. Wells, a journalist and activist who was born into slavery less than a year before the Emancipation Proclamation and devoted much of her career to exposing the horrors of lynching. In an 1892 pamphlet based on her articles and lectures, Wells vigorously contested the widespread misconception that lynching was a form of vigilante justice motivated mainly by outrage at sexual assaults on white women. In most cases, she noted, the victims were not even accused of rape. And even when they were, the evidence was typically slight, often conflating consensual interracial relationships with criminal violence.[35]

What recourse did black people have when the authorities tolerated such murders, whatever the pretext? "Of the many inhuman outrages of this present year," Wells wrote, the only cases "where the proposed lynching did *not* occur" involved situations "where the men armed themselves in Jacksonville, Fla., and Paducah, Ky., and prevented it. The only times an Afro-American who was assaulted got away [have] been when he had a gun and used it in self-defense."[36]

For Wells, the lesson was clear: "A Winchester rifle should have a place of honor in every black home, and it should be used for that protection which the law refuses to give. When the white man who is always the aggressor knows he runs as great risk of biting the dust every time his Afro-American victim does, he will have greater respect for Afro-American life. The more the Afro-American yields and cringes and begs, the more he has to do so, the more he is insulted, outraged and lynched."

"I BOUGHT A WINCHESTER DOUBLE-BARRELED SHOTGUN"

Wells was not an isolated extremist. Her position echoed Frederick Douglass, the *Daily Georgian*, and the *New Orleans Republican*, and it was endorsed by other leading civil rights activists. "Nearly all my schoolmates in the South carried pistols," the sociologist W.E.B. Du Bois, like Wells a founding member of the National Association for the Advancement of Colored People (NAACP), recalled in his autobiography. "I never owned one. I could never conceive myself killing a human being. But in 1906 I rushed back from Alabama to Atlanta where my wife and six-year-old child were living. A mob had raged for days killing Negroes. I bought a Winchester double-barreled shotgun and two dozen rounds of shells filled with buckshot. If a white mob had stepped on the campus where I lived I would without hesitation have sprayed their guts over the grass."[37]

In a 1936 article for the NAACP organ *The Crisis*, Roy Wilkins, who would later serve as the organization's executive secretary and executive director, celebrated the "stubborn, thrilling, crazy bravery" of William Wales and his sister Cora, who were confronted by a white mob that surrounded their home in Gordonsville, Virginia, after they declined to accommodate a cemetery expansion by surrendering their property to the local government. "A mob of 5,000 persons including all the sheriffs, constables, deputies and state police for miles around, armed with everything from machine guns on down, was held at bay by a 60-year-old Negro man and his 62-year-old sister for six hours," Wilkins wrote. "The pitched battle of two against 5,000 was finally won by the mob only after a gasoline-soaked torch was tossed into the house and the occupants burned to death."[38]

While that act of armed resistance ultimately proved futile, others were more successful. In 1925, for example, Detroit physician Ossian

Sweet and his friends used guns against a violent mob bent on evicting him and his family from a white neighborhood. After Sweet was charged with murder, the NAACP hired the famous trial lawyer Clarence Darrow to defend him, his brother Henry, and others involved in the standoff. An all-white jury acquitted Henry Sweet, prompting prosecutors to drop the charges against all the other defendants.[39]

In backing Ossian Sweet and other African Americans who used guns in response to racist aggression, the NAACP recognized the importance of armed self-defense, which was especially salient for civil rights activists in the South. Robert F. Williams, an ex-Marine who was president of the NAACP's Monroe, North Carolina, chapter in the late 1950s, took that logic a step further by organizing a rifle club he dubbed the Black Armed Guard.

In 1957, Williams recalled in his 1962 book *Negroes With Guns*, he and other NAACP members in Monroe "shot up an armed motorcade of the Ku Klux Klan, including two police cars, which had come to attack the home of Dr. Albert E. Perry," vice president of the NAACP's local chapter. After Klansmen fired at Perry's house, Williams and his men fired back. That same year, Williams said, he used a pistol and a rifle to ward off an attack on black picketers at a segregated swimming pool by an angry crowd threatening to "kill the niggers."[40]

Williams was suspended by the NAACP in 1959 because of angry public remarks in which he endorsed vigilante violence. Because "we cannot take these people who do us injustice to the court," Williams said after a Union County, North Carolina, jury acquitted a white man charged with attempted rape of a black woman, "it becomes necessary to punish them ourselves. In the future we are going to have to try and convict them on the spot. We cannot rely on the law. We can get no justice under the present system. If we feel that injustice is done, we must right then and there, on the spot, be prepared to inflict punishment on these people. Since the federal government will not bring a halt to lynching in the South, and since the so-called courts lynch our people legally, if it's necessary to stop lynching with lynching, then we must be willing to resort to that method."[41]

Two years later, Williams was charged with kidnapping a Klansman and his wife, who were surrounded by an angry crowd when they drove into Williams's neighborhood. Williams, who always maintained that he had ushered the couple into his house for their own protection, fled the country to escape prosecution. From his exile in Cuba, he said he supported the use of force only in self-defense and recognized the value of nonviolent resistance.

"Massive civil disobedience is a powerful weapon under civilized conditions, where the law safeguards the citizens' right of peaceful demonstrations," Williams wrote. "In civilized society the law serves as a deterrent against lawless forces that would destroy the democratic process. But where there is a breakdown of the law, the individual citizen has a right to protect his person, his family, his home and his property. To me this is so simple and proper that it is self-evident."[42]

"WE HAD BETTER DO SOMETHING FOR OURSELVES"

That point also seemed self-evident to the Deacons for Defense and Justice, an organization that provided armed security for civil rights workers and protesters during the 1960s. Civil rights activists routinely risked their lives, a danger that was underlined by incidents such as the 1955 murder of the Reverend George Lee, the 1963 murder of Medgar Evers, and the 1964 murders of James Chaney, Andrew Goodman, and Michael Schwerner. The Deacons, who formed in 1964 and eventually established more than 20 chapters in Alabama, Arkansas, Louisiana, and Mississippi, were determined to guard against that threat.[43]

The original Deacons, mostly World War II and Korean War veterans, were alarmed by Klan activity in Jonesboro, Louisiana. Earnest Thomas, the Jonesboro group's vice president, traced its roots to a Klan parade, accompanied by a police escort, through a black neighborhood. "We decided that if the power structure could do that for the Klan," he told *The New York Times* in 1965, "then we had better do something for ourselves."[44]

Richard Haley, Southern director for the Congress of Racial Equality (CORE), acknowledged that the strategy embraced by the Deacons, who helped protect CORE workers, might seem at odds with his organization's commitment to nonviolence. "I still have to believe in my own mind that nonviolence is more effective than even the Deacons," he told *The New York Times*. "But I couldn't say to Earnest Thomas, 'I want you to lay aside any protection you have and go along with my policy.' In fact, it is likely that if any situation arises, I would be kind of happy to go along with this." In short, Haley said, "protected nonviolence is apt to be more popular with the participants than unprotected."[45] Hartman Turnbow, a Mississippi activist who in 1964 used a rifle to drive off an attack on his home by night riders, put it more bluntly in a prescient comment to Martin Luther King Jr. that year: "This nonviolent stuff ain't no good. It'll get you killed."[46]

Even King, the very embodiment of nonviolent resistance, defended the use of force in self-defense. Writing in 1960, King condemned "the anger-motivated drive to strike back violently" in response to racist oppression, rejecting what he took to be Williams's position, that "we must be cringing and submissive or take up arms." But King, like Wells, understood that guns could provide "that protection which the law refuses to give."[47]

King noted that "all societies, from the most primitive to the most cultured and civilized," recognize "violence exercised merely in self-defense" as "moral and legal." He added that "the principle of self-defense, even involving weapons and bloodshed, has never been condemned, even by Gandhi, who sanctioned it for those unable to master pure nonviolence." King drew a distinction between retaliatory violence by black militants, which he worried would alienate potential allies, and armed self-defense. "When the Negro uses force in self-defense," he wrote, "he does not forfeit support—he may even win it, by the courage and self-respect it reflects."

That position was not merely theoretical for King. After his home in Birmingham, Alabama, was bombed in January 1956, law professor Nicholas Johnson notes, members of King's church "came with guns and sat up in shifts guarding his house." Activist Bayard Rustin, himself a pacifist, "recalled the parsonage was 'a virtual garrison' with pistols, rifles, and shotguns in every corner of the living room." The Reverend Glenn

Smiley confirmed that "the place is an arsenal," adding that "the whole movement is armed in a sense."[48]

After the bombing, King had doubts about the protection provided by the local police department. Accompanied by two fellow Baptist ministers, Ralph Abernathy and H.H. Hubbard, King sought a pistol permit for "a night watchman at his home." Despite the potentially deadly threats that King faced as a leader of the Montgomery bus boycott, the county sheriff, Mac Sim Butler, said no. "I went to the sheriff to get a permit for those people who are guarding me," King told fellow protest organizers at a February 1956 meeting. "In substance, he was saying, 'You are at the disposal of the hoodlums.'"[49]

Butler's decision illustrated the lingering power of gun control to disarm African Americans. Even when framed in race-neutral terms, laws that gave local officials broad discretion over who was allowed to carry guns for self-defense could be selectively deployed against disfavored groups. Such laws persisted in several states as late as 2022, when the U.S. Supreme Court deemed them inconsistent with the Second Amendment.[50]

Activists who dared to carry guns for self-protection without official permission were subject to arrest. In 1939, the NAACP reported that J.A. Briar, the 69-year-old president of its Greenville, South Carolina, chapter, had been "charged with carrying a concealed weapon." The NAACP described Briar as "the latest victim of the terror the Klan and other groups are using against Negroes in Greenville and vicinity."[51]

The civil rights leader T.R.M. Howard, who was famously well-armed, was stopped for speeding in 1947. Although his five companions laid their pistols on the floor in the hope of avoiding a concealed-carry charge, each was fined $100 (about $1,500 in current dollars). Howard reportedly dodged a fine by keeping his gun hidden in a secret compartment.[52]

"IGNORANT CELESTIALS" AND "HOT-HEADED" ITALIANS

Discriminatory enforcement is a recurring theme in the history of restrictions on public possession of firearms, and African Americans are not the only minority group that has been targeted in the name of crime control. On a Saturday night in December 1875, William Douglass—the same police captain who, a few weeks before, had mounted San Francisco's first raid on an opium den (see Chapter 1)—gathered 30 officers for a Chinatown operation aimed at enforcing the city's recently enacted ban on concealed weapons.[53]

That ordinance, which the Board of Supervisors had approved the previous July, made it a misdemeanor for anyone other than public officials or travelers to carry a concealed weapon without the police commissioner's written permission. Another ordinance made it illegal for theatrical performances to continue past 1 a.m. Based on that double legal authority, Douglass's men invaded two Chinese theaters on Jackson Street shortly after that hour.[54]

Why Chinese theaters? Under the none-too-subtle headline "Disarming the Chinese," the *San Francisco Chronicle* explained that "the Mongolian portion of our community are lamentably inactive in the performance of duties imposed upon them by law, and particularly energetic and demonstrative in doing certain acts sternly prohibited." Even while castigating the residents of Chinatown for "this disregard of ordinances," the *Chronicle* conceded that "in many cases" it was "attributable to a lack of knowledge of their existence on the part of ignorant Celestials who do not learn of some new prohibition until they are brought before the Police Judge, who teaches them the lesson at [an] extravagant price."[55]

Douglass and 15 officers, accompanied by "a trio of newspaper reporters," charged into the Royal Theater, causing a "cry of alarm" and "a scene of the wildest confusion." The cops patted down every patron but came up empty. Douglass ordered a search of the theater, which discovered "a half dozen bowie knives, two pistols, and a nice assortment of iron bars"—weapons that had apparently been ditched by panicked theatergoers.[56]

The haul from a similarly sweeping raid in Buffalo, New York, was even less impressive. On a Sunday night in March 1888, a police captain "sent consternation into the Italian colony" by dispatching "forty-two stalwart bluecoats" to "bring in all the male Dagos that looked as if they carried knives," the *Buffalo Courier* reported. The cops "raided every known Italian lodging-house" on eight streets and arrested "over 200 swarthy-looking, jabbering foreigners" but found just two knives.[57]

That incident reflected growing fears of armed, allegedly crime-prone Italian immigrants, which eventually helped inspire New York's Sullivan Law, a 1911 measure that required a police permit to own or carry concealable handguns. The law also made it a felony for aliens to possess firearms or other potentially deadly weapons in public.

"The Sullivan Law was passed, in good part, as an effort to disarm Italian immigrants, [who] many believed were predominately responsible for violent crime in New York City in the early 20th century," a 2022 Supreme Court brief from a group of "Italo-American jurists and attorneys" noted. "There are always several reasons for legislation, but the historical record shows that much of the impetus for the law came from a reaction to crime many associated with first- and second-generation Italian immigrants."[58]

The first person to be convicted under the Sullivan Law, Marino Rossi, "was arrested for carrying a .38 revolver while in New York City on his way to New Haven for work." Although he explained that he was "an honest working man" and was carrying the gun for self-protection, that did not matter under the law.[59]

Upon sentencing Rossi to a year in prison, Judge Warren Foster, a leading supporter of the Sullivan Law, explained that its enforcement was aimed at dissuading Italians like Rossi from carrying guns: "It is unfortunate that this is the custom with you and your kind, and that fact, combined with your irascible nature, furnishes much of the criminal business in this country. . . . I and my colleagues on the bench intend to stamp out this habit, and with this end in view it is our object to let the community know that the violators of the Sullivan law are going to be severely punished." *The New York Times* applauded Foster's lecture to Rossi and "his hot-headed countrymen," saying "the Judge's warning to the Italian community was timely and exemplary."[60]

"Armed Bands of Citizens"

Half a century later, California legislators responded to a different scary group by making it a crime to carry a loaded firearm, openly or concealed, without a license. Although the assemblyman who proposed that 1967 bill, Don Mulford (R–Alameda County), disclaimed any racial motive, the context of its introduction and passage was more than a little suggestive. The Black Panther Party for Self-Defense had been founded in Oakland, which is part of Alameda County, the previous year. The Panthers had made a habit of "policing the police" through openly armed patrols that were meant to deter the use of excessive force and other abuses. The group's co-founder, Huey P. Newton, inspired by Robert F. Williams, had studied California's gun laws, so he knew that open carry was allowed without a license.

Mulford, a conservative Republican who took a dim view of the Panthers, wanted to rectify that situation. When Newton appeared on a local talk radio show in 1967, one of the callers was Mulford, who promised to "get" the Panthers and stop their patrols. According to the bill itself, legislators were concerned that "the State of California has witnessed, in recent years, the increasing incidence of organized groups and individuals publicly arming themselves for purposes inimical to the peace and safety of the people of California."[61]

The Mulford Act was deemed an "urgency statute" under the California Constitution after the Panthers took things up a notch by sending an armed delegation of 24 men to the state Capitol, where about a dozen of them barged into the Assembly as it was debating a different bill on May 2, 1967. The "urgency statute" designation, which required approval by two-thirds majorities in both houses, signified that the legislation was "necessary for immediate preservation of the public peace, health, or safety." It meant that the bill would take effect immediately after it was enacted instead of the following January.[62]

Although the Panthers were protesting Mulford's bill, their ostentatious display of guns, which was recorded by the newspaper photographers and TV cameramen who accompanied them, seemed to clinch the measure's approval. "Our job is to make the laws," Assembly Speaker Pro Tem Carlos Bee (D–San Joaquin County) said, "and this type of thing does no good." Assemblyman Bill Greene, a black Democrat from Los Angeles, concurred: "This action was not militant. It was senseless. No person, black or white, can condone this action."[63]

The Assembly passed the Mulford Act in June, followed by the Senate in July. Governor Ronald Reagan signed the bill into law two days later. Reagan, who as president would condemn gun control laws that burden law-abiding citizens without having any impact on criminals, declared that "there's no reason why on the street today a citizen should be carrying loaded weapons."[64] According to Mulford, the National Rifle Association (NRA), which later would adamantly oppose broad restrictions on the right to carry guns for self-defense, also was on board.

"I am sure you are aware that I am very grateful to the National Rifle Association for its help in making my gun control bill, AB 1591, a workable piece of legislation, yet protecting the Constitutional rights of citizens," Mulford wrote in a constituent letter dated June 15, 1967. In a letter the same day to a critic of the bill, Mulford said it "enjoyed the full support of the National Rifle Association." He disagreed with the critic's contention that existing laws were adequate. "If this were true," he wrote, "we would not have armed bands of citizens frightening school children, invading courts, invading police departments, invading the halls of the Legislature, with loaded weapons."[65]

Newton described the Mulford Act as "legislation aimed at keeping the black people disarmed and powerless at the very same time that racist police agencies throughout the country are intensifying the terror, brutality, murder, and repression of black people."[66] Although Mulford denied any such motivation, Assemblyman Willie Brown (D–Oakland), who would later serve as the Assembly's speaker and San Francisco's mayor, did not buy it. He noted that Mulford previously had opposed similar gun restrictions but changed his mind when "Negroes showed up in his district—Oakland—with arms."[67] Mulford seemed to confirm Brown's point in an interview two decades later, saying, "Don't forget in those days . . . you had the Black Panthers running around with loaded guns in the streets and a number of other acts of violence or near violence."[68]

"Disarming the Negro Laborers"

In addition to deciding who could publicly carry guns, states sometimes restricted access to certain types of firearms or banned their sale altogether. An 1879 Tennessee law, for example, prohibited the sale of handguns except for "army or navy pistols"—large, high-quality handguns that were owned by many former Confederate officers and cavalrymen, who "tended to come from the upper strata of society," gun policy scholars David Kopel and Joseph G.S. Greenlee note. Because those models were relatively expensive, "the effect of the 1879 Tennessee law was to make new handguns unaffordable to poor people of all races. The vast majority of the former slaves were poor, and so were many whites. While some Jim Crow era laws had a focused racial impact, the Tennessee statute was one of many Jim Crow laws that disadvantaged black people *and* poor whites, both of whom were viewed with suspicion by the ruling classes."[69]

In 1881, Arkansas enacted a similar ban, which also covered dirks, Bowie knives, sword canes, and brass knuckles, all in an effort "to preserve the public peace and prevent crime."[70] In 1893, Florida began requiring a county-issued license to own repeating rifles, a requirement it extended to pistols in 1901. The licensing process entailed a $100 bond, equivalent to more than $3,600 in current dollars, so that rule, like the bans on inexpensive handguns, would have been prohibitive for people of modest means.[71] Similarly, Don Kates notes, "Alabama in 1893 and Texas in 1907 imposed extremely heavy business and/or transaction taxes on handgun sales," creating "economic barriers to ownership." In 1902, South Carolina restricted the sale of handguns, allowing purchases only by "sheriffs and their special deputies—i.e., company goons and the KKK."[72]

The Florida law applied to anyone who "shall carry around" or "have in his manual possession" a pistol or repeating rifle. In a 1941 case, the Florida Supreme Court narrowly construed that language, precluding the prosecution of a man who had a pistol in the glove compartment of his car. Concurring Justice Rivers H. Buford went further than the majority, deeming the law "unconstitutional because it offends against the Second Amendment to the Constitution" and a similar provision of the Florida Constitution.[73]

"I know something of the history of this legislation," added Buford, who was a state legislator when the law was amended in 1901. "The original Act of 1893 was passed when there was a great influx of negro laborers in this State drawn here for the purpose of working in turpentine and lumber camps. The same condition existed when the Act was amended in 1901 and the Act was passed for the purpose of disarming the negro laborers and to thereby reduce the unlawful homicides that were prevalent in turpentine and saw-mill camps and to give the white citizens in sparsely settled areas a better feeling of security. The statute was never intended to be applied to the white population and in practice has never been so applied."

Buford elaborated on that point: "We have no statistics available, but it is a safe guess to assume that more than 80% of the white men living in the rural sections of Florida have violated this statute. It is also a safe guess to say that not more than 5% of the men in Florida who own pistols and repeating rifles have ever applied to the Board of County Commissioners for a permit to have the same in their possession and there had never been, within my knowledge, any effort to enforce the provisions of this statute as to white people, because it has been generally conceded to be in contravention of the Constitution and non-enforceable if contested."

When Congress approved the Gun Control Act of 1968, some observers perceived a similar motivation. Among other things, that law prohibited mail-order gun sales and banned importation of firearms that were not deemed "suitable for sporting purposes," a category that included inexpensive handguns known as "Saturday night specials." The law "was passed not to control guns but to control blacks," the left-leaning journalist Robert Sherrill, who was generally supportive of gun control and critical of the NRA's resistance to it, charged in his 1973 book *The Saturday Night Special*. Alarmed by the inner-city riots of 1967 and 1968, Sherill surmised, legislators wanted to "shut off weapons access to blacks." Since "they probably associated cheap guns with ghetto blacks and thought cheapness was peculiarly the characteristic of imported military surplus and the mail-order traffic," he said, "they decided to cut off these sources while leaving over-the-counter purchases open to the affluent."[74]

Writing a few years later, conservative policy analyst Barry Bruce-Briggs saw merit in Sherill's characterization. "It is difficult to escape the conclusion that the 'Saturday night special' is emphasized because it is cheap and is being sold to a particular class of people," he wrote. "The name is sufficient evidence—the reference is to 'niggertown Saturday night.'" Nicholas Johnson likewise writes that the label "combined references to cheap little guns dubbed 'Suicide Specials' and the tumult of 'Niggertown Saturday Night.'"[75]

Legal scholars Jennifer Behrens and Joseph Blocher cast doubt on that widely cited etymology in 2024, noting that references to "Saturday night specials" or "Saturday night pistols" long predated the 1960s and that such terms were used in apparently race-neutral contexts. "Scholars and litigants should stop repeating this particular origin story" without "clearer evidence" to support it," they concluded, although they noted that "none of this shows that gun regulations—including of cheap, easily concealable firearms—were *not* motivated in part by racism."[76]

Explicitly racist at first, gun control laws in the United States evolved into restrictions that were written in race-neutral terms (as required by the Fourteenth Amendment) but still had a disproportionate impact on African Americans, either by design or in practice. As we will see in the next chapter, drug policy followed a similar course, imposing racially skewed burdens long after open expressions of bigotry were no longer politically or socially acceptable.

CHAPTER THREE

The Drug War in Black and White

"A Grave Miscarriage of Justice"

On a Monday evening in December 1988, Richard Anderson, a 49-year-old Oakland longshoreman, was driving to a birthday party at his sister's house when he saw a teenager he knew, Michael Lucero, at a phone booth. Lucero gestured for Anderson to stop and asked for a ride to a local Burger King. In exchange for a few dollars in gas money, Anderson agreed. It turned out that Lucero was carrying a paper bag containing about 100 grams of crack cocaine, which he sold to a man he had arranged to meet at the restaurant. The buyer was an undercover federal agent.[1]

Because of his incidental and apparently unwitting connection to a drug deal, Anderson, who had no prior criminal record, was sentenced to 10 years in federal prison. That stunning outcome was dictated by a 1986 law that established a 10-year mandatory minimum sentence for trafficking in 50 grams or more of crack. If the exchange had involved the same amount of cocaine powder, no such minimum would have applied, and Anderson's punishment would have been much less severe.

U.S. District Judge William Schwarzer, a Republican appointee "known for his stoic demeanor," choked back tears as he imposed the legally required sentence in September 1989. He called it "a grave miscarriage of justice" caused by "rules making judges clerks—or not even that, computers—automatically imposing sentences without regard to what is just and right." He added, "It behooves us to think that it may profit us very little to win the war on drugs if, in the process, we lose our soul."[2]

Two years after Schwarzer cried at the injustice wrought by federal crack penalties, Senator Joe Biden (D–Del.) bragged about them in a speech to his colleagues. Standing on the floor of the U.S. Senate in June 1991, Biden held up a quarter. "If you have a piece of crack cocaine no bigger than this quarter that I am holding in my hand," he said, "you go to jail for five years. You get no probation. You get nothing other than five years in jail. The judge does not have a choice."[3]

To be clear: The future president was not marveling at the unfairness of that punishment; he was touting his anti-drug bona fides. In fact, Biden complained that the Justice Department under President George H.W. Bush's attorney general, Richard Thornburgh, was not using that penalty aggressively enough. If the police arrest you "with that much" in New York City and "they take you to the Justice Department," he said, "guess what the Justice Department, Mr. Thornburgh, says? 'We are not going to prosecute you. You have to have 10 times that much for us to prosecute you in New York City.'"[4]

Biden's complaint was part of his broader argument that Democrats, although frequently portrayed as soft on crime, could be tougher than Republicans. Biden struck that pose after Bush announced an escalation of the war on drugs in September 1989 while holding up a plastic bag of crack, which the president described as an "innocent-looking" substance that was "turning our cities into battle zones."[5] Biden, who was tapped to deliver a televised Democratic response, questioned the administration's anti-drug zeal. "Quite frankly," he said, "the president's plan's not tough enough, bold enough, or imaginative enough to meet the crisis at hand," which he called "the number one threat to our national security."[6]

In his 1991 Senate speech, Biden was showing how "tough" and "bold" he could be by reminding his colleagues about his support for the Anti-Drug Abuse Act of 1988, which prescribed a five-year mandatory minimum sentence for anyone caught with as little as five grams of crack cocaine—a bit more than the weight of a sugar packet. Unlike mandatory minimums for other drugs, that penalty applied to simple possession, meaning prosecutors did not have to allege that a defendant was involved in distributing crack. Because "we said crack cocaine is such a bad deal," as Biden put it, even crack users who did not sell the drug could go to prison for five years, and he thought that should happen more often.[7]

The law establishing that draconian punishment built on the highly punitive approach embodied in the Anti-Drug Abuse Act of 1986, which Biden helped write as the senior Democrat on the Senate Judiciary Committee.[8] Among other things, the 1986 law prescribed mandatory minimum sentences for drug trafficking offenses. That sentencing scheme treated the smoked version of cocaine as if it were 100 times worse than the snorted kind, even though these were just two different ways of consuming the same drug. Possessing five grams of crack with intent to distribute it triggered the same five-year mandatory minimum as 500 grams of cocaine powder; likewise, the 10-year mandatory minimum required five kilograms of cocaine powder but only 50 grams of crack.[9]

During his 1991 remarks, Biden was bursting with pride about his role in passing such legislation. "Since 1986," he noted, "Congress has passed over 230 new or expanded penalties for drug and criminal offenses in these United States—230 new penalties." The anti-drug laws, he boasted, were enacted "through the leadership of Senator [Strom] Thurmond, myself, and others."[10]

Even in 1991, some legislators objected to Biden's approach. Although Senator Howard Metzenbaum (D–Ohio) agreed that crack was "the worst terror on our streets today," he questioned the justice of requiring "five years with no chance of parole for possessing a teaspoonful of crack weighing as much as two pennies." He cited a couple of cases that illustrated his concerns about mandatory minimums.[11]

"Sylvia Jenkins, a Washington secretary, was sent to prison for five years because her son had hidden some drugs in her attic," Metzenbaum said. "Even though she had little culpability, the mandatory minimum penalty . . . required that harsh sentence." U.S. District Judge Stanley Harris, a Ronald Reagan appointee who was charged with sentencing Jenkins, objected to the penalties that Biden's handiwork required him and his colleagues to impose. "I've always been considered a fairly harsh sentencer," he said. "But it's killing me that I'm sending so many low-level offenders away for all this time."[12] Metzenbaum also mentioned Richard Anderson's case.

At the time, Biden was unfazed by such stories. But in a speech he gave nearly three decades later, just before he entered the 2020 presidential race, he conceded that the distinction between smoked and snorted cocaine "was a big mistake when it was made." Although "we thought we were told by the experts that crack . . . was somehow fundamentally different," he explained, "it's not different." That misconception, he added, "trapped an entire generation."[13]

Biden was speaking at the National Action Network's Martin Luther King Jr. breakfast in Washington, D.C., so he did not need to explain that his "big mistake" had disproportionately affected black people like Anderson, who accounted for the vast majority of federal crack defendants. Although that pattern was clear by the early 1990s, Biden did not fully repent until 2007, when was seeking his party's presidential nomination and introduced a bill that would have eliminated the sentencing disparity between smoked and snorted cocaine.[14]

Biden liked to brag about his anti-crime alliance with Senator Strom Thurmond (R–S.C.) and Senator James Eastland (D–Miss.), both of whom had records as staunch segregationists, and he was still citing that work as an inspiring example of bipartisan collaboration as late as 2019.[15] But whatever Thurmond and Eastland's motives might have been, it seems safe to say that Biden, who eventually was troubled by the disparate impact of the policies he supported as a senator, did not pursue them based on racial animus. That goes double for the African-American politicians who initially supported his anti-crack agenda, which they thought would help rather than hurt their communities.

In this context, it is misleading to describe the ongoing war on drugs as racist, which suggests that current policy makers are motivated, consciously or not, by bigotry. The concept of "systemic racism" attempts to avoid that problem, although it confusingly implies that racism is possible even without racists. It is nevertheless fair to say that the manifold racial disparities produced by the war on drugs do not seem consistent with equal treatment under the law. Especially given the dark history of drug prohibition, it is not hard to see why civil rights groups argue that "racial justice" demands reform of that legal regime.[16]

"Rapidly Spreading to the Suburbs"

Although national drug prohibition in the United States began with the Harrison Narcotics Tax Act of 1914, Richard Nixon is often credited with launching the modern war on drugs in 1971, when he described "drug abuse" as "America's public enemy number one." To "fight and defeat this enemy," the president said at a press conference, "it is necessary to wage a new, all-out offensive."[17]

Contrary to his reputation, Nixon's drug policies were more nuanced and humane than the policies that Joe Biden began pushing in the 1980s. While Biden thought five years in prison was an appropriate punishment for crack consumers and argued that "we have to hold every drug user accountable," Nixon drew a distinction between drug dealers, who he thought deserved "severe punishments," and drug users, whom he portrayed as victims deserving "compassion" and rehabilitation. Toward the latter end, Nixon sought increased funding for drug treatment. He wanted to "tighten the noose around the necks of drug peddlers, and thereby loosen the noose around the necks of drug users."[18]

Still, if you are looking for racist motives behind the war on drugs, Nixon seems like a promising example. Privately, his White House tapes revealed, he was given to racist and anti-Semitic rants. In 1971, he complained that "every one of the bastards that are out for legalizing marijuana is Jewish." He wondered "what the Christ is the matter with the Jews," speculating that "it's because most of them are psychiatrists."[19] The Jews "are just a very aggressive and abrasive and obnoxious personality," he told an adviser in 1973. That same year, he made his policy on Jewish appointees clear: "No Jews. We are adamant when I say no Jews." He complained that his secretary of state, William P. Rogers, had "sort of a blind spot on the black thing," thinking "they are coming along," which Nixon thought might be true "if you're talking in terms of 500 years." Regarding Jamaica, Nixon declared, "Blacks can't run it . . . and they won't be able to for a hundred years, and maybe not for a thousand. . . . Do you know, maybe, one black country that's well run?"[20]

Judging from comments by John Ehrlichman, Nixon's domestic policy adviser, the president's antipathy toward African Americans influenced his decision to play up the drug issue. "You want to know what this was really all about?" Ehrlichman said in a 1994 interview with journalist Dan Baum. "The Nixon campaign in 1968, and the Nixon White House after that, had two enemies: the antiwar left and black people. You understand what I'm saying? We knew we couldn't make it illegal to be either against the war or black, but by getting the public to associate the hippies with marijuana and blacks with heroin, and then criminalizing both heavily, we could disrupt those communities. We could arrest their leaders, raid their homes, break up their meetings, and vilify them night after night on the evening news. Did we know we were lying about the drugs? Of course we did."[21]

According to Ehrlichman, heroin was the drug that Nixon associated with African Americans. By the mid-1980s, crack had taken heroin's place as the scariest drug menace, and it too was linked to black people as both consumers and dealers. This smokable form of the drug, which can be readily made by heating a mixture of cocaine powder, water, and baking soda, first emerged in the inner-city neighborhoods of Los Angeles, Miami, and New York in 1984 and 1985. Unlike cocaine powder, it was cheap in per-dose terms, and it produced a shorter, more intense experience.[22]

By 1986, news outlets were describing crack as instantly addictive. In a March 17 cover story, *Newsweek* credulously quoted a drug expert who called crack "the most addictive drug known to man" and averred that it caused "instantaneous addiction." *Newsweek* warned that crack "has transformed the ghetto" and "is rapidly spreading to the suburbs."[23]

Later that month, *The New York Times* reported that "teen-agers in New York City and its suburbs" were using this "especially potent and addicting form of cocaine" in "dramatically increasing numbers." The *Times* said crack use was rampant not only in poor black areas like "the Bedford-Stuyvesant section of Brooklyn" but also in "the wealthiest suburbs of Westchester County." In fact, according to a New Jersey Health Department official quoted by the *Times*, crack was "all over the place."[24] The paper reiterated that point in April, noting crack's "popularity among Westchester teen-agers" and quoting a warning from a local legislator: "If we don't stop crack now, it will destroy our young people."[25] A June 8 headline hit the same theme: "Crack Addiction Spreads Among the

Middle Class."[26] That same day, the *Times* reported that "the use of crack has reached epidemic proportions" on Long Island.[27]

Newsweek called the use of crack and other illegal drugs "The Plague Among Us," declaring that "nearly everyone now concedes that the plague is all but universal."[28] *U.S. News & World Report* used similar language, saying "illicit drugs pervade American life"—"a situation that experts compare to medieval plagues."[29]

"Vicious Violence"

These reports recapitulated themes that were conspicuous during the early history of U.S. drug laws (see Chapter 1). According to the mainstream press, a dangerously addictive drug habit that originally was confined to a minority group was spreading to the white, middle-class majority. And as it moved from "the ghetto" to "the suburbs," this "plague" posed a special threat to "teen-agers."

As sociologists Craig Reinarman and Harry G. Levine note, one clue that such reports could not be trusted was that the same publications would sometimes contradict themselves.[30] "Don't tell the kids," *Newsweek* whispered in 1990, "but there's a dirty little secret about crack: as with most other drugs, a lot of people use it without getting addicted. In their zeal to shield young people from the plague of drugs, the media and many drug educators have hyped the very real dangers of crack into a myth of instant and total addiction."[31] In 1989, *The New York Times* noted that "law-enforcement officials and young people say crack and most other narcotics are rarely seen in the suburbs, whether modest or wealthy." Crack, it said, "is confined mainly to poor urban neighborhoods."[32]

Even at the peak of the crack cocaine "epidemic" in the early 1990s, according to federal survey data, just 0.7 percent of Americans 12 or older reported using the drug in the previous year, while less than half as many reported past-month use.[33] As of 2023, 3.5 percent of respondents said they had ever tried crack, while just 0.2 percent said they had used it in the previous month.[34] In other words, 94 percent of people who had used crack were not still using it even as often as once a month. Even allowing for underreporting, these numbers are not consistent with the tales of a drug so irresistible that it was instantly producing addicts and spreading inexorably across the country.

Press coverage of crack also tied it to violence, a concern that figured in agitation against cocaine and marijuana in the early twentieth century (see Chapter 1). From the mid-1980s to the early 1990s, one story after another cited "drug-related violence" as a by-product of crack. "Wherever it appears," *Newsweek* reported in 1986, crack "spawns vicious violence among dealers and dopers." Referring to "the crime it has loosed in our streets," the magazine's editor-in-chief called crack use "an authentic national crisis—an assault on the law and the peace, a waste of life and treasure."[35] In the late 1980s, newspapers and magazines routinely quoted law-enforcement sources who blamed crack for rising homicide rates, especially in Washington, D.C., the nation's "murder capital."

Since the "dealers and dopers" who worried *Newsweek* were typically black, this fear harked back to the "cocaine-crazed negroes" of Edward Huntington Williams's nightmares. But while there is no denying that the crack trade was often violent, the common impression that the violence was caused by the drug's pharmacological effects had little basis in reality. A 1989 analysis of "crack-related" homicides in New York City found that the overwhelming majority—85 percent—grew out of black-market disputes. About 7 percent were committed in the course of crimes aimed at supporting crack habits. Just one of the 118 homicides involved a perpetrator who was high on crack.[36]

The evidence, in short, did not support claims that crack was "the most addictive drug known to man," that it was spreading "all over the place" like a "plague," or that it triggered murderous impulses. Those fears nevertheless drove a draconian political response in Washington, D.C., catalyzed largely by the June 1986 death of Len Bias, a star University of Maryland basketball player who had just been drafted by the Boston Celtics.[37]

"LEN BIAS DIED FOR A PURPOSE"

Bias died of cardiac arrhythmia after snorting cocaine powder.[38] But some press coverage and commentary erroneously suggested that he had been smoking crack. "There is speculation that Bias may have been freebasing or using 'crack,' which is smoked and is nearly twice the concentration in a normal intake of cocaine powder," *New York Times* sports writer Ira Berkow reported. Syndicated columnist Jimmy Breslin likewise mentioned Bias in a piece about the crack business in New York City, quoting a crack user who said, "I never heard of anybody droppin' dead from crack, like this boy in Maryland."[39]

A week after Bias died, Rep. Charles Rangel (D–N.Y.) and the Reverend Jesse Jackson said the tragedy "underscored the need for a national drive to combat drug abuse," as *The New York Times* put it. Rangel, who chaired the House Select Committee on Narcotics Abuse and Control, criticized the Reagan administration for not doing enough on that front. "Even though the administration claims to have declared a war on drugs, the only evidence we find of this war [is] the casualties," Rangel said. "If indeed a war has been declared, I asked the question, 'When was the last time we heard a statement in support of this war from our commander in chief?'"[40]

Rangel and Jackson were speaking at a Washington, D.C., press conference, where they were joined by University of Maryland basketball coach Lefty Driesell and Red Auerbach, president of the Boston Celtics. "Len Bias died for a purpose," Driesell said. "And the purpose was to bring attention to this committee, to the president, and to the world that drugs can kill. We need to stop cocaine from coming into the country."[41]

The message of that press conference complicates any narrative that portrays the modern war on drugs as a racist project. The heightened concern about drugs was prompted by the death of a young black man, and it was voiced by a prominent black legislator, joined by a well-known civil rights leader. The day after Rangel and Jackson's press conference, that concern was amplified by the cocaine-related death of another African-American athlete, Cleveland Browns defensive back Don Rogers.[42]

Rangel's solution included more funding for "drug abuse education," subsidies for state and local drug enforcement, and a White House conference aimed at producing "a national policy to combat drug abuse," which he imagined would convene within six months. But Congress moved faster than that, approving the Anti-Drug Abuse Act of 1986 a few months after Rangel and Jackson demanded action. When Congress passed the bill that September, just 16 representatives and two senators voted against it. An amended version passed the House by unanimous consent and passed the Senate by a voice vote the following month, and President Ronald Reagan signed it into law on October 27, 1986.

Rangel voted for the bill, along with a dozen other members of the Congressional Black Caucus. In a 1989 *Ebony* profile that dubbed him "The Front-Line General in the War on Drugs," he summed up the attitude behind that position. "We need outrage!" he told the magazine. "I don't know what is behind the lackadaisical attitudes towards drugs, but I do know that the American people have made it abundantly clear: They are outraged by the indifference of the U.S. government to this problem."[43]

Jackson's stance was similar. When he ran for the 1988 Democratic presidential nomination, he described himself as "the general in this war to fight drugs."[44] But by 2011, he was calling for an end to that war, describing it as "a complete failure" that had squandered taxpayer money, fostered "violence and corruption," and incarcerated "millions of citizens who pose no threat to anyone" for "nonviolent acts that were not even crimes a century ago."[45]

Rangel also had second thoughts about his get-tough approach to drugs. In 1999, he introduced a bill that would have eliminated the mandatory minimum sentences for crack cocaine trafficking and possession.[46] What changed his mind?

"In response to the onslaught of cocaine abuse in the 1980s," Rangel explained in 2007, "the nation crafted a drug policy totally lacking in compassion, and worse, that was totally unfair to the weakest, and most disadvantaged, in society. The sudden, frightening epidemic of a new street drug—crack cocaine—and the drug induced death of basketball star Len Bias in 1986—impelled besieged lawmakers to enact stiff punishments for crack cocaine offenses, including long mandatory minimum jail sentences. Instead of reducing drug addiction and crime, those laws, however well-intentioned, swelled prison populations, created a sentencing divide that victimized young Black men, left a generation of children fatherless, and drove up the costs of a justice system focused more on harsh punishment than rehabilitation."[47] Or as Rangel put it in a 2022 documentary, "it seemed like a good idea at the time," but "clearly, it was overkill."[48]

"NEUTRAL ON THEIR FACE"

The problems that Rangel eventually perceived were apparent by the late 1980s, when federal judges like Schwarzer and Harris started openly objecting to mandatory crack sentences. They became clearer during the next few years, when sentencing data showed it was mainly black men who were receiving those penalties.

Similar state laws also generated controversy. A 1989 Minnesota law established a presumptive sentence of four years in prison for possessing three grams or more of crack, compared to a presumptive sentence of probation for possessing less than 10 grams of cocaine powder. While 97 percent of crack defendants in Minnesota were black, 80 percent of cocaine powder defendants were white. That racial disparity, a Minnesota judge ruled in 1990, was inconsistent with the state constitution's guarantee of equal protection. The following year, the Minnesota Supreme Court agreed, finding no "rational basis" for the distinction between the two forms of cocaine.[49]

The U.S. Sentencing Commission (USSC), an independent judicial agency charged with writing sentencing guidelines for federal judges and advising legislators on criminal penalties, discussed the Minnesota decision in a 1991 report to Congress. "Objections have been raised in several federal district courts that the mandatory minimum penalties for 'crack' cocaine discriminate on racial grounds," the USSC noted. "Although the drug laws are racially neutral on their face, critics of the 'crack' provisions contend that the statutes have a racially discriminatory effect." Those critics, it said, argued that the distinction between crack and cocaine powder "is irrational and, therefore, the discriminatory effect of the legislation is unconstitutional."[50]

Although the commission did not endorse that argument, it became increasingly skeptical of the rationale for extra-harsh crack sentences and increasingly troubled by the resulting racial disparities. "While some aspects of crack cocaine use and distribution suggest that a higher penalty for crack offenses compared to powder cocaine offenses is appropriate, the present 100-to-1 quantity ratio is too great," the USSC said in a 1995 report to Congress. "Among other problems, the 100-to-1 quantity ratio creates anomalous results by potentially punishing low-level (retail) crack dealers far more severely than their high-level (wholesale) suppliers of the powder cocaine that served as the product for conversion into crack."[51]

Notwithstanding the special concern provoked by the emergence of crack, the commission noted, "powder cocaine and crack cocaine are two forms of the same drug, containing the same active ingredient." That meant their pharmacological effects were similar, which made claims about crack-induced violence suspect. The USSC noted that "systemic violence" associated with the black market accounted for the vast majority of "crack-related" homicides. That sort of violence was distinct from "economically compulsive crime" by crack users and "pharmacologically driven crime" committed under the drug's influence. The commission's review of the relevant research indicated that "neither powder nor crack cocaine excite[s] or agitate[s] users to commit criminal acts and that the stereotype of a drug-crazed addict committing heinous crimes is not true for either form of cocaine."[52]

Based on the unsubstantiated assumption that crack was far more dangerous than cocaine powder, Congress created a sentencing scheme that had a strikingly disproportionate impact on black defendants. In 1993, the USSC reported, "blacks accounted for 88.3 percent of federal crack cocaine distribution convictions." By contrast, cocaine powder defendants were mostly white (32 percent) or Hispanic (39 percent).[53]

That disparity, the commission said, "does not mean" that "the penalties are racially motivated" or that Congress "acted with any discriminatory intent." Unlike the Minnesota Supreme Court, it noted, "all [federal] appellate courts" had rejected equal protection claims based on racially skewed cocaine sentencing. The "high percentage of Blacks convicted of crack cocaine offenses" was nevertheless "a matter of great concern," the report said.[54]

"When one form of a drug can be rather easily converted to another form of the same drug and when that second form is punished at a quantity ratio 100 times greater than the original form, it would appear reasonable to require the existence of sufficient policy bases to support such a sentencing scheme regardless of racial impact," the commission noted. "Moreover, when such an enhanced ratio for a particular form of a drug has a disproportionate effect on one segment of the population, it is particularly important that sufficient policy bases exist in support of the enhanced ratio."[55]

"REAL REGARDLESS OF INTENT"
USSC Vice Chairman Michael Gelacak underlined that point in a 1997 report. "Even though the Commission has conceded that there was no intent by the Legislature that penalties fall disproportionately on one segment of the population, the impact of these penalties nonetheless remains," he wrote. "If the impact of the law is discriminatory, the problem is no less real regardless of the intent. This problem is particularly acute because the disparate impact arises from a penalty structure for two different forms of the same substance."[56]

Subsequent data from the sentencing commission confirmed that defendants subject to the especially severe penalties for crack distribution were overwhelmingly black.[57] That reality was reflected in the sentences that federal defendants received. In fiscal year 1990, for instance, 75 percent of black drug defendants were convicted of offenses that carried mandatory minimums, compared to 54 percent of white drug defendants.[58]

In fiscal year 2010, black defendants were still more likely than white defendants to be convicted under mandatory minimum provisions. And while just 39 percent of the black defendants were able to avoid those penalties based on "substantial assistance" to law enforcement or the "safety valve" that Congress created in 1994 for low-level, nonviolent offenders with minimal criminal histories, 64 percent of white drug offenders qualified for such relief. The upshot was that black drug offenders were more than twice as likely to receive mandatory minimums.[59]

As you would expect, those minimums made a big difference. The average sentence for drug defendants who received them in fiscal year 2010 was 11 years, compared to about five years for those who were granted relief. Overall, the average sentence for black crack offenders was nearly 10 years, compared to less than six years for white crack offenders.

The average sentences for cocaine powder offenses were lower: about eight years for black defendants and five years for white defendants.[60]

Black defendants, in other words, were at a double disadvantage. They accounted for the overwhelming majority of crack offenders, who were subject to heavier penalties than cocaine powder offenders. And even within each cocaine category, they were apt to receive longer sentences than white defendants. The sentencing commission suggested that the latter disparity was driven partly by racial differences in criminal histories, which affected the penalties recommended by federal sentencing guidelines and eligibility for the safety valve.[61]

Congress did not address crack sentences until 2010, 15 years after the USSC began recommending reform (a position it repeatedly reiterated over the years). And even then, Congress did not eliminate the gap, as Biden sought to do in 2007. The Fair Sentencing Act of 2010, which passed the House by a voice vote and passed the Senate by unanimous consent with support from the Obama administration, eliminated the mandatory minimum for simple possession and reduced the weight ratio for trafficking offenses, making it 18 to 1 rather than 100 to 1.[62]

That change did not apply to crack offenders who had already been sentenced, meaning that thousands of people continued to serve prison terms that nearly everyone agreed were too long. The FIRST STEP Act of 2018, which was supported by the Trump administration and passed both houses of Congress by overwhelming margins, addressed that omission, making the 2010 reform retroactive.[63]

Those two changes meant less time behind bars for thousands of mostly black crack offenders, including some 6,000 convicted in the three years after the Fair Sentencing Act and more than 4,000 who, thanks to the FIRST STEP Act, were released earlier than their original sentences would have required. African Americans accounted for more than three-quarters of the first group and 92 percent of the second group.[64]

That relief came too late for Keith Jackson, the teenager who inadvertently supplied the prop for President Bush's 1989 crack speech. Federal drug agents lured Jackson to Lafayette Square so that Bush could dramatically claim that the bag of crack he displayed on TV had been bought at "a park just across the street from the White House." Far from frequenting that park, Jackson did not even know where the White House was; he had to ask the agent who set him up for directions. "We had to manipulate him to get him down there," the agent told *The Washington Post*. "It wasn't easy."[65]

The following year, Jackson, then 19, was sentenced to 10 years in federal prison for selling crack within 1,000 feet of a school. Bush did not understand why people were upset that his underlings, at his behest, had tricked Jackson into committing that crime. "I think it was great because it sent a message to the United States that even across from the White House they can sell drugs," the president said. "I can't feel sorry for this fellow."[66]

"Much More Likely to Be Searched"

The crack debacle is just one example of a drug prohibition regime that produces racially skewed outcomes from start to finish. Before people can be sentenced for violating the drug laws, they have to be convicted. Before they can be convicted, they have to be arrested. And before they can be arrested, they have to be caught, which often results from searches for contraband. How do those happen?

Often they happen during routine traffic stops. The U.S. Supreme Court has given police broad leeway to pull people over based on suspected violations of state motor vehicle codes, which include myriad rules governing the maintenance and operation of cars. Those rules are so numerous, picayune, vague, and subjective that it is hard to drive for any length of time without breaking one or more of them.[67]

In practice, that means cops can stop pretty much any vehicle on the road. According to the Supreme Court, that is consistent with the Fourth Amendment as long as police claim to be enforcing traffic laws, even if their real intent is to look for evidence of an unrelated crime.[68] Civil forfeiture laws, which allow police to pad their budgets by seizing money or other property that is allegedly tainted by crime (typically a drug offense), give them an additional incentive to make pretextual traffic stops.[69]

Research indicates that the risk of such harassment is not evenly distributed across racial groups. Looking at 12 years of data from North Carolina, political scientist Frank Baumgartner and his colleagues found "dramatic disparities in the rates at which black drivers, particularly young males, are searched and arrested as compared to similarly situated whites." For example, "blacks are 200% more likely to be searched and 190% more likely to be arrested after being pulled over for a seat belt violation; 110% more likely to be searched or arrested following a stop for vehicle regulatory violations; and 60% more likely to be searched or arrested after being stopped for equipment issues."[70]

The racial differences were especially large for discretionary searches based on consent or probable cause, as opposed to protective pat-downs or searches conducted pursuant to a warrant or after an arrest. Discretionary searches of black drivers were less likely to find drugs than discretionary searches of white drivers, which suggested that the extra suspicion African Americans encountered had no rational basis. Furthermore, the racial disparities grew over the years, while the likelihood of finding drugs did not.

These differences persisted after the data were adjusted for other variables that might affect the likelihood of being searched. "Controlling for why and when they were stopped, which officer pulled them over, and whether or not they had contraband in the car, young men of color are much more likely to see adverse outcomes," Baumgartner and his co-authors reported. "Minorities are much more likely to be searched and arrested than similarly situated whites, controlling for every variable that the state of North Carolina mandates to be collected when traffic stops are carried out."

Other studies reinforce these findings. After surveying drivers in the Kansas City area in 2003 and 2004, political scientist Charles Epp and his colleagues classified police encounters based on the legal justification (or lack thereof) and the amount of discretion involved. They found that black drivers were no more likely than white drivers to report clear-cut "traffic safety stops" (e.g., for running a red light or stop sign, driving at night with headlights off, or exceeding the speed limit by seven or more miles an hour) but were nearly three times as likely to report seemingly pretextual "investigatory stops" (e.g., for an unilluminated license plate, driving too slowly, or no reason mentioned by the officer).[71]

During investigatory stops, Epp and his colleagues reported, black drivers were five times as likely as white drivers to be searched. They also were more likely to be handcuffed and threatened with arrest and more likely to describe the officer's demeanor as rude, hostile, or insulting. Black drivers perceived investigatory stops as less legitimate than traffic safety stops, while white drivers made no such distinction. The more stops black drivers had experienced, the less they trusted the police, an effect that was not apparent among white drivers.

"Drivers are well aware of the profound racial disparities in police stops, and this awareness shapes perceptions of the police and their own place in society," Epp and his co-authors write. "Police stops confirm whites' common assumption that they are full citizens deserving respect and leniency; they teach African Americans that they are targets of suspicion."[72]

Information collected by the Pennsylvania State Police reveals similar disparities. "Year after year," *The Philadelphia Inquirer* reported in 2020, "troopers were roughly two to three times more likely to search black or Hispanic drivers than white drivers." And when searches were conducted, "troopers were far less likely to find contraband" if the drivers were black or Hispanic rather than white, suggesting that the evidentiary threshold for searching black and Hispanic drivers was lower.[73]

It is possible to reduce these disparities through determined effort, starting with data collection and analysis. In 2018, according to police data, black drivers in Portland, Oregon, were subjected to discretionary searches more than 12 percent of the time, compared to a rate of about 5 percent for white drivers. But by 2022, the Portland Police Bureau had reduced both the overall search rate and the racial gap: The discretionary-search rate was 1.8 percent for black drivers and 1.1 percent for white drivers.[74]

"The Numbers Are What the Numbers Are"

Similar patterns show up in searches of pedestrians. New York City's "stop, question, and frisk" program, although ostensibly aimed at seizing illegally possessed firearms, more frequently discovered marijuana, contributing to a spike in low-level pot busts. Both trends overwhelmingly involved young black or Latino men.

During Mayor Michael Bloomberg's administration, the number of stop-and-frisk encounters skyrocketed from about 97,000 in 2002 to a peak of nearly 686,000 in 2011.[75] That dramatic increase overlapped with an upward trend in low-level marijuana possession arrests that began under Bloomberg's predecessor, Rudy Giuliani. The number of arrests rose from about 1,500 in 1993, the year before Giuliani took office, to more than 51,000 in 2000, his second-to-last year. It then dropped off, dipping below 30,000 in 2004 before climbing again and reaching a peak of more than 51,000 in 2011, which was also the peak year for stop and frisk.[76]

This requires some explanation, since New York legislators supposedly decriminalized marijuana possession way back in 1977. Under that law, possessing 25 grams or less of marijuana (about nine-tenths of an ounce) was a civil offense punishable by no more than a $100 fine. But until 2019, possessing marijuana that was "burning or open to public view" was still a misdemeanor. In addition to catching people who happened to be smoking pot or waving their weed around, cops could manufacture misdemeanors by instructing people they stopped to take out any contraband they might have or by searching them (ostensibly for weapons) and pulling out a joint or a bag. Voilà: The marijuana was now "open to public view," an arrestable offense.

Such tricks did not seem fair to the marijuana users they ensnared, their lawyers, or civil liberties groups. In response to those complaints, Police Commissioner Ray Kelly issued a September 2011 directive that told his officers to cut it out. "The public display of marihuana must be an activity undertaken of the subject's own volition," Kelly said, explaining that the charge was not legally appropriate "if the marihuana recovered was disclosed to public view at an officer's discretion."[77]

Based on interviews with "veteran New York City legal aid and public defender attorneys and supervisors from Manhattan, Brooklyn and the Bronx," sociologist Harry G. Levine estimated that "two-thirds to three-quarters of the people arrested for misdemeanor possession" were busted in circumstances that Kelly said made an arrest invalid.[78] But Kelly said he would not hazard a guess as to how often that was happening.

"There was an allegation at a City Council hearing that I attended, that officers were telling individuals who were stopped to empty their pockets, and when they showed they had marijuana, that they were being arrested for a misdemeanor, and that's not the intent of the law," the commissioner told reporters. "If you have it in plain sight, then it is a misdemeanor. If you're directed by an officer to take it out of your pocket, that's not the intent of the law. That's what that directive was meant to address. It's very difficult to quantify whether or not that was happening. So . . . the numbers are what the numbers are."[79]

Whatever the impact of Kelly's directive, those numbers started dropping the following year. Between 2011 and 2015, the number of low-level marijuana possession arrests in New York City fell from more than 50,000 to fewer than 17,000, which coincided with a dramatic decline in stop-and-frisk encounters. In 2019, the year that state legislators eliminated the "public view" loophole, the NYPD arrested about 1,100 people for marijuana possession, which represented a 98 percent drop since 2011.[80] As of 2021, when New York legalized public possession of three ounces or less by adults 21 or older, people who met those criteria no longer had to worry about getting arrested.

All told, New York City's pot-bust binge generated more than 700,000 arrests from 1994 to 2019. More than four-fifths of the arrestees were black or Latino. In other words, Bloomberg—a white billionaire who in a 2001 interview with *New York* magazine lightheartedly acknowledged that he himself had used marijuana, saying, "You bet I did, and I enjoyed it"—presided over a pot crackdown that overwhelmingly affected people with darker skin of much more modest means.[81]

After he was elected mayor, Bloomberg reiterated that he had smoked pot "when I was younger," like "most people in my generation." But he said he regretted his remark in the *New York* interview because it was later featured in ads sponsored by the National Organization for the Reform of Marijuana Laws. "I do not think that decriminalizing marijuana is a good idea," he said. "I am very much in favor of enforcing laws on the books. I've always thought if we don't want to enforce laws on the books, we should remove them from the books. But when you have laws, you breed contempt if you don't enforce them."[82] Bloomberg apparently did not consider the contempt that results from wildly uneven enforcement of widely flouted laws.

"A Racial Justice Issue"

Racially skewed marijuana arrests were not limited to New York City. Based on an analysis of more than eight million marijuana arrests from 2001 through 2010, the American Civil Liberties Union (ACLU) found that black people were nearly four times as likely to be arrested for possession as white people, although surveys find that rates of cannabis consumption in the two groups are similar. While the racial gap varied across the country, it was apparent in nearly every county with more than 30,000 residents where black people accounted for at least 2 percent of the population.[83]

The war on weed "has needlessly ensnared hundreds of thousands of people in the criminal justice system, had a staggeringly disproportionate impact on African-Americans, and comes at a tremendous human and financial cost," the ACLU concluded in its 2013 report. "The price paid by those arrested and convicted of marijuana possession can be significant and linger for years, if not a lifetime. Arrests and convictions for possessing marijuana can negatively impact public housing and student financial aid eligibility, employment opportunities, child custody determinations, and immigration status."[84]

The ACLU revisited this subject in 2020, updating its findings with additional data through 2018. "Stark racial disparities in marijuana possession arrests have remained unchanged nationwide," it reported. "On average, a Black person is 3.64 times more likely to be arrested for marijuana possession than a white person." That was only slightly lower than the figure that the ACLU had calculated in its previous report (3.73). And "just as before," it found that "such racial disparities in marijuana possession arrests exist across the country, in every state, in counties large and small, urban and rural, wealthy and poor, and with large and small Black populations."[85]

By the beginning of 2018, eight states had legalized recreational marijuana. Unsurprisingly, the total number of marijuana arrests fell dramatically in those states after legalization. But even in those states, certain marijuana-related conduct, such as public consumption and possession in excess of specified amounts, remained illegal. Overall, the ACLU found, the racial arrest gap in states that had legalized marijuana shrank but did not disappear. On average, black people were 1.72 times as likely as white people to be arrested for marijuana possession, down from 2.2 in 2010.[86]

"Marijuana legalization has always been a racial justice issue," the ACLU said. "Whereas marijuana use by white people has been de facto legal in much of the country, in Black and Brown communities, police have routinely stopped people, particularly youth—at the park, on the street, in the train, on the bus, at school, near school, by the community center, on the porch, or while driving—searching (usually in vain) for something illegal, and, if they found marijuana, arresting and hauling people to jail. Such police harassment not only criminalizes people of color for engaging in an activity that white people participate in with relative impunity, it is a means of surveillance and social control counterproductive to public safety and community health. Indeed, repeated police encounters prove traumatic and dehumanizing for those who endure them."[87]

Racial disparities in drug law enforcement extend beyond marijuana arrests. African Americans accounted for about 28 percent of total drug arrests in 2023, twice their share of the general population.[88] That is substantially lower than the numbers seen in the late 1980s and early 1990s, when the black share was 40 percent or more.[89] The vast majority of drug arrests (82 percent in 2023) involve possession, as opposed to sale or production.[90] Yet survey data indicate similar rates of past-year and past-month drug use among black and white respondents.[91]

Information about involvement in drug sales is more limited. But in a 1991 survey, 1.4 percent of black adults admitted selling drugs in the previous year, compared to 0.7 percent of white adults.[92] Since the black share of the total population that year was about 12 percent, you might expect that African Americans would account for something like a quarter of arrests for drug sales. Yet they actually accounted for two-fifths of drug arrests at the time, about a third of which involved sale or production.[93] And in 1990, black defendants accounted for 57 percent of drug trafficking convictions in state courts, which handle the vast majority of such cases.[94]

In contrast with the 1991 survey, a 1997 survey found that black teenagers were only slightly more likely than white teenagers to report that they had sold drugs in the previous year. Based on those results and survey data on drug use, a 2016 Brookings Institution report posited that "blacks and whites sell and use drugs at similar rates." Yet the authors found that "blacks are 2.7 times as likely as whites to be arrested for a drug-related crime," "receive sentences that are almost 50 percent longer," and "are 6.5 times as likely to be incarcerated for drug-related offenses at the state level."[95]

At the federal level, according to the U.S. Sentencing Commission, black drug defendants receive longer sentences, on average, than white drug defendants, even after "controlling for available personal and offense characteristics." The gap is largely due to differences in the likelihood of receiving a sentence that includes prison: Black men were 35 percent less likely than white men to receive a probation-only sentence.[96]

THE NEW JIM CROW?

Civil rights activist Michelle Alexander, in her 2010 book *The New Jim Crow*, argued that such disparities reflect the systemic racism of the war on drugs, a de facto continuation of once-explicit discrimination against African Americans.[97] In addition to questioning the implication of racist design, Alexander's critics argued that she had exaggerated the impact of drug prohibition on mass incarceration.[98] Drug offenders represent a large share of federal prisoners: 44 percent as of 2024.[99] But they account for a much smaller share of state prisoners: 13 percent as of 2021.[100] Overall, according to a 2024 report from the Prison Policy Initiative, about 360,000 people were incarcerated for drug offenses. That represented roughly one-fifth of people in U.S. prisons or jails.[101]

That static picture, however, does not reflect the cumulative impact of drug-related incarceration. Writing in 2015, Brookings Institution scholar Jonathan Rothwell noted that "drug crimes have been the predominant reason for new admissions into state and federal prisons in recent decades." From 1993 through 2011, "there were three million admissions into federal and state prisons for drug offenses." During the same period, "there were 30 million arrests for drug crimes, 24 million of which were for possession." Even allowing for repeat offenders, Rothwell wrote, "these figures show how largely this problem looms over the lives of many Americans, and especially black Americans."[102]

All of which brings us back to the question we started with: To what extent is prohibition's disproportionate impact on African Americans attributable to racial bias, as opposed to good intentions gone awry? Black politicians like Charles Rangel, who said he was responding to a "frightening epidemic of a new street drug," surely did not intend that the severe penalties they supported would create "a sentencing divide that victimized young Black men." Supporters of New York City's stop-and-frisk program likewise insisted that they were trying to protect residents of high-crime neighborhoods, although that seemingly reasonable allocation of police resources resulted in routine harassment of mostly innocent black and Latino men while contributing to a surge in penny-ante pot busts that overwhelmingly involved those same groups.

There are other possible explanations for these disparities that do not involve racial prejudice. If black drug users and dealers tend to be more conspicuous than white drug users and dealers because they are more likely to consume or sell drugs out in the open, for example, that could help account for their higher risk of arrest, especially if there are more cops in black neighborhoods because other sorts of crime are more common there. If black drug defendants are less likely than white drug defendants to have competent legal representation because they are disproportionately poor, that could help explain why they are more likely to be incarcerated once they are arrested and why they tend to serve longer prison terms.

Still, some disparities are hard to explain in race-neutral terms. A 2020 study of nearly 100 million traffic stops across the United States found that "black drivers were less likely to be stopped after sunset, when a 'veil of darkness' masks one's race, suggesting bias in stop decisions." The researchers also considered how often motorists were searched and how often those searches discovered contraband. They found "evidence that the bar for searching black and Hispanic drivers was lower than that for searching white drivers." And while searches were less common in jurisdictions that had legalized marijuana, "the bar for searching black and Hispanic drivers was still lower than that for white drivers."[103]

In a 2019 paper, economist Cody Tuttle looked at federal crack sentencing patterns before and after Congress raised the thresholds for mandatory minimums. Tuttle found "a sharp increase" in cases where defendants were sentenced near the new, 280-gram cutoff for the 10-year mandatory minimum, an increase that was "disproportionately large for black and Hispanic offenders." He concluded that "the increased bunching for minority offenders" around the new threshold was "driven by prosecutorial discretion." Decisions about how to charge crack trafficking offenses varied between and within districts, and about 30 percent of prosecutors accounted for the racial disparity. While that gap "cannot be explained by differences in education, sex, age, criminal history, seized drug amount, or other elements of the crime," Tuttle reported, it corresponded well with "a measure of state-level racial animus" based on geographic variations in Google searches for "a specific racial slur and its plural form."[104]

Even if U.S. drug policy is no longer driven by bigotry at the legislative level, in other words, it entails broad discretion for police officers and prosecutors, some of whom are apt to be influenced by racial prejudice. That phenomenon, combined with other factors that make black people more vulnerable to drug law enforcement, creates a situation in which African Americans bear the brunt of the government's efforts to prevent consumption of psychoactive substances that politicians have deemed intolerable. As Michael Gelacak put it in 1997: "If the impact of the law is discriminatory, the problem is no less real regardless of the intent." As we will see in the next chapter, enforcement of gun laws has resulted in similarly striking disparities.

Chapter Four

Gun Control in Black and White

"People Don't Know What's Going On"
After moving to a Washington, D.C., neighborhood near Capitol Hill in February 2002, Shelly Parker, a black emergency room nurse turned software designer, was troubled by local gang activity and decided to do something about it. "She wanted her neighborhood to be a safer and more comfortable place for law-abiding citizens," Brian Doherty writes. "She made a nuisance of herself to local drug dealers, walking the streets wearing an orange hat as a one-woman citizen patrol, calling cops when she saw illegal activity, and installing a security camera for her yard."[1]

Parker's activities did not endear her to the neighborhood drug dealers. By that June, Doherty notes, "her car window had been broken, her security camera had been stolen, and a drug gang lookout [had] rammed a car into her back fence." A subsequent incident was even scarier. "One night," NPR reported, "a 7-foot-2-inch-tall drug dealer who lived with his mother on the block tried to break into her house and threatened to kill her. She chased him away by setting off the alarm, and when the police came, one of the officers told her to 'get a gun.'"[2]

That was easier said than done in the District of Columbia, where a local ordinance required that all guns be registered with the police; prohibited possession of handguns that had not been registered prior to September 24, 1976; and required that residents who had rifles or shotguns at home keep them in a condition that was not conducive to self-defense: "unloaded and disassembled or bound by a trigger lock or similar device." On its face, the law made it a crime even to unlock and load a gun to ward off a home invasion. Violating those rules was a misdemeanor punishable by a maximum fine of $1,000, up to a year in jail, or both. A second violation of the handgun ban was a felony punishable by a fine up to $5,000 and/or up to five years in prison.[3]

"What I want is simply to be able to own a handgun in my home, in the confines of the walls of my home—nothing else," Parker told NPR.[4] Because the city had made that option illegal, Parker became the lead plaintiff in a lawsuit arguing that its ordinance violated the Second Amendment right "to keep and bear arms."[5]

Parker ultimately was excluded from the case because an appeals court determined that she lacked standing to sue: Unlike Dick Heller, a white security guard who had unsuccessfully sought permission to keep his on-the-job handgun at home, she never actually applied for a registration certificate (which inevitably would have been denied).[6] But although Parker was replaced by Heller as the lead (and only) plaintiff, the case she helped initiate led to the U.S. Supreme Court's landmark 2008 decision in *District of Columbia v. Heller*, which recognized a constitutional right to keep handguns at home for self-defense.[7]

Otis McDonald, a retired University of Chicago maintenance engineer, faced a problem similar to the one Parker had confronted in Washington. An Army veteran and hunter who was familiar with firearms, McDonald legally owned shotguns, but he wanted to keep a handgun at home for protection against the criminals who plagued his Chicago neighborhood. As a community activist promoting alternative policing strategies, he had been repeatedly threatened with violence. The safeguard he wanted to employ was nevertheless forbidden in Chicago, where residents could not legally keep handguns unless they had been registered before April 16, 1982.[8]

"I don't understand how somebody in today's society can take away a law-abiding citizen's inherent rights and think it will do any good when you look at it across the country and it hasn't done any good," McDonald told a local newspaper in 2010. "I don't think guns against guns are the answer to our problems, but you have to look at it realistically. We are in a war, and what do we do? Guns in the houses are not doing all this killing.

It's not law-abiding citizens with guns who are doing all the violence. It bothers me to think people don't know what's going on."[9]

McDonald's frustration drove him to join three other Chicago residents and two gun rights groups in a lawsuit that culminated in another important Second Amendment decision two years after *Heller*. In *McDonald v. Chicago*, the Supreme Court held that state and local governments, not merely federal enclaves like the District of Columbia, were required to respect the right that the justices had upheld in *Heller*.[10] That ruling was consistent with what the framers of the Fourteenth Amendment seem to have had in mind and with prior decisions that applied other Bill of Rights provisions to the states.

These cases involved African Americans who wanted to keep handguns at home but were prohibited from doing so because the cities where they lived had decided that residents could not be trusted with what the Supreme Court called "the quintessential self-defense weapon." Yet in *Heller*, the NAACP Legal Defense & Educational Fund (LDF)—which grew out of litigation that, among other things, sought to vindicate the right of armed self-defense against racist aggressors—took the government's side. In *McDonald*, the organization filed a brief that supported neither the plaintiffs nor the government.

Those positions were hard to reconcile with the words and actions of civil rights leaders ranging from Frederick Douglass to Martin Luther King Jr., who understood the value of guns as self-defense tools. The LDF's stance glossed over the reality that gun control, even when divorced from its racist roots, disproportionately burdened black people in several ways. They were especially likely to live in jurisdictions with both strict gun laws and high crime rates. They were especially likely to live in neighborhoods where police focused their resources. They were especially likely to be legally disqualified from owning guns. And largely for those reasons, they were especially likely to be arrested and imprisoned for violating firearm regulations, even when they had no history of violence and posed no threat to public safety—even when they only wanted, like Parker and McDonald, to own guns for protection of themselves, their homes, and their families.

Gun Laws "Protect Black People"

"In densely populated urban centers like the District of Columbia," the LDF said in *Heller*, "gun violence deprives many residents of an equal opportunity to live, much less succeed. The effects of gun violence on African-American citizens are particularly acute." The organization was therefore motivated to defend "the authority of locally elected officials to enact regulations intended to promote public health and safety by reducing gun deaths, gun injuries, and gun-related violence."[11]

At this point, the U.S. Court of Appeals for the D.C. Circuit already had concluded that "the Second Amendment protects an individual right to keep and bear arms."[12] The LDF urged the Supreme Court to reject that interpretation and instead rule that "the right protected by the Second Amendment is one that exists only in the context of a lawfully organized militia," as state and federal courts had "almost unanimously" concluded.

According to that "collective right" view, the Second Amendment's prefatory clause ("A well regulated militia, being necessary to the security of a free state . . .") meant that "the right of the people to keep and bear arms" was fundamentally different from "the right of the people peaceably to assemble" (protected by the First Amendment), "the right of the people" to be secure from "unreasonable searches and seizures" (protected by the Fourth Amendment), and the unspecified rights "retained by the people" under the Ninth Amendment. Unlike those rights, advocates of this reading said, the rights guaranteed by the Second Amendment were *not* individual rights; they were limited to service in the militia.

The Supreme Court, which had never squarely addressed the issue before, ultimately rejected the interpretation urged by the LDF. Both the text and the history of the Second Amendment, Justice Antonin Scalia concluded in the majority opinion, indicated that it was understood to guarantee an individual right, which included the right to keep handguns "in defense of hearth and home."[13]

On its face, the LDF's position was puzzling. According to its brief, the organization "since its founding" had been "committed to transforming this nation's promise of equality into reality for all Americans, with a particular emphasis on the rights of African Americans."[14] As we saw in

Chapter 2, that struggle included an insistence on "the right to keep and bear arms to defend their homes, families or themselves," as the *Loyal Georgian* put it in 1866 (quoting the Freedmen's Bureau)—a right that belonged to "all men, without distinction of color."

In rejecting that tradition, the LDF essentially argued that African Americans' collective interest in crime control, which it thought could be achieved through firearm regulation, trumped any individual's interest in protecting himself against crime when the government was manifestly failing to prevent it. Recognizing an individual right to arms, the LDF worried, "unduly limits the ability of States and municipalities struggling to address the problem of gun violence, a problem of particular interest to this nation's African-American community."[15]

The LDF conceded that "the history surrounding the adoption of early gun control laws" may have been "tainted by racial discrimination" and acknowledged "concerns about this nation's past or present-day problems with racial discrimination" in enforcement of such laws. But it said the solution to "discriminatory enforcement of firearm laws" was to scrutinize such practices, "as necessary," under the Fourteenth Amendment's guarantee of equal protection or the Fifth Amendment's guarantee of due process.[16]

In *McDonald*, the LDF again declined to defend the Second Amendment rights of African Americans. Its brief instead cautioned against applying the Second Amendment to the states via the Fourteenth Amendment's moribund "privileges or immunities" clause, as opposed to the Supreme Court's usual reliance on the latter amendment's guarantee of due process to "incorporate" freedoms protected by the Bill of Rights.[17] And in a 2022 case involving New York's requirement that residents show "proper cause" to publicly carry handguns for self-defense, the LDF reiterated the position it had taken in *Heller*. Such laws aimed to "protect Black people," it said, and if they had a racially disproportionate impact the answer was enforcement of equal protection rather than broad recognition of the right to bear arms.[18]

The LDF's brief in *New York State Rifle & Pistol Association v. Bruen* emphasized the threat that guns in the hands of violent criminals posed to black people rather than the protection that guns might afford to potential victims of those criminals. "The effects of gun violence on Black Americans are particularly acute," it said, "as Black people, and specifically Black men, are disproportionately likely to experience a gun injury or death." The LDF's description of how guns were used in Southern states after the Civil War was similarly one-sided, emphasizing the threat that guns in the hands of white supremacists posed to black people rather than the protection that guns could provide against those aggressors.[19]

"HE HAD A GUN BECAUSE OF CRIME"

New York's statute, a descendant of the Sullivan Law, made it a felony, punishable by up to 15 years in prison, to carry a loaded firearm outside one's home or place of business without a permit. It gave local authorities broad discretion to issue or deny carry permits based on a vague and subjective standard. In that respect, it resembled the laws that Southern states historically had used to disarm African Americans, including the law that a local sheriff had used to deny the pistol permit that Martin Luther King Jr. sought for the men who were guarding his home in Birmingham.

The National African American Gun Association (NAAGA), a group founded in 2015 to educate people about "the rich legacy of gun ownership by African Americans" and "defend the inalienable right to self defense for African Americans," noted the King episode in a brief supporting the challenge to New York's law. NAAGA's *Bruen* brief reviewed the long history of deploying gun laws to uphold white supremacy by leaving black people defenseless against racist assaults. "The historical exclusion of African Americans from exercise of the right to bear arms by total bans or by discretionary licensing laws reflected their status as slaves or non-citizens," it noted. "Protecting the right of the people at large, particularly the freedmen, to carry arms was a primary objective of the Fourteenth Amendment."[20]

Black Guns Matter (BGM), a group founded in 2016 that "focuses on teaching African Americans about gun safety and armed self-defense," made similar points in its *Bruen* brief. The New York law "shares its origins with laws that disfavor certain groups, keeping them marginalized on the periphery of society," BGM said. Noting that "armed self-defense has always been vitally important to the African American community," it added that "the need for armed self-defense is most critical" when the government "fails to offer assistance."[21]

That need, BGM said, was reflected in gun purchases by black men and women, which increased substantially in response to the surge in violent crime during the COVID-19 pandemic and the unrest that followed the May 2020 murder of George Floyd by Minneapolis police. That jump in gun sales, it said, "signals a realization by African Americans that reliance upon the government is inadequate to address the challenges they face in their own communities and shows the current, modern importance of armed self-defense to the African American community."[22]

In another brief opposing New York's law, the Black Attorneys of Legal Aid and several other public defender groups highlighted the practical consequences of the state's tight restrictions on public possession of handguns. "Each year," they said, "we represent hundreds of indigent people whom New York criminally charges for exercising their right to keep and bear arms. For our clients, New York's licensing requirement renders the Second Amendment a legal fiction. Worse, virtually all our clients whom New York prosecutes for exercising their Second Amendment rights are Black [or] Hispanic." That situation, the brief said, "is no accident," since "New York enacted its firearm licensing requirements to criminalize gun ownership by racial and ethnic minorities," and "that remains the effect of its enforcement by police and prosecutors today."[23]

The public defenders said the de facto ban on carrying guns for self-defense in New York City had a "brutal" impact on residents of high-crime neighborhoods: "New York police have stopped, questioned, and frisked our clients on the streets. They have invaded our clients' homes with guns drawn, terrifying them, their families, and their children. They have forcibly removed our clients from their homes and communities and abandoned them in dirty and violent jails and prisons for days, weeks, months, and years. They have deprived our clients of their jobs, children, livelihoods, and ability to live in this country. And they have branded our clients as 'criminals' and 'violent felons' for life. They have done all of this only because our clients exercised a constitutional right."[24]

One of those clients was Benjamin Prosser, a young man who "had repeatedly been the victim of violent stranger assaults and robberies on the street." When Prosser "started a job that required that he travel two hours for work every day, he decided to carry a firearm." Although "he did not possess it with any intent to engage in violence," the public defenders said, "his experiences taught him that he needed a weapon to be safe." But as with Marino Rossi, the first person convicted under New York's Sullivan Law, Prosser's intent did not matter. He was arrested for violating New York's gun restrictions and, facing a potential prison sentence of three-and-a-half to 15 years, pleaded guilty to a lesser charge. Although his formal sentence was limited to probation, his conviction still qualified him as a "violent felon," a status that permanently barred him from owning a gun and invited "discrimination by employers, landlords, and whoever else conducts a background check."[25]

Another defendant was Sam Little, a father in his thirties who was working on a college degree in child psychology. Little "had repeatedly witnessed and been victimized by violence," the brief noted. "He had friends who had been shot and murdered, and he himself had been shot—both when he was a teenager and then several years later. Once, Mr. Little was slashed across the face with a knife." One night, he "left his home to go a friend's birthday party, which was in the same neighborhood where he had previously been slashed. To ensure his safety, Mr. Little brought a firearm." Police stopped and frisked him while he was walking down the street, and he was ultimately convicted of a firearm offense that sent him to jail for eight months. The prosecution ended Little's college education, nixed a job offer, and permanently limited such opportunities.[26]

Even Democrats who generally supported gun control were troubled by such cases. Before he was elected as Manhattan's district attorney in 2021, Alvin Bragg acknowledged the unjust consequences of arresting people like Prosser and Little. "We need to recognize that not every person charged with possessing an illegal gun in New York City is a driver of violence," Bragg said on his campaign website. When he was growing up, he recalled, his father kept a handgun at home to "ward off burglary attempts." Bragg's father "had an illegal gun not because he liked guns or because he was 'dangerous'; he had a gun because of crime in the neighborhood."[27]

Although Bragg retreated from that stance after he was elected, Philadelphia District Attorney Larry Krasner expressed similar concerns about arrests for illegal gun possession. Such arrests "must be targeted to distinguish between drivers of gun violence who possess firearms illegally and otherwise law-abiding people who are not involved in gun violence," he said in 2022. When "people do not feel protected by the police," Krasner noted, they may "view the risk of being caught by police with an illegal gun as outweighed by the risk of being caught on the street without one."[28]

Black Guns Matter founder Maj Toure says his Second Amendment advocacy was inspired by his experiences as a rapper trying to sell records, which involved developing local contacts in cities such as New York, Detroit, and Los Angeles. Those collaborators, he recalls, were frequently waylaid by gun charges. "Where's Steve?" he would ask. Upon learning that "he caught a gun charge," Toure would naively ask, "Who'd he shoot?" The reply: "He didn't shoot anybody. He just had the gun." This was "a constant theme," Toure says. If no one was threatened, assaulted, or robbed, he would wonder, "What is the crime here?"[29]

"Creating Criminals"

The Supreme Court's June 2022 decision in *Bruen* rejected the policy that forced New Yorkers to choose between protecting themselves and obeying the law. The court recognized that "the right of the people to keep and bear arms" includes a right to "carry a handgun for self-defense outside the home." While 43 states had established "objective criteria" for allowing people to carry guns, Justice Clarence Thomas noted in the majority opinion, New York was one of seven states where that permission was contingent on demonstrating "a special need." That additional requirement, Thomas said, impermissibly gave local officials broad discretion to prevent "ordinary, law-abiding citizens" from exercising the Second Amendment right to "carry weapons in case of confrontation."[30]

That was not the outcome the LDF wanted, and that fact requires some explanation given "the rich legacy of gun ownership by African Americans" that groups like NAAGA and Black Guns Matter admire. Beginning in the late 1960s, mainstream black organizations, which had long embraced the right of armed self-defense, became full-throated supporters of gun control. In his book about "the black tradition of arms," law professor Nicholas Johnson identifies three main reasons for that shift.[31]

Moderate black leaders, who had always tried to maintain a distinction between armed self-defense and political violence, found that the emergence of militant groups like the Black Panthers made drawing that line harder. After "a strong black political class rose on the wave of a progressive coalition," Johnson says, newly empowered African-American leaders tended to take their policy cues from that coalition, which supported tighter restrictions on firearms. And "as black-on-black violence commanded increasing attention, gun bans promised a solution with the compelling logic of no guns equals no gun crime."[32] The upshot was an alliance that seems natural today but looks surprising from a longer historical perspective.

The LDF, which emerged from litigation pioneered by the NAACP, has been independent from the older group since 1957. But the NAACP itself, founded in 1909 by civil rights leaders who emphatically supported the right of armed self-defense, sued gun manufacturers in 1999 for fostering violent crime by "oversupplying" firearms—a claim that a federal jury rejected in 2003.[33] Jesse Jackson, who in 1988 became the first black candidate for a major party's presidential nomination to win primary contests, was arrested in 2007 for blocking the entrance to a suburban gun store that he said helped Chicago residents evade the city's handgun ban.[34] Three years later, the Supreme Court overturned that ban in response to Otis McDonald's challenge.

Like the NAACP and Jackson, the vast majority of black politicians favor gun control—and not just the laws already on the books. In 2021, for example, Rep. Sheila Jackson Lee (D–Texas), who had represented downtown Houston in Congress since 1995, introduced a bill that would have created an elaborate nationwide system to license gun owners, register firearms, and punish violators with harsh mandatory minimum penalties: a $75,000 fine, 15 years in prison, or both.[35]

Jackson Lee's attitude toward gun control was strikingly at odds with her attitude toward drug control. She had repeatedly sponsored or co-sponsored bills that would have removed marijuana from the list of federally proscribed substances, eliminating a ban first imposed in 1937. "Across this nation," she said in 2020, "thousands of men and women have suffered needlessly from the federal criminalization of marijuana, particularly in communities of color [that] have borne the burden of collateral consequences for those ensnared in criminal legal systems that have damaged our society across generations. This is unacceptable, and we must change our laws."[36]

Jackson Lee's critique of the war on drugs extended beyond marijuana. "We come together today armed not only with the knowledge that our criminal justice system is deeply flawed, but with the commitment to fix these flaws," she said when she proposed a package of drug sentencing reforms in 2015. "The cost of this system is incredibly high, not just in dollars spent, but also in dollars lost. Every person taken out of a community and placed into a prison is a person who cannot contribute to a family, a community, and our society. Worse, this system takes an incredible human toll, with the cycle of incarceration in a constant state of destruction. Today, with this legislation, we unify to reject a system that is often more effective at creating criminals and collateral damage than actual justice."[37]

Such concerns were conspicuously missing six years later, when Jackson Lee saw nothing wrong with sending gun owners to prison for 15 years or more if they failed to comply with the daunting and complicated regulations that she thought would help reduce violent crime. And notwithstanding her concern about "creating criminals," her bill would have turned millions of peaceful gun owners into felons.

The legislation would have required registration of all firearms, including information about where they would be stored and the identities of everyone who might use them. It also would have required that all gun owners obtain federal licenses, limited to people 21 or older who passed a "psychological examination" as well as a criminal background check, completed at least 24 hours of training, and paid an $800 "fee" for liability insurance.

If current or would-be gun owners did not successfully complete that process, the bill would have made it a felony for them to possess firearms. Successful applicants would have had to renew their licenses every year at first, then every three years once they had been licensed for at least five years. If a gun owner neglected to renew his license, he would have been subject to the same penalties as someone who never got one.

The system that Jackson Lee imagined is highly impractical. Gun owners would be understandably reluctant to identify themselves and their firearms so they could be entered in a federal database and required to apply for licenses. Politicians pursuing far less ambitious gun control schemes have found that voluntary compliance is the exception rather than the rule.[38] Since the Justice Department would not have the resources to go after millions of recalcitrant gun owners even if it knew who they were, the result would be arbitrary application of Jackson Lee's draconian penalties to the few who happened to attract the government's attention.

Who would those people tend to be? The record of gun law enforcement in the United States provides a clue, and it is not encouraging for anyone who worries, like Jackson Lee did, about racial bias in policing and the drug war's impact on "communities of color."

"Suspicionless Stops and Frisks"
We have already discussed how the New York Police Department's "stop, question, and frisk" program contributed to a dramatic increase in petty marijuana arrests. But the program's ostensible aim was to reduce deadly violence by enforcing the state law that the Supreme Court ultimately overturned in *Bruen*, which made it essentially impossible for ordinary people to legally carry handguns, even for self-defense, in New York City. The main justification for all those stops and frisks was to fight crime by finding and seizing illegally possessed guns—something that police almost never actually did.

During Mayor Michael Bloomberg's administration, you may recall, the number of pedestrian stops septupled, from about 97,000 in 2002 to a peak of nearly 686,000 in 2011. In 2003, when the NYPD made about 161,000 stops, it found guns just 0.38 percent of the time. By 2011, the gun seizure rate had fallen to 0.033 percent. That year, 87 percent of the stops involved black or Latino pedestrians, and 56 percent of the encounters included pat-downs. But when pedestrians were frisked, ostensibly because police had reason to believe they were armed, officers discovered a weapon of any kind less than 2 percent of the time.[39]

According to Bloomberg, those minuscule and falling gun seizure rates showed the program was working. "The number of guns that we've been finding has continued to go down, which says the program at this scale is doing a great job," he told radio host John Gambling in May 2012. "The whole idea here, John, is not to catch people with guns; it's to prevent people from carrying guns. . . . The fact that we're getting fewer guns says the program is working. And the program will really have succeeded when we don't get any guns."[40] Although Bloomberg apparently did not realize it, he was conceding that the stop-and-frisk program was blatantly unconstitutional.

The legal justification for the program was based on *Terry v. Ohio*, the 1968 decision in which the Supreme Court first allowed investigatory stops without probable cause.[41] That constitutional compromise, law professor Rachel Barkow argues, was motivated by public concerns about rising crime and the resulting political backlash against the court's pro-defendant rulings in cases like *Mapp v. Ohio* (excluding evidence obtained by illegal searches) and *Miranda v. Arizona* (requiring police to inform arrestees of their constitutional rights) rather than careful consideration of the Fourth Amendment's text and history.[42] Chief Justice Earl Warren alluded to that context in the majority opinion, noting "the practical and constitutional arguments pressed with great vigor on both sides of the public debate over the power of the police to 'stop and frisk'—as it is sometimes euphemistically termed—suspicious persons."

In *Terry*, Detective Martin McFadden had observed two black men, John Terry and Richard Chilton, repeatedly walk back and forth in front of a Cleveland jewelry store, peering into a display window each time and conferring in between with each other and a white man, Carl Katz. Suspecting that they were casing the store and planning to rob it, McFadden stopped the men and received a "mumbled" reply when he asked for their names. The detective immediately grabbed Terry and frisked him, discovering a pistol in his overcoat, which led to a concealed-weapon charge.

The Supreme Court held that the stop and the search were consistent with the Fourth Amendment because they were based on "specific and articulable facts" that, "taken together with rational inferences from those facts," justified McFadden's suspicions. It said police may stop someone when they reasonably suspect he is engaged in criminal activity and may pat him down when they have "reasonable grounds" to believe he is "armed and dangerous."[43]

Were New York City cops stopping people based on "reasonable suspicion"? Since the vast majority of stops—nine out of 10 in 2011—did not result in a summons or arrest, that seemed doubtful.[44] When they patted people down, did cops have "reasonable grounds" to think they would find weapons? Since 98 percent of the pedestrians frisked in 2011 did not have weapons, that seemed even more doubtful. And in that 2012 radio interview, Bloomberg admitted that "the whole idea" behind the pat-downs was "not to catch people with guns" but rather to *deter* them from carrying guns. Whatever you might think of that strategy's effectiveness, it was clearly inconsistent even with the latitude granted by *Terry*.

Four years before Bloomberg inadvertently conceded that the NYPD was routinely violating the Fourth Amendment, the Center for Constitutional Rights had filed a federal class action lawsuit making precisely that argument. The lawsuit also argued that the stop-and-frisk program violated the Fourteenth Amendment's guarantee of equal protection because "these suspicionless stops and frisks have and are being conducted predominantly on Black and Latino individuals, on the basis of racial and/or national origin profiling."[45]

The lead plaintiff in that lawsuit was David Floyd, a 28-year-old black man who had been repeatedly stopped and frisked by the NYPD. The first time that happened was on a Friday afternoon in April 2007, when he was walking down Beach Avenue a few doors from his house in the Bronx. Two police officers confronted him, demanding to know who he was, where he was going, what he was doing, and whether he was carrying any weapons. Floyd, who at the time was a freelance film editor, presented his driver's license and explained that he was walking home. Unsatisfied, one of the officers searched Floyd, feeling under his shirt and inside his pants pockets. He found nothing illegal.[46] Testifying in federal court six years later, Floyd said the incident left him feeling "frustrated

[and] humiliated, because it was on my block where I live, and I wasn't doing anything."[47]

"It Was Again the Humiliation"
Floyd was stopped and frisked again in February 2008, the month after he filed his original lawsuit. Floyd, who lived in a small house on his godmother's property, was approached by the tenant who was renting a basement apartment in her house, which was directly in front of his. The tenant said he had been locked out of his unit and asked Floyd to fetch the keys from his godmother's upstairs apartment. Since Floyd did not know which key was the right one, he returned with all the spare keys he could find. As Floyd was standing with the tenant in front of his godmother's house, trying to find the correct key, three officers approached them and asked what they were doing. Before they could explain the situation, the cops ordered them against a wall with their hands spread.[48]

After Floyd explained what was happening, the officers searched his pockets and asked for his ID. They wondered why his driver's license had an address different from his godmother's property. To clear things up, Floyd retrieved the tenant's ID from the locked basement apartment, after which the officers left.

Initially, the officers who interrogated Floyd that time might reasonably have wondered what he was doing. But they ordered him against the wall before he had a chance to explain, and they searched him without any reason to believe he was armed even after he clarified that he lived on the property and was helping the tenant. It is hard to imagine that police would have been equally aggressive when confronted by the same situation in a white, middle-class neighborhood.

"It was again the humiliation," Floyd testified in 2013. And this time, he said, "it wasn't down the block. It wasn't in another neighborhood. It was on the property that I lived on. . . . I felt that I was being told I shouldn't leave my home."[49]

Floyd's experience of being repeatedly stopped and frisked for no apparent reason was common during this period. In 2011 alone, the New York Civil Liberties Union noted, the NYPD stopped young black men

168,126 times, which "exceeded the entire city population of young black men" by about 10,000.[50]

As Bloomberg saw it, this sort of routine harassment was justified by the broader goal of discouraging young men from carrying guns. In August 2013, the federal judge who heard Floyd's case disagreed, ruling that the stop-and-frisk program violated the right to be free from unreasonable searches and seizures. U.S. District Judge Shira Scheindlin also concluded, based on data showing who was stopped and what happened afterward, that the program violated the right to equal protection.[51]

Scheindlin's analysis of data on 4.4 million stops made between January 2004 and June 2012 strongly suggested that reasonable suspicion was the exception rather than the rule. During this period, she noted, only 12 percent of people subjected to the "demeaning and humiliating" experience of being treated like a criminal were arrested or issued a summons. Even more striking, although police were supposed to frisk a subject only if they reasonably believed he was armed, 52 percent of these encounters included pat-downs, only 1.5 percent of which discovered a weapon. Even when officers reached into subjects' clothing after feeling what they thought was a weapon, they were right just 9 percent of the time.[52]

The officially recorded justifications for stops provided further evidence that New York cops' suspicions were frequently less than reasonable. "Between 2004 and 2009," Scheindlin noted, "the percentage of stops where the officer failed to state a specific suspected crime rose from 1% to 36%." Since stops are always supposed to be based on a reasonable suspicion of criminal activity and cops were free to make stuff up, unchallenged, on the forms they filled out, the fact that they failed to even name the crime they claimed to have suspected more than a third of the time suggested a pretty casual attitude toward the Fourth Amendment. The reasons they offered for suspecting someone was up to no good were similarly vague. Two of the most popular were "high crime area" and "furtive movements."[53]

"A Very Broad Concept"

What counted as "furtive movements"? "Two officers testified to their understanding of the term," Scheindlin noted. "One explained that 'furtive movement is a very broad concept,' and could include a person 'changing direction,' 'walking in a certain way,' '[a]cting a little suspicious,' 'making a movement that is not regular,' being 'very fidgety,' 'going in and out of his pocket,' 'going in and out of a location,' 'looking back and forth constantly,' 'looking over their shoulder,' 'adjusting their hip or their belt,' 'moving in and out of a car too quickly,' '[t]urning a part of their body away from you,' '[g]rabbing at a certain pocket or something at their waist,' 'getting a little nervous, maybe shaking,' and 'stutter[ing].' Another officer explained that 'usually' a furtive movement is someone 'hanging out in front of [a] building, sitting on the benches or something like that' and then making a 'quick movement,' such as 'bending down and quickly standing back up,' 'going inside the lobby . . . and then quickly coming back out,' or 'all of a sudden becom[ing] very nervous, very aware.'"[54]

That "very broad concept" gave officers much more leeway than the Supreme Court had allowed in *Terry*. "If officers believe that the behavior described above constitutes furtive movement that justifies a stop," Scheindlin wrote, "then it is no surprise that stops so rarely produce evidence of criminal activity."[55]

The fact that people stopped by police turned out to be innocent nine times out of 10 also figured in Scheindlin's equal protection analysis. Bloomberg and NYPD officials said the vast majority of people stopped by the cops (83 percent during the period Scheindlin considered) were black or Latino because the vast majority of criminal suspects were black or Latino. Bloomberg, in fact, argued that crime statistics justified an even greater racial disparity, saying cops should be stopping fewer white people and more people with darker skin, even though the numbers indicated that the reasons for stopping blacks and Latinos already were flimsier than the reasons for stopping whites, who were more likely to be caught with weapons or other contraband when searched.[56]

Scheindlin did not buy Bloomberg's argument. "The City and its highest officials believe that blacks and Hispanics should be stopped at the same rate as their proportion of the local criminal suspect population," she wrote. "But this reasoning is flawed because the stopped population is overwhelmingly innocent—not criminal. . . . While a person's race may be important if it fits the description of a particular crime suspect, it is impermissible to subject all members of a racially defined group to heightened police enforcement because some members of that group are criminals. The Equal Protection Clause does not permit race-based suspicion."[57]

Scheindlin also rejected Bloomberg's deterrence rationale. She noted testimony by Eric Adams, then a state legislator and later New York's mayor, who said Police Commissioner Ray Kelly had told him the department's stops focused on blacks and Latinos "because he wanted to instill fear in them" that "every time they leave their home, they could be stopped by the police." Kelly "has even suggested that it is permissible to stop racially defined groups just to instill fear in them that they are subject to being stopped at any time for any reason—in the hope that this fear will deter them from carrying guns in the streets," Scheindlin said. "The goal of deterring crime is laudable, but this method of doing so is unconstitutional."[58]

Bloomberg was outraged by Scheindlin's decision. "There is just no question that stop-question-frisk has saved countless lives," he said. "And we know that most of the lives saved, based on the statistics, have been black and Hispanic young men." He complained that Scheindlin "ignored the real-world realities of crime" and "made it clear that she wasn't at all interested in the crime reductions here or how we achieved them."[59]

There is little evidence that the stop-and-frisk program had the impact that Bloomberg claimed.[60] But as Scheindlin emphasized, that empirical question had nothing to do with the legal question of whether the program was consistent with the Fourth and Fourteenth Amendments. "This Court's mandate is solely to judge the constitutionality of police behavior, not its effectiveness as a law enforcement tool," she noted. "Many police practices may be useful for fighting crime—preventive detention or coerced confessions, for example—but because they are unconstitutional they cannot be used, no matter how effective."[61]

The city, which initially asked the U.S. Court of Appeals for the 2nd Circuit to overrule Scheindlin, dropped its appeal in 2014 after Bill de Blasio succeeded Bloomberg as mayor. The city agreed to various reforms, including an independent monitor charged with making sure the NYPD was respecting its constitutional limits.[62] Beginning in 2012, the annual number of stop-and-frisk encounters dropped precipitously. By 2021, it had fallen below 9,000. The number rose to more than 15,000 in 2022, but that was still about 98 percent lower than the 2011 peak.[63]

As the number of stops waned, so did Bloomberg's confidence that the program had done "a great job." In November 2019, a week before the former Republican launched his disastrous campaign for the 2020 Democratic presidential nomination, Bloomberg delivered a *mea culpa* to the congregation of an African-American church in Brooklyn. "I was wrong, and I am sorry," he said. Contrary to his expectations, he noted, "crime did not go back up" when the number of stops fell dramatically. Nor was that the only way in which Bloomberg had erred. "I got something important really wrong," he confessed. "I didn't understand . . . the full impact that stops were having on the black and Latino communities. I was totally focused on saving lives—but as we know: good intentions aren't good enough."[64]

"WILDLY OVERINCLUSIVE"

Despite that experience, Bloomberg continued to push stricter gun control, seemingly oblivious to its racially disproportionate impact. As a presidential candidate, he advocated a national "red flag" law, a federal ban on "assault weapons," and a national background-check requirement for private gun sales. Everytown for Gun Safety, which is funded mainly by Bloomberg, advocates similar policies.

Judging from surveys, expanded background checks are perhaps the least controversial idea favored by Bloomberg and his allies. Federal law currently requires background checks only for firearm sales by federally licensed dealers—people who make a living by selling guns. According to polling, around nine out of 10 Americans think that requirement should be extended to all gun transfers, including private sales, which in practice would mean they would have to be completed via licensed dealers.[65]

Even such seemingly massive support does not necessarily tell us how people will vote when they have a chance to enact such policies through ballot initiatives. As *The New York Times* noted in 2022, the gap between "expected support" for "universal background checks" (based on polling) and "actual support" (based on election results) was 28 points in

California, 22 points in Washington, 36 points in Nevada, and 35 points in Maine.[66] Those gaps may reflect the difference between answering a survey question about a gun policy in the abstract and casting a vote for a specific measure after a campaign in which the pros and cons have been debated.

It is not hard to understand why expanded background checks might be popular, at least in theory. The FBI's National Instant Criminal Background Check System, created by the Brady Handgun Violence Protection Act of 1993, aims to identify would-be gun buyers who are legally barred from owning firearms, based on the assumption that they would pose a threat to public safety if they were armed. But that assumption is highly doubtful, because the categories of "prohibited persons" are defined broadly and arbitrarily.

Under current federal law, prohibited persons include anyone who was ever convicted of a crime punishable by more than a year of incarceration, which generally corresponds to the distinction between misdemeanors and felonies. Disqualifying offenses include not only violent crimes such as robbery and aggravated assault but also nonviolent crimes such as mail fraud, embezzlement, and obstruction of justice. They also include offenses, such as drug dealing, that not only do not involve violence but do not entail the violation of anyone's rights. No matter the details or date of the offense, a felony conviction permanently deprives the offender of his Second Amendment rights.[67] That rule, law professor Adam Winkler notes, is "wildly overinclusive" because "many felonies are not violent in the least, raising no particular suspicion that the convict is a threat to public safety."[68]

Prohibited persons also include anyone who lives in the United States without the government's permission; anyone who has been involuntarily committed to a psychiatric institution, regardless of how long ago that happened and even if he was never deemed a threat to others; and any "unlawful user" of a "controlled substance." That last category includes all cannabis consumers, even if they live in states that have legalized medical or recreational use. It also includes people who use controlled substances prescribed for someone else, such as someone who takes a relative's leftover Vicodin to alleviate pain caused by a back or shoulder injury.[69]

As far as the federal government is concerned, all of those people, even if they have no history of violence, have demonstrated that they cannot be trusted with guns. That policy disproportionately affects African Americans in several ways.

A 2017 study estimated that 33 percent of male African Americans had been convicted of a felony, compared to 8 percent of the general population.[70] In other words, millions of black men have permanently lost their Second Amendment rights, even if their crimes were nonviolent, occurred long ago, or both. And although black and white Americans use illegal drugs at similar rates, black people are much more likely to be arrested for possession, which means their drug use is more likely to be publicly documented.[71]

These differences are reflected in gun arrests and convictions. In 2023, according to the FBI, African Americans accounted for nearly half of arrests for weapon offenses—more than three times their share of the general population.[72] At the end of 2021, according to the Bureau of Justice Statistics, black offenders accounted for 43 percent of state prisoners serving time for weapon crimes, more than twice the share for white offenders.[73] And in fiscal year 2021, according to the U.S. Sentencing Commission (USSC), 55 percent of defendants sentenced for federal firearm offenses were black.[74]

What does it take to be incarcerated for a firearm offense? The USSC reported that 89 percent of the federal defendants were legally disqualified from owning guns, typically because of a felony record. Half of those prohibited persons committed "aggravating criminal conduct." But in the other cases, the defendant's "status as a prohibited person" was the sole "basis of the conviction."[75]

One of the aggravating factors was using a gun (which includes merely possessing it) "in connection with a crime of violence or drug trafficking crime." The average sentence in those cases was nearly 10 years, which starkly illustrates the interaction between gun and drug laws. Without aggravating factors, the average sentence was three years.[76]

Even in the latter cases, you might surmise, the defendants' prior criminal records probably indicated violent tendencies that justified sending them to prison for possessing a gun. But that is not necessarily true. Overall, 61 percent of firearm offenders had been convicted of violent crimes such as assault, robbery, homicide, and rape. Many of these defendants surely posed a continuing threat to public safety. But nearly two-fifths of the firearm offenders had no record of violent crime. Many prior convictions involved drug offenses or previous weapon offenses. Five percent of the defendants were disqualified from owning a gun because they were illegal drug users.[77]

Disarming people convicted of violent felonies makes more sense than disarming people convicted of fraud, insider trading, or nonviolent drug offenses. But the permanent deprivation imposed by federal law leaves no room for rehabilitation, even though it is well-established that recidivism declines dramatically with age.[78]

Consider Darrell Hargraves, a black Missouri man who completed an 11-year federal sentence for attempted armed robbery in 2006. He turned his life around at middle age, applying the construction and electrical wiring skills he had learned in prison to make a legitimate living in Kansas City. After Hargraves was caught with a gun in his toolbox during a routine traffic stop in 2017, he was prosecuted under federal law, which sent him back to prison for another four-and-a-half years.[79]

Why was Hargraves carrying a gun? He bought it after he was assaulted while working on a home in 2012. "My belief at the time was that I had to protect myself, despite [it] being a violation of the law," he told *The Kansas City Star* in 2020, while serving his sentence for illegal firearm possession. "Self-preservation prevailed, which brings me to where I am today."[80]

"Lock Up the Bad People"

Millions of American gun owners are prohibited persons who could be prosecuted for multiple federal felonies. For them, obtaining or possessing a gun is punishable by up to 15 years in prison. If they lie on the federal form required for firearm sales by federally licensed dealers, that is two additional felonies—one punishable by up to 10 years in prison, the other by up to five years. They can even be charged with "trafficking in firearms," which Congress counterintuitively has defined broadly enough to include prohibited persons who obtain guns. That offense, like illegal gun possession, carries a maximum penalty of 15 years. All told, the same underlying conduct theoretically could result in four felony convictions with combined maximum sentences of nearly half a century.[81]

In practice, illegal gun owners rarely are convicted of multiple firearm charges, although prosecutors can use the threat of them to coerce guilty pleas. And when those prohibited persons are convicted, their sentences typically are much shorter than the maximums allowed by law. But the vast majority of gun offenses are never prosecuted at all.

As of 2010, an estimated 19 million Americans had felony records.[82] That same year, the estimated number of illegal drug users in the United States (mainly cannabis consumers) was about 39 million, and the number in 2023 was substantially higher: about 70 million.[83] Based on surveys indicating that roughly one-third of American adults own guns, we can surmise that something like 20 million drug users illegally possessed firearms that year.[84] How many of them were punished for that crime?

The FBI counted about 159,000 state weapon charges in 2022.[85] The U.S. Sentencing Commission reported about 8,200 federal firearm prosecutions in fiscal year 2021.[86] Three-quarters of federal firearm cases involve gun possession by people with felony records. But although the number of illegal drug users is far larger, the Justice Department prosecuted an average of just 120 a year for possessing firearms from 2008 to 2017, accounting for less than 2 percent of federal gun cases.[87]

As with drug law violations, the risk of prosecution, while low overall, is not evenly distributed. Black people are much more likely to be arrested and imprisoned for gun offenses than white people, just as they are much more likely to be arrested and imprisoned for drug offenses.

There is some evidence that racial bias plays a role in these disparities, starting with the data on who is stopped and searched that we discussed in Chapter 3. Race may also make a difference at the sentencing stage. According to the U.S. Sentencing Commission, black defendants tend to receive more severe punishment for federal firearm offenses than white defendants, even after "available personal and offense characteristics" are taken into account. The difference is mainly due to probation-only sentences, which black men were 40 percent less likely to receive than white men.[88]

In a 2003 analysis of state sentences for firearm offenses in Maryland, criminologist Jill Farrell found that black defendants were more likely to receive mandatory minimums than white defendants even when she controlled for other relevant variables. "It appears that race matters to the decision, above and beyond offense severity, prior record, what county the defendant was convicted in, and case processing variables," Farrell wrote. She conceded that unmeasured variables, such as the strength of the evidence or the way a gun was used, might account for some of this difference. But she argued that her findings "support the notion that mandatory minimum penalties open the door for unwarranted disparities."[89]

As in the war on drugs, there are alternative explanations for racial disparities in gun law enforcement, including decisions about how to deploy police and prosecutorial resources. Consider what happened in Washington, D.C., when the city launched an anti-gun initiative in 2020. The program encouraged federal prosecution of people with felony records who illegally possessed firearms. Under the D.C. Code, that offense is punishable by at least a year in prison—three years if the original felony was violent.[90] But sentences under federal law tend to be even more severe: five years, on average, in fiscal year 2021.[91]

D.C.'s felon-in-possession crackdown, which was backed by the District's African-American mayor, Muriel Bowser, was originally advertised as a citywide measure. But in practice, the program focused entirely on three police districts that overlapped with wards that were 64 percent to 92 percent black. By comparison, black people represented 45 percent of the District's total population. D.C. Council Member Charles Allen complained that the program "targeted District residents of color," imposing "harsh penalties on Black residents whose neighborhoods have historically been underinvested in and overpoliced."[92]

Larry Krasner, Philadelphia's district attorney, likewise has highlighted the racially disproportionate impact of crackdowns on illegal gun possession. "A law enforcement strategy prioritizing seizing guns locally does little to reduce the supply of guns, and, if it entails increasing numbers of car and pedestrian stops, has the potential to be counterproductive by alienating the very communities that it is designed to help," he noted in 2022. "People of color are disproportionately stopped in Philadelphia and arrested for illegal gun possession in Philadelphia and statewide." African Americans, who represented 44 percent of Philadelphia's population, accounted for about 80 percent of people arrested for illegal gun possession in the city.[93]

Something similar happened in Missouri, where Darrell Hargraves was federally prosecuted for possessing a gun. Under Project Safe Neighborhoods, a Justice Department program, the number of such cases increased dramatically: They accounted for 43 percent of Missouri's federal caseload by 2021, up from 20 percent when the program was launched in 2001. In the Western District of Missouri, which includes Kansas City, 54 percent of defendants convicted of illegal gun possession were black. The share was even higher in the Eastern District, which includes St. Louis: 81 percent.[94]

Like New York City's stop-and-frisk program, Project Safe Neighborhoods was well-intentioned: Police and prosecutors were trying to help residents of rough neighborhoods like the one where Hargraves lived by reducing violent crime. But the result was a crackdown that disproportionately penalized residents of those neighborhoods, including people who, like Hargraves, responded to high crime rates by arming themselves in self-defense. As law professor Bonita Gardner noted in 2007, "Project Safe Neighborhoods singles out African Americans by targeting only those communities in which African Americans live."[95]

The National Rifle Association (NRA), which you might expect to defend the Second Amendment rights of city dwellers beset by crime, was instead enthusiastic about locking them up. NRA Executive Vice President Wayne LaPierre was a fan of Project Exile, a precursor to Project Safe Neighborhoods that began in the late 1990s in Richmond, Virginia. Around 90 percent of Project Exile defendants were black.[96] "By prosecuting them, they prevent the drug dealer, the gang member, and the felon from committing the next crime," LaPierre told *The Wall Street Journal* in 2008. "Leave the good people alone and lock up the bad people."[97]

Maj Toure, who as a libertarian disagrees with progressives about a lot of things, found Michelle Alexander's critique of the war on drugs in *The New Jim Crow* compelling, and he sees a similar racial dynamic at work in gun control. "The outcome is still the same" even when "a black cop" is enforcing the law, he says. "The road to hell is paved with good intentions."[98] Whatever you make of these disparities or the argument that they violate equal protection, there are many other reasons to worry about the constitutional implications of the twin crusades against drugs and guns, as we will see in the next chapter.

Chapter Five

Drugs, Guns, and the Constitution

Timothy Leary's Bad Trip

Two years after Harvard gave him the boot and three years before Congress banned LSD, Timothy Leary set out on a road trip from Millbrook, New York, in a rented station wagon. The 45-year-old psychedelic enthusiast was accompanied by his girlfriend, Rosemary Woodruff, and his two teenaged children, Susan and Jack. They had planned a month-long family vacation in Yucatán, Mexico, after which Leary and Woodruff would stay behind to work on his newly commissioned autobiography. Leary and his companions arrived in Laredo, Texas, on the evening of December 22, 1965, and crossed the international bridge to Nuevo Laredo, Mexico.[1]

At the customs station on the Mexican side of the bridge, Leary learned that the visa he needed would not be approved until the next day. That turned out to be the least of his troubles.

"All the grass is out of the car, right?" Leary asked as he started driving the station wagon back across the bridge. Jack had flushed his, but Woodruff said she had been unable to retrieve her "silver box" of pot from her bag because "there were two uniformed porters leaning against the car." Since trying to toss the contraband off the side of the bridge seemed inadvisable, Susan hid it in her clothing.[2]

At the inspection point on the U.S. side, Leary explained that he "didn't enter Mexico" and had nothing to declare. After a suspicious customs agent picked up what looked like a cannabis seed from the car floor near Leary's feet, the encounter escalated into searches of the vehicle, the passengers, and their luggage. A "personal search" of Susan discovered "a silver snuff box containing semi-refined marihuana and three partially smoked marihuana cigarettes"—about half an ounce, all told.[3]

Leary claimed ownership of the stash, which earned him a 30-year prison sentence.[4] That astonishingly severe penalty was based on two federal charges: transportation of illegally imported marijuana and failure to pay a transfer tax on the contraband. Those puzzling charges provide a window on the constitutionally dubious origins of federal drug prohibition.

Leary said he had bought the pot in New York and did not know where it was grown. But the government alleged that he had transported marijuana "knowing the same to have been imported or brought into the United States contrary to law." How did Leary allegedly know that? At his March 1966 trial in Laredo, U.S. District Judge Ben Connally told the jurors they could convict Leary based on either of two legal theories.

Since Leary admitted driving into Mexico with the marijuana and driving back, Connally said, the jurors could conclude that he knew it was "brought into the United States contrary to law." Alternatively, the jurors could assume that the pot Leary obtained in New York was grown in Mexico and that Leary knew that. The statute under which he was charged said mere possession of marijuana was enough to establish knowledge of its illegal importation unless "the defendant explains his possession to the satisfaction of the jury." That presumption, Leary argued on appeal, violated his Fifth Amendment right to due process.

The other charge against Leary was even weirder. Under the Marihuana Tax Act of 1937, unregistered recipients of cannabis were required to pay, in advance, a transfer tax of $100 per ounce, which would entitle them to a government-issued stamp indicating that the tax had been paid. To complete that process, they had to fill out an "order form." The Internal Revenue Service was required to keep copies of those forms and make them available to state or local law enforcement agencies.

Those requirements put cannabis consumers in a double bind. If they failed to pay the tax, they were committing a federal felony. But if they paid the tax, they were revealing information that could be used to prosecute them under state law. That dilemma did not seem fair to Leary, who argued that the tax demand violated the Fifth Amendment by requiring him to incriminate himself.

In 1969, the U.S. Supreme Court unanimously agreed with Leary on both points. The justices overturned his conviction for transporting illegally imported marijuana, noting that it might have been based on an unconstitutional presumption of knowledge. They also threw out the Marihuana Tax Act conviction, saying it violated the Fifth Amendment's prohibition of compelled self-incrimination.[5]

Congress responded to the court's ruling in *Leary v. United States* with the Controlled Substances Act of 1970, which among other things flatly prohibited marijuana possession.[6] You might wonder why Congress did not take that straightforward approach to begin with. Why emphasize the possibly foreign provenance of marijuana or create a fanciful tax scheme that notionally required pot dealers and their customers to keep the government apprised of their illegal transactions?

Those indirect approaches were inspired by questions about the constitutionality of federal drug prohibition—questions that Congress took seriously during the first few decades of the twentieth century but had stopped asking by the time it approved the Controlled Substances Act. Those doubts explain why the Marihuana Tax Act, like the Harrison Narcotics Tax Act of 1914, was framed as a revenue measure rather than a ban.

Federal gun control raised similar issues and inspired a similar solution. The National Firearms Act of 1934, the first significant attempt at federal gun regulation, was enacted as part of the Internal Revenue Code. Like the early federal drug laws, it ostensibly was all about raising money for the government and, toward that end, imposed registration and tax requirements, violations of which triggered criminal penalties.[7]

The perceived need to restrict drugs and guns has driven politicians to rethink the proper role of government, justifying interventions that previously were deemed beyond the enumerated powers granted to Congress and even beyond the broad "police power" retained by the states.[8] But the constitutional controversies provoked by drug and gun laws are not limited to the question of where federal or state legislators get the authority to regulate those things. As Leary's case illustrates, enforcement of drug prohibition frequently collides with the limits imposed by the Bill of Rights. So does gun control, which raises a question that has become increasingly salient in recent years: At what point do firearm regulations conflict with "the right of the people to keep and bear arms"?

Those constitutional guarantees are highly inconvenient for politicians, cops, and prosecutors who are determined to stamp out the illegal drug trade and restrict access to firearms. It is therefore not surprising that both crusades have eroded civil liberties, a tendency that would make those policies objectionable even if they had an equal impact on people of different racial and ethnic groups. The constitutional compromises demanded by drug and gun control should trouble all Americans, whether or not they have any interest in using drugs or owning guns.

"THE GUISE OF A REVENUE POWER"

When Congress considered the Smoking Opium Exclusion Act in 1909, Senator Joseph W. Bailey (D–Texas) strenuously objected. The bill "is upon its face an effort to suppress the practice of smoking opium," he noted, "and that is clearly a police regulation." It was an "attempt by the federal government through the custom houses to regulate and suppress a bad habit among the people." But "the federal government has no general police powers."[9]

Bailey was not impressed by the argument that Congress was exercising its power to impose and collect duties on imported goods. "The fact that this is a part of tariff legislation could not alter the power of the federal government with respect to it," he said. "In other words, if it is a question that the federal government has the power to deal with, it may deal with it in the way of a tax or in the way of regulation; but the Government has no right to regulate through a tax a matter which it has no right to regulate directly. To levy a tax for the purpose of regulation under the guise of a revenue power is simply to abuse the taxing power of the federal government."

Bailey allowed that the measure might be defended as an exercise of the power to regulate international commerce, based on the premise that opium for smoking, like "diseased meat," is not "in a merchantable condition." But since the ban covered all smoked opium, regardless of its quality, he was skeptical of that rationale, which he suspected was a cover for the law's true aim.

"The nations of the world, which have no government like ours—no divisions and subdivisions which must be respected—have called a conference, and they want to regulate the health and morals of their people," Bailey observed, alluding to the International Opium Commission that was meeting in Shanghai as he spoke. But under the U.S. Constitution, he said, "matters relating to the health and morals of the community are committed exclusively to the states, and in no wise are subject to the control of the federal government."

When Senator Henry Cabot Lodge (R–Mass.) defended the bill as "a measure of hygiene and protection," Bailey thought that comment proved his point. "If it is a matter of health," he said, "it is not within the jurisdiction of the federal government, and I must object to the consideration of the bill."

Although Bailey's complaint failed to persuade his colleagues, it was grounded in a widely shared understanding of congressional power. "In the early twentieth century," the historian Isaac Campos notes, "drug prohibitions (including alcohol [prohibition]) were understood as being a quite radical intrusion by the state into the personal affairs of Americans. On the federal level such laws were clearly understood to be unconstitutional. This is why the federal laws were tax laws . . . rather than explicit prohibitions, and this is why alcohol prohibition required a constitutional amendment."[10]

Eventually, thanks to the Supreme Court, the power to "regulate commerce with foreign nations" and "among the several states" would become an all-purpose excuse for pretty much anything Congress wanted to do. But that transformation had barely begun in 1909, when even the legislators who thought the opium bill was constitutional felt a need to dress it up as a tariff measure.

Six years earlier, the Supreme Court had narrowly approved a federal ban on interstate distribution of lottery tickets.[11] Bailey did not think much of that decision, joining the dissenters in viewing the law as an exercise of the police power reserved to the states. Four years after

Congress approved the Smoking Opium Exclusion Act, the justices upheld the Mann Act, which made it a felony to "knowingly transport" a woman or girl "in interstate or foreign commerce" for "the purpose of prostitution or debauchery, or for any other immoral purpose."[12]

Both of those cases, however, involved interstate activity. The Supreme Court had yet to read the Commerce Clause broadly enough to allow an outright ban on drug-related conduct that never crossed state lines. "There are no Federal laws on the growth or use of marijuana, the plant being grown so easily that there is almost no interstate commerce in it," *The New York Times* noted in 1931. Even Federal Bureau of Narcotics Commissioner Harry Anslinger, who at the time was urging states to ban marijuana cultivation, "said the [federal] government under the Constitution cannot dictate what may be grown within individual States."[13] And when Anslinger later lobbied for a federal law (the same law that tripped up Timothy Leary in 1965), it was based on the tax-power rationale that was popular at the time, despite the objections of skeptics like Bailey.

The Supreme Court had blessed that rationale in 1928, when it upheld the Harrison Narcotics Tax Act. The justices acknowledged that "merely calling an Act a taxing act can not make it a legitimate exercise of taxing power" when "the words of the act show clearly its real purpose is otherwise." But they rejected the argument that the Harrison Act was a transparent cover for exercising police powers that Congress was never granted, deeming the law's official rationale and the "substantial revenue" it raised enough to make it constitutional.[14] That stretch, law professor A. Christopher Bryant argued in 2012, qualified as "the most disingenuous Supreme Court opinion, ever."[15]

The Supreme Court's evolving understanding of the Commerce Clause would eventually render such subterfuge obsolete. That evolution reached a new peak in a 1942 case that involved a crop much more mundane than opium or marijuana.

Congress "Can Regulate Virtually Anything"

In 1941, an Ohio farmer named Roscoe Filburn violated federal law by growing too much wheat. Specifically, Filburn sowed 23 acres of winter wheat, a dozen more than he had been allotted under the Agricultural

Adjustment Act of 1938. The penalty was 49 cents for each of 239 unauthorized bushels, totaling $117.11 (equivalent to about $2,600 today). Filburn refused to pay.[16]

The recalcitrant farmer argued that Congress had exceeded its constitutional authority by telling him how much wheat he could grow, even for his own use on his own property. Since he used the extra wheat to feed his family and his livestock, he said, it never left his farm and therefore was never part of interstate commerce. According to the Supreme Court, however, that did not matter.

Five years before, the justices had narrowly upheld the National Labor Relations Act of 1935, ruling that the Commerce Clause reached economic activities, such as hiring and firing practices, that were "intrastate in character when separately considered" if they had "such a close and substantial relation to interstate commerce that their control is essential or appropriate to protect that commerce from burdens and obstructions."[17] The court extended that logic in the wheat case, *Wickard v. Filburn*.

When farmers grow wheat for their own consumption, the justices reasoned, their conduct collectively has "a substantial influence" on the interstate "price and market conditions" that Congress sought to regulate. "Even if appellee's activity be local and though it may not be regarded as commerce," Justice Robert H. Jackson wrote for the unanimous court in 1942, "it may still, whatever its nature, be reached by Congress if it exerts a substantial economic effect on interstate commerce."[18]

That "substantial effects" test was a breathtakingly broad license for federal action, and during the ensuing decades Congress repeatedly invoked it to justify legislation that otherwise would have been blatantly unconstitutional, including the Controlled Substances Act. "A major portion of the traffic in controlled substances flows through interstate and foreign commerce," Congress noted when it passed that law. But even "incidents of the traffic which are not an integral part of the interstate or foreign flow, such as manufacture, local distribution, and possession," it said, "nonetheless have a substantial and direct effect upon interstate commerce."[19]

How so? "After manufacture, many controlled substances are transported in interstate commerce," Congress noted. It added that "controlled substances distributed locally usually have been transported in interstate commerce immediately before their distribution"; that "controlled substances possessed commonly flow through interstate commerce immediately prior to such possession"; that "local distribution and possession of controlled substances contribute to swelling the interstate traffic in such substances"; that "substances manufactured and distributed intrastate cannot be differentiated from controlled substances manufactured and distributed interstate"; and that "federal control of the intrastate incidents of the traffic in controlled substances is essential to the effective control of the interstate incidents of such traffic."[20]

Through the magic of "substantial effects," Congress transformed conduct that was neither interstate nor commercial, including mere possession of illegal drugs, into federal crimes. It no longer had to pretend that it was collecting taxes, and it no longer had to aver that people caught with illegal drugs were knowingly transporting contraband that had been imported from another country.

A 2005 case involving medical marijuana vividly illustrated how far the super-elastic Commerce Clause invented by the Supreme Court could be stretched. The plaintiffs were Angel Raich and Diane Monson, two patients who used marijuana for symptom relief in compliance with California law. Monson grew her own marijuana, while Raich relied on two caregivers who grew it for her. Raich and Monson argued that Congress exceeded its power to regulate interstate commerce when it purported to ban noncommercial production and possession of homegrown cannabis that always remained within a single state.

"Our case law firmly establishes Congress' power to regulate purely local activities that are part of an economic 'class of activities' that have a substantial effect on interstate commerce," Justice John Paul Stevens wrote for the majority in *Gonzales v. Raich*. He said *Wickard* "establishes that Congress can regulate purely intrastate activity that is not itself 'commercial,' in that [the commodity] is not produced for sale, if it concludes that failure to regulate that class of activity would undercut the regulation of the interstate market in that commodity."[21]

Like Filburn, Raich and Monson "are cultivating, for home consumption, a fungible commodity for which there is an established, albeit illegal, interstate market," Stevens wrote. He perceived a "likelihood" that marijuana produced for medical use in California would be diverted to the interstate market, thereby evading the "closed regulatory system" that the Controlled Substances Act had established.[22]

"While the diversion of homegrown wheat tended to frustrate the federal interest in stabilizing prices by regulating the volume of commercial transactions in the interstate market, the diversion of homegrown marijuana tends to frustrate the federal interest in eliminating commercial transactions in the interstate market in their entirety," Stevens wrote. "In both cases, the regulation is squarely within Congress' commerce power because production of the commodity meant for home consumption, be it wheat or marijuana, has a substantial effect on supply and demand in the national market for that commodity."[23]

Justice Clarence Thomas was dismayed by the majority's reasoning. "Diane Monson and Angel Raich use marijuana that has never been bought or sold, that has never crossed state lines, and that has had no demonstrable effect on the national market for marijuana," Thomas wrote in his dissent. "If Congress can regulate this under the Commerce Clause, then it can regulate virtually anything—and the Federal Government is no longer one of limited and enumerated powers."[24]

"WE WILL TAX THE MACHINE GUN"

The constitutional rationale for federal gun legislation underwent a similar transformation. The National Firearms Act of 1934 was aimed at restricting access to weapons and accessories that Congress viewed as especially dangerous: machine guns, short-barreled rifles and shotguns, and "muffler[s] or silencer[s]." Despite the bill's public safety motivation, it was framed as a revenue measure rather than a crime control law: an act "to provide for the taxation of manufacturers, importers, and dealers in certain firearms and machine guns," "to tax the sale or other disposal of such weapons," and, toward those ends, "to restrict importation and regulate interstate transportation thereof."[25]

The law required suppliers of the covered products to register with the local "collector of internal revenue" and pay an annual occupational tax. It also imposed a $200 tax on transfers, which was designed to be prohibitive, amounting to more than $4,600 in current dollars. To facilitate collection of that tax, the National Firearms Act required current owners to register with the Bureau of Internal Revenue and report any subsequent transfers. The law made it a federal offense to carry a covered weapon across state lines unless it was registered.

During House hearings on the bill in the spring of 1934, legislators and witnesses repeatedly invoked John Dillinger, the machine-gun-wielding bank robber who would be killed by federal agents at Chicago's Biograph Theater a few months later. Attorney General Homer S. Cummings also expressed concern about the availability of "bullet-proof vests" to criminals like Dillinger and wondered "if that could be made a matter of prohibition under some theory that permits the federal government to handle it." But "of course," he added, "we have no inherent police powers to go into certain localities and deal with local crime. It is only when we can reach those things under the interstate commerce provision, or under the use of the mails, or by the power of taxation, that we can act."[26]

Cummings explained how "the power of taxation" worked in this context: "If we made a statute absolutely forbidding any human being to have a machine gun, you might say there is some constitutional question involved. But when you say, 'We will tax the machine gun,' and when you say that the absence of a license showing payment of the tax has been made indicates that a crime has been perpetrated, you are easily within the law."[27]

Four years later, Congress dispensed with the tax pretense. The Federal Firearms Act of 1938 explicitly sought to "regulate commerce in firearms," and not just incidentally. It created a licensing system for gun manufacturers, importers, and dealers, making it illegal to "transport, ship, or receive any firearm or ammunition in interstate or foreign commerce" without a federal license. The law also invoked the Commerce Clause in a more dubious way, making it illegal for anyone who was "a fugitive from justice" or had been convicted of "a crime of violence" to "receive any firearm or ammunition which has been shipped or transported in interstate or foreign commerce." It treated possession as "presumptive evidence" of receipt.[28]

That provision, which Congress expanded in 1961 to cover nonviolent crimes punishable by more than a year in prison, created a precedent for the broad categories of "prohibited persons" established by the Gun Control Act of 1968, which were further expanded by subsequent legislation.[29] The official aim of the 1968 law was "to provide for better control of the interstate traffic in firearms" and thereby "provide support to Federal, State, and local law enforcement officials in their fight against crime and violence." The law retained the language about receiving a gun supplied through interstate commerce, which on its face would not include a firearm that never crossed state lines. But in 1986, Congress changed that provision to cover possession (not just receipt) of a gun "in or affecting commerce," further straining the already tenuous connection to an enumerated power.[30]

You might think an essentially meaningless phrase like that has no real import. But according to federal courts, such boilerplate is constitutionally crucial.

In the 1995 case *United States v. Lopez*, the Supreme Court ruled that Congress had exceeded its power to regulate interstate commerce when it passed the Gun-Free School Zones Act of 1990, which made it a felony to possess a firearm within 1,000 feet of a school. "The Act neither regulates a commercial activity nor contains a requirement that the possession be connected in any way to interstate commerce," Chief Justice William Rehnquist noted in the majority opinion. "If we were to accept the Government's arguments, we are hard pressed to posit any activity by an individual that Congress is without power to regulate." Rehnquist also noted that the law "contains no jurisdictional element which would ensure, through case-by-case inquiry, that the firearm possession in question affects interstate commerce."[31]

Congress responded by amending the law to specify that it applies only to "a firearm that has moved in or that otherwise affects interstate or foreign commerce."[32] It also added a bunch of "findings" that emphasized the national economic impact of gun violence. The U.S. Court of Appeals for the 8th Circuit thought Congress had cured the problem identified by Rehnquist. Because the law "contains language that ensures, on a case-by-case basis, that the firearm in question affects interstate commerce," the appeals court ruled in 1999, it is "a constitutional exercise of Congress's Commerce Clause power." The U.S. Court of Appeals for the 9th Circuit concurred in 2005, noting that "incorporating a jurisdictional element into the offense has traditionally saved statutes from Commerce Clause challenges."[33]

Congress, in short, initially forgot that it was supposed to be regulating "interstate or foreign commerce." But after the Supreme Court reminded it, the invocation of that phrase was enough to fix the law, even though nothing of substance had changed.

Two years after it ruled against the original version of the Gun-Free School Zones Act, the Supreme Court issued another gun-related decision that likewise had little practical impact on federal firearm regulation. In *Printz v. United States*, the court said a provision of the 1993 Brady Handgun Violence Prevention Act impermissibly "commandeered" local police officials by requiring them to run background checks on gun buyers until the FBI's National Instant Criminal Background Check System (NICS) was up and running, which happened the year after the Supreme Court's decision.[34] The FBI's management of NICS resolved the court's concern about state autonomy without affecting the underlying policy of blocking gun purchases for frequently arbitrary reasons.

THE *BRUEN* BURDEN

That policy and many other firearm regulations looked newly vulnerable after the Supreme Court clarified the Second Amendment test for gun control laws in the 2022 case *New York State Rifle & Pistol Association v. Bruen*. The decision upheld the right to bear arms outside the home, which the court said New York had violated by requiring residents to demonstrate "proper cause" before they could legally carry guns for self-defense. In reaching that conclusion, the justices rejected the "interest-balancing" approach that federal courts had commonly used to uphold gun control laws by weighing the burdens they imposed against their purported benefits.

"When the Second Amendment's plain text covers an individual's conduct, the Constitution presumptively protects that conduct," Justice Thomas wrote for the majority in *Bruen*. "The government must then justify its regulation by demonstrating that it is consistent with the Nation's historical tradition of firearm regulation. Only then may a court conclude that the individual's conduct falls outside the Second Amendment's 'unqualified command.'"[35]

New York and other states with similar laws responded by making carry permits easier to obtain but much harder to use, banning guns from long lists of "sensitive places." That end run provoked court challenges, several of which were at least partly successful. In 2022, 2023, and 2024, federal courts in New York, New Jersey, Maryland, Hawaii, and California blocked enforcement of various location-specific gun bans, saying the states had failed to meet the *Bruen* test.[36]

That test may also pose a threat to the Gun-Free School Zones Act. The Supreme Court has repeatedly recognized schools themselves as "sensitive places" where the government can, consistent with the Second Amendment, prohibit possession of firearms. But does that mean the government is also free to ban guns in public places that are *not* schools but happen to fall within myriad statutorily defined "school zones" that extend a fifth of a mile in every direction? With 130,000 or so K–12 schools scattered through communities across the country, those zones cover a lot of territory. While the statute makes an exception for people "licensed" to carry firearms, many states allow lawful gun owners to be armed in public without obtaining permits.[37]

Bruen likewise reinforced the case against the federal law that strips people of their Second Amendment rights for reasons that have little or nothing to do with the danger they might pose to public safety. Congress planted the seeds of that policy in 1938, when it barred people with certain criminal records from obtaining guns.[38] But the original list was limited to violent crimes such as murder, manslaughter, rape, kidnapping, robbery, and assault with a deadly weapon. The current list is much longer, extending to any crime punishable by more than a year of incarceration.[39]

While disqualifying crimes typically are felonies, that is not always the case. In 1995, for instance, Bryan Range pleaded guilty to fraudulently obtaining $2,458 in food stamps by understating his income. He returned the money, paid a $100 fine and $288 in court costs, and served three years of probation. But although Range did not initially realize it, that conviction also carried a lifelong penalty under federal law: Because his Pennsylvania misdemeanor theoretically could have been punished by up to five years in prison, he lost his right to own a gun. Under *Bruen*, the U.S. Court of Appeals for the 3rd Circuit concluded in 2023, that consequence violated the Second Amendment.[40] The following year, the U.S. Court of Appeals for the 9th Circuit likewise overturned the firearm conviction of Steven Duarte, a California man who was prohibited from owning guns because of prior convictions for nonviolent offenses.[41]

Even prior to *Bruen*, some federal judges had questioned the breadth of the rule that Range and Duarte challenged. In a 2017 dissent she wrote as a federal appeals court judge, Supreme Court Justice Amy Coney Barrett said a felony mail fraud conviction did not justify the permanent loss of Second Amendment rights. "History is consistent with common sense: it demonstrates that legislatures have the power to prohibit dangerous people from possessing guns," Barrett wrote. "But that power extends only to people who are *dangerous*."[42]

Who counts as "dangerous" in this context? That was one of the issues raised by a case the Supreme Court considered in 2023. The case involved the federal ban on gun possession by people who are subject to domestic violence restraining orders.[43] Although that might seem like a commonsensical safeguard, the U.S. Court of Appeals for the 5th Circuit deemed it unconstitutional, saying it was not "relevantly similar" to the historical precedents cited by the government.[44]

Writing for a unanimous panel, 5th Circuit Judge Cory T. Wilson noted that the law "works to disarm not only individuals who are threats to other individuals but also every party to a domestic proceeding (think: divorce court) who, with no history of violence whatever, becomes subject to a domestic restraining order that contains boilerplate language" prohibiting the use or threat of force. Judge James C. Ho amplified that point in his concurring opinion, noting that protective orders are easily obtained, are "often used as a tactical device in divorce proceedings," are "a tempting target for abuse," and in some cases had been used to disarm the *victims* of domestic violence, leaving them "in greater danger than before."[45]

The Supreme Court dodged these issues in 2024, when it concluded that the law was constitutional in at least some of its applications, including the prosecution challenged in that case. "Our tradition of firearm regulation allows the Government to disarm individuals who present a credible threat to the physical safety of others," Chief Justice John Roberts wrote for the majority in *United States v. Rahimi*, leaving for another day the question of whether the Second Amendment allows the government to disarm people without evidence of such a threat.[46]

"Dangerous" Cannabis Consumers

Pushing the concept of dangerousness even further, the Biden administration argued that it encompassed the 60 million or so Americans who use marijuana each year.[47] All of those cannabis consumers were committing federal felonies if they owned guns, even if they lived in states that had legalized marijuana.[48] Defending that policy in federal court, the Justice Department, unlike Harry Anslinger, did not claim that marijuana makes people violent. But it did liken cannabis consumers to "dangerous lunatics," depicting them as irresponsible and untrustworthy scofflaws whose medical or recreational choices justified taking away their gun rights.[49]

That position was consistent with the assumptions of the legislators who added illegal drug users to the federal list of prohibited persons in 1968. The Senate report on that legislation mentioned "narcotic addicts," along with unsupervised "juveniles," "mental defectives," and "armed groups who would supplant duly constituted public authorities," as a category of people "whose possession of firearms" was "contrary to the public interest."[50] During a legislative debate in May 1968, Senator Joseph Tydings (D–Md.) expressed the hope that Congress would "give the law-enforcement officers of our nation the assistance they need in controlling the unrestricted traffic in firearms into the hands of convicted felons, hoodlums, junkies, narcotic addicts, and other persons who should not possess them."[51] Although Tydings referred to "junkies" and "addicts," the Gun Control Act's ban applied to any "unlawful user" of marijuana, depressants, stimulants, or narcotics, no matter the pattern of use.[52]

The Biden administration's insistence that cannabis consumers had no Second Amendment rights fit easily within that rhetorical tradition. But it was hard to reconcile with President Joe Biden's view that marijuana use should not be treated as a crime at all, let alone one grave enough to justify the loss of constitutional rights. In October 2022, when Biden issued a mass pardon for people convicted of simple marijuana possession under federal law, he said it would help eliminate "needless barriers to employment, housing, and educational opportunities."[53] Yet he not only supported the "needless barrier" to armed self-defense that marijuana users faced under federal law; he seemed to think people who violated that law were not being punished severely enough. In June 2022, Biden signed a bill that increased the maximum penalty for illegal gun possession from 10 to 15 years and created a new potential charge against drug users who buy guns, likewise punishable by up to 15 years in prison.[54]

The Biden administration's position also seemed inconsistent with the early historical precedents that the government's lawyers cited. The closest analogs they could identify were laws enacted in the seventeenth, eighteenth, and nineteenth centuries that prohibited drinkers from publicly carrying or firing guns while intoxicated. Those laws were a far cry from a categorical ban on gun possession by cannabis consumers, which applies even in their own homes and even when they are sober. That policy is akin to decreeing that drinkers may not own guns, which would be plainly inconsistent with the Second Amendment.

In 2023, federal judges in Texas, Oklahoma, and North Carolina concluded that the Justice Department's defense of prosecuting cannabis consumers for illegal gun possession failed to meet the government's burden under *Bruen*.[55] The U.S. Court of Appeals for the 5th Circuit agreed with that assessment in another case later that year. Writing for a unanimous 5th Circuit panel, Judge Jerry E. Smith conceded that "Founding-era governments took guns away from persons perceived to be dangerous." But a broad application of that principle, he noted in *United States v. Daniels*, would be perilous to civil liberties.[56]

"The legislature cannot have unchecked power to designate a group of persons as 'dangerous' and thereby disarm them," Smith wrote. "Congress could claim that immigrants, the indigent, or the politically unpopular were presumptively 'dangerous' and eliminate their Second Amendment rights without judicial review. That would have 'no true limiting principle' ... and would render the Second Amendment a dead letter."⁵⁷

Biden's dogged defense of the federal ban on gun possession by any "unlawful user" of a "controlled substance" (the language adopted in 1986) put him on a collision course with his own son. After a diversion agreement fell through in 2023, the Justice Department charged Hunter Biden with three federal felonies based on his purchase of a revolver in 2018, when he was an admitted crack user.⁵⁸ At the time of that transaction, those three offenses carried combined maximum penalties of 25 years in prison. Seeking dismissal of the gun charges, Biden's lawyers noted that the ban he violated was widely flouted, rarely enforced, and, judging from the 5th Circuit's decision, constitutionally dubious.⁵⁹

In 2024, a federal judge rejected Biden's argument that the gun charges should be dismissed on Second Amendment grounds. U.S. District Maryellen Noreika noted that the 5th Circuit's decision was limited to the facts of a specific case and that the U.S. Court of Appeals for the 8th Circuit had recently rejected a facial challenge to the gun possession ban, likening drug users to people who are "mentally ill and dangerous." She nevertheless said Biden could argue that the law was unconstitutional as applied to him once he was convicted.⁶⁰ That happened in June 2024, reigniting a legal dispute that pitted Biden against his father until the president ended it by pardoning his son that December.⁶¹

Bruen also reinvigorated constitutional challenges to laws that limit magazine capacity or ban firearms with specified characteristics. In September 2023, Roger Benitez, a federal judge in California, ruled that the state's 10-round magazine limit was not "consistent with the Nation's historical tradition of firearm regulation."⁶² A month later, Benitez reached the same conclusion regarding California's "assault weapon" ban, which applies to semi-automatic rifles with features such as pistol grips, flash suppressors, and folding or adjustable stocks.⁶³

In both cases, Benitez had little trouble concluding that the targeted products were "in common use" for "lawful purposes," meaning they were covered by "the Second Amendment's plain text." Millions of law-abiding Americans have owned magazines that hold more than 10 rounds, which come standard with many firearms, and the guns that California banned, which are among the most popular rifles sold in the United States.[64] Turning to the second step of the *Bruen* test, Benitez concluded that the historical examples cited by California, which included "trap gun" bans and restrictions on gun powder storage, were not "relevantly similar" to the statute it was defending. Federal judges in other states have deemed "assault weapon" bans unconstitutional for similar reasons.[65]

This sort of analysis raises questions that invite judicial disagreement. Judges must decide, for example, how much weight to give laws from different historical periods and when the analogs cited by the government are numerous, similar, and representative enough to establish a relevant historical tradition. The *Bruen* test nevertheless makes it harder for judges to uphold a gun control law based on their own assessment of its costs and benefits, which in practice tends to conflate legal conclusions with personal policy preferences.

In defending gun laws against post-*Bruen* challenges, government lawyers inadvertently underlined the hazards of giving legislators broad leeway to regulate firearms. The Justice Department argued, for example, that the Second Amendment applies only to "law-abiding, responsible citizens," meaning that people who commit "serious crimes," defined by "felony-level punishment," are not part of "the people" who have a right to arms.[66] If so, legislators have an open-ended power to curtail Second Amendment rights based on how they decide to define and classify criminal offenses.

"At root," the 3rd Circuit noted when it restored Bryan Range's gun rights, "the Government's claim that only 'law-abiding, responsible citizens' are protected by the Second Amendment devolves authority to legislators to decide whom to exclude from 'the people.' We reject that approach because such 'extreme deference gives legislatures unreviewable power to manipulate the Second Amendment by choosing a label.'"[67]

The Justice Department also cited racist gun restrictions as relevant historical precedents. It argued that the contemporary categories of prohibited persons fit a tradition of disarming people whom legislators deemed "dangerous" or "untrustworthy." Although racially discriminatory gun laws "likely would not pass constitutional muster today," the government's lawyers said, they "demonstrate that the Second Amendment was not historically understood to pose an obstacle to disarming, as a class, certain persons deemed dangerous."[68] It would be more accurate to say such laws reflected a belief that black people and Native Americans were not entitled to the same constitutional rights as white people.

Spiritual Highs and Legal Blows

While the Constitution explicitly recognizes a right to own guns, there is no comparable provision that specifically guarantees a right to use drugs. "Arguably," the philosopher Douglas Husak suggests, "the framers neglected to include rights to consume food and other substances because they believed these rights were too obvious to mention."[69] Arguments that such rights are covered by more general protections, such as the Ninth Amendment, the Fourteenth Amendment's guarantee of "privileges or immunities," or an inferred right to privacy, initially seemed promising. But with the notable exception of a 1975 Alaska Supreme Court decision based on that state's explicit constitutional protection of privacy, such direct challenges to drug prohibition ultimately did not make much headway.[70] State and federal attempts to stop people from using drugs nevertheless raise numerous other constitutional issues.

Religious liberty is the very first freedom mentioned in the Bill of Rights. Defending himself against federal marijuana charges in 1966, Timothy Leary unsuccessfully argued that he had a First Amendment right as "an initiated Hindu" to use the herb as a "sacrament."[71] *The New York Times* condemned Leary's "specious" claim that freedom of conscience includes the freedom to alter your consciousness. Religious liberty, the *Times* said, "should not protect the use of marijuana" or "other drugs."[72]

Congress evidently disagreed. In 1978, it approved the American Indian Religious Freedom Act, which codified regulations that accommodated the Native American Church's peyote rituals.[73] But that law did not help Alfred Smith and Galen Black, two church members in Oregon, when they were fired from their jobs as drug counselors in 1984 because of their peyote use. Oregon's peyote ban did not include any religious exceptions. So when Smith and Black applied for unemployment compensation, the state turned them down, concluding that they had been fired for cause. That decision, Smith and Black argued, violated their First Amendment right to the free exercise of religion.

The Supreme Court rejected that claim in 1990, saying the Free Exercise Clause does not require exemptions from "neutral, generally applicable" laws. In reaching that conclusion, the court repudiated the test it had previously applied to government actions that impose a substantial burden on religious freedom, under which they had to be the least restrictive means of serving a compelling state interest.[74] Congress responded with the Religious Freedom Restoration Act of 1993 (RFRA), which aimed to re-establish the "compelling interest" test.[75] That law had overwhelming support from religious groups across the political spectrum and was approved by Congress almost unanimously.

In 1997, the Supreme Court ruled that RFRA was unconstitutional insofar as it applied to the states, but it remained binding on the federal government.[76] And nine years later, the court unanimously ruled that the law protected the American branch of a syncretic Brazil-based church, O Centro Espírita Beneficente União do Vegetal, from federal interference with its rituals, even though the group's sacramental tea, ayahuasca, contained the otherwise illegal psychedelic drug dimethyltryptamine.[77] That decision opened the door for other religious groups to make similar claims.[78]

Freedom of speech, which comes right after freedom of religion in the First Amendment, also has been threatened by the war on drugs. After California legalized medical marijuana in 1996, the Clinton administration threatened to punish doctors who recommended the drug to their patients by revoking the federal authorization they needed to prescribe controlled substances. In 2002, the U.S. Court of Appeals for the 9th Circuit upheld an injunction against that policy, noting that it was apt to have a chilling effect on constitutionally protected speech.[79]

The same could be said of an anti-drug law that Congress approved in 2003. The Illicit Drug Anti-Proliferation Act, originally known as the RAVE Act, was the brainchild of then-Senator Joe Biden (D–Del.). His legislation expanded a 1986 provision, known as the "crack house" statute, that made it a felony, punishable by up to 20 years in prison, large fines, and property forfeiture, to "manage or control any building, room, or enclosure" and knowingly make it available for illegal drug use. Biden thought that language was inadequate to go after rave promoters—"the scum who should be put in jail"—because they often used spaces owned by other people. His new version extended the law to cover temporary venues used for raves or other events where people consume drugs.[80]

A month after Biden's bill was enacted, the Drug Enforcement Administration (DEA) used it to shut down a fundraising concert in Billings, Montana, sponsored by two groups critical of the war on drugs: the National Organization for the Reform of Marijuana Laws and Students for Sensible Drug Policy. During a July 2003 confirmation hearing for DEA Administrator Karen Tandy, Biden pronounced himself "disturbed" by that use of his law. He asked Tandy to explain how she planned to "reassure people who may be skeptical of my legislation that it will not be enforced in a manner that has a chilling effect on free speech."[81]

Skipping over the Second Amendment, which we have already discussed in connection with drug prohibition, and the Third, which restricts the quartering of troops in private homes, we arrive at the Fourth Amendment, which prohibits "unreasonable searches and seizures." As you might expect, the interests of police officers keen to discover contraband frequently conflict with that command.

"Most People Consent"

To facilitate the war on drugs, the Supreme Court has blessed all sorts of invasive practices. Among other things, the court has approved pretextual traffic stops, detention of drivers based on suspicion of drug activity, warrantless tracking of cars via surreptitious radio transmitters, warrantless searches of vehicles and any containers or packages within them (including purses), warrantless searches of mobile homes occupied as residences, warrantless searches of "open fields" and barns, admission of evidence discovered through faulty search warrants that police thought were valid, warrantless rummaging through people's trash, warrantless surveillance of private property by low-flying aircraft, random drug testing of public school students, warrantless searches of students' belongings, search warrants based on information from undisclosed sources, searches triggered by a police dog's purported reaction to cars or luggage, and the "long, uncomfortable, and humiliating" detention of travelers based on nothing more than a suspicion that they are smuggling drugs inside their bodies.[82]

By the late 1980s, such decisions had become so common that defense attorneys perceived a "drug exception" to the Fourth Amendment.[83] You can get a sense of the cumulative power that exception has given drug warriors by considering the risks that Americans run when they dare to drive somewhere.

The vulnerability of motorists to detention, interrogation, and searches evolved gradually, starting with a drug bust involving an intoxicant that today is legal in every state. On December 15, 1921, federal prohibition agents in Michigan stopped an Oldsmobile Roadster that was traveling west on the road from Detroit to Grand Rapids. They had seen two suspected bootleggers, George Carroll and John Kiro, driving that car a few months earlier. The agents searched the car and found 68 bottles of whiskey and gin hidden behind the upholstery of the seats. Carroll and Kiro argued that the search violated the Fourth Amendment and that the liquor should not have been admitted as evidence against them.[84]

The Supreme Court disagreed, saying "contraband goods concealed and illegally transported in an automobile or other vehicle may be searched for without a warrant" as long as police have "probable cause for believing" the car contains contraband. As the court saw it, such leeway was a practical necessity. "It is not practicable to secure a warrant" in such cases, Chief Justice William Howard Taft said in the majority opinion, "because the vehicle can be quickly moved out of the locality or jurisdiction in which the warrant must be sought."

Taft's willingness to accommodate prohibition agents went only so far, however. "It would be intolerable and unreasonable," he said, "if a prohibition agent were authorized to stop every automobile on the chance of finding liquor, and thus subject all persons lawfully using the highways to the inconvenience and indignity of such a search." Yet thanks to subsequent Supreme Court rulings, the current situation for American motorists strongly resembles that "intolerable" scenario.

According to the Supreme Court, police can lawfully stop a driver if they have probable cause to believe he has committed a traffic violation, no matter how trivial, even when the true purpose of the stop is an unrelated drug investigation.[85] That is a very broad license, because state transportation codes include hundreds of rules governing the operation and maintenance of motor vehicles.

Many of those rules are picayune. Among other things, they may specify acceptable tire wear, restrict window tints, forbid air fresheners that dangle from rearview mirrors, and dictate the distance from an intersection at which a driver must signal a turn. Other rules are open to interpretation. They might, for instance, mandate a "safe distance" between cars, require that cars be driven in a "reasonable and prudent" manner, or ban any windshield crack that "substantially obstructs" the driver's view.

"The upshot of all this regulation," law professor David A. Harris notes, "is that even the most cautious driver would find it virtually impossible to drive for even a short distance without violating some traffic law. A police officer willing to follow any driver for a few blocks would therefore always have probable cause to make a stop."[86]

To get from a stop to a search, police can begin with seemingly friendly chitchat that morphs into questions about what the driver is doing, where he is going, and whether he has anything illegal in the car. While drivers are not obligated to answer questions that go beyond the ostensible purpose of the stop, the pressure of the situation encourages them to cooperate.

The same is true if police ask for permission to search the car. "The initial friendly chat helps put the driver in the frame of mind of responding to the trooper on a friendly basis, making cooperation and the giving of consent more likely," Harris observes. "And it usually works. Whether out of a desire to help, fear, intimidation, or a belief that they cannot refuse, most people consent."[87]

"War on Motorists"

Drivers who have just denied that there is anything illegal in their cars may worry that refusing permission for a search will look suspicious. But the general pattern of compliance is especially striking in cases where a motorist allows a search that he knows will discover illegal drugs. Why would anyone agree to a search, knowing it will result in his arrest, if he truly believes he is free to refuse?

Even while maintaining the fiction that such searches are voluntary, the Supreme Court has rejected the idea that police should have to inform people that they have a right to say no. In 1996, the court deemed such a rule "unrealistic" even when the original purpose of a traffic stop has been accomplished and the driver is theoretically free to go.[88]

In that case, Montgomery County, Ohio, Sheriff's Deputy Roger Newsome stopped Robert Robinette for speeding and, after giving him a warning, added a Columbo-esque query: "One question before you get gone: Are you carrying any illegal contraband in your car? Any weapons of any kind, drugs, anything like that?"

Robinette said no, which was predictably followed by Newsome's request to search his car. Robinette "consented," even though he had marijuana and an MDMA tablet in the car, which led to his arrest. In the Supreme Court's view, Robinette should have understood that he was no longer being detained after he got the warning for speeding, meaning he was under no obligation to stick around, let alone allow a search he knew would send him to jail.

Tactics like Newsome's are common. In 2023, a federal judge concluded that the Kansas Highway Patrol (KHP) had "waged war on motorists" by subjecting them to pretextual traffic stops on Interstate 70. That highway connects Colorado and Missouri, where marijuana is legal, through Kansas, where it is not. "The war is basically a question of numbers: stop enough cars and you're bound to discover drugs," U.S. District Kathryn Vratil wrote. "And what's the harm if a few constitutional rights are trampled along the way?"[89]

Vratil found that Kansas troopers had unlawfully prolonged traffic stops, often based on "absurd" reasons for suspecting drug activity. "Troopers occupy a position of power and authority during a traffic stop," she noted. "When a trooper quickly reapproaches a driver after a traffic stop and continues to ask questions, the authority that a trooper wields—combined with the fact that most motorists do not know that they are free to leave and KHP troopers deliberately decline to tell them that they are free to leave—communicates a strong message that the driver is not free to leave."

Even when a constitutionally savvy driver says no to a car search, that need not be the end of the matter if a drug-detecting dog is available. The Supreme Court has said that deploying a canine narc does not count as a search and therefore requires no special justification.[90] The court has approved the use of such dogs during routine traffic stops, provided it does not "unreasonably" prolong the driver's detention.[91] And the court has said an alert by a properly trained dog is enough to provide probable cause for a search, notwithstanding substantial evidence that such alerts are often erroneous, imagined, invented, or triggered by the handler's subconscious cues.[92] In practice, these rulings mean that when a driver declines to allow a search, an officer can still get permission from a dog.

Highway Robbery

One factor driving pretextual traffic stops is civil asset forfeiture, a system of legalized larceny that allows police to seize cash, cars, and other assets that are allegedly connected to crime. Under federal law and many state laws, police and prosecutors get to keep most or all of the proceeds from forfeitures they initiate and use that money to supplement their budgets. That means cops have a financial incentive to stop and search people who may have property they can seize. And once property is seized, the system is rigged against owners trying to recover their property in ways that seem inconsistent with the Fifth Amendment's guarantee of due process.

The experience of William Davis and John Newmerzhycky, Californians who were stopped by Iowa state troopers in April 2013 while returning home from a World Series of Poker event in Joliet, Illinois, was unusual because of the size of the heist and because they ultimately got their money back. But the circumstances were otherwise typical of the roadside robbery authorized by civil forfeiture laws.[93]

Trooper Justin Simmons, who was part of an "interdiction team" looking for contraband and money to seize, ostensibly stopped the two men because Newmerzhycky, who was driving, failed to signal properly as he passed another car. Simmons let Newmerzhycky off with a warning, meaning he was notionally free to go. But Simmons was not really done.

"Hey, John?" the trooper said as Newmerzhycky started returning to his car. "Do you have time for a couple of questions? Do you have something illegal in the car?"

Things quickly went downhill from there. Newmerzhycky denied having any contraband, Simmons asked for permission to search the car, Newmerzhycky said no, and Simmons summoned an officer with a drug-sniffing dog, which supposedly alerted to the trunk, justifying a search that turned up $100,000 in poker winnings, plus a small amount of medical marijuana. The cops seized the money on the theory that large sums of cash, although perfectly legal for travelers to carry, are inherently suspicious—a theory that figures in many forfeiture cases.[94]

Davis and Newmerzhycky challenged the forfeiture in federal court. More than three years after the seizure, the state settled the lawsuit by agreeing to return all the money and pay the men another $50,000 for their trouble.[95]

More commonly, police grab property that is worth considerably less than $100,000. Based on data from 21 states, the Institute for Justice found that the average value of cash seizures was $1,276, which is less than a lawyer typically would charge to contest a forfeiture. After a seizure, the owner bears the burden of challenging the forfeiture, a complicated and daunting process that often costs more than the property is worth. Unlike criminal defendants, forfeiture victims have no right to an attorney if they cannot afford one. And assuming they manage to mount a challenge, the government's burden of proof is lighter than it would be in a criminal case.[96]

Even when owners eventually get their property back, it can take months or years. In February 2019, for example, police in Satsuma, Alabama, pulled over Halima Culley's son and arrested him for possession of marijuana and drug paraphernalia. They seized the car, which belonged to Culley, and tried to keep it under Alabama's civil forfeiture law. Although Culley ultimately got her car back as an "innocent owner," that process took 20 months.[97]

That same month, a friend borrowed Lena Sutton's car. He was pulled over in Leesburg, Alabama, and arrested for methamphetamine possession. Like Culley, Sutton successfully invoked the "innocent owner" defense to get her car back after police seized it. But that did not happen for more than a year.[98] In the meantime, her lawyer told the U.S. Supreme Court in October 2023, "she missed medical appointments, she wasn't able to keep a job, she wasn't able to pay a cell phone bill, and as a result" she "was not in a position to be able to communicate about the forfeiture proceedings."[99]

Culley and Sutton argued that due process requires a prompt hearing to determine whether the government has probable cause to retain seized property while a forfeiture case is pending. The justices disagreed, ruling that due process requires nothing more than "a timely forfeiture hearing" on the ultimate question of whether the government can permanently keep the property.[100]

As that decision reflects, the Supreme Court generally has not demanded much in the way of due process for civil forfeiture. That is largely because the practice has a long history in the United States, although it was limited mainly to piracy and customs cases until relatively recently. Beginning in the 1980s, it became a major tool of the war on drugs, which made it much more lucrative for the government and much more dangerous for innocent property owners.[101]

Thanks to reforms inspired by egregious forfeiture abuses, owners of seized assets nowadays can argue that they should get their property back because it was used for illegal purposes without their permission or knowledge, although they typically have the burden of proving their innocence—a stark reversal of the situation in a criminal case.[102] But according to the Supreme Court, even that modest protection is not constitutionally required. In a 1974 case, the court upheld the forfeiture of a yacht that was seized because someone who leased it brought a bit of marijuana aboard.[103] Two decades later, the justices saw no constitutional problem with seizing a woman's car because her husband had used it to pick up a prostitute.[104]

Since civil forfeiture is "remedial" rather than "punitive," the Supreme Court has said, combining it with a criminal sentence based on the same underlying conduct generally does not violate the Fifth Amendment's prohibition of double jeopardy.[105] Despite that distinction, the court said in 1993, a civil forfeiture *can* amount to an "excessive fine" under the

Eighth Amendment when its purpose is at least partly punitive.[106] And that constraint, according to a decision issued 26 years later, applies to state as well as federal forfeitures.[107] That case involved an Indiana man, Tyson Timbs, whose $42,000 Land Rover was seized because he used it in connection with a $225 heroin sale to an undercover cop. The forfeiture of Timbs's car, the Indiana Supreme Court ultimately ruled, was an excessive fine because it was both punitive and grossly disproportionate.[108]

"Entirely Rational"

Theoretically, a grossly disproportionate prison sentence, if it amounts to "cruel and unusual punishment," also can violate the Eighth Amendment. But the U.S. Supreme Court has said such claims are viable only in "exceedingly rare" and "extreme" cases.[109] How extreme? More extreme than a mandatory life sentence for possessing a pound and a half of cocaine, which the justices upheld in 1991.[110]

Given that precedent, it is not very surprising that Weldon Angelos, the young Utah record producer and part-time pot dealer we met at the beginning of this book, did not get far with an Eighth Amendment challenge to the mandatory 55-year prison sentence he received in 2004. Under a federal law aimed at armed drug dealers, that penalty was dictated by two basic facts: Angelos owned guns, and he sold 24 ounces of marijuana to a police informant in three separate transactions.[111] Paul Cassell, the federal judge who was forced to impose the sentence, called it "unjust, cruel, and even irrational." But as Cassell himself noted, that did not necessarily mean it was "cruel and unusual" as the Supreme Court had interpreted the phrase.[112]

When Angelos appealed his sentence, a long list of former federal judges, attorneys general, and Justice Department officials filed a brief in support of his Eighth Amendment argument.[113] The U.S. Court of Appeals for the 10th Circuit was unimpressed. The Eighth Amendment "forbids only extreme sentences that are 'grossly disproportionate' to the crime," the 10th Circuit noted, and the Supreme Court had made it clear that "the gross disproportionality principle reserves a constitutional violation for only the extraordinary case."[114]

The appeals court's reasoning in approving Angelos's punishment highlighted the way that drug and gun laws interact to magnify the injustice of each. The Supreme Court, the 10th Circuit noted, had said the "basic purpose" of the statute that generated Angelos's 55-year sentence was "to combat the 'dangerous combination' of 'drugs and guns.'"[115] According to the congressman who introduced the original version of that provision, which was incorporated into the Gun Control Act of 1968, the idea was "to persuade the man who is tempted to commit a federal felony to leave his gun at home."[116] But even a defendant who left his gun at home could still face the statute's draconian penalties if he also kept drugs, drug money, or ancillary items such as bags or scales there.

The jury that convicted Angelos, the 10th Circuit noted, found that he not only "possessed a handgun during the course of the first two controlled purchases" (which Angelos says was not true) but also "possessed firearms at his apartment in conjunction with drug-trafficking materials." The appeals court added that "all of these firearms appear to have facilitated his drug trafficking by, if nothing else, providing protection from purchasers and others." Because Angelos sold marijuana, in other words, his constitutional right to armed self-defense became a felony that could send him to prison for half a century.

The 10th Circuit emphasized that the Supreme Court had deemed it "entirely rational for Congress to penalize the mere presence of a firearm during a drug transaction." As the justices saw it, it did not matter "whether guns are used as the medium of exchange for drugs sold illegally or as a means to protect the transaction or dealers." Either way, "their introduction into the scene of drug transactions dramatically heightens the danger to society."[117]

In 2016, after years of lobbying by prominent legal, political, and cultural figures, Angelos was quietly freed from prison. He had served nearly 13 years and expected to serve 35 more, taking into account "good time" credit. His release was not the result of judicial intervention or the presidential clemency that Cassell had repeatedly recommended. It happened because Robert Lund, the lead prosecutor on the case, agreed to support a sentence reduction. After defending the original sentence for years, Lund, now a state judge in Utah, had second thoughts about its fairness.[118]

Congress also had second thoughts. Two years after Angelos regained his freedom, it approved the FIRST STEP Act, a package of criminal justice reforms that, among other things, changed the statute under which Angelos had been sentenced. The enhanced 25-year mandatory minimum for subsequent offenses now requires a prior conviction, meaning gun charges can no longer be "stacked" the way they were in his case.[119] Angelos, now a cannabis reform activist, worked with members of Congress to ensure that provision was included in the law.[120]

Almost everyone, including the prosecutor who had thrown the book at Angelos, eventually agreed that his sentence was unjust. But the courts said it was not "extreme" and "extraordinary" enough to constitute cruel and unusual punishment. That legal reality brings home a point that becomes abundantly clear when you consider the penal consequences of the twin crusades against drugs and guns: Once cruel punishment becomes common, it is still cruel, but it is no longer unusual.

Ross Ulbricht ran into a similar problem when he challenged the life sentence he had received for creating a website that enabled people around the world to anonymously buy politically disfavored intoxicants with bitcoin.[121] President Donald Trump, who pardoned Ulbricht in January 2025 after he had served 11 years in federal prison, joined many other critics across the political spectrum in viewing a life sentence for a nonviolent, first-time drug offender as "ridiculous."[122] But when Ulbricht argued that his punishment was "procedurally and substantively unreasonable," a federal appeals court disagreed. While "only exceptional cases justify such a severe sentence" and "we might not have imposed the same sentence ourselves in the first instance," 2nd Circuit Judge Gerald Lynch wrote in 2017, it was "'within the range of permissible decisions' that the district court could have reached."[123]

Lynch allowed that "reasonable people may and do disagree about the social utility of harsh sentences for the distribution of controlled substances, or even of criminal prohibition of their sale and use at all." He conceded "it is very possible" that "we will come to regard these policies as tragic mistakes and adopt less punitive and more effective methods of reducing the incidence and costs of drug use." But he added that "the democratically elected representatives of the people have opted for a policy of prohibition, backed by severe punishment," which "results in the routine incarceration of many traffickers for extended periods of time."

Those penalties, which Lynch admitted might very well look like "tragic mistakes" in retrospect, are the end result of a process that produces many other casualties on the way. As the next chapter details, the war on drugs endangers innocent bystanders as well as people who defy the judgment of our "democratically elected representatives."

Chapter Six

Drug-Related Violence

"The Baby Didn't Deserve This"

When Alecia Phonesavanh heard her 19-month-old son, Bou Bou, screaming, she thought he was simply frightened by the armed men who had burst into the house in the middle of the night. Then she saw the charred remains of the portable playpen where the toddler had been sleeping, and she knew something horrible had happened.[1]

Phonesavanh and her husband, Bounkham, had been staying with his sister, Amanda Thonetheva, in Cornelia, a small town in northeastern Georgia, for two months. It was a temporary arrangement after the couple's house in Wisconsin was destroyed by a fire. They and their four children, ranging in age from one to seven, occupied a garage that had been converted into a bedroom.[2]

Around 2 a.m. on May 28, 2014, a SWAT team consisting of Habersham County sheriff's deputies and Cornelia police officers broke into that room without warning. One of the deputies, Charles Long, tossed a flash-bang grenade, a "distraction device" that is meant to discombobulate criminal suspects with a blinding flash and deafening noise, into the dark room. It landed in Bou Bou's playpen and exploded in his face, causing severe burns, disfiguring injuries, and a deep chest wound.[3]

After the grenade exploded, the Phonesavanhs later reported, the officers forcibly prevented them from going to Bou Bou's aid and lied about the extent of his injuries, attributing the blood in the playpen to a lost tooth. The boy's parents did not realize how badly he had been hurt until they arrived at the hospital where the police took him. Bou Bou, who was initially placed in a medically induced coma, had to undergo a series of reparative surgeries that doctors said would continue into adulthood.[4]

Habersham County Sheriff Joey Terrell said his men never would have used a flash-bang if they knew children were living in the home. They were looking for Wanis Thonetheva, Amanda's 30-year-old son, who allegedly had sold $50 worth of methamphetamine to a police informant a few hours earlier. But Thonetheva, who no longer lived in his mother's house, was not there. Nor did police find drugs, drug money, weapons, or any other evidence of criminal activity.

"The baby didn't deserve this," Terrell conceded. "The family didn't deserve this." Although "you try and do everything right," he said, "bad things can happen. That's just the world we live in. Bad things happen to good people." He blamed Thonetheva, who he said was "no better than a domestic terrorist."[5]

As is often the case with drug raids, the initial, self-serving police account proved to be inaccurate in several crucial ways. Although Thonetheva supposedly was armed and dangerous, he proved to be neither: He was unarmed when he was arrested later that night at his girlfriend's apartment without incident (and without the deployment of a "distraction device"). Although Terrell claimed police had no reason to believe they were endangering children, even cursory surveillance could easily have discovered that fact: There were children's toys, including a plastic wading pool, in the yard, where Bounkham frequently played with his kids. In the driveway was a minivan containing four child seats that was decorated with decals depicting a mother, a father, three little girls, and a baby boy.[6]

Four months after the raid, a local grand jury faulted the task force that executed it for a "hurried" and "sloppy" investigation that was "not in accordance with the best practices and procedures."[7] Ten months after that, a federal grand jury charged Nikki Autry, the deputy who obtained the no-knock warrant for the raid, with lying in her affidavit. "Without her false statements, there was no probable cause to search the premises for drugs or to make the arrest," said John Horn, the acting U.S. attorney for the Northern District of Georgia. "And in this case, the consequences of the unlawful search were tragic."[8]

The negligence and misconduct discovered after the paramilitary home invasion that burned and mutilated Bou Bou Phonesavanh are common features of "botched" drug raids that injure or kill innocent people, including nationally notorious incidents such as the 2020 death of Breonna Taylor in Louisville, Kentucky. But beyond the specific failures detailed in the wake of such outrages is the question of what these operations are supposed to accomplish even when they go as planned. More than a century of experience with drug prohibition suggests that its benefits are not commensurate with its costs, to put it mildly. And that's assuming you accept the morally dubious premise that violence is an appropriate response to peaceful transactions between consenting adults.

"A Pattern of Excess"

Although Terrell initially said the government would cover Bou Bou's medical bills, which according to his family exceeded $1 million, the Habersham County Board of Supervisors reneged on that promise. A federal lawsuit that Alecia and Bounkham Phonesavanh filed on their son's behalf in February 2015 ultimately resulted in settlements totaling $3.6 million.[9] But no one was ever held criminally liable for the raid.

The Habersham County grand jury decided not to recommend criminal charges against anyone involved in the operation. The grand jurors "gave serious and lengthy consideration" to possible charges against Autry, who conducted the "hurried" and "sloppy" investigation that resulted in the search warrant. But after she resigned "in lieu of possible termination" and "voluntarily surrendered" the certification that authorized her to work as a police officer, the jurors decided that resolution was "more appropriate than criminal charges and potential jail time."[10]

A federal investigation, by contrast, found evidence that Autry had broken the law. A July 2015 indictment charged her with willfully depriving Bou Bou, his parents, Thonetheva, and his mother of their Fourth Amendment rights under color of law. That crime is generally punishable by up to a year of imprisonment, but the maximum penalty rises to 10 years when "bodily injury results" from the offense, as it did in this case.[11]

In her search warrant affidavit, Autry claimed a confidential informant who was known to be "true and reliable" had bought methamphetamine from Thonetheva at his mother's house. Autry also said she had personally confirmed "heavy traffic in and out of the residence." None of that was true.[12]

The informant on whom Autry ostensibly relied was "brand new" and therefore did not have a track record demonstrating his trustworthiness. It was not the informant but his roommate who supposedly bought the meth. And Autry did not monitor the house to verify that a lot of people were going in and out.[13]

Without those inaccurate details, Magistrate Judge James Butterworth testified during Autry's federal trial, he would not have approved the warrant she sought. Assistant U.S. Attorney Bill McKinnon argued that Autry, whom he described as "an overzealous police officer" with "no respect for the people she's investigating," made up those key details to manufacture probable cause for a search.[14] "If there had never been a search warrant, Bou Bou would've never been injured," McKinnon said in his closing argument. "There's a direct causation."[15]

Autry testified that the affidavit was prepared by a supervisor but acknowledged that she had reviewed it and had not suggested any changes. Her attorneys portrayed that failure as unintentional. They argued that Autry, the only officer to face charges as a result of the raid, became a scapegoat for other people's errors. They noted that Long, the deputy who threw the grenade that nearly killed Bou Bou, had violated protocol by failing to illuminate the room before using the explosive device. "There's a pattern of excess in the ways search warrants are executed," defense attorney Michael Trost told the jury. "That's what led to the injuries to this child."[16]

The jurors, who acquitted Autry in December 2015, may have been swayed by that argument, which also figured in the local grand jury's report. "While no member of this grand jury condones or wishes to tolerate drug dealers and the pain and suffering that they inflict upon a community, the zeal to hold them accountable must not override cautious and patient judgment," it said. "This tragedy can be attributed to well intentioned people getting in too big a hurry, and not slowing down and taking enough time to consider the possible consequences of their actions."

Like Trost, the Habersham County grand jury perceived "a pattern of excess" in drug law enforcement. "There should be no such thing as an 'emergency' in drug investigations," it said. "There is an inherent danger both to law enforcement officers and to innocent third parties in many of these situations.... No amount of drugs is worth a member of the public being harmed, even if unintentionally, or a law enforcement officer being harmed."

The grand jury recommended that suspects be "arrested away from a home" whenever that is "reasonably possible" without creating "extra risk" to police or the public. "Going into a home with the highest level of entry should be reserved for those cases where it is absolutely necessary," the grand jurors said, noting the risk that cops will be mistaken for robbers. "Neither the public nor law enforcement officers should be in this dangerous split second situation unless it is absolutely necessary for the protection of the public."

Failure Begets Persistence

The implications of that critique are more radical than the grand jurors, who took for granted the righteousness of the war on drugs, probably realized. If "no amount of drugs" justifies a risk of injury to police or bystanders, enforcing prohibition at gunpoint is inherently problematic. And if drug dealing does not constitute an "emergency" that requires extraordinary measures, the rhetoric and tactics that police and politicians routinely employ against that activity are fundamentally misguided.

Leaving aside those deeper questions, what are police trying to achieve when they mount an operation like this one? As the grand jury implicitly conceded, busting one dealer has no measurable impact on the availability of drugs: If police nab someone like Wanis Thonetheva, someone else will surely take his place. But from 1995 through 2023, police in the United States arrested people for producing or selling illegal drugs millions of times.[17] Did that massive undertaking make a dent in the drug supply big enough to reduce consumption?

Survey data suggest it did not. The federal government estimated that 25 percent of Americans 12 or older used illegal drugs in 2023, up from 11 percent in 1995.[18] Meanwhile, the age-adjusted overdose death rate rose more than tenfold.[19]

The economics of prohibition explain why drug law enforcement does not work as intended. Although politicians like Joe Biden and Donald Trump frequently promise to "stop the flow" of illegal drugs, the government has never managed to do that and never will. Prohibition sows the seeds of its own failure by enabling traffickers to earn a hefty "risk premium," a powerful financial incentive that drives them to find ways around any roadblocks (literal or figurative) that drug warriors manage to erect. The fact that the government cannot even keep drugs out of prisons suggests the magnitude of the challenge facing agencies that try to intercept drugs before they reach consumers.

Realistically, those agencies can only hope to impose additional costs on traffickers that will ultimately be reflected in retail prices. If those efforts substantially raise the cost to consumers, they might have a noticeable effect on rates of drug use. But that strategy is complicated by the fact that illegal drugs acquire most of their value close to the consumer. The cost of replacing destroyed crops and seized shipments is therefore relatively small, a tiny fraction of the "street value" trumpeted by law enforcement agencies. As you get closer to the retail level, the replacement cost rises, but the amount that can be seized at one time falls.[20]

Given that dilemma, it is not surprising that throwing more money at source control and interdiction never seems to have a substantial, lasting effect on drug prices in the United States. From 1981 to 2012, for example, the average, inflation-adjusted retail price for a pure gram of heroin fell by 86 percent. During the same period, the average retail price for cocaine and methamphetamine fell by 75 percent and 72 percent, respectively.[21] In 2021, the Drug Enforcement Administration (DEA) reported that methamphetamine's "purity and potency remain high while prices remain low," that "availability of cocaine throughout the United States remains steady," and that "availability and use of cheap and highly potent fentanyl has increased."[22]

Undaunted by this losing record, law enforcement agencies across the country continue to invade people's homes in search of drugs, endangering police officers and innocent bystanders as well as criminal suspects. The clearer it becomes that blunt force is ineffective at preventing substance abuse, it seems, the more determined drug warriors are to deploy it.

SWAT teams, originally intended for special situations involving hostages, active shooters, or riots, today are routinely used to execute drug searches.[23] Examining a sample of more than 800 SWAT deployments by 20 law enforcement agencies in 2011 and 2012, the American Civil Liberties Union found that 79 percent involved searches, typically for drugs.[24] Research by criminologist Peter Kraska has yielded similar numbers. SWAT teams proliferated between the 1980s and the first decade of the twenty-first century, Kraska found, becoming common in small towns as well as big cities. Meanwhile, he estimated, the annual number of SWAT raids in the United States rose from about 3,000 to about 45,000, and 80 percent involved the execution of search warrants.[25]

Even when drug raids do not technically involve SWAT teams, they frequently feature "dynamic entry" in the middle of the night. Although that approach is supposed to reduce the potential for violence through surprise and a show of overwhelming force, it often has the opposite effect. As the Habersham County grand jury noted, these operations are inherently dangerous, especially since armed men breaking into a home after the residents have gone to bed can easily be mistaken for criminals, with potentially deadly consequences.

"Somebody Kicked in the Door"

The March 2020 raid that killed Breonna Taylor, a 26-year-old EMT and aspiring nurse, vividly illustrated that danger. Like the raid that sent Bou Bou Phonesavanh to the hospital, it involved a dubious search warrant that was recklessly executed.

Louisville police had substantial evidence that Taylor's former boyfriend, Jamarcus Glover, was selling drugs. But the evidence that she was involved amounted to guilt by association: She was still in contact with Glover, who continued to receive packages at her apartment. Joshua Jaynes, the detective who obtained the search warrant, said he had "verified through a US Postal Inspector" that packages had been sent to Glover at Taylor's address. But Jaynes later admitted that was not true. Rather, he said, another officer had "nonchalantly" mentioned that Glover "just gets Amazon or mail packages there." A postal inspector in Louisville said there was nothing suspicious about Glover's packages, which reportedly contained clothing and shoes. But to obtain the search warrant, Jaynes intimated that they might contain drugs or drug money.[26]

That was not the only problem with the warrant. Jaynes successfully sought a no-knock warrant without supplying the sort of evidence that the Supreme Court has said is necessary to dispense with the usual requirement that police knock and announce themselves before entering someone's home. In 1997, the court unanimously held that the Fourth Amendment does not allow a "blanket exception" to that rule for drug investigations. Rather, it said, police must "have a reasonable suspicion that knocking and announcing their presence, under the particular circumstances, would be dangerous or futile, or that it would inhibit the effective investigation of the crime by, for example, allowing the destruction of evidence."[27] While Jaynes made that general assertion in his affidavit, he did not include any evidence to back it up that was specific to Taylor.

Despite their no-knock warrant, the three plainclothes officers who approached Taylor's apartment around 12:40 a.m. on a Friday in March 2020 banged on the door before smashing it open with a battering ram. They said they also announced themselves, but that claim was contradicted by nearly all of Taylor's neighbors. Taylor's boyfriend, Kenneth Walker, was in bed with her at the time. He later said he heard no announcement and had no idea that the men breaking into the apartment were police officers. Alarmed by the banging and the ensuing crash, he grabbed a handgun and fired a single shot at the intruders, striking Sergeant Jonathan Mattingly in the thigh.[28]

The three officers responded with a hail of 32 bullets, including six fired by Mattingly, 16 fired by Detective Myles Cosgrove, and 10 fired by Detective Brett Hankison, who was standing outside the apartment. Hankison fired blindly through a bedroom window and a sliding glass door, both of which were covered by blinds and curtains. Six of the rounds struck Taylor, who was unarmed and standing near Walker in a dark hallway. Investigators later concluded that Cosgrove had fired the bullet that killed Taylor.[29]

Walker called his mother and 911 about the break-in that night. "Somebody kicked in the door and shot my girlfriend," he told a police dispatcher.[30] He initially was charged with attempted murder of a police officer, but local prosecutors dropped that charge two months later, implicitly conceding that he had a strong self-defense claim.[31] An investigation by Kentucky Attorney General Daniel Cameron concluded that Mattingly and Cosgrove also had fired in self-defense, a judgment that reflects the dangerously chaotic situation the officers created by breaking into the apartment in the middle of the night.[32] The only officer to face state criminal charges was Hankison, who was fired three months after the raid because of his reckless shooting.[33] He was charged with three counts of wanton endangerment that September but acquitted by a state jury in March 2022.[34]

Taylor's family, which sued the city of Louisville the month after the raid, announced a $12 million settlement in September 2020.[35] Three months later, Louisville's interim police chief, Yvette Gentry, fired Cosgrove, saying he had fired "in three distinctly different directions," which indicated he "did not identify a target" and instead "fired in a manner consistent with suppressive fire, which is in direct contradiction to our training, values and policy."[36] Gentry also fired Jaynes, saying he had lied in his search warrant affidavit about the source of information concerning Glover's packages.[37]

The fallout continued in August 2022, when the U.S. Justice Department announced charges against two former and two current officers who were involved in the raid or the investigation that preceded it. Hankison was charged with willfully violating the Fourth Amendment under color of law by blindly firing 10 rounds through "a covered window and covered glass door," thereby endangering Taylor, Walker, and three neighbors in an adjoining apartment. Jaynes was charged under the same statute based on his affidavit, which the Justice Department said "contained false and misleading statements, omitted material facts, relied on stale information, and was not supported by probable cause." Prosecutors filed the same charge against Sergeant Kyle Meany, who approved the affidavit.[38]

Jaynes and Meany were also accused of trying to cover up the lack of probable cause for the warrant by lying to investigators, which was the basis of several other charges. Jaynes, for example, was charged with falsifying records in a federal investigation and with conspiracy for "agreeing with another detective to cover up the false warrant affidavit after Taylor's death by drafting a false investigative letter and making false statements to criminal investigators." The other detective, Kelly Goodlett, was accused of "conspiring with Jaynes to falsify the search warrant for Taylor's home and to cover up their actions afterward."[39]

Goodlett, who pleaded guilty a few weeks after she was charged, said Jaynes had never verified that Glover was receiving "suspicious packages" at Taylor's apartment.[40] Hankison's federal prosecution ended with a mistrial in November 2023 because the jury could not reach a verdict.[41] A year later, another federal jury convicted Hankison of willfully violating Tayor's Fourth Amendment rights. Because the charge "involved the use of a dangerous weapon and an attempt to kill," he faced a maximum sentence of life in prison.[42]

In August 2024, a federal judge dismissed two felony counts that enhanced the penalties Jaynes and Meany faced for aiding and abetting a violation of Taylor's Fourth Amendment rights. U.S. District Judge Charles R. Simpson III emphasized that it was "the late-night, surprise manner of entry" that precipitated the exchange of gunfire. Even if the warrant had been valid, he reasoned, the outcome would have been the same.[43]

"A Pattern of Deceit"

The Breonna Taylor shooting, which involved a black woman killed by white police officers, became a leading exhibit for the Black Lives Matter movement. But something similar happened a year earlier in Houston, and in that case it was a black police officer who lied to justify a drug raid that killed a middle-aged white couple. That same officer, it turned out, also had a history of framing black defendants. Whatever role racial bias plays in policing, it clearly is not the only incentive for the abuses that the war on drugs fosters.

On a Monday evening in January 2019, plainclothes Houston narcotics officers broke into the home of Dennis Tuttle and Rhogena Nicholas without warning. One of the cops immediately used a shotgun to kill the couple's dog. Police said Tuttle, who according to his relatives was napping with his wife at the time, picked up a revolver and fired four rounds, hitting one cop in the shoulder, two in the face, and one in the neck—an impressive feat for a disabled 59-year-old Navy veteran surprised by a sudden home invasion. The officers responded with dozens of rounds, killing Tuttle and Nicholas, who was unarmed.[44]

After that deadly raid, Houston Police Chief Art Acevedo put the blame squarely on Tuttle and Nicholas, whom he portrayed as dangerous drug dealers. They were operating a locally notorious "drug house," he claimed, and "the neighborhood thanked our officers" for doing something about it. Based on a tip from a resident who "had the courage" to report that "they're dealing dope out of the house," he said, the Houston Police Department's Narcotics Division "was able to actually determine" that "street-level narcotics dealing" was happening at the house, where police "actually bought black-tar heroin."[45]

Acevedo praised the officers who killed Tuttle and Nicholas as "heroes," paying special attention to Gerald Goines, the 34-year veteran who had conducted the investigation that led to the raid. Goines had been shot in the neck and face after breaching the door and entering the house to assist his wounded colleagues. "He's a big teddy bear," Acevedo gushed. "He's a big African American, a strong ox, tough as nails, and the only thing bigger than his body, in terms of his stature, is his courage. I think God had to give him that big body to be able to contain his courage, because the man's got some tremendous courage."[46]

Acevedo's story began to unravel almost immediately. Neighbors said they had never seen any evidence of criminal activity at the house, where Tuttle and Nicholas had lived for two decades.[47] Police found personal-use quantities of marijuana and cocaine at the house but no heroin or any other evidence of the drug dealing Goines had described in his application for a no-knock search warrant. Nor did the search discover the 9mm semi-automatic pistol that Goines claimed his confidential informant had seen, along with a "large quantity of plastic baggies" containing heroin, at the house the day before the raid, when the informant supposedly had bought the drug there. And although Goines said he had been investigating the alleged "drug house" for two weeks, he still did not know who lived there: He described the purported heroin dealer as a middle-aged "white male, whose name is unknown."[48]

Within two weeks of the raid, it became clear that Goines had invented the heroin sale. Later it emerged that the tip he was investigating came from a neighbor who likewise had made the whole thing up. Those revelations resulted in criminal charges against Goines, the neighbor, and several of Goines's colleagues on Narcotics Squad 15, including Steven Bryant, who had backed up the account of a heroin purchase that never happened.[49]

The scandal prompted local prosecutors to drop dozens of pending drug cases and reexamine more than 2,000 others in which Goines or Bryant had been involved.[50] The investigation by the Harris County District Attorney's Office, which revealed a "pattern of deceit" going back years, led to the release or exoneration of drug defendants who had been convicted based on Goines's plainly unreliable word. One of them, Frederick Jeffery, had received a 25-year sentence for possessing five grams of methamphetamine. The house search that discovered the meth was based on a warrant that Goines obtained by falsely claiming an informant had bought marijuana at that address. It was the same informant who supposedly bought heroin from Tuttle.[51]

In addition to fictional drug purchases, Goines's search warrant applications frequently described guns that were never found. Over 12 years, *The Houston Chronicle* reported, Goines obtained nearly 100 no-knock warrants, almost always claiming that informants had seen firearms in the homes he wanted to search. But he reported recovering guns only once—a suspicious pattern that no one seems to have noticed.[52]

More than five years after police killed Tuttle and Nicholas, a state jury convicted Goines on two counts of felony murder for instigating the deadly raid by filing a fraudulent search warrant affidavit. During the trial, Goines's lawyers sought to blame the victims, arguing that the couple would still be alive if Tuttle had not grabbed his gun. The prosecution argued that Tuttle did not realize the intruders were cops and reacted as "any normal person" would to a violent home invasion. The jury, which sentenced Goines to 60 years in prison, clearly favored the latter narrative.[53]

After the state murder charges were filed in 2019, Acevedo said Goines and Bryant had "dishonored the badge." But he remained proud of the other officers who participated in the raid. "I still think they're heroes," he said. "I consider them victims." Acevedo argued that Goines's colleagues had "acted in good faith" based on a warrant they thought was valid. He even asserted that "we had probable cause to be there," which plainly was not true.[54]

Three months later, Goines and Bryant were charged with federal civil rights violations. The indictment also charged Patricia Ann Garcia, the neighbor whose tip prompted Goines's investigation, with making false reports. Bryant and Garcia later pleaded guilty.[55]

"We have zero indication that this is a systemic problem with the Houston Police Department," Acevedo said after the state charges were announced. "This is an incident that involved the actions of a couple of people." He reiterated that take after the federal indictment, dismissing "the chances of this being systemic."[56]

Harris County District Attorney Kim Ogg saw things differently. "Houston Police narcotics officers falsified documentation about drug payments to confidential informants with the support of supervisors," she said in July 2020. "Goines and others could never have preyed on our community the way they did without the participation of their supervisors; every check and balance in place to stop this type of behavior was circumvented."[57]

On the same day that Ogg announced charges against three narcotics supervisors, Acevedo released the results of a long-overdue internal audit of the Houston Police Department's Narcotics Division, which found widespread sloppiness, if not outright malfeasance. Given "the number and variety of errors," criminologist Sam Walker told *The Houston Chronicle*, the Narcotics Division "looks like an operation completely out of control."[58]

A federal civil rights lawsuit that Nicholas's mother and brother filed in January 2021, which named Acevedo as a defendant, described Narcotics Squad 15 as "a criminal organization" that had "tormented Houston residents for years." According to the lawsuit, the narcotics officers' crimes included "search warrants obtained by perjury," "false statements submitted to cover up the fraudulent warrants," "improper payments to informants," "illegal and unconstitutional invasions of homes," "illegal arrests," and "excessive force."[59]

"It Was a Very Fun Game"

The abuses in Houston came to light only because of a disastrous raid that killed two suspects and injured four officers. If Goines had not been shot during the police assault on Tuttle and Nicholas's home, he could have planted evidence to validate his false claims, in which case most people would have believed the story that Acevedo initially told. Goines would have been free to continue framing people he thought were guilty. Although several drug suspects had accused him of doing that over the years, their complaints were not taken seriously.

How often does this sort of thing happen? There is no way to know. Prosecutors, judges, and jurors tend to discount the protestations of drug defendants, especially if they have prior convictions, and automatically accept the testimony of cops like Goines, who are presumed to be honest and dedicated public servants. Yet the Houston scandal and similar revelations in cities such as New York, Baltimore, Philadelphia, Chicago, Los Angeles, and San Francisco suggest that police corruption and "testilying" are more common than people generally think.[60]

"Police officer perjury in court to justify illegal dope searches is commonplace," law professor Peter Keane, a former San Francisco police commissioner, observed in 2011. "One of the dirty little not-so-secret secrets of the criminal justice system is undercover narcotics officers intentionally lying under oath. It is a perversion of the American justice system that strikes directly at the rule of law. Yet it is the routine way of doing business in courtrooms everywhere in America."[61]

Acevedo insisted that the problem in Houston was not "systemic." Yet the evidence collected by local prosecutors indicated that supervisors abetted the misconduct of dishonest narcotics officers. Meanwhile, prosecutors and judges overlooked red flags in Goines's warrant applications and testimony. Similar problems were evident after the raids that killed Breonna Taylor and injured Bou Bou Phonesavanh. These are systemic issues.

So are the incentives created by the war on drugs. By criminalizing peaceful transactions between consenting adults, drug prohibition creates opportunities for Goines-style fakery that would not otherwise exist.

When someone is murdered, there is a body. When someone is assaulted, there are injuries. When someone is robbed, there is stolen property. In all of those cases, there are identifiable victims, and there may also be independent witnesses who are motivated to come forward because they have an interest in punishing and deterring predatory crime. But when a crime consists of nothing but handing a police officer or an informant something in exchange for money, the evidence often consists of nothing but that purported buyer's word, along with drugs that easily could have been obtained through other means. This situation invites dishonest cops to invent drug offenses and take credit for the resulting arrests, as Goines did for years with impunity. When your job is creating crimes by arranging illegal drug sales, it is not such a big leap to create crimes out of whole cloth, especially if you are convinced that your target is a drug dealer.

This line of work also offers many opportunities for other kinds of police corruption, such as taking bribes to look the other way and stealing drugs or drug money.[62] That sort of corruption is rampant in countries such as Mexico and Honduras, where drug lords can escape capture or break out of prison with help from the same officials who are supposed to be chasing them down and locking them up.[63] But drug-related financial corruption is by no means limited to foreign law enforcement agencies.

José Irizarry, a former DEA agent, received a 12-year prison sentence in 2021 after pleading guilty to 19 federal crimes, including money laundering, wire fraud, bank fraud, and identity theft. While working in Miami and Cartagena, Irizarry admitted, he had helped drug cartels divert about $9 million from DEA money laundering investigations. "In return," federal prosecutors said, "Irizarry received bribes and kickbacks worth at least $1 million for himself and his family, which was used to purchase jewelry, luxury cars, and a home."[64]

In interviews with the Associated Press before he began his prison sentence, Irizarry painted a picture of rampant corruption within the DEA. He accused fellow agents of "joining him in skimming millions of dollars from drug money laundering stings to fund a decade's worth of luxury overseas travel, fine dining, top seats at sporting events and frat house-style debauchery." While not all of Irizarry's claims could be confirmed, much of his account was consistent with an earlier scandal involving DEA "sex parties" in Colombia and with ongoing FBI investigations.[65]

Irizarry said he and his colleagues treated their work as an excuse to party because they recognized that their mission was futile. "You can't win an unwinnable war," he said. "DEA knows this, and the agents know this. . . . There's so much dope leaving Colombia. And there's so much money. We know we're not making a difference." In short, he said, "the drug war is a game," and "it was a very fun game that we were playing."[66]

Other federal cases have involved DEA supervisors who leaked information to defense attorneys in exchange for bribes, a DEA agent who instructed a drug trafficker to buy a $43,000 truck so he could seize it for his own use, and a Customs and Border Protection agent who received $50,000 in bribes over a decade to facilitate drug smuggling.[67] At the local level, police officers in cities such as Baltimore, Los Angeles, New York, and Philadelphia are periodically caught supplementing their salaries by taking bribes or selling drugs.[68] And then there is the perennial problem of correctional officers who smuggle drugs into prisons.[69]

Prohibition sets the stage for financial corruption by creating a highly lucrative black market that gives traffickers the incentive and means to protect their businesses by paying off the people charged with disrupting them. And since drug dealers can hardly complain to the authorities when their merchandise or money is stolen, they are vulnerable to police robbery and extortion. Similar incentives fostered official corruption during national alcohol prohibition.

In a 1931 report, the National Commission on Law Observance and Enforcement, a.k.a. the Wickersham Commission, noted that "the margin of profit" from illegal alcohol sales "makes lavish expenditure in corruption possible" and "puts heavy temptation in the way of everyone engaged in enforcement or administration of the law." As a result, "public corruption through the purchase of official protection for this illegal traffic is widespread and notorious." The commission described "police corruption in every type of municipality, large and small"; the "systematic collection of tribute" from bootleggers; and the spread of corruption to "services which in the past had been above suspicion." While "there was much corruption in connection with the regulation of the liquor traffic before prohibition," the commission concluded, "the corruption was not so widespread and flagrant as it now is."[70]

Prohibition's Bloody Trail

Another conspicuous feature of alcohol prohibition was violence between criminal organizations vying for shares of the black market. On the morning of February 14, 1929, for example, four men, two of whom were wearing police uniforms, fatally shot six members and one associate of George "Bugs" Moran's North Side Gang after lining them up against the wall of a Chicago garage. It was the culmination of escalating violence between Moran's gang and Al Capone's Chicago Outfit, which had been warring for years.[71]

The shocking St. Valentine's Day Massacre, which made front-page headlines across the country, reflected a broader trend. After 1910, the nationwide homicide rate rose sharply. The beginning of that upward trend, the economist Milton Friedman noted, coincided with World War I, which is consistent with the observation that "wars tend to lead to a rise in crime." But even after the war, "the homicide rate kept on going up very rapidly and reached a peak in precisely the year in which prohibition was ended, 1933." The rate then fell sharply and remained relatively low until the late 1960s.[72] Friedman saw those trends as prima facie evidence that alcohol prohibition boosted violence, which is consistent with the dynamics of black markets. When there is no legal, peaceful way to protect your business or resolve commercial disputes, the result tends to be self-help along the lines of the St. Valentine's Day Massacre.[73]

Friedman also noted that the U.S. homicide rate "rose very rapidly after [Richard] Nixon introduced his drug war," suggesting that stepped-up enforcement of drug prohibition had a similar effect. That also makes sense, because arresting drug dealers or breaking up drug cartels invites frequently bloody competition to take their place. Beginning in 2008, for instance, Mexico saw a dramatic increase in homicides related to drug trafficking, amounting to something like 60,000 or 70,000 additional homicides by 2013. The surge in deadly violence was driven largely by a government crackdown that disrupted drug markets, generating conflict between cartels trying to claim revenue that was suddenly up for grabs.[74]

For similar reasons, violence tends to be more common in emerging or growing drug markets, which helps explain the surge in "crack-related" homicides during the 1980s and 1990s. As we saw in Chapter 3, the vast majority of those homicides were related to black-market disputes.[75] In other words, they were "crack-related" in the same sense that the St. Valentine's Day Massacre was "alcohol-related."

A 2023 study likewise found that rising opioid-related deaths from 1999 to 2015, which the researchers used as a proxy for demand, were associated with rising homicide rates. "While the crack markets of the 1980s and 1990s were particularly dangerous, most illegal markets entail a risk of violence," the authors noted. And although illegal drug markets may not be "the only source of the interpersonal violence associated with the opioid epidemic," they "elevate risk for violent conflict generally and lethal violence in particular."[76]

The corruption and violence associated with black markets stem from artificially high profits that enrich criminal organizations at the expense of everyone else, including drug consumers. Since prohibition is essentially a price support program for gangsters, consumers typically pay much more per dose than they would in a legal market. That is a problem not just for drug users but also for victims of drug-related theft. Although estimates are variable and uncertain, crimes committed to support drug habits may account for more than a quarter of robberies, perhaps a third of burglaries, and around two-fifths of larceny cases.[77] Inflated drug prices magnify the burden of such crimes.

To estimate the impact of prohibition on drug prices, the economist Jeffrey Miron compared the ratio of retail prices to farmgate prices (the cost of crops used to make the final product) for heroin and cocaine to the ratio for coffee, chocolate, and beer. Assuming the relevant comparison is to unprocessed goods such as coffee beans bought at a grocery store, he found, "the data suggest that black market cocaine and heroin cost perhaps hundreds of times their legalized prices." But if "the appropriate benchmark is more processed goods such as espresso at Starbucks, then the data suggest black market cocaine is 2 times the legal price and black market heroin is 6 times the legal price." The best estimate, Miron suggested, "is likely between these two extremes."[78]

Miron also compared the retail prices of black-market cocaine and heroin to the prices of cocaine, morphine, and heroin legally sold for medical or research purposes. Based on that method, he reported, "the data imply that cocaine is four times as expensive as it would be in a legal market, and heroin perhaps nineteen times."

Illegal drug traffickers face hazards that legal businesses do not, including seizure of their products, property, and profits as well as the risk of arrest, prosecution, and incarceration. The measures they take to avoid those outcomes, such as concealment, additional security, bribes, and elaborate smuggling methods, cost money too. But as Miron notes, black-market dealers avoid the taxes and regulations imposed on legal businesses, which "partially offsets the increased costs created by prohibition."

Sometimes more than partially. States such as California, where the black market still accounted for an estimated two-thirds of marijuana sales eight years after voters approved recreational legalization, have discovered that high taxes and burdensome regulations give unauthorized dealers a competitive advantage.[79] "In virtually every state that has legalized cannabis, elaborate regulations and high taxes make legal weed much more costly to produce than illegal weed, and much more expensive for consumers," economists Robin Goldstein and Daniel Sumner noted in 2022.[80] They found that "legal retailers are able to give illegal retailers the most spirited competition" in the three states where recreational sales had been legal the longest: Colorado, Oregon, and Washington, all of which had "cheap legal weed."[81]

Eventually, Goldstein and Sumner predicted, the legal cannabis industry would have more success at displacing the black market: "As the industry expands and matures, technology and business practices will improve. In spite of heavy regulation and taxation, legal weed will start to look more typical, like other innovative agribusiness industries. Costs and prices will come down, making legal weed more competitive pricewise with illegal products."[82]

"Legalized Murder"

One advantage of legal marijuana products is the assurance provided by laboratory testing and labeling, including information about THC content and other ingredients. In 2019, a rash of disabling and life-threatening lung injuries underlined the importance of such information. The Centers for Disease Control and Prevention (CDC) gave the condition an awkward and misleading name: "e-cigarette or vaping product–associated lung injury," a.k.a. EVALI. Although journalists and public health officials initially implied that EVALI was caused by nicotine vaping, the CDC's investigators eventually identified the main culprit as vitamin E acetate, an additive used in black-market THC vapes.[83]

The problem reflected by that episode was familiar: People who buy illegal drugs, unlike consumers of legal intoxicants such as liquor or state-regulated marijuana, typically do not know exactly what they are getting. Back when the alcohol trade was illegal in the United States, for example, consumers ran the risk of drinking booze contaminated by dangerous levels of methanol, which can cause blindness, kidney failure, and death. Sloppy distilling practices were one potential source of methanol exposure during alcohol prohibition. Another was consumption of industrial alcohol, which by law had to be "denatured" with methanol to deter diversion. Bootleggers did not always effectively remove the methanol, which resulted in casualties that became a point of contention between supporters and opponents of prohibition.[84]

"The Government is under no obligation to furnish the people with alcohol that is drinkable when the Constitution prohibits it," Wayne B. Wheeler, general counsel of the Anti-Saloon League, argued in 1926. "The person who drinks this industrial alcohol is a deliberate suicide." Senator Edward I. Edwards (D–N.J.) saw the situation differently. "I call it legalized murder," he said, "and the Government is an accessory to the crime."[85]

For Wheeler, deaths resulting from the government-mandated poisoning of industrial alcohol were a necessary price of preventing Americans from drinking. "The very fact that men will gamble with their lives to get a drink of liquor shows how deeply this habit was fixed on the people under the old license system," he said. "To root out a bad habit like that costs many lives and long years of effort."[86]

Americans decisively repudiated Wheeler's crusade by repealing the Eighteenth Amendment 14 years after it took effect. But more than a century after it started, drug prohibition still "costs many lives" by preserving a black market where the quality and potency of drugs is highly variable and unpredictable. That problem has manifested in many ways over the years, including levamisole, a veterinary anti-parasite drug, in cocaine; butylone, a "designer" psychedelic, in MDMA; xylazine, a veterinary tranquilizer, in fentanyl; and bromazolam, a synthetic benzodiazepine, sold as Xanax.[87] But the deadliest example resulted from the confluence of government efforts to prevent diversion of pain medication with the rise of illicit fentanyl.

In response to an increase in opioid-related deaths during the first decade of the twentieth-first century, state and federal officials sought to discourage the prescription of narcotic analgesics like hydrocodone and oxycodone. Those efforts included increased scrutiny of doctors' prescribing practices, raids of clinics identified as "pill mills," pain treatment guidelines issued by the CDC, statutory and regulatory limits, and restrictive policies imposed by insurers, pharmacists, and medical groups under government pressure. The crackdown succeeded in reducing opioid prescriptions, which fell by more than half from 2012 to 2023.[88] But it left many patients to suffer needlessly as doctors became increasingly reluctant to prescribe the medication they needed to relieve their pain, and it did not succeed in reducing the number of opioid-related deaths.[89]

To the contrary, the upward trend that prompted the anti-opioid campaign not only continued but accelerated. The opioid-related death rate, which rose by 80 percent between 2002 and 2012, more than tripled between 2012 and 2022. That year, the CDC counted nearly 82,000 opioid-related deaths, three-and-half times the number in 2012.[90]

"We Knew That This Was Going to Be an Issue"

What went wrong? In addition to leaving bona fide pain patients in the lurch, restricting access to prescription opioids pushed nonmedical users toward black-market substitutes that were much more dangerous. It replaced legally produced, reliably dosed pharmaceuticals with iffy products of unknown provenance and composition. Worse, that trend coincided with the proliferation of fentanyl as a heroin booster and substitute. While legal fentanyl is commonly and safely used in medical treatment, it is 30 to 50 times as potent as heroin, so its presence in the illegal drug supply made potency even more variable, increasing the risk of lethal dosing errors.[91] Eventually, fentanyl was showing up not only in powder sold as heroin but also in cocaine, methamphetamine, and counterfeit pills resembling legal medications such as Percocet and Xanax.[92]

The impact of these developments was illustrated by what happened after OxyContin, a long-acting version of oxycodone, was reformulated in 2010. That change, which was aimed at discouraging diversion by frustrating attempts to crush the pills for snorting or injection, was immediately followed by an increase in heroin-related deaths. Economists David Powell and Rosalie Liccardo Pacula found that trend was especially pronounced in states with relatively high pre-2010 rates of nonmedical OxyContin use. In subsequent years, they reported, "reformulation stimulated illicit drug markets to grow and evolve," ultimately resulting in more fentanyl-related deaths.[93]

"We knew that this was going to be an issue, that we were going to push addicts in a direction that was going to be more deadly," Carrie DeLone, Pennsylvania's former physician general, confessed in 2017. Her justification: "You have to start somewhere."[94]

Fentanyl's rise, like the shift from legal pain pills to black-market opioids, was driven by drug law enforcement. Consumers were not clamoring for fentanyl instead of heroin. But from the perspective of drug traffickers trying to avoid detection and minimize costs, fentanyl has several advantages over heroin. It is much more potent, which makes it easier to smuggle, and it can be produced much more cheaply and inconspicuously, since it does not require the cultivation and processing of opium poppies. Fentanyl pressed into pills that look like pharmaceuticals give consumers a false assurance of safety while costing traffickers much less than the real thing.[95]

Although attempts to "stop the flow" of illegal drugs were always doomed, fentanyl's potency, which allowed many doses to be smuggled in small packages, made that task even harder. "US government agencies have made considerable efforts to interdict fentanyl and its precursors from entering the US market, but the combination of its small size and high value makes this difficult," the economist Roger Bate noted in 2018. "Mexican gangs and Chinese criminal enterprises find it easy to hide the products through a variety of transit methods." Even if law enforcement agencies "managed to stop 100 percent of direct [fentanyl] sales to the US," he observed, "enterprising dealers [would] simply sell into nations such as the UK, repackage the product, and then resell it into the US. Intercepting all packages from the UK and other EU nations to the US will not be possible." And "whether or not drugs are available to the general public via the mail, drug dealers have domestic production and overland and sea routes and other courier services that deliver the product to the US."[96]

The trend toward increased opioid potency echoed what happened during alcohol prohibition, when consumption shifted from beer and wine toward liquor. The black market favored distilled spirits because they allowed bootleggers to ship more doses in any given volume.[97] Enforcement of drug prohibition likewise has driven a series of shifts: from opium to heroin, from heroin to fentanyl, and from fentanyl to fentanyl analogs, some of which are even more potent.[98] Prohibition-inflated prices, meanwhile, encouraged drug injection, which is the most efficient route of administration but poses additional risks, including skin and soft-tissue infections and transmission of blood-borne diseases such as AIDS and hepatitis—hazards that were amplified by drug paraphernalia laws and restrictions on access to hypodermic syringes.[99] Adding insult to injury, medical help for people who overdosed after injecting drugs might be delayed because bystanders worried that they could face criminal charges, including homicide if the overdose proved fatal.[100]

Prohibition, in short, makes drug use much more dangerous, and efforts to enforce prohibition make it more dangerous still. That perverse effect pervades drug law enforcement, from source control and interdiction to local arrests. Incarceration of drug users, for example, raises the risk of fatal overdoses because forced abstinence reduces tolerance. As a result, people who were recently released from prison are especially vulnerable to overdoses.[101] Busting drug dealers disrupts local markets, forcing users to rely on unfamiliar dealers, which also makes overdoses more likely.[102]

A determined drug warrior could survey the damage caused by prohibition and, like Wayne Wheeler, dismiss it as the price that must be paid to discourage bad habits. But few prohibitionists today would argue that someone who dies after taking fentanyl disguised as Percocet is "a deliberate suicide." At the same time, putting all the blame on dishonest drug dealers overlooks the government's role in creating the black market where those dealers thrive.

One thing that's especially notable about the costs that prohibition imposes on drug users, ranging from the risk of arrest to a heightened risk of lethal overdoses, is that the people who bear those burdens are not the people who benefit from them. Prohibition makes life worse—in many cases, a lot worse—for people who defy it. Those harms supposedly are justified by the goal of protecting people who are deterred by prohibition from bad choices they might otherwise make. As the philosopher Douglas Husak has observed, that tradeoff is morally dubious even if you accept paternalism as a legitimate rationale for government intervention.[103]

Invented Crimes

The burdens of prohibition do not fall exclusively on people who like illegal drugs. Everyone else pays too, in the form of squandered taxpayer money, diverted law enforcement resources, official corruption, black-market violence that endangers innocent bystanders, theft driven by artificially high drug prices, and eroded civil liberties. By the time the Wickersham Commission issued its 1931 report, most Americans, including many who had supported the Eighteenth Amendment, had decided that such costs outweighed any benefits from deterring alcohol abuse.[104]

Alcohol prohibition, which banned production and sale but did not criminalize consumption and made malleable exceptions for religious and medical use, was mild compared to the war on drugs. But the Wickersham Commission noted that the policy, combined with the corruption it fostered and the resentment aroused by heavy-handed enforcement, had bred disrespect for the law, as reflected by widespread disobedience, jury nullification, and the rebellion of jurisdictions that had effectively opted out of the anti-alcohol crusade. Even before the Eighteenth Amendment was repealed, five states had repealed laws aimed at enforcing it.[105]

Beginning in 1996, when California became the first state to legalize the medical use of marijuana, cannabis prohibition faced a similar crisis. By 2024, 38 states had legalized medical use, and two dozen, accounting for most of the U.S. population, had taken the further step of allowing recreational use.[106] In 2023, a record 70 percent of American adults told Gallup they favored repealing marijuana prohibition, which nevertheless remained in place at the federal level.[107]

These reversals underlined the arbitrariness of attempts to prevent people from consuming politically disfavored intoxicants. Alcohol was contraband for 14 years, and then it suddenly wasn't. Recreational marijuana suppliers were treated as criminals in every state until 2014, when the first licensed pot shops opened in Colorado and Washington. While the opinions of voters and politicians changed, the moral justification for using force to stop adults from drinking alcohol or smoking pot did not.

That is the central issue raised by drug prohibition: Is the potentially harmful use of psychoactive substances the sort of problem that justifies a violent response? Drug prohibition authorizes police to enter people's homes and threaten them with guns based on nothing more than the suspected presence of illegal substances. That authority results in police conduct that otherwise would be instantly recognized as criminal, including assault, theft, trespassing, burglary, kidnapping, and murder. The war on drugs makes police officers enemies to be feared rather than allies to be welcomed.

The fact that drug warriors have manifestly failed to achieve their avowed goals after more than a century of dedicated effort is certainly relevant in assessing the effectiveness of the policies they support. So is the fact that those policies have made matters worse in many respects. But those observations do not conclusively prove that the quantifiable costs of prohibition outweigh the quantifiable benefits of preventing substance abuse, to the extent that the threat of legal penalties actually does that.

Such analyses are plagued by measurement problems and debatable counterfactual suppositions. But if it is fundamentally wrong to invade people's homes, threaten them with deadly force, and lock them in cages because they are suspected of conduct that is treated as a crime based on legislative whims that could change next year or a few decades from now, no collectivist calculus can make it right.

Gun control raises similar questions. As the next chapter explains, firearm laws, like drug laws, often impose costs on people who pose no threat to public safety, and there is not much evidence that they produce countervailing benefits.

Chapter Seven

The False Promise of Gun Control

"Weapons of War"

James Huberty, a 41-year-old survivalist who had recently lost his job as a security guard, spent the morning of July 18, 1984, at the San Diego Zoo with his wife, Etna, and their two daughters. The family ate lunch at a McDonald's restaurant in the Clairemont neighborhood before returning to their home in San Ysidro. After Etna lay down to rest, Huberty approached her and said, "I want to kiss you goodbye." When she asked him where he was going, he said he was "hunting humans."[1]

Just before 4 p.m., Huberty drove his black Mercury Marquis sedan to a San Ysidro McDonald's, where he used three guns—a Browning 9mm pistol, a Winchester 12-gauge shotgun, and an Uzi 9mm semi-automatic carbine—to shoot 40 people. Twenty-one of them died, including an eight-month-old boy and a nine-year-old girl. Seventy-seven minutes after the shooting began, a police sniper killed Huberty with a single shot to the chest.[2]

California Assemblyman Art Agnos, a San Francisco Democrat who would later serve as that city's mayor, cited the San Ysidro massacre to support the case for his 1985 bill banning what he called "assault weapons"—semi-automatic versions of military firearms, such as the Uzi used by Huberty. Unlike the rifles that soldiers carry, which are capable of automatic fire, these civilian models fire just one round per trigger pull. But Agnos thought they should be regulated as strictly as machine guns, which ordinary civilians could not legally possess in California without a permit that was essentially impossible to obtain.

"The only use for assault weapons is to shoot people," Agnos told the California Assembly's Public Safety Committee in June 1985. San Jose Police Chief Joseph McNamara concurred. "These are weapons of war," he said. "They are made to kill people, and they are all over California. There is no legitimate use for these. Nobody hunts deer with them."[3]

Thus began a long-running public policy debate that was repeatedly revived after subsequent mass shootings. "From Aurora to Sandy Hook, San Bernardino to Las Vegas, Sutherland Springs to Parkland, one common thread that runs through mass shootings is the use of AR-15 military-style assault weapons," Senator Dianne Feinstein (D–Calif.) said in February 2018, a week after a gunman killed 17 people at Marjory Stoneman Douglas High School in Parkland, Florida. "These weapons are designed to kill the greatest number of people in the shortest amount of time, and we need to get these weapons of war off our streets."[4]

Although "assault weapons" fire no faster than any other semi-automatic, such as a Glock 19 pistol or a Ruger 10/22 hunting rifle, politicians often conflated them with machine guns, which are strictly regulated under federal law and have not been legally produced for civilians in the United States since 1986.[5] They argued that "assault weapons" were good for nothing but mass shootings and gang warfare, despite the fact that such guns are rarely used in homicides.[6] They said these rifles were "weapons of choice" for mass shooters, who in fact were much more likely to use handguns, and claimed they were uniquely deadly, even though the category is defined based on features that make little or no difference in the hands of a murderer.[7]

Josh Sugarmann, founder and executive director of the Violence Policy Center, laid out this strategy of misdirection and obfuscation in a 1988 report on "Assault Weapons and Accessories in America." Sugarmann observed that "the weapons' menacing looks, coupled with the public's confusion over fully automatic machine guns versus semi-automatic assault weapons—anything that looks like a machine gun is assumed to be a machine gun—can only increase the chance of public support for restrictions on these weapons."[8]

Sugarmann added that because "few people can envision a practical use for these guns," the public should be more inclined to support a ban on "assault weapons" than a ban on handguns. While handguns are by far the most common kind of firearm used to commit crimes, they are also the most popular choice for self-defense.[9] Prohibiting "assault weapons" therefore sounded more reasonable.

This approach has been intermittently effective. In Gallup polls from 1996 to 2019, support for banning "semi-automatic guns known as assault rifles" ranged from 36 percent to 57 percent.[10] Support for such laws also has fluctuated in polling by the Associated Press, ranging from 51 percent in 2022 to 60 percent in 2019, and Quinnipiac University, ranging from 47 percent in 2023 to 67 percent in 2018.[11] Quinnipiac recorded that peak shortly after the Parkland shooting. The perpetrator of that attack, Nikolas Cruz, used a Smith & Wesson M&P15 rifle, which is similar to the Colt AR-15, a semi-automatic version of the M16 carried by U.S. soldiers.[12]

Politicians, like voters, tend to see mass shootings as evidence in favor of banning military-style rifles. Although Agnos's bill was rejected by the California Assembly in 1985, the legislature approved a similar ban in 1989.[13] That was the year a 24-year-old drifter named Patrick Purdy used a Norinco Type 56S rifle, a semi-automatic version of a Chinese gun modeled after the AK-47, in an attack that killed five children at a Stockton elementary school.[14] Eight other states—Connecticut, Delaware, Illinois, Maryland, Massachusetts, New Jersey, New York, and Washington—eventually followed California's example, often enacting or broadening bans after mass shootings.[15] In 1994, Congress passed a federal "assault weapon" ban sponsored by Feinstein.[16]

The federal law, which expired in 2004, banned production and sale of 18 firearm brands or models by name, along with "copies or duplicates" of them. The law also covered guns meeting specified criteria. Any semi-automatic rifle that accepted detachable magazines, for example, was deemed an "assault weapon" if it had two or more of five listed features: a folding or telescoping stock, a pistol grip, a bayonet mount, a grenade launcher, or a "flash suppressor or threaded barrel designed to accommodate a flash suppressor." State laws typically take a similar approach, banning features that may be useful to law-abiding gun owners but do not affect a rifle's basic operation: With or without them, a rifle fires the same ammunition at the same rate with the same muzzle velocity.

As you might expect given the arbitrary distinctions drawn by such laws, there is little evidence that they reduce gun deaths. The same is true of other frequently proposed regulations, such as expanded background checks for gun buyers and "red flag" laws that authorize judges to disarm people who are deemed a danger to themselves or others. Attempts to reduce violent crime by restricting access to firearms are complicated by two basic realities: Americans already own around half a billion guns, and the Supreme Court has repeatedly upheld their general right to those arms under the Second Amendment.[17]

Given those facts, drastic restrictions on firearms, such as handgun bans or confiscation of weapons from people who cannot demonstrate a government-recognized "special need," are practically, politically, and legally impossible. And even when legislators approve relatively modest regulations that can pass muster with the courts, they mainly affect law-abiding people who are inclined to follow the rules—as both Joe Biden and Donald Trump have noted at different times. People who want guns for criminal purposes obviously have no compunction about breaking the law, and they are highly motivated to evade barriers such as background checks, bans on gun ownership by people with felony records, and restrictions on public possession.

Although mass shootings account for a tiny percentage of gun homicides in the United States, they loom large in the firearm policy debate.[18] Here the challenge of preventing violence through gun regulation is compounded by the difficulty of predicting which of the country's many oddballs and malcontents might someday seek revenge or notoriety by shooting up a workplace, school, church, or shopping mall. The perpetrators of such horrifying crimes usually do not have the sort of criminal or psychiatric records that would prevent them from legally buying firearms.[19] And while "red flags" are easy to spot in retrospect, they are much harder to identify before the fact than people tend to assume.

"Just As Deadly"

Biden, whose 1994 crime bill incorporated Feinstein's "assault weapon" ban, frequently urged Congress to reinstate the law after it expired. Yet even as he argued that the ban had reduced mass shooting deaths, he conceded that it had no impact on the lethality of legally available firearms. The problem, he explained in a 2019 *New York Times* essay, was that gun manufacturers easily "circumvent[ed]" the law by "making minor modifications to their products—modifications that [left] them just as deadly."[20] But the same analysis applied to the new, supposedly improved legislation that Biden favored, which slightly modified the list of prohibited features and made just one enough to render a rifle illegal.

Because those bills still would ban guns based on arbitrarily selected characteristics, they would leave mass murderers with plenty of alternatives that are "just as deadly." A bill that Feinstein introduced in 2023, for example, specifically exempted the Iver Johnson M1 carbine and the Ruger Mini-14 rifle, but only when they have fixed stocks.[21] Under that bill, adding a folding or adjustable stock to these rifles would transform them from legitimate firearms into proscribed "assault weapons," even though that change does not make them any more deadly or suitable for mass murder. A folding stock makes a rifle shorter for transport or storage, while an adjustable stock allows a more comfortable fit for shooters of different sizes.

Feinstein's original ban frowned on bayonet mounts. Her subsequent bills deleted that much-ridiculed detail but added barrel shrouds, coverings that protect the shooter's hand from the heat generated by firing a rifle. Feinstein also added rocket launchers to the equally fanciful grenade launchers on her list of prohibited accessories. Crimes committed with rifle-mounted grenade or rocket launchers are about as common in the United States as crimes committed with rifle-mounted bayonets. Even if someone decided to attach a grenade or rocket launcher to his rifle, he would have a hard time finding something to launch with it, since grenades and rockets are strictly regulated as "destructive devices" under the National Firearms Act.[22]

Other commonly disfavored features, such as adjustable stocks, barrel shrouds, flash suppressors (which reduce the light generated by firing a rifle and can be useful in nighttime hunting or self-defense situations), and pistol grips (which improve ergonomics and rifle control) are more practical, which is why some gun owners want them.[23] But their advantages do not make much difference in the context of a mass shooting.

Like bans on inexpensive handguns, "assault weapon" bans aim to eliminate firearms that supposedly are favored by criminals. But as the philosopher Douglas Husak observes, "The same characteristics that make a kind of gun useful for criminal purposes are those that make it useful for legitimate purposes as well—most notably, for self-protection." It therefore is "impossible to identify a kind of gun that is widely used unlawfully but lacks a legitimate purpose."[24]

Law professor Adam Winkler likens the federal "assault weapon" ban to "a law designed to reduce dog bites that only outlawed the sale of Doberman pinschers with clipped ears." While "those dogs are vicious looking and certainly capable of doing serious harm," he writes, "this law wouldn't improve public safety, given that other similarly dangerous dogs aren't affected and one could own a Doberman without clipped ears." Bans on rifles with scary-looking features, he concludes, are likewise "a triumph of symbolism over substance."[25]

In short, the distinction that Biden perceived between "assault weapons" and guns that do not fall into that politically defined category was as suspect as the distinction he once drew between the snorted and smoked forms of cocaine. His complaint about the limitations of the 1994 "assault weapon" ban implicitly admitted as much.

Federal judges have noted the point that Biden conceded and then immediately forgot. In 2011, for instance, Brett Kavanaugh, who joined the U.S. Supreme Court in 2018 but was then a judge on the U.S. Court of Appeals for the D.C. Circuit, dissented from a decision upholding the District of Columbia's "assault weapon" ban. As he noted in that opinion, the D.C. law, like Feinstein's bills, covered a "haphazard" set of arbitrarily selected guns "with no particular explanation or rationale for why some made the list and some did not."[26]

In 2021, U.S. District Judge Roger Benitez observed that "the firearms deemed 'assault weapons' are fairly ordinary, popular, modern rifles." And contrary to the way politicians had portrayed them, those guns accounted for a tiny share of weapons used in homicides. FBI homicide statistics "do not track assault rifles," Benitez wrote, "but they do show that killing by knife attack is far more common than murder by any kind of rifle."[27] From 2015 through 2019, according to the FBI, rifles of any sort, only a subset of which would qualify as "assault weapons," were used to commit about 2 percent of homicides. More than 10 percent of homicides involved "knives or cutting instruments," while handguns accounted for at least 45 percent. They were used in 90 percent of gun homicides where the type of firearm was specified.[28]

If the rifles that politicians like Biden and Kamala Harris deem intolerable are not commonly used to kill people, what are they used for? In a 2021 survey of gun owners, about 30 percent reported that they had ever owned AR-15s or similar rifles. The results suggested that such guns number in the tens of millions, which is consistent with the industry's tally of "modern sporting rifles" sold in the United States since 1990 (more than 30 million as of January 2025). When asked why they had bought those rifles, two-thirds of the survey respondents said they used them for recreational target shooting, while half mentioned hunting and a third mentioned competitive shooting. Sixty-two percent said they used the rifles for home defense, and 35 percent cited defense outside the home.[29]

These guns clearly are "in common use" for "lawful purposes like self-defense," meaning they qualify as "arms" covered by the Second Amendment under the Supreme Court's 2008 ruling in *District of Columbia v. Heller*. Even though handguns are used to commit murder much more often than "assault weapons," the Court held in *Heller* that Americans have a constitutional right to own them. "Most handguns are semi-automatic," Kavanaugh noted during his Supreme Court confirmation hearing in 2018, when Feinstein grilled him about his position on "assault weapon" bans. "The question was can you distinguish, as a matter of precedent," between semi-automatic handguns and semi-automatic rifles. Kavanaugh pointed out that "semi-automatic rifles are widely possessed in the United States; there are millions and millions." That suggests they do not qualify as "dangerous and unusual weapons," which the Supreme Court had said can be banned without violating the Second Amendment.[30]

Even while expressing dismay at the constraints that the Supreme Court's Second Amendment rulings have imposed on gun control, a federal judge in 2024 thought it was clear that New Jersey's ban on AR-15s was unconstitutional under those precedents. U.S. District Judge Peter

Sheridan noted a 2022 estimate that Americans owned about 24 million "AR-15s and similar sporting rifles," and he highlighted testimony that such guns are "well-adapted for self-defense." Like the law at issue in *Heller*, Sheridan noted, New Jersey's law "acts effectively as the total prohibition on a commonly used firearm for self-defense." And under *Heller*, he said, "a categorical ban on a class of weapons commonly used for self-defense is unlawful."[31]

Constitutional issues aside, do "assault weapon" bans work as advertised? "It is premature to make definitive assessments of the [federal] ban's impact on gun crime," criminologist Christopher Koper said in a 2004 report commissioned by the Justice Department. Koper noted that the use of "assault weapons" in gun crimes (primarily pistols rather than rifles) had declined in the six cities he and his colleagues examined, although that change "was offset throughout at least the late 1990s by steady or rising use of other guns" equipped with "large capacity magazines" (LCMs).[32]

LCMs typically are defined as magazines that hold more than 10 rounds, which come standard with many of the most popular rifles and pistols. The 1994 "assault weapon" ban also covered production and sale of LCMs. "The failure to reduce LCM use has likely been due to the immense stock of exempted pre-ban magazines," Koper said. "Because the ban has not yet reduced the use of LCMs in crime, we cannot clearly credit the ban with any of the nation's recent drop in gun violence." If the law were renewed, he said, "the ban's effects on gun violence are likely to be small at best and perhaps too small for reliable measurement." In a 2024 review of the relevant research, the RAND Corporation found "inconclusive evidence for the effects of assault weapon bans on mass shootings" and "limited evidence that high-capacity magazine bans reduce mass shootings."[33]

"Stronger Background Checks"

After the 2015 mass shooting that killed 14 people in San Bernardino, California, President Barack Obama recommended "common-sense gun safety laws," including "stronger background checks," to prevent such crimes.[34] But it turned out that the killers had obtained the rifles they used in that attack from a neighbor who bought them legally. Since the neighbor was allowed to buy guns, "stronger background checks" would not have made a difference.

That situation was not unusual. The vast majority of guns used in mass shootings are obtained legally, either by the killers themselves or by their relatives or acquaintances. Mass murderers typically do not have the sort of criminal or psychiatric records that would disqualify them from buying firearms. And even when they do or are not allowed to buy guns for other reasons (because they are too young, for example), they can get them through intermediaries. According to a National Institute of Justice report on public mass shootings from 1966 through 2019, 77 percent of the perpetrators "purchased at least some of their guns legally," while 13 percent made "illegal purchases." In mass shootings at K–12 schools, more than 80 percent of the killers "stole guns from family members."[35]

Ordinary criminals likewise are rarely stymied by background checks. A 2022 analysis of shootings in Philadelphia did not find a single gun that was purchased from a licensed dealer, which would entail a background check. The main sources were illegal transfers and theft, which is consistent with other research on guns used by criminals.[36] According to a 2019 report from the Bureau of Justice Statistics, just 10 percent of prison inmates who had obtained guns reported buying them from licensed dealers, and their success in doing that means they passed background checks. The rest obtained firearms through various informal sources, including relatives, friends, theft, and "the underground market."[37]

Expanding background checks to cover private sales in addition to sales by federally licensed dealers would not change this picture much. According to surveys, Americans overwhelmingly agree with Obama that "universal background checks" are a "common-sense" way to reduce gun violence.[38] But when people already are breaking the law to sell or obtain guns, adding another legal requirement is not likely to change their behavior. And the experience with state laws that notionally require background checks for all firearm sales indicates that they are widely flouted.

If people were following that requirement, you would expect to see a surge in background checks after these laws are implemented. A 2018 study found evidence of such an effect in Delaware but not in Colorado or Washington.[39] Why don't gun owners comply with these laws? Some may be unaware of the requirement, while others may object to the additional time, effort, and expense that compliance would entail, since it means completing the sale through a licensed dealer with access to the background check system. And since police generally do not know who owns guns or when they decide to sell one, enforcing the requirement is a challenge.

A 2019 study of 34 states found that laws requiring background checks for private gun sales were associated with a 15 percent reduction in "overall homicide rates," although the authors noted that "further research is necessary to determine whether these associations are causal ones."[40] By contrast, another study published the same year found that California's "comprehensive" background check requirement "was not associated with a net change in the firearm homicide rate over the ensuing 10 years."[41]

In a 2024 analysis of the relevant studies, the RAND Corporation found "moderate" evidence that "universal background checks may reduce total homicides" and "limited" evidence that they "may reduce firearm homicides." The impact of that policy was "uncertain" in several of the studies. The analysis also considered research on the impact of requiring licensed dealers to conduct background checks. It rated the evidence that "dealer background checks may reduce firearm homicides" as "moderate" and the evidence that they reduce "violent crime and total homicides" as "inconclusive."[42]

There are several possible explanations for these unimpressive findings. The evidence from surveys of convicted criminals indicates that they can readily obtain guns from informal sources, no matter what the law says about screening buyers. Even when they are not knowingly supplying criminals, gun owners may be disinclined to follow new requirements for disposing of their own property, as the data from Colorado and Washington suggest. And the broad criteria that block gun sales when background checks *are* conducted do not reliably identify buyers who pose a threat to public safety.

The federal rule that disqualifies anyone convicted of a crime punishable by more than a year of incarceration, Adam Winkler notes, is "wildly overinclusive," encompassing many people with no history of violence. "Perjury, securities law violations, embezzlement, obstruction of justice, and a host of other felonies do not indicate a propensity for dangerousness," he writes. "It is hard to imagine how banning Martha Stewart or Enron's Andrew Fastow from possessing a gun furthers public safety."[43]

Similarly, Donald Trump lost his Second Amendment rights based on 34 felony convictions that involved falsification of business records.[44] The upshot was that a man entrusted with control of the nation's vast military might, including its nuclear weapons, was not allowed to own a gun, which makes no sense no matter what you think about the case that resulted in those convictions. And while the loss of that right might not matter much to someone with armed, taxpayer-funded protection, the same cannot be said of ordinary people who are legally barred from possessing firearms, including nonviolent drug offenders, cannabis consumers, people who live in the United States without the government's permission, people who at some point were involuntarily treated for suicidal impulses, and people who committed violent offenses long ago but are now peaceful and productive.

In 2022, the FBI completed 9.3 million background checks for gun purchases and blocked nearly 132,000 gun sales—1.4 percent of the total.[45] How many of those would-be buyers had "a propensity for dangerousness"? Not many, judging from the way that prosecutors charged with enforcing federal gun laws typically react to these attempted purchases.

People who lie on the form that buyers must complete when they purchase guns from a federally licensed dealer are guilty of at least two felonies, punishable by combined maximum penalties of 15 years in prison, even if the transaction is not completed.[46] Yet these cases are rarely prosecuted. From fiscal year 2008 through fiscal year 2017, federal prosecutors filed an average of just 300 cases a year under both provisions.[47]

In fiscal year 2017, the Government Accountability Office reported, the Bureau of Alcohol, Tobacco, Firearms, and Explosives (ATF) "referred about 13,000 firearms denials to its field divisions for investigation," resulting in just 12 prosecutions as of June 2018. Another 10 cases were "pending or awaiting prosecution" at that point. U.S. attorneys "said that denial cases are difficult to prosecute and offer less value for public safety than other prosecutions."[48]

In 2002 and 2003, a report from the Justice Department's inspector general noted, the FBI blocked a total of 122,000 gun sales, which represented 0.7 percent of background checks. Only 154 of the would-be gun owners—0.1 percent—were prosecuted. "These cases lack 'jury appeal' for various reasons," the report noted. One of those reasons: "The factors prohibiting someone from possessing a firearm may have been nonviolent or committed many years ago."[49]

When the FBI cannot complete a background check on a gun buyer within three business days, the dealer is allowed to complete the sale. Sometimes it turns out that buyers were not legally allowed to own guns, in which case the ATF is tasked with seizing the weapons. The Justice Department's inspector general noted that there were often delays in retrieving weapons from prohibited buyers, partly because "ATF special agents did not consider most of the prohibited persons who had obtained guns to be dangerous and therefore did not consider it a priority to retrieve the firearm promptly."

If ATF agents did not think most of the prohibited buyers were dangerous, one might reasonably wonder why they were prohibited to begin with. The fact that federal prosecutors almost never file charges against prohibited persons who attempt to buy guns, whom they evidently do not view as a grave enough threat to be worth the time and effort, raises the same question.

Those judgments should give pause to politicians who assume that prohibited persons are uniformly dangerous. Senator Tom Cotton (R–Ark.), for example, has proposed a mandatory minimum five-year sentence for illegal gun possession, saying it would help protect the public from "violent felons." Yet that description applies only to a relatively small subset of Americans who are legally barred from owning guns. You might think a legislator who promised to "always defend our Second Amendment rights" would be reluctant to double down on a law that takes away those rights for reasons unrelated to public safety.[50]

Contrary to what avowed Second Amendment champions like Cotton seem to think, the net cast by background checks is clearly too wide, catching many people who are not dangerous. At the same time, the holes in that net are big enough that criminals have little difficulty arming themselves, regardless of what the law officially requires. "Red flag" laws, which aim to disarm people who allegedly pose a danger to themselves or others, are plagued by similar problems.

"What Did We Prevent?"

Shortly after 5 a.m. on November 5, 2018, two police officers arrived at Gary Willis's house in Glen Burnie, Maryland. They were there to take away his guns. They ended up killing him instead.[51]

According to the Anne Arundel County Police Department, the 61-year-old man, who at that hour presumably had just been awakened by the officers' knocking, answered the door with a gun in his hand. He put it down when he saw who was there. Upon learning that the two officers had come to serve him with an "extreme risk protective order" that barred him from possessing firearms, police said, Willis became "irate" and picked up the weapon again. As one officer tried to wrestle the gun away from Willis, it went off, whereupon the other officer shot him.[52]

Police Chief Timothy Altomare argued that the incident illustrated the need for Maryland's red flag law, which had taken effect barely a month before. "If you look at this morning's outcome," he told the Annapolis *Capital Gazette*, a newspaper whose headquarters had been the site of a mass shooting the previous June, "it's tough for us to say, 'Well, what did we prevent?' Because we don't know what we prevented or could've prevented. What would've happened if we didn't go there at 5 a.m.?"[53]

For one thing, Willis probably would still be alive. Altomare invited the public to speculate that Willis might have used a gun to kill someone. Yet at the time of his death, the only evidence to support that concern seems to have been a complaint from his sister, who reportedly obtained the gun confiscation order against her brother after a family argument during which he said something that alarmed her. Willis had no opportunity to challenge that claim, and he had no idea he had been stripped of his Second Amendment rights until police arrived at his door early in the morning with the court order in hand.

Based on interviews with relatives, local news outlets reported that the order stemmed from an argument the day before about the care of Willis's elderly mother. According to a local TV reporter, "Gary Willis struggle[d] with alcoholism" but "family say he wasn't dangerous, just strongly opinionated."[54] Michele Willis, Gary's niece, gave a similar account in an interview with *The Baltimore Sun*, saying her uncle was someone who "like[d] to speak his mind" but "wouldn't hurt anybody." She added that his fatal encounter with the police seemed senseless. "I'm just dumbfounded now," she said. "They didn't need to do what they did."[55]

As of 2024, Maryland was one of 21 states with red flag laws, which authorize court orders that temporarily bar people from obtaining or possessing guns when they are deemed a threat to themselves or others.[56] Most of those laws were enacted after the Parkland massacre, which provoked recriminations about warning signs that critics said should have prompted interventions that could have prevented the attack.[57] After the August 2019 mass shootings in El Paso and Dayton, President Trump endorsed red flag laws as a way of disarming would-be mass murderers.[58] His successor, Joe Biden, who in 2022 signed a law that provided federal funding to implement such laws, promoted them for the same reason.[59]

According to a 2024 research review, however, the court orders authorized by red flag laws usually are aimed at preventing suicide rather than homicide.[60] The evidence on whether they succeed in doing that is limited and mixed. There is no solid evidence that they prevent homicides, even though the oldest red flag law was enacted by Connecticut in 1999, following a mass shooting at the Connecticut Lottery Corporation's headquarters the previous year.[61]

One thing is clear: Taking away people's guns based on predictions of what they might do with them raises thorny due process concerns. That is especially true with laws like Maryland's, which authorize broad categories of people to seek gun confiscation orders based on scant evidence and effectively put the burden on gun owners to demonstrate that they *don't* pose a threat to themselves or others. While the benefits of these laws are mostly speculative, they inevitably deprive law-abiding people of the constitutional right to armed self-defense, even when it is quite unlikely that they would use guns to hurt themselves or anyone else.

A Rigged Process

Maryland's law, which was enacted two months after the Parkland attack and took effect in October 2018, authorizes law enforcement officers, physicians, mental health specialists, and various relatives, intimates, and cohabitants to seek court orders. That list includes housemates, spouses, dating partners, people who have "a child in common with the respondent," and anyone "related to the respondent by blood, marriage, or adoption." A temporary order, lasting up to a week, can be issued if there are "reasonable grounds" to believe the respondent poses "an immediate and present danger" to himself or others.[62]

At that stage, as Gary Willis discovered, *respondent* is a misnomer. The initial order is ex parte, meaning its target does not have a chance to respond. A judge can extend the ex parte order for up to six months if there is "good cause." A final order, which lasts up to a year and can be extended for another six months, can be issued after a hearing based on "clear and convincing evidence" that the respondent "poses a danger" to himself or others. In light of that language, *extreme risk protective order* is also a misnomer, since any level of danger—low, high, or middling—suffices to obtain one.

At least at this point, the respondent is allowed to rebut the claims against him. But his odds of prevailing, depending on the state, range from bad to terrible. Overall, public health researcher April Zeoli and her collaborators found in a 2024 review of the relevant research, "the majority of petitions at the ex parte and final stages are granted, with many reports finding large majorities being granted, particularly among ex parte orders."[63]

In 2023, Maryland courts granted one-week temporary orders 73 percent of the time, and about two-thirds of those orders were reissued, extending the time without an adversarial hearing for up to half a year. When hearings to consider final orders were held, petitions were granted about 65 percent the time.[64]

In Florida, where the legislature approved a red flag law less than a month after the Parkland shooting, approval rates are much higher than Maryland's. From March 2018 through June 2022, Florida judges granted all applications for temporary "protective orders," which last up to two weeks, and issued final orders, which last up to a year, about 98 percent of the time.⁶⁵

You might suspect that difference can be attributed to the fact that Florida limits petitioners to law enforcement officials, who are supposed to independently assess information provided by relatives, friends, or acquaintances of allegedly dangerous or suicidal individuals. "In states that authorize civilians to petition," Zeoli and her co-authors report, "judges appear to be more likely to grant petitions initiated by law enforcement officers than those filed by civilians." But even in those states, they note, law enforcement officials account for "the overwhelming share of petitioners."⁶⁶ That may help explain why judges in New York, where the list of potential petitioners is about as long as Maryland's, nevertheless had approved more than 97 percent of applications for temporary or final orders as of January 2025.⁶⁷

After the Buffalo mass shooting that killed 10 people in 2022, legislators expanded New York's 2019 red flag law, adding health care practitioners to the list of potential petitioners. The amended law also required law enforcement agencies to seek orders whenever they have "credible information" that "an individual is likely to engage in conduct that would result in serious harm."⁶⁸ The total number of applications exploded from 342 in 2021 to more than 2,500 in 2022, more than 5,000 in 2023, and nearly 5,400 in 2024.⁶⁹

In addition to the question of who can (or must) file a petition, red flag laws vary in the maximum length they allow for temporary orders, which ranges from six days in New York to 30 days in Oregon (assuming the respondent seeks a hearing). The maximum length of final orders also varies: A year is typical, but a few states have a six-month limit, while final orders can last up to five years in California and indefinitely in Connecticut and New Jersey, where respondents must file a successful challenge to regain their gun rights.⁷⁰

States likewise have different standards of proof. For temporary orders, they range from probable cause (the standard for a search or an arrest) to "clear and convincing evidence." For final orders, most red flag laws require clear and convincing evidence, but a "preponderance of the evidence" (meaning any likelihood greater than 50 percent) suffices in five states and the District of Columbia.[71]

Even when clear and convincing evidence is required for a final order, the thing to be proven—usually a "significant" risk but in some states a mere "risk," "danger," or "risk of danger"—is vague and undefined. And when you combine those terms with the standard of proof, it becomes clear that people can lose their Second Amendment rights even when the likelihood that they would otherwise harm themselves or someone else is quite low. If a 10 percent risk counts as significant, for example, the preponderance-of-the-evidence standard reduces it to around 5 percent.

Unlike criminal defendants, respondents cannot count on legal assistance when they navigate this complicated and daunting process. Colorado is the only state that guarantees state-funded representation for respondents who cannot afford a lawyer or choose not to spend thousands of dollars on one.[72]

Another challenge for respondents is that judges are keen to avoid the regret and negative publicity entailed by declining to issue an order against someone who later uses a gun to kill himself or murder someone. That possibility tends to loom large when a judge is presented with someone who is allegedly dangerous. The risk of unjustifiably (but temporarily) barring someone from possessing firearms pales by comparison.

"I'M NOT A VIOLENT PERSON"

That risk is nevertheless real. Given the way the process is rigged against respondents, they can easily be deprived of a constitutional right based on sincere but mistaken concerns, malicious complaints by people with an ax to grind, or hasty judgments by overzealous police officers.

Consider Chris Velasquez, a University of Central Florida student who owned no firearms, had no history of violence, and had never threatened anyone but who nevertheless was an early target of his state's red flag law because he wrote some stupid things on Reddit. In a thread titled "You guys are too weak to be a school shooter," Velasquez replied, "Maybe for now but not forever." Later, he posted "RIP Paddock my hero" in a thread about the autopsy of Las Vegas mass shooter Stephen Paddock and wrote "Cruz is a hero!" in reference to Nikolas Cruz, perpetrator of the Parkland massacre.[73]

Those three comments resulted in a March 2018 interview with a university police officer, Jeffrey Panter, during which Velasquez explained that he was just "trolling" and trying to look tough but regretted his tasteless comments. "I'm not a violent person," Velasquez told Panter. "I would never, ever act out in violence against anybody in a mass shooting or anything of the sort." He called the Parkland massacre "a senseless tragedy" and noted that a mass shooter may get his "15 minutes of fame" but will "eventually be remembered as a piece of crap." Listening to the interview, you do not get the impression that Velasquez had ever seriously contemplated committing a crime of this sort, let alone made any plans or taken any steps in that direction.[74]

Panter refused to accept Velasquez's explanation or his assurances. During the interview, he pressured, cajoled, and manipulated Velasquez into agreeing with statements that, taken out of context, made it seem like he genuinely admired Paddock and Cruz, that he identified with Cruz because both of them had been bullied as kids, and that he had repeatedly fantasized about returning to his former middle school or high school in Orlando and shooting it up.

A mandatory psychiatric assessment after the interview found that Velasquez did not meet Florida's criteria for involuntary treatment, which would have required clear and convincing evidence that, because of "mental illness," there was a "substantial likelihood" that he would "inflict serious bodily harm" on himself or others "in the near future."[75] Panter nevertheless referred the case to the Orlando Police Department, where Sergeant Matthew Ochiuzzo twisted Velasquez's online comments and his interview with Panter into a portrait of a deeply troubled man who was just one disappointment away from committing mass murder.[76]

On a list of 15 possible grounds for issuing a risk protection order, Ochiuzzo checked five, including "there is evidence that the respondent is seriously mentally ill," "respondent has committed a recent act or threat of violence," and "respondent has used or threatened to use any weapons against him or herself or others." None of that was true.

Ochiuzzo claimed Velasquez "disclosed that he has had thoughts and urges to commit a mass shooting since his sophomore year of high school." But Velasquez never said that. To the contrary, when Panter asked about his state of mind in high school, he said, "I didn't have any thoughts of a school shooting."

Ochiuzzo also claimed "the respondent indicated that he wanted to commit the mass shootings so that he could feel the 'adrenaline rush' from the shooting." In reality, Velasquez repeatedly said he would never commit such a crime.

Based on an affidavit that was highly misleading and in some respects blatantly inaccurate, 9th Judicial Circuit Judge Bob LeBlanc issued a temporary risk protection order against Velasquez.[77] But at a hearing about two weeks later, when Velasquez finally had a chance to defend himself, LeBlanc found the city had failed to provide clear and convincing evidence that Velasquez posed "a significant danger."[78]

Velasquez's lawyer, Kendra Parris, said LeBlanc realized the threat described by Ochiuzzo was never more than theoretical. "The judge asked, 'Did he actually make any threats, or was this all in response to hypothetical questions?'" she said. "And of course, it was all in response to hypothetical questions. Fortunately, the judge noted that this essentially amounted to thought policing and declined to issue the order."[79]

"They're Treating Me as If I'm a Criminal"

Although that decision may look like a victory for due process, Parris noted that LeBlanc could have reached a different conclusion, since Florida's law says judges "may consider any relevant evidence." The statute gives 15 examples but says the list is not exhaustive.[80]

The law also leaves crucial terms undefined. Ochiuzzo claimed Velasquez was "seriously mentally ill," for example, even though he had no diagnosis and a psychiatrist found he did not meet the criteria for commitment. Nor is it clear what "a significant danger" means in this context. Even assuming that judges apply such standards with precision, should they consider a 5 percent risk "significant"? One percent? Ten percent?

"Because we can't figure out what 'significant' means, you have this high burden of proof," Parris said, but it relates to a probability that may be "extraordinarily low," based on any evidence a judge considers relevant. "The 'clear and convincing evidence' standard is meaningless, because the criteria are open-ended. The court literally can look at anything."[81]

One of Parris's clients, who lived in Broward County, Florida, posted a photo of an AR-15 rifle he had built, accompanied by the comment, "It's done. Hooray." On another occasion, he posted a comment criticizing teenaged gun control activists, who he said were trying to take away people's Second Amendment rights. Those two posts were enough to obtain a temporary gun confiscation order, although Parris ultimately persuaded the city to drop its petition for a final order.[82]

Another client, former professional football player Oliver Hoyte, did not have the benefit of a lawyer at his hearing, but he really could have used one. After an argument with his aunt and her boyfriend, he said, they told police he had threatened them with a gun. In addition to that claim, Tampa police presented several other unverified allegations against Hoyte—including some they had never questioned him about, he said. They even cited a 2013 case in which he was *acquitted* of aggravated assault. He said video evidence contradicted the testimony of a man who claimed Hoyte had pulled a gun on him.[83]

"I feel like I should have the right to representation," Hoyte said. "The judge said, 'You do have the right to representation, but the court is not going to appoint it for you.'"

Police confiscated Hoyte's Taurus 9mm pistol, and he was forbidden to buy any other firearms for a year. As a result, Hoyte said, he did not feel safe visiting certain neighborhoods, including the one where his family lived. "I'm not on an equal footing with everyone else," he said. "I don't have the right to bear arms, and I haven't done anything wrong. I haven't been convicted of any crime. I haven't been hospitalized. I haven't harmed anyone. This law is wrong because it eliminates due process. They're treating me as if I'm a criminal."

Another Florida case involved a former hospital administrator, Kevin Morgan, who was in the midst of an acrimonious divorce. His estranged wife claimed he was depressed, suicidal, and obsessed with the apocalypse, which he thought was imminent. She said he was stockpiling food, gold, guns, and ammunition in anticipation of the end times; that he talked about seeing, hearing, and wrestling with demons; and that he had performed a ritual that involved rubbing "oils" on their children and the walls of their house. She reported that he was abusing the drugs he had been prescribed for chronic pain, had talked about dismembering his former wife, had intimated he would do the same to her if she ever disrespected him, and had threatened to kill her with succinylcholine, a paralytic agent used during surgery and intubation.[84]

On the strength of such alarming claims, Morgan's wife obtained a temporary domestic violence protection injunction, an involuntary psychiatric evaluation order under the Florida Mental Health Act, and a temporary risk protection order under the state's red flag law.[85] All three were ex parte orders. As with Velasquez, the psychiatric evaluation found that Morgan did not meet the criteria for commitment.[86] A follow-up evaluation, which found no evidence of drug abuse, described Morgan's behavior as "compliant," his mood as "stable," his thought process as "organized," and his judgment and impulse control as "good." The licensed mental health counselor who completed that report noted the pending divorce, adding that Morgan "is being mentally and emotionally abused by his wife."[87]

When it was time for a judge to decide whether the initial gun confiscation order should be extended for a year, Morgan got a hearing, and the lurid picture painted by his wife disintegrated. By the end of the hearing, the lawyer representing the Citrus County Sheriff's Office, which was seeking the final order, conceded that he had not met the law's evidentiary standard, and the judge agreed.[88]

Notably, Morgan had the able assistance of Mike Blackstone, a Crystal River lawyer who also was handling his divorce and charged him a discounted rate for the red flag case, which Blackstone estimated ordinarily would cost $2,500 to $5,000 in legal fees.[89] And notwithstanding Morgan's ultimate victory, the extremely high approval rate by judges in Florida suggests the deck is stacked against respondents like him. "All the pressure is on the other side," Parris observed. "There's absolutely no downside to just going ahead and issuing the order."[90]

"Urgent, Individualized Intervention"

What is the upside? The hope is that red flag orders will stop would-be mass murderers before it is too late. But they have repeatedly failed to do so in states such as California, Illinois, Indiana, and New York, even when killers had said or done things that in retrospect looked like obvious red flags.[91]

A 2019 study of California's red flag law described 21 cases in which fear of a mass shooting prompted police or relatives to seek "gun violence restraining orders" from 2016 (when the law took effect) through 2018. Judging from "print, broadcast, and Internet media searches using Google," the authors said, the respondents in those cases did not subsequently commit any noteworthy violent crimes.[92]

Those 21 examples accounted for 13 percent of the cases for which the researchers were able to obtain court records but just 5 percent of applications during the three years covered by the study. "It is impossible to know whether violence would have occurred had [court orders] not been issued, and we make no claim of a causal relationship," the researchers wrote. "Nonetheless, the cases suggest that this urgent, individualized intervention can play a role in efforts to prevent mass shootings."

By and large, the warning signs described in the study seem legitimately alarming, although it is not clear how many of the threats were serious or how determined the respondents were to carry them out. At one extreme, for example, there was a "31-year-old man who was known in his Muslim community as a supporter of the Islamic State," who was "on the Terrorist Screening Center Watchlist," who "made repeated threats of mass violence," and who had recently purchased a semi-automatic pistol.

At the other extreme, perhaps, was a 14-year-old high school student "with a history of racist comments at school" who posted "videos on Instagram of himself using firearms, favorable comments about school violence and shootings, racist comments, and suggestions of animal cruelty." After he was taken into custody for a psychiatric screening, he "claimed that he had been joking." Police nevertheless seized his father's guns.

Since none of these people (even the more serious-sounding ones) appeared to have obtained guns by indirect means after they were barred from legally buying or possessing them, it seems fair to say they were not highly motivated. Then again, that is the only sort of would-be mass murderer who could be stymied by a red flag law.

A 2022 study that analyzed a sample of 6,787 red flag cases from six states raised similar questions. April Zeoli and her co-authors identified 662 cases—about one-tenth of the total—that involved alleged threats to three or more victims. "While we cannot know how many of the 662 ERPO [emergency risk protection order] cases precipitated by a threat would have resulted in a multiple victim/mass shooting event had ERPO laws not been used to prohibit the purchase and possession of firearms," they said, "the study provides evidence at least that ERPOs are being used in six states in a substantial number of these kinds of cases that could have ended in tragedy."[93]

How often do people follow through on such threats? "We are unaware of any literature documenting how many individuals threaten mass shootings but do not go on to attempt or commit them," Zeoli et al. said, "although we suspect that there are many more threats than completed events."

That is certainly true when it comes to suicides. In 2021, according to survey-based estimates from the Centers for Disease Control and Prevention (CDC), 12.3 million American adults "seriously thought about suicide," 3.5 million "made a plan," and 1.7 million made an attempt. But the CDC counted a total of 48,183 completed suicides that year. In other words, about 0.4 percent of people who seriously contemplated suicide and 1.4 percent of people who made a plan actually killed themselves.[94]

That point is especially salient in the context of red flag orders. Zeoli et al. noted that earlier studies of red flag laws "reported that 32% of ERPOs in Connecticut and 21% in Indiana were issued to mitigate a threat of harm to others."[95] That means 68 percent of respondents in Connecticut and 79 percent of respondents in Indiana were deemed a threat to themselves. Judging from the CDC's numbers, very few of them would have acted on the alleged suicidal tendencies that prompted the orders.

Data from Florida reinforce the impression that gun confiscation orders are usually motivated by the belief that respondents pose a threat to themselves rather than other people. About 55 percent of risk protection orders issued in Volusia County from 2019 through 2023 involved a "suicidal person" or a "mental health incident" without mention of threats to others.[96] Similarly, an analysis of 359 petitions for gun confiscation orders in Colorado from January 2020 to mid-November 2022 found that "the respondent was accused of threatening others, either explicitly or indirectly," about half the time.[97]

By contrast, threats to others predominated in studies of orders issued during the first year after Colorado's law took effect, over five years in Oregon, and over three years in California, although the last study was limited to respondents "with accessible court records." These cases often combined both kinds of threats. In Oregon, for example, half of the petitions "cited both threats of assault and [threats of] self-harm," 34 percent "cited threats of assault exclusively," and 12 percent "cited threats of self-harm exclusively."[98]

In most studies, according to the systematic research review that Zeoli and her colleagues published in 2024, "self-harm risk was reported as the motivating behavior behind more than half of ERPO petitions."[99] They noted Zeoli et al.'s 2022 study finding that "roughly 10% of more than 6,600 petitions" in six states "were filed in response to threats to shoot at least three individuals."

"An Unavoidable False Alarm Rate"
Overall, these findings belie the general impression that the main goal of red flag laws is to prevent homicide—and mass shootings in particular. "Even though risk-based firearm seizure laws have typically been enacted in response to mass homicides," the authors of a 2018 study noted, "the laws have functioned primarily as a means of seizing firearms from suicidal individuals."[100]

That study found that Indiana's red flag law was associated with a 5 percent reduction in the overall suicide rate. But "Connecticut's estimated reduction in firearm suicides was offset by increased nonfirearm suicides." Using a different (and contested) method, a 2017 study led by medical sociologist Jeffrey Swanson estimated that one suicide was prevented in Connecticut by every 10 to 20 gun seizures.[101] A 2019 study of Indiana's law, also led by Swanson, reached a similar conclusion: one suicide prevented for every 10 "gun-removal actions."[102]

Taking those results at face value, they imply that 90 to 95 percent of people who are subject to gun confiscation orders because they are deemed a threat to themselves would *not* otherwise have killed themselves. "Is this a fair public health tradeoff?" Swanson et al. wondered in their Connecticut study. When I pressed Swanson on that question, he suggested that Indiana needed to improve due process for respondents in these cases. "The state's apparent failure to comply with the statutory guideline of holding a hearing within 14 days puts a damper on the success story of suicide prevention," he said. "This should be the focus of efforts to improve implementation of the law."[103]

None of these studies produced evidence that red flag laws reduce homicides, which is the risk that legislators typically claim to be addressing. A 2024 RAND Corporation analysis deemed the evidence regarding red flag laws and suicide "limited." Among the studies that met RAND's inclusion criteria, an interstate comparison found "significant reductions in total suicides and firearm suicides" of 4 and 6 percent, respectively. Another publication (the 2018 study of Connecticut and Indiana) "showed small and uncertain effects on firearm suicide rates and on nonfirearm suicide rates." A 2021 California study likewise found "uncertain effects" from San Diego County's especially aggressive use of gun confiscation orders.[104] RAND reached similar conclusions regarding red flag laws and homicide, deeming the evidence "uncertain" and "inconclusive."[105]

Since mass shootings are rare events, it is not surprising there is no solid evidence that red flag laws help prevent them. But although that possibility cannot be ruled out, implementation of these laws faces challenges that have long bedeviled criminologists and mental health specialists.

In a 2019 *New York Times* essay, psychiatrist Richard Friedman noted that "experienced psychiatrists fare no better than a roll of the dice at predicting violence."[106] Research backs up that assessment. "Over thirty years of commentary, judicial opinion, and scientific review argue that predictions of danger lack scientific rigor," law professor Alexander

Scherr noted in 2003. "Scientific studies indicate that some predictions do little better than chance or lay speculation, and even the best predictions leave substantial room for error about individual cases. The sharpest critique finds that mental health professionals perform no better than chance at predicting violence, and perhaps perform even worse."[107]

If "mental health professionals" are really bad at predicting violence, it seems unlikely that judges would do better, and that problem is compounded in the case of mass shootings. "The rare nature of mass shootings creates challenges for accurately identifying salient predictors of risk," RAND Corporation researchers Rosanna Smart and Terry Schell noted in 2021. "The low base rates of these events also ensure that policies targeting individuals based on risk factors would result in an extremely high rate of false positives; even the best available risk factors can identify only a subpopulation in which the risk of committing a mass shooting is on the order of one in a million."[108]

A 2012 study that the Department of Defense commissioned after the 2009 mass shooting at Fort Hood in Texas made the same point in an appendix titled "Prediction: Why It Won't Work." While "there may be pre-existing behavior markers that are specifiable," it said, those markers "are of low specificity and thus carry the baggage of an unavoidable false alarm rate, which limits feasibility of prediction-intervention strategies."[109] In other words, even if certain "red flags" are common among mass shooters, almost none of the people who display those signs are bent on murderous violence.

That "unavoidable false alarm rate" is a problem for politicians who think red flag laws are the key to preventing mass shootings or other types of gun violence. Due process safeguards that make it harder to obtain gun confiscation orders conflict with the urge to cast the net as wide as possible, lest a potential murderer be missed. But the wider the net is cast, the greater the danger that people will lose their constitutional rights for no good reason.

Common Sense?

I have focused on "assault weapon" bans, expanded background checks, and red flag laws because they are leading examples of what politicians like to call "common-sense gun safety legislation." But their limitations illustrate the broader point that, given the constitutional and practical constraints on gun control, passing new laws cannot reasonably be expected to have much of an impact on homicide or suicide rates.

Even gun laws that have been on the books for so long that people take them for granted do not necessarily make sense upon closer examination. The National Firearms Act of 1934, for example, originally would have covered pistols and revolvers as well as machine guns, on the theory that handguns were especially suitable for crime because they were easy to conceal. The rule regarding rifle and shotgun length was designed to prevent people from circumventing the pistol and revolver restrictions by cutting down long guns. But once handguns were removed from the bill, that rationale did not make much sense.[110]

The RAND Corporation's review of research on the effectiveness of gun control does identify at least one policy that seems to work. It found "supportive" evidence in favor of child-access prevention laws, which make it illegal to store guns in a way that allows unsupervised access by minors. According to RAND's analysis, there is "moderate" evidence that such laws reduce suicide among young people and "supportive" evidence that they reduce firearm accidents and homicides in that age group. It said the evidence of such benefits in the general population, by contrast, was "limited" or "inconclusive."[111]

By and large, the solutions touted by politicians who favor stricter gun regulation do not have a firm empirical basis. That problem is partly due to inadequate or flawed research. A 2020 RAND report "parsed the results of 27,900 research publications on the effectiveness of gun control laws," statistician Aaron Brown notes. "From this vast body of work, the RAND authors found only 123 studies, or 0.4 percent, that tested the effects rigorously."[112]

There is also a deeper problem. Gun control, like drug control, frequently entails broad restrictions that burden the general population in the hope of reaching a small subset of concern. Both kinds of policies focus on things that can be used for good or ill instead of targeting the harm that is sometimes caused by their misuse. In the process, they impose costs that politicians tend to minimize or ignore. The next chapter outlines a more carefully tailored approach that aims to reduce the harm caused by gun violence and substance abuse while minimizing the harm caused by government intervention.

Chapter Eight

Hope for Help

"Are You an Unlawful User?"
A few years after her husband died, Vera Cooper, the owner of a plumbing business in Milton, Florida, tried to buy a .22-caliber pistol for self-protection. She felt vulnerable as a widow in her seventies living alone and had been alarmed by an employee who threatened revenge after she fired him. But before she could complete the gun purchase, she had to fill out a federal form aimed at preventing firearm sales to "prohibited persons."[1]

Among other things, the form asks, "Are you an unlawful user of, or addicted to, marijuana or any depressant, stimulant, narcotic drug, or any other controlled substance?" It adds a warning: "The use or possession of marijuana remains unlawful under Federal law regardless of whether it has been legalized or decriminalized for medicinal or recreational purposes in the state where you reside."[2]

That posed a problem for Cooper, who used cannabis to treat chronic knee pain and insomnia as a patient registered with Florida's medical marijuana program. After she answered the drug question honestly, the gun dealer told her she had to choose between her state-approved medicine and her constitutional right to armed self-defense. Because she did not think that was fair, Cooper joined a federal lawsuit challenging the policy.[3]

That lawsuit, filed in April 2022, was spearheaded by Nikki Fried, a Democrat who ran Florida's Department of Agriculture and Consumer Services. In that position, Fried oversaw both the state's cannabis industry and the issuance of concealed weapon licenses. Since the dilemma that patients like Cooper faced sat at the intersection of marijuana and guns, Fried argued, it was her responsibility to help resolve it.

At the time, Fried was seeking the Democratic nomination to oppose Republican Governor Ron DeSantis when he ran for reelection that year. But that did not stop DeSantis, a conservative not otherwise known for his enlightened views on drug policy, from endorsing Fried's cause. "The governor stands for protecting Floridians' constitutional rights— including 2nd Amendment rights," his office said the day that Fried filed her lawsuit. "Floridians should not be deprived of a constitutional right for using a medication lawfully."[4]

DeSantis reiterated that position in January 2024, when he was vying with Donald Trump for the Republican presidential nomination. During a campaign stop in New Hampshire, DeSantis was asked about the federal ban on gun possession by cannabis consumers. "I don't think that's constitutional, to be honest with you," he replied. "If you're using a legal product, I don't see how that can nullify a constitutional right."[5]

While Florida and 37 other states recognized marijuana as "a legal product," of course, the federal government did not. But DeSantis's stance was consistent with two principles valued by conservatives: the right to arms guaranteed by the Second Amendment and the state autonomy guaranteed by federalism. The same principles explain why several Republicans in Congress supported legislation, dubbed the Second Amendment Protection Act, that would eliminate the disability that prevented Cooper from legally buying a pistol.[6]

Even the National Rifle Association (NRA), which for many years avoided taking a position on this issue, finally took the plunge in 2022. Although the organization had not directly supported the Florida lawsuit or other attempts to vindicate the Second Amendment rights of cannabis consumers, the NRA's director of media relations told me, "It would be unjust for the federal government to punish or deprive a person of a constitutional right for using a substance their state government has, as a matter of public policy, legalized."[7]

Other gun rights groups did not need prodding. In 2023, the Firearms Policy Coalition (FPC), which specializes in mounting constitutional challenges to gun control laws, offered to help the president's son, Hunter Biden, after he was charged with violating the same ban that Cooper confronted. That charge stemmed from Biden's purchase of a revolver in October 2018, a period when he was using crack cocaine. "If Hunter is looking for gun lawyers to challenge the federal law he's charged with violating.... we know some people," the FPC said. After Biden was convicted in June 2024, the group "reiterated its offer of assistance."[8]

Marijuana Moment, a publication founded by longtime cannabis activist Tom Angell, covered the Florida lawsuit, Biden's prosecution, and related cases extensively.[9] The fight against the gun ban for cannabis consumers, *Marijuana Moment*'s Kyle Jaeger repeatedly assured his readers, was "not about expanding gun rights, per se."[10] But as the Biden administration struggled to defend the policy of disarming anyone who uses marijuana, Jaeger highlighted every twist and turn, emphasizing the Justice Department's increasingly absurd portrayal of cannabis consumers as untrustworthy, irresponsible, and dangerous.[11]

In a July 2024 brief opposing Cooper's lawsuit, for example, the government's lawyers averred that medical marijuana patients who own guns "endanger public safety in multiple ways." They "may mishandle firearms—or use firearms to commit crimes—because of 'drug-induced changes in physiological functions, cognitive ability, and mood,'" the brief said. They "may 'commit crime in order to obtain money to buy drugs'— and thus pose a danger of using firearms to facilitate such crime." And "violent crime may occur as part of the drug business or culture."[12]

That alarming portrait bore little resemblance to Cooper or the other two Florida plaintiffs: Nicole Hansell, an Afghanistan veteran who used marijuana to treat PTSD and severe anxiety, and Neill Franklin, a retired police officer who wanted to use marijuana for pain relief, but not at the cost of surrendering his Second Amendment rights.[13] The Justice Department implicitly portrayed all three plaintiffs as potential public menaces because they might be inclined to handle guns while stoned, commit crimes to support their drug habits, or (for some reason) buy marijuana from violent drug dealers instead of state-licensed dispensaries.

The Biden administration's stubborn defense of this position inspired an opposing coalition that transcended party and ideology. That coalition, in turn, gave hope to those of us who argue that critics of drug control and critics of gun control have more in common than they usually realize. But even if these two politically disparate groups can agree that both policies are frequently irrational and unjust, the question remains: What are the alternatives?

I don't pretend to have any easy answers. But the beginning of wisdom in drug policy lies in recognizing some important distinctions: between use and abuse, between drugs themselves and the harm they may cause when misused, between self-inflicted harm and conduct that threatens or hurts others, and between harm caused by substance abuse and harm caused by efforts to prevent it. Similar distinctions can and should be applied to gun policy, guided by the overall goal of minimizing harm, including the harm inflicted by misguided interventions.

The Possibility of Harm

The philosopher Douglas Husak notes that drug and gun laws both punish "inchoate offenses," meaning they prohibit conduct that is not necessarily harmful. They "do not proscribe harm itself," he writes, "but rather the *possibility* of harm—a possibility that need not (and typically does not) materialize when the offense is committed." Remarking on the political divide between critics of drug control and critics of gun control, he observes that "skepticism about the justifiability of criminal proscriptions is brushed aside as we move back and forth between the topics of guns and drugs." But if we take seriously "our interest in not being subjected to hard treatment and reprobation," he argues, we should be equally skeptical of using criminal sanctions in both areas, regardless of how we feel about drugs or guns.[14]

"Perhaps the most worrisome feature of statutory schemes to prohibit gun or drug possession is the willingness to use the criminal law to prevent the risk of harm, even though that harm would materialize in only a tiny fraction of the cases in which persons are subject to punishment," Husak writes. "The net of criminal liability is deliberately cast far and wide to catch enormous numbers of offenders," even though "only a small percentage of those who are punished would ever have caused the harm to be prevented."

Husak notes that "current constitutional law requires the state to have a compelling interest before it will allow important, fundamental interests to be restricted." He wonders why we should "concede that our fundamental liberties to speak or to exercise our religious beliefs are more important and thus entitled to a greater degree of protection than our interest in not being punished." Given the choice, he suggests, "many persons would prefer to surrender their right to freedom of speech than their right not to be subjected to hard treatment and censure." And "if we agree that our interest not to be punished is equally valuable, *all* criminal laws should be required to satisfy the same justificatory test that applies to deprivations of our fundamental liberties."

Under that test, criminal laws would pass muster only if they were narrowly tailored to serve a compelling state interest. As Husak notes, drug and gun laws fail that test.

"Our current system of gun control is overinclusive because individuals are prohibited from owning guns simply because of their membership in (allegedly) high-risk groups," Husak writes. "In the case of [prohibited] drugs, this problem is compounded because the group consists of the entire universe. An adequate theory of criminalization would not allow a person to be punished for creating an unacceptable risk of harm in the absence of good reason to believe that he posed that very risk."

That lack of tailoring, Husak argues, makes gun and drug laws morally suspect. "If we take punishment seriously," he writes, "we should object to impositions of the penal sanction that are overinclusive—such as inchoate offenses of gun or drug possession." He concludes that "inchoate offenses of gun or drug possession are almost certainly unjustified."

While Husak does not explicitly distinguish between types of harm, the classical liberal philosopher John Stuart Mill famously argued that forcible government intervention is justified only to stop people from harming others. "The sole end for which mankind are warranted, individually or collectively, in interfering with the liberty of action of any of their number, is self-protection," he wrote in his 1859 essay *On Liberty*. "The only purpose for which power can be rightfully exercised over any member of a civilised community, against his will, is to prevent harm to others. His own good, either physical or moral, is not a sufficient warrant."[15]

Applying that principle, Mill took a dim view of alcohol prohibition, and his critique logically extends to bans on other psychoactive substances and paternalistic policies generally. But prohibitionists argue that alcoholics and other drug abusers *do* cause "harm to others," which they cite as a secondary justification. That rationale is an open-ended license for state intervention, since almost any sort of self-harm can be said to adversely affect other people.

The totalitarian implications of that argument can be avoided by distinguishing between "harm to others" that violates their rights (such as the harm caused by theft, assault, or reckless driving) and "harm to others" that does not (such as the harm caused by economic competition, hurtful words, or neglect of personal relationships). That distinction reflects a constrained view of government's proper role, which libertarians argue should be limited to protecting people from aggression, defined to include theft and fraud as well as the use or threat of violence.[16] But one need not entirely accept that view to recognize the moral challenge posed by the use of force, the dangers of overcriminalization, or the wisdom of focusing on actual, not just potential, harm.

"A Magical Thought"

In 2016, Maine legislators responded to escalating drug-related deaths by approving a bill allowing pharmacists to dispense naloxone, an opioid antagonist that quickly reverses heroin and fentanyl overdoses. Paul LePage, Maine's Republican governor, vetoed the bill, which he worried would encourage drug use. "Naloxone does not truly save lives; it merely extends them until the next overdose," he wrote in his veto letter. "Creating a situation where an addict has a heroin needle in one hand and a shot of naloxone in the other produces a sense of normalcy and security around heroin use that serves only to perpetuate the cycle of addiction."[17]

Legislators decisively rejected LePage's argument when they mustered the requisite two-thirds majority to override his veto.[18] In doing so, they took a stand in favor of harm reduction, a strategy that aims to reduce drug-related harm rather than drug use per se.[19] While politicians like LePage might prefer that no one use heroin, the war on drugs had failed to achieve that goal for more than a century. Given that reality,

Maine's lawmakers overwhelmingly thought, it made sense to make naloxone as readily available as possible. Some heroin users would still overdose, but they would be less likely to die as a result.

More generally, insisting on abstinence as the only solution to drug-related hazards is a risky strategy, leaving out anyone who is not prepared to stop using drugs entirely. Nora Volkow, director of the National Institute on Drug Abuse, has remarked on the dangers of that approach in the context of addiction treatment programs. "This very polarized categorical perspective, that it's either you go abstinent or we don't pay any attention to you and we send you to jail, is catastrophic," she said at a 2023 drug policy conference. That attitude, she argued, has "contributed to what we're seeing as a horrific problem in our country with horrible fatalities like we've never seen." While abstinence is "great" as a "theoretical ideal," Volkow said, trying to "impose that as a reality for everyone" is "sort of like a magical thought and not practical." She warned that the "inflexibility" of demanding abstinence, as opposed to incremental improvements that can reduce the risk of fatal outcomes, "costs a lot of lives."[20]

The argument between LePage and Maine's legislature harked back to an earlier controversy over the distribution of sterile hypodermic syringes. The logic there was similar: Given that people would continue to inject drugs, it was better that they do so with fresh equipment, thereby reducing the risk of skin and soft tissue injury caused by bacteria and the risk of infection by communicable diseases such as AIDS and hepatitis when needles are shared. Those dangers were magnified by restrictions on the legal availability of hypodermic syringes and by drug paraphernalia laws that treated their possession as a crime.

U.S. programs offering clean needles in exchange for used ones began informally (and illegally) in the early 1980s.[21] Like LePage, opponents of needle exchange programs argued that making drug use less dangerous would encourage it. If Congress allowed federal anti-AIDS funds to be used for this purpose, Senator Jesse Helms (R–N.C.) argued in 1988, it would be "saying it is OK, in effect, to use drugs."[22] That year, in response to such arguments, Congress imposed a ban on federal funding of needle exchange programs.[23] Congress modified that rule in 2015 to allow funding for the programs as long as it was not used to purchase the needles themselves.[24] By 2018, more than 300 "syringe service programs" (SSPs) were operating in the United States, typically run by private organizations under the supervision of local and state health departments.[25]

Needle exchange gained legitimacy largely because of extensive research indicating that it helped reduce the spread of infectious disease. "Nearly 30 years of research has shown that comprehensive SSPs are safe, effective, and cost-saving, do not increase illegal drug use or crime, and play an important role in reducing the transmission of viral hepatitis, HIV and other infections," the Centers for Disease Control and Prevention (CDC) noted in 2024. "Research shows that new users of SSPs are five times more likely to enter drug treatment and about three times more likely to stop using drugs than those who don't use the programs. SSPs that provide naloxone also help decrease opioid overdose deaths. SSPs protect the public and first responders by facilitating the safe disposal of used needles and syringes."[26]

Perhaps partly thanks to that precedent, wide distribution of naloxone, which can be administered through intravenous injection, with an intramuscular auto-injector, or via a nasal spray, caught on faster as a legal harm-reduction measure. The Food and Drug Administration (FDA) approved the nasal spray, sold under the brand name Narcan, in 2015.[27] By 2019, when the FDA approved a generic version of the spray, 33 states and the District of Columbia had authorized pharmacists to dispense naloxone without a doctor's prescription through standing orders or similar policies.[28] Four years later, the FDA approved over-the-counter sales of the nasal spray.[29]

Annual opioid-related deaths, which nearly tripled in the 13 years between 2002 and 2015, more than doubled in the ensuing seven years.[30] In the face of that dismal and accelerating trend, state and federal officials rejected the objections of politicians like LePage. But other harm-reduction measures proved more controversial.

DRUGS, SEX, AND DRIVING

Like needle exchange programs, supervised consumption sites, where people use drugs they bring with them in a safe setting monitored by staff members who can provide medical help if it is needed, began informally in the United States. That was largely because they were arguably illegal under the federal "crack house" statute, which was originally part of the Biden-backed Anti-Drug Abuse Act of 1986 and was broadened by a 2003 law that the Delaware senator and future president wrote (see Chapter 5). That law made it a felony to "maintain any place, whether permanently or temporarily, for the purpose of . . . using any controlled substance."[31]

In 2019, William McSwain, the U.S. attorney for the Eastern District of Pennsylvania, sued to stop Safehouse, a private organization, from opening a supervised injection site in Philadelphia, arguing that it would violate the crack house statute.[32] A federal judge disagreed in 2020, but an appeals court reversed that decision the following year, agreeing with McSwain that Safehouse could be prosecuted if it went ahead with its plan.[33] Under a new administration headed by the same politician who had written the law that McSwain cited, the Justice Department seemed more accommodating. In 2022, a spokesman said the department was "evaluating supervised consumption sites, including discussions with state and local regulators about appropriate guardrails for such sites, as part of an overall approach to harm reduction and public safety."[34]

At that point, states had begun to experiment with this strategy. In 2021, the Rhode Island legislature authorized "safe injection sites" with local permission, and the Providence City Council approved the state's first such facility in 2024.[35] In 2023, Minnesota legislators authorized "safe recovery sites," and the organization Minnesota Overdose Awareness began operating one in Minneapolis the following year.[36] Two months later, Vermont's legislature overrode Governor Phil Scott's veto of a similar bill, clearing the way for a site in Burlington.[37]

Although legislation along these lines stalled in New York's legislature, two supervised consumption sites in New York City, operated by the organization OnPoint NYC, opened in November 2021 with the blessing of local officials. Between December 2021 and December 2024, OnPoint reported, the two sites served 5,804 people, mostly heroin, fentanyl, or cocaine injectors, on 171,712 occasions. Trained staff responded 1,696 times to prevent fatal overdoses or other adverse effects, administering naloxone 329 times and using supplemental oxygen 1,166 times. There were no fatalities at the sites or at hospitals that subsequently treated OnPoint participants.[38]

Research in other countries, where supervised drug consumption sites have operated for decades, reinforces the promise of such programs. "One study found a 26% net reduction in overdose deaths in the area surrounding a supervised injection site in Vancouver, Canada, compared with the rest of the city," physicians Jorge Finke and Jie Chan noted in a 2022 *American Family Physician* editorial. "A supervised injection site in Barcelona, Spain, was associated with a 50% reduction in overdose mortality from 1991 to 2008."[39] Similarly, a 2024 study found that supervised consumption sites in Toronto were associated with a 42 percent decline in the citywide overdose mortality rate over two years—a change that was concentrated in the neighborhoods near the sites, which saw a 67 percent drop.[40]

Finke and Chan cited other potential benefits: "People who inject drugs are significantly less likely to share needles if they regularly use supervised injection sites. These sites could be effective in reducing the rates of HIV and hepatitis C in people who inject drugs. Supervised injection sites can also reduce the number of publicly discarded syringes, and they improve public safety." They noted that "concerns about these sites leading to increased criminal activity or drug use are not supported by the evidence." To the contrary, a Vancouver study "observed an abrupt, persistent decrease in crime after the opening of a supervised injection site."

If this concept is still a tough sell, that is mainly because of moral objections to drug use and any policy that could be seen as condoning it, even if that policy consists mainly of refraining from prosecuting people for providing a safer alternative to injecting drugs in public restrooms, parks, or parking lots.[41] In that respect, this controversy resembles disputes over sex education or condom distribution aimed at teenagers, which provoke complaints from parents who do not want their kids to have sex at all. Whatever you might prefer, the other side argues, some teenagers are bound to have sex, and it is better that they do so equipped with knowledge and prophylactics that make bad outcomes, such as unwanted pregnancies and sexually transmitted diseases, less likely.

However you come down in that debate, it is instructive to consider another context where harm reduction is generally uncontroversial: traffic safety. We could try to reduce the death toll from car accidents by discouraging people from driving. Alternatively, we could focus on innovations and interventions that reduce the risk of traffic fatalities, such as road improvements, seat belts, safer car design, and efforts to curb intoxicated driving through law enforcement, moral suasion, and social pressure. The latter approach, the one that historically has been favored in the United States, has been remarkably successful at reducing traffic deaths, which fell from 33.4 to 1.5 per 10,000 motor vehicles between 1913 and 2022. The United States has seen a similarly steep reduction in traffic deaths per 100 million miles traveled, which fell from 21.7 in 1923 to 1.3 in 2022.[42]

Is drug use more like adolescent sex or more like driving? That obviously depends on value judgments. But in making those judgments, it is important to keep in mind that illegal drug use typically does not lead to life-disrupting habits that cause serious harm.[43] By that measure, it is morally indistinguishable from alcohol consumption, which can result in addiction, injury to drinkers, and harm to others but usually does not. People typically manage to use alcohol and other drugs without causing serious problems for themselves or others. That choice reflects their judgment that the benefits outweigh the risks, and that judgment deserves the same respect as any other self-regarding decision.

In the context of drinking, harm reduction measures such as using a designated driver, public transportation, or a ride share service to travel to and from bars are widely accepted. And when it comes to nicotine consumption, public health authorities recognize that cigarette smokers can dramatically reduce the health risks they face by vaping instead.[44] Instead of demanding abstinence, those strategies seek to reduce the harm associated with drug consumption. So do programs such as needle exchanges, distribution of naloxone and fentanyl test strips, testing of club drugs, education about the hazards of drug mixing, and supervised consumption sites. And even when drug use is especially hazardous, as we can surmise it is for the average OnPoint NYC client, there is little sense, morally or practically, in supporting policies that make it more dangerous still.

Decriminalization Versus Legalization

One of those policies makes drug users, unlike drinkers, subject to criminal punishment merely for possessing or consuming psychoactive substances. On that score, drug prohibition is more severe than the alcohol prohibition regime imposed by the Eighteenth Amendment and the Volstead Act, which banned commercial production and distribution without criminalizing drinkers. States began reconsidering the policy of treating cannabis consumers as criminals in the 1970s, and most of them—31 as of 2024—eventually made low-level possession a civil infraction, a minor misdemeanor with no possibility of jail, or no offense at all (in the two dozen states that had legalized recreational use by adults).[45]

The logic of decriminalizing marijuana use while continuing to treat marijuana production and distribution as felonies was compelling to legislators, especially at a time when harsh pot laws were ensnaring a growing number of white, middle-class adolescents and young adults. But that policy was always morally suspect, since it punished people who engaged in the conduct that legislators wanted to deter less severely than people who merely facilitated that conduct. This was rather like letting murderers off with a slap on the wrist while coming down hard on their accomplices.

The most ambitious U.S. attempt to expand decriminalization came when Oregon voters approved a 2020 ballot initiative that eliminated criminal penalties for low-level possession of all drugs. Measure 110, which was backed by 58 percent of voters, replaced that threat with a $100 civil fine that drug users could avoid by agreeing to a "health assessment" at an "addiction recovery center," which could result in a nonmandatory treatment referral.[46] Four years later, after polls indicated that most Oregonians thought that reform was a mistake, Oregon legislators overwhelmingly voted to restore criminal penalties for simple possession.[47]

Although that repudiation suggested decriminalization in Oregon had been a disaster, the main reasons for the reversal had little to do with Measure 110. Critics complained about drug-related public nuisances, which could have been addressed, like alcohol-related public nuisances, without treating consumption itself as a crime. Opponents of Measure

110 also noted that drug-related deaths in Oregon continued to rise after decriminalization. But other Western states that had not decriminalized drug use saw similar trends, which seemed to reflect the delayed arrival of illicit fentanyl in that region.[48]

Defenders of Measure 110 argued that it was not given a proper chance to achieve its goals, which they said were hampered by tardy and inadequate funding for drug treatment.[49] But it was not surprising that opioid-related deaths kept rising in Oregon, because decriminalization did nothing to address the iffy and unpredictable composition of illegal drugs. Harm reduction measures such as increased access to naloxone, distribution of fentanyl test strips, and supervised consumption sites likewise do not eliminate that hazard, although they can help mitigate it. By contrast, drug users who replace illicit drugs with methadone or buprenorphine through "medication-assisted treatment" (MAT) are much less likely to die from overdoses. According to a 2019 review of the evidence, "treatment using agonist medication is associated with an estimated mortality reduction of approximately 50 percent."[50]

One major drawback of MAT is that many people do not stick with it. A 2016 review reported a wide range of retention rates, with some studies finding that more than 60 percent of patients had dropped out after a year.[51] "Retention rates are quite low," two researchers noted in 2021. "Overall, 40% to 50% of patients treated with methadone or buprenorphine relapse within a 6-month period of treatment initiation."[52] Intriguingly, the 2016 review found that "methadone was associated with better retention than buprenorphine/naloxone" but "heroin-assisted treatment was associated with better retention than methadone among treatment-refractory patients."

Heroin is not legally available for MAT in the United States, where methadone and buprenorphine are the only options. Might retention be improved by offering a wider range of opioids, including legal, reliably dosed versions of the street drugs that people otherwise prefer? Going a step further, what if people could obtain those drugs without enrolling in a treatment program?

We don't have to speculate about how that option might affect the risk for any given drug user. The fatal overdose rate for consumers of black-market drugs is much higher than the rate for nonmedical consumers of opioid pharmaceuticals, as you would expect given the difference in quality and consistency. In 2022, the CDC counted about 12,000 deaths involving "natural and semisynthetic opioids," the category that includes pain medications such as Vicodin and Percocet.[53] Federal survey data indicated that around 8.5 million Americans used drugs like those for nonmedical purposes that year.[54] By comparison, the CDC counted nearly 80,000 deaths involving heroin or illicit fentanyl in 2022. According to the same federal survey, fewer than two million Americans used those drugs that year. Even if you think the latter estimate is off by a lot because of underreporting and a sample that excludes many opioid users, that is a huge difference in risk.

That comparison suggests the potential benefits of going beyond decriminalizing drug use by legalizing the drug supply. The fear, of course, is that even a dramatic reduction in the risk to individual drug users would be swamped by an increase in their total number, leading to more drug-related deaths on balance. But judging from the government's estimates, that scenario would require something like a tenfold increase in the number of opioid users. And that's assuming people who would use these drugs only if they were legal would be just as prone to dangerous consumption patterns, such as heavy use, injection, and drug mixing, as people who are undeterred by prohibition.

However you rate the likelihood of that outcome, there remains the moral question of whether saving one group of people from the consequences of their own bad choices can justify exposing a different group of people to much greater hazards than they otherwise would face, including legal risks and black-market violence as well as the unpredictability of illegal drugs. That collectivist calculus ignores the injustice of punishing people for conduct that *might* cause harm even though it typically does not. It gives no weight to individual autonomy—the principle that, as Mill put it, "the individual is sovereign" over "his own body and mind."[55] And given the abysmal track record of the war on drugs, that calculus is almost certainly wrong even on its own terms.

Even without drug prohibition, the law can and should impose limits on drug-related behavior, applying distinctions that are familiar in the context of alcohol. Those justifiable limits include age restrictions on sales, prohibition of driving while impaired, regulation of public behavior, and punishment of conduct, such as theft and assault, that violates people's rights, regardless of what substance the perpetrator may have consumed. And as with alcohol, the force of law can and should be supplemented by education, social pressure, and economic incentives that encourage responsible behavior. Although some advocates of harm reduction may disagree, their logic ultimately points in this direction: toward a legal regime in which people are simultaneously free and accountable.

"A Public Health Menace"

Harm reduction is a concept familiar to public health specialists, who apply it in a wide range of contexts, including sexually transmitted diseases, unwanted pregnancy, traffic safety, and nicotine consumption. But when it comes to firearms, supporters of stricter regulation often employ public health rhetoric in a less discriminating way, describing guns as "a public health menace" or "a virus that must be eradicated."[56] That attitude is not merely offensive to anyone who owns guns or values the constitutional right to armed self-defense; it is utterly unrealistic in a society where guns number in the hundreds of millions.

Recognizing that reality, *New York Times* columnist Nicholas Kristof has proposed "a harm-reduction model familiar from public health efforts to reduce deaths from other dangerous products such as cars and cigarettes." That approach, he says, "would start by acknowledging the blunt reality that we're not going to eliminate guns any more than we have eliminated vehicles or tobacco, not in a country that already has more guns than people." If "done right," Kristof writes, harm reduction "avoids stigmatizing people as gun nuts and makes firearms less a part of a culture war."[57]

Despite those insights, Kristof's recommendations consist mainly of doubling down on current policies. Among other things, he favors requiring a license to own a gun, prohibiting gun sales to adults younger than 21, "universal background checks," "tightly restricting AR-15-style weapons and large-capacity magazines," disarming people via red flag laws, and extending the ban on gun possession by people with felony records to include people convicted of violent misdemeanors.

Several of these proposals are constitutionally dubious, and most of them suffer from a familiar problem: They are overinclusive, imposing broad restrictions that mainly affect the law-abiding majority while attempting to restrain a violent minority that can easily evade government-imposed restrictions. "The persons who pose the greatest risk of gun violence are probably those who will go to the greatest lengths to circumvent the law and obtain a gun despite whatever legal machinery is designed to prevent them from doing so," Husak observes. This is the problem that Joe Biden recognized back in 1985, before he embraced a gun control agenda that wishes it away.

It seems both sensible and fair to restrict the gun rights of people who have been convicted of violent crimes, perhaps including misdemeanors as well as felonies. It is less clear that a lifetime ban can be justified unless we assume that rehabilitation is impossible. When someone like Darrell Hargraves, who was convicted of attempted armed robbery as a young man, completes his sentence and becomes a peaceful, productive citizen, neither justice nor public safety is served by sending him back to prison decades later because he dared to arm himself for self-defense.[58]

It makes even less sense to permanently disarm someone based on crimes, such as mail fraud or drug dealing, that do not involve violence, or based on psychiatric records that do not involve threats to others. Until legislators rectify the absurdly broad criteria that disqualify people from legally owning firearms, any attempt to expand background checks for gun buyers, to the extent that it actually results in more background checks, will compound the illogic and injustice of the current system.

Gun control focuses on the tools that criminals use—tools that typically are used for lawful purposes. Criminals, of course, also use many other tools that fit the same description, such as knives, baseball bats, crow bars, and cars. If we are truly interested in harm reduction, it makes more sense to focus on the outcomes that actually worry us. As law professor John Pfaff puts it, "a better way to focus on gun violence is to target the *violence* more than the *guns*."[59] Here the outlook is by no means hopeless.

Why Does Crime Go Down?
Beginning in the early 1990s, the United States saw a precipitous decline in violent and property crime. By 2013, the homicide rate was less than half as high as it had been two decades earlier. Despite ups and downs since then, the homicide rate as of 2023 was still about 42 percent lower than the peak recorded in 1991. The country also saw substantial reductions in robbery, aggravated assault, and property crime rates.[60] In 2023, the U.S. homicide rate fell by about 12 percent, the largest annual decrease ever recorded.[61] Preliminary numbers for 2024 indicated a continued decline in violent and property crime (with the exception of shoplifting).[62]

These numbers contradicted Donald Trump's July 2024 claim that "our crime rate is going up," supposedly thanks largely to the Biden administration's border policies, and his claim the following month that "homicides are skyrocketing."[63] But they also posed a perplexing puzzle, especially when it came to explaining the long-term downward trend.

In a 2004 article focusing on the decline in crime during the 1990s, economist Steven Levitt reported that the most commonly cited explanation was "innovative policing strategies." He added that "the crime decline is also frequently attributed to increased imprisonment, changes in the market for crack cocaine, the aging of the population, tougher gun control laws, the strong economy and increases in the number of police." Levitt argued that four factors "can account for virtually all of the observed decline in crime: increases in the number of police, the rising prison population, the waning crack epidemic and the legalization of abortion."[64] The abortion explanation, which Levitt and fellow economist John J. Donohue had first proposed a few years before, was based on "strong evidence that unwanted children are likely to be disproportionately involved in criminal activity."[65]

Reviewing the evidence in 2015, the Brennan Center for Justice conceded "it is possible that legalized abortion could have affected the crime decline in the 1990s," although any such effect "likely waned in the 2000s," since by then "the first cohort that would have been theoretically affected by abortion, 10 years after the 1990s, would be well beyond the most common crime committing age." The Brennan Center's analysts agreed with Levitt that economic growth was not an important explanation for the crime decline, estimating that just 0 to 5 percent of the drop could be attributed to higher employment, while per capita income growth might account for 5 to 10 percent.[66]

Levitt estimated that "the increase in police between 1991 and 2001 can account for a crime reduction of 5–6 percent across the board." The Brennan Center concluded that more cops had a "modest, downward effect on crime in the 1990s, likely 0 to 10 percent" of the total drop. But that effect, it said, "likely became negligible in the 2000s because of a plateau and subsequent slight decrease in the number of police officers during that decade."

Levitt concluded that the "incapacitation effect" of "the increase in incarceration over the 1990s" could account for a reduction of about 8 percent in property crime and 12 percent in homicide and violent crime generally, representing "about one-third of the observed decline in crime." Here the Brennan Center's conclusions, based on additional data and analysis, were starkly different.

"Increased incarceration accounted for approximately 6 percent of the reduction in property crime in the 1990s," the report's authors estimated. "Increased incarceration has had no effect on the drop in violent crime in the past 24 years. In fact, large states such as California, Michigan, New Jersey, New York, and Texas have all reduced their prison populations while crime has continued to fall." The report highlighted evidence of "diminishing returns" from incarceration, to the point that "increased incarceration at today's levels has a negligible crime control benefit."

When that report was published, the total number of people in U.S. prisons and jails was nearly 2.2 million.[67] By 2024, the number had declined to about 1.9 million.[68] But as Supreme Court Justice Neil Gorsuch noted in a book published that year, the United States remained "a world leader when it comes to incarceration," with a rate "eight times as high as the median rate in western European democracies." More people were serving life sentences in the United States than "were serving *any* sentence in 1970," and "one out of every 47 adults" was under "some form of correctional supervision," including parole and probation.[69]

A 2014 Brookings Institution report explained why the marginal benefit from imprisoning more people can be expected to decline as the prison population expands. "The crime-reduction gains from higher incarceration rates depend critically on the incarceration rate itself," it noted. "When the incarceration rate is low, marginal gains from increasing the incarceration rate are higher. This follows from the fact that when prisons are used sparingly, incarceration is reserved for those who commit the most serious crimes. By contrast, when the incarceration rate is high, the marginal crime-reduction gains from further increases tend to be lower, because the offender on the margin between incarceration and an alternative sanction tends to be less serious. In other words, the crime-fighting benefits of incarceration diminish with the scale of the prison population."[70]

The evidence also suggests that lengthening prison terms, like sentencing more people to prison, is not cost-effective. "We've known for a long time that swiftness and certainty are more important than severity," the criminologist Mark Kleiman noted in 2011. "What's not adequately understood is that severity is the enemy of swiftness and certainty. A severe punishment can't be swift because there's a lot of due process involved, and it can't be certain, because you're chewing up a lot of resources. That 25-year mandatory sentence under the California 'three strikes' law—that's 25 people who can't be locked up for a year. It's a little strange that the people who are loudest about opposing wasteful government spending haven't noticed that long prison terms are wasteful government spending."[71]

Kleiman was referring to conservatives, but even then they were beginning to come around on this issue. Right on Crime, a joint project of the Texas Public Policy Foundation, the American Conservative Union Foundation, and Prison Fellowship, was founded in 2007. It "makes the case for conservative criminal justice reform," which it argues is perfectly consistent with crime control.[72] The evidence supports that view: States such as Texas and Louisiana have seen falling crime rates even as they reduced their prison populations.[73]

Whatever the role of incarceration in the crime decline since the early 1990s, it seems clear that incapacitation works only to the extent that the government locks up people who otherwise would be committing predatory crimes. That is another reason to question the wisdom (as well as the justice) of imprisoning people who are guilty of nothing other than exchanging prohibited intoxicants for money. The war on drugs is also implicated in another factor that Levitt identified as an important reason for the drop in crime: He estimated that "the decline of crack explains about 15 percent of the fall [in] homicide." As we saw in Chapter 3, the violence associated with the crack trade in the 1980s and 1990s was mainly a product of prohibition.

Violence Interruption

Levitt found "little or no evidence that changes in gun control laws in the 1990s can account for falling crime." Given the "active black market in guns," he wrote, "the apparent ineffectiveness of gun control laws should not come as a great surprise to economists." It is also worth noting that from 1993 to 2013, when the homicide rate fell by more than half, the estimated number of guns owned by Americans rose by about the same percentage.[74]

What about "innovative policing strategies"? In 2004, Levitt deemed the evidence inconclusive. "While the impact of policing strategies on crime is an issue on which reasonable people might disagree given the lack of hard evidence," he wrote, "my reading of the limited data that are available leads me to the conclusion that the impact of policing strategies on New York City crime are exaggerated, and that the impact on national crime is likely to be minor."

A decade later, the Brennan Center found the evidence more compelling. In particular, the report noted evidence in favor of CompStat, a crime tracking program that New York City began using in 1994. CompStat, which has been copied by other cities, involves weekly meetings in which department leaders allocate police resources based on information about crime patterns that is updated every day. CompStat "played a role in bringing down crime in cities," the Brennan Center concluded. "Based on an analysis of the 50 most populous cities, this report finds that CompStat-style programs were responsible for a 5 to 15 percent decrease in crime in those cities that introduced it." A 2024 study similarly concluded that "Compstat has helped bring down crime rates by around 10%, with both violent and property offenses significantly decreasing" after its adoption.[75]

Various community-based programs also show promise in reducing gun violence. "Focused deterrence" strategies, for example, are modeled after Operation Ceasefire, a Boston initiative that sought to interrupt cycles of gang violence in the 1990s. This approach aims to "identify chronic violent offenders and prevent them from engaging in future violence" by warning them of "impending swift and certain legal action if violence continues" while "simultaneously offer[ing] social services and support to change risky behavior."[76] A 2018 review and meta-analysis found that such programs were associated with a "statistically significant, moderate crime reduction effect."[77]

A 2023 evaluation of Safe Streets, a "violence interrupter" program in Baltimore, found that it was "associated with a statistically significant average reduction in homicides of 32%" during its first four years.[78] According to the Center for Gun Violence Solutions at Johns Hopkins University's Bloomberg School of Public Health, early results suggest that "cognitive behavioral interventions," "violence reduction councils," and addressing environmental conditions such as "inadequate street lighting" and "large numbers of vacant buildings and blighted lots" can reduce gun violence.[79] A 2022 report on shootings in Philadelphia noted several studies supporting that last approach, which indicate that it "leads[s] to reductions in violence" and "other positive outcomes."[80]

These programs target a kind of violence that is far more common than the public mass shootings that tend to attract much more attention and inspire more fear in the general population. For reasons we discussed in Chapter 7, preventing the latter sort of violence poses daunting practical challenges, because it is very difficult to predict who, among the country's many troubled and angry people, is apt to commit such horrifying crimes. For every lonely, depressed, and resentful teenager who decides to shoot up a high school, for instance, there are millions of others who will never do such a thing. But outreach and intervention programs that seek to help that much larger population—by discouraging bullying or offering psychological services, for example—are worthwhile even if they have no measurable impact on mass shootings.

There is likewise no easy public policy solution to suicides, which account for most gun-related deaths (54 percent in 2021).[81] In 2021, the CDC counted more than 48,000 suicides, nearly twice the number of homicides.[82] About 55 percent of those suicides involved firearms, and gun control advocates argue that reducing access to that particular, especially effective means would reduce the annual death toll.[83] Yet according to an analysis of international data, "there is nearly no correlation between firearm availability and the rate of successful suicides."[84]

General restrictions on guns seem poorly targeted to address this problem, and narrower approaches such as red flag laws are still bound to be overbroad. As we saw in Chapter 7, the CDC's numbers indicate that, even when people go so far as to make a plan for suicide, just 1.4 percent go through with it.[85] "Even among those classified as 'high-risk,'" psychiatrist-epidemiologist Gonzalo Martinez-Ales and his colleagues noted in 2020, "most will never engage in suicidal behaviors, and attempts to identify particular persons who will commit suicide tend to yield striking false-positive rates."[86]

Martinez-Ales was grappling with possible explanations for recent increases in the U.S. suicide rate, which rose by 37 percent from 2000 to 2022, from 10.4 to 14.2 per 100,000 Americans.[87] That trend, which followed a sharp decline in the 1990s, obviously reflects factors other than the rate of household gun ownership, which according to survey data was slightly lower in 2021 than it was in 2000.[88] Martinez-Ales et al. noted that "the increase in suicides by firearm was less pronounced than the increase in suicides by other means, such as suffocation," which suggests that "variations in access to lethal means" did not contribute to the rise in suicides. The authors, who considered several other theories and found them wanting, urged "a new generation of suicide research that examines causal factors beyond the proximal and clinical and fosters a socially conscious reimagining of [suicide] prevention."

While that does not sound very encouraging, Martinez-Ales and his co-authors noted that "brief contact interventions," which aim merely to "ensure contact between the patient and treatment providers over a sustained period of time," seem to be "a particularly cost-effective psychosocial approach to suicide risk reduction." A systematic review published the same year looked at research on the effectiveness of various suicide prevention methods, including "community approaches," "psychotherapeutic interventions," and "pharmacotherapeutic and multi-level interventions." Based on an analysis of 15 controlled studies, the authors concluded that "suicide prevention interventions are effective in preventing completed and attempted suicides and should be widely implemented." They recommended further investigation of multilevel interventions in light of "their greater effects and synergistic potential."[89]

COVID-19 SPIKES

In the first year of the COVID-19 pandemic, Americans saw many dramatic changes, including surges in homicides and drug-related deaths. The homicide rate rose by a whopping 30 percent in 2020—the biggest annual increase in more than a century.[90] The drug-related death rate rose by 31 percent, which was the biggest annual increase ever recorded.[91]

The homicide rate fell sharply in 2023 and, according to preliminary estimates, fell again in 2024, apparently reverting to the pre-pandemic norm.[92] Drug-related deaths continued to rise for two years after 2020, although the increases in 2021 and 2022 (16 percent and 1.2 percent, respectively) were much smaller than the 2020 spike, before falling by about 3 percent in 2023.[93] According to provisional estimates, the drug death toll fell dramatically in 2024: The estimated number of deaths during the year ending in September 2024 was 24 percent lower than the number during the previous 12 months—the largest such drop ever recorded.[94]

Commonly proposed explanations for both of these surges centered around the economic and social dislocations caused by the pandemic itself and by government reactions to it. People were out of work, out of school, cooped up at home, separated from social networks, and deprived of engaging activities. Those conditions, observers surmised, were conducive to violent conflict *and* substance abuse. The plausibility of that theory reflects the fundamental truth that how people treat themselves and others depends partly on conditions that can be improved—in this case, perhaps, by the passing of a pandemic but in other cases, perhaps, by deliberate, rational effort.

The COVID-19 explanation for the homicide spike provoked considerable debate. The pandemic "may have stimulated more homicides," statisticians Mohammad Fazel-Zarandi and Arnold Barnett conceded in 2024. But based on their analysis of homicide victims and perpetrators in 50 large cities, they reported that "the growth in murder was by no means concentrated in the cities that seemingly suffered the most from the pandemic in terms of deaths, lockdown severity, or unemployment." At the same time, their analysis cast doubt on the hypothesis that the spike was related to the fallout from the May 2020 death of George Floyd in Minneapolis, including the unrest that followed it, the "Defund the Police" movement, and a resulting "police pullback."[95] Proponents of that theory argued that it made more sense, because the rise in homicides did not begin until late May.[96]

According to a 2024 Brookings Institution analysis, however, "the national homicide rate was already on track to reach a peak far above the previous year even before Floyd was killed." The authors found that "the spike in murders during 2020 was directly connected to local unemployment and school closures in low-income areas." They reported that "cities with larger numbers of young men forced out of work and teen boys pushed out of school in low-income neighborhoods during March and early April" saw "greater increases in homicide from May to December that year, on average." They speculated that "the persistence of these changes can also explain why murders remained high in 2021 and 2022 and then fell in late 2023 and 2024."[97]

The COVID-19 explanation for the 2020 surge in drug deaths seemed to be less controversial. "The COVID-19 pandemic and disruption in access to prevention, treatment, and harm reduction services have likely contributed to this increase," CDC researchers concluded in 2022.[98] While opioid-related deaths were already rising, *The New York Times* reported in April 2021, "the pandemic unquestionably exacerbated the trend, which grew much worse last spring: The biggest jump in overdose deaths took place in April and May, when fear and stress were rampant, job losses were multiplying and the strictest lockdown measures were in effect."[99]

The New York Times cited research that found many drug users had increased their consumption during the pandemic. They also were more likely to take drugs on their own, which increases the risk of a fatal outcome, and most reported consuming mixtures of drugs, "another red flag." A 2024 study likewise found that "volatile drug use during the COVID-19 pandemic was common, appeared to be driven by structural vulnerability, and was associated with increased overdose risk."[100] Another study published the same year concluded that "policies limiting in-person activities significantly increased" drug death rates.[101]

If pandemic-related restrictions were largely responsible for the surge in drug deaths, it is less clear why deaths declined so precipitously in 2024, which was well after those restrictions were lifted. Addressing that puzzle, Nabarun Dasgupta and two other drug researchers deemed it "unlikely" that antidrug operations along the U.S.-Mexico border had helped reduce overdoses. They noted that recent border seizures had mainly involved marijuana and methamphetamine rather than illicit fentanyl, the primary culprit in overdoses, and that retail drug prices had been falling in recent years—the opposite of what you would expect if interdiction were effective.[102]

While replacing street drugs with methadone or buprenorphine reduces overdose risk, Dasgupta et al. said, it did not look like expanded access to MAT could account for the drop in deaths. But they thought it was "plausible" that broader distribution of naloxone had played a role, and they suggested a few other possible explanations that do not hinge on deliberate interventions.

If opioid users by 2024 tended to be more experienced than they were when fentanyl began proliferating as a heroin booster and substitute, they might have been less likely to overdose thanks to increased tolerance and/or greater caution. If the introduction of the animal tranquilizer xylazine as a fentanyl adulterant decreased the typical number of doses per day, which Dasgupta et al. thought was plausible given the former drug's pharmacological effects, that also could have reduced the risk of overdosing. So might a shift from injection to smoking. And although lower retail prices are the opposite of what drug warriors are trying to achieve, they mean that people are less likely to oscillate between using drugs when they can afford them and abstaining when they come up short. That pattern increases the risk of an overdose because tolerance declines during periods of abstinence, whether they result from arrest and jail, disruption of the local drug supply, or financial factors like high prices.

Whatever caused the subsequent drop, it seems clear that pandemic-related isolation, psychological stress, and economic difficulty help explain the 2020 spike in drug-related deaths. This widely accepted take is consistent with what we know about drug use and addiction. In ordinary times, mainstream news outlets like *The New York Times* are quick to explain addiction by reference to the inherent powers of certain drugs. But as experts like the psychologist Stanton Peele have been pointing out for half a century, the risk of addiction is not evenly distributed: It is heightened by social, economic, and personal circumstances that make drug use especially appealing.[103]

The pandemic may have magnified the problems that make drug use more attractive, but it did not create them. Contrary to the conventional narrative, which blamed the "opioid crisis" on an oversupply of pain pills, "drug-related deaths have been rising since the late 1950s," a 2019 report on "deaths of despair" from the Joint Economic Committee noted.[104] The increase in opioid-related fatalities was the latest manifestation of that long-term trend. When it comes to drug-related "deaths of despair," the root problem is the despair, not the drugs.

Republican presidential candidate Vivek Ramaswamy acknowledged that point during a 2023 debate. As a response to opioid deaths, he recommended "faith-based approaches that restore purpose and meaning in the next generation of Americans."[105] Ramaswamy was right to emphasize the importance of "purpose and meaning," the absence of which contributes to unhealthy preoccupations with drugs. But contrary to his implication, religion is just one source of purpose and meaning, which also can be found through secular pursuits and interpersonal connections.

As Peele emphasizes, people with intact and loving families, strong social support, good jobs, and stable lives that include involvement with meaningful activities are much less likely to develop harmful relationships with drugs than people without those things. When it comes to crime, the picture is more complex: Some theorists emphasize the importance of personality traits such as impulsivity, which may be influenced by genetics and biology, while others tend to focus on environmental factors that may include early trauma, family dynamics, and growing up in a dangerous neighborhood.[106] A third approach combines these two orientations, considering how personality traits interact with different environments.[107] But to the extent that crime is affected by changing circumstances, as suggested by what happened during and after the pandemic, some of the factors that influence drug abuse can also be expected to influence violent behavior.

Whether and how the government should be involved in trying to foster the conditions that reduce the risks of drug abuse and violence is a matter of wide disagreement. Progressives see a large role for government, while conservatives like Ramaswamy (and libertarians) traditionally have preferred the private, voluntary efforts of neighbors, religious groups, and charitable organizations. Both sides nevertheless should be able to agree that the government should *not* pursue policies that fail to do what they are supposed to do, policies that punish people for conduct that is not inherently criminal, policies that inflict harm without rhyme or reason.

"It Was Very Weird"

Four years after Weldon Angelos was sentenced to prison for half a century, the Supreme Court acknowledged that the Second Amendment protects an individual right to arms. Four years later, Colorado and Washington became the first states to legalize marijuana for recreational use, a step that 22 others had taken by 2024. If federal prosecutors had not reconsidered their defense of his sentence, Angelos still would have been in prison at that point and would have stayed there into the 2050s—all because he engaged in a business that is now legal in nearly half the states while exercising a constitutional right recognized by the nation's highest court.

When states began to legalize recreational cannabis, Angelos recalls, he and a fellow inmate who had received a 22-year federal sentence for selling medical marijuana in California "were both watching this take place." State-licensed marijuana businesses "were allowed to sell large amounts of cannabis and have guns there for security, and they're not being prosecuted," he notes. "It was very weird that this was being allowed to happen while he was doing 22 and I was doing 55 for the exact same thing."[108]

Under current federal law, of course, state-licensed marijuana merchants *could* be prosecuted—not just for selling pot but also for taking precautions against robberies. That threat is magnified by federal prohibition, which makes banks leery of serving cannabis suppliers, forcing them to rely heavily on cash.[109] Adding insult to injury, the same federal law that Angelos was convicted of violating makes it a felony for those businesses to "have guns there for security."[110]

In 2022, Christopher Kavanaugh, the U.S. attorney for the Western District of Virginia, bragged about a federal guilty plea by a Roanoke drug dealer who had been acquitted of murder in state court. Even though a state jury had concluded that he acted in self-defense, the plea deal called for a 12-year federal prison sentence. "Drug dealers with firearms should take heed," Kavanaugh warned. "You cannot shoot someone during a drug deal and then claim self-defense when you are carrying that firearm in furtherance of drug trafficking."[111]

In the eyes of the federal government, state-licensed marijuana dispensaries that employ armed guards likewise are "drug dealers with firearms." Four months before Kavanaugh issued his press release, a security guard at the Euphorium marijuana shop in Covington, a Seattle suburb, shot and killed an armed robber who had taken a fellow employee hostage.[112] "Anybody that would put their life out there to protect someone else is absolutely a hero," Lindsey Evans, the store's general manager, told a Seattle TV station.[113] But federal law does not view that guard as heroic. For discharging a gun that facilitated drug trafficking, he could face a 10-year mandatory minimum if the Justice Department decided to prosecute him. And since he "cause[d] the death of a person through the use of a firearm," he could face a maximum sentence of life in prison or the death penalty under the same statute.[114]

Angelos, who lives in Utah, now owns a California cannabis brand that he dubbed Reeform, a nod to his work lobbying for changes to federal law and helping imprisoned marijuana offenders apply for clemency. President Donald Trump granted him a "full and unconditional pardon" in December 2020, and Angelos received a letter from the Justice Department saying all his civil rights, including his Second Amendment rights, had been restored.[115] But Angelos—who thinks "it makes zero sense to take anyone's gun rights permanently," especially for a victimless crime—has not yet tried to buy a firearm. "I do have a [cannabis] brand," he notes. And although he is not involved in production or sales, he wants to be "extra careful" until the courts resolve the issue of whether marijuana-related firearm disabilities are constitutional.[116]

Angelos's three children, a baby girl and two little boys when he went to prison, were 13, 17, and 19 by the time he was released. Twelve and a half years in prison hurt Angelos, his family, and everyone who cared about him without helping anyone. An appeals court nevertheless deemed his original sentence, which was more than four times as long, reasonable in light of congressional concern about the "dangerous combination" of "drugs and guns." The "entirely rational" policies responsible for that travesty revealed an even more dangerous combination: the fear that breeds injustice and the inertia that perpetuates it.

Acknowledgments

I have been writing about drug policy and gun policy for more than three decades, so you could say this book has been in the works for most of my career. I owe a debt to *Reason* magazine, which gave me the opportunity to explore both subjects in depth, and in particular to Virginia Postrel, who hired me as an assistant editor back in 1989. Virginia encouraged me to write a 1994 *Reason* essay based on a talk I had given about the similarities between gun control and the war on drugs. That exercise planted the seeds that eventually sprouted into *Beyond Control*.

I am also grateful to *Reason*'s current editor, Katherine Mangu-Ward, and Reason Foundation President David Nott for accommodating my work on the book and to several other colleagues who provided a sounding board, offered advice, and/or helped with the research, including Nick Gillespie, Ron Bailey, Brian Doherty, Jesse Walker, Billy Binion, and Robby Soave. Dan Cavanaugh, an archivist at the University of Virginia's law library, provided crucial help by scanning the 1917 U.S. Department of Agriculture report on marijuana in Texas, which I discuss in chapter 1.

Weldon Angelos, whose legal odyssey at the intersection of drugs and guns figures prominently in the beginning, middle, and end of *Beyond Control*, spared time for an interview that fleshed out his story, an inspiring example of turning adversity into activism. I also benefited from a candid and colorful conversation with Black Guns Matter founder Maj Toure, who sees the parallels between drug policy and gun policy more clearly than most people. The book draws on illuminating conversations with various other sources I have consulted over the years, including Florida attorneys Kendra Parris and Mike Blackstone, their clients, and

Acknowledgments

Stanton Peele, whose pathbreaking work on addiction has long guided my thinking about drug policy.

Dale Gieringer, Jeff Miron, David Pozen, David Kopel, and Stephen Halbrook generously agreed to read chapters covering material in their areas of expertise. Their detailed comments were very helpful in correcting errors and sharpening my argument.

My wife, Michele, provided encouraging feedback throughout the project and not only put up with my obsessions but shared my excitement whenever I found vivid material while wading through old newspaper articles and other dusty documents. My editor at Prometheus Books, Jake Bonar, likewise shared my excitement about the project. He and production editor Meredith Dias patiently guided me through the editing process, which thanks to their support was nearly painless.

Notes

Introduction: The Twin Crusades

1. Andrea Jones, "The Nation's Shame: The Injustice of Mandatory Minimums," *Rolling Stone*, October 7, 2014.
2. Eva S. Nilsen, "Indecent Standards: The Case of *U.S. Versus Weldon Angelos*," *Roger Williams University Law Review*, Winter 2006, 11:2, pp. 537–63.
3. Interview with Weldon Angelos, August 14, 2024.
4. Ibid.
5. 18 USC 924(c); *United States v. Angelos*, 345 F. Supp. 1227 (D. of Utah 2004).
6. Interview with Angelos.
7. Ibid.
8. U.S. Sentencing Commission, *2023 Sourcebook of Federal Sentencing Statistics*, 2024, Table 11.
9. Interview with Angelos.
10. *United States v. Angelos*.
11. Douglas N. Husak, "Guns and Drugs: Case Studies on the Principled Limits of the Criminal Sanction," *Law and Philosophy*, September 2004, 23:5, pp. 437–93.
12. Interview with Maj Toure, August 26, 2024.
13. Jacob Sullum, "The Case Against Biden," *Reason*, November 2020, pp. 26–31.
14. Elise Viebeck, "How an Early Biden Crime Bill Created the Sentencing Disparity for Crack and Cocaine Trafficking," *The Washington Post*, July 28, 2019.
15. Joe Biden, "Democratic Response to Drug Policy Address," C-SPAN, September 5, 1989.
16. *Congressional Record*, August 23, 1994, 140:17, p. 23850.
17. Inimai Chettiar and Michael Waldman, eds., *Solutions: American Leaders Speak Out on Criminal Justice*, Brennan Center for Justice, 2015, pp. 3–6.
18. Arlette Saenz, "Biden: 'I Haven't Always Been Right' on Criminal Justice," CNN, January 21, 2019.
19. "Justice," Biden campaign website, 2020; Democratic presidential debate, November 20, 2019.
20. "Clemency Recipient List," White House, April 26, 2022; "Commutations Granted by President Joseph Biden (2021–Present)," Office of the Pardon Attorney, U.S. Department of Justice; "Clemency Statistics," Office of the Pardon Attorney.
21. "A Proclamation on Granting Pardon for the Offense of Simple Possession of Marijuana," White House, October 6, 2022.

Notes (Introduction)

22. "Number of Federal Offenders Convicted Only of 21 U.S.C. § 844 Involving Marijuana, Fiscal Years 1992–2021," U.S. Sentencing Commission, October 12, 2022.

23. "Remarks by President Biden in State of the Union Address," White House, March 7, 2024; Diana Kawka, "Expungement: The Missing Federal Piece," *Minnesota Journal of Law & Inequality* blog post, May 10, 2023.

24. "Press Briefing by Press Secretary Jen Psaki," White House, March 30, 2021; Kamala Harris, "Repeating the Same Mistakes of the Past," *Medium*, January 5, 2018; Marijuana Justice Act of 2017, S. 1689, introduced on August 1, 2017 (Harris became a cosponsor in May 2018); Marijuana Opportunity Reinvestment and Expungement Act, S.2227, introduced by Harris on July 23, 2019.

25. "Statement from President Biden on Marijuana Reform," White House, October 6, 2022.

26. Joe Biden on Twitter, October 6, 2022.

27. Department of Health and Human Services, "Basis for the Recommendation to Reschedule Marijuana Into Schedule III of the Controlled Substances Act," August 29, 2023.

28. "Schedules of Controlled Substances: Rescheduling of Marijuana," Drug Enforcement Administration, Docket No. DEA-1362, A.G. Order No. 5931-2024.

29. David Ovalle et al., "Attorney General Moves to Reclassify Marijuana As Lower-Risk Drug," *The Washington Post*, April 30, 2024.

30. Kyle Jaeger, "Top Federal Drug Policy Expert Says Marijuana's Schedule I Status Inhibits Research," *Marijuana Moment*, April 2, 2019.

31. Vince Sliwoski, "Three Myths and Three Facts on the HUGE Marijuana Rescheduling Recommendation," Harris Sliwoski, August 31, 2023.

32. David H. Carpenter, "Marijuana Banking: Legal Issues and the SAFE(R) Banking Acts," Congressional Research Service, November 15, 2023.

33. Kyle Jaeger, "Congressional Leaders' Bill Extends State Medical Marijuana Protections and Calls for Studying Legalization Models," *Marijuana Moment*, March 4, 2024.

34. Michelle Minton, "The Implications of Federal Cannabis Rescheduling," Reason Foundation, January 2024.

35. 18 USC 922(g)(3); Abigail F. Kolker and Lisa N. Sacco, "Marijuana and Restrictions on Immigration," Congressional Research Service, September 17, 2020.

36. Kate Bryan, "Cannabis Overview," National Conference of State Legislatures, April 9, 2024.

37. Kyle Jaeger, "Americans' Support for Marijuana Legalization Stabilizes With Bipartisan Majorities in Favor, Gallup Poll Finds," *Marijuana Moment*, November 1, 2024.

38. "President Biden's State of the Union Address," White House, March 1, 2022.

39. Gus Carlson, "To Beat Drugs, Make Them Legal, Kill Off Profits, Trump Declares," *The Miami Herald*, April 14, 1990, p. 1.

40. Anti-Drug Abuse Act of 1988, Public Law 100-690.

41. *This Week*, ABC News, November 8, 2015.

42. "Criminal Justice Reform," Hillary Clinton 2016 campaign website.

Notes (Introduction)

43. Donald Trump, remarks at the Conservative Political Action Conference, February 27, 2015; Jenna Johson, "Trump Softens Position on Marijuana Legalization," *The Washington Post*, October 29, 2015.
44. Donald Trump on Truth Social, August 31, 2024.
45. Donald Trump on Truth Social, September 8, 2024.
46. "Drug Epidemic," Trump campaign video, February 6, 2016.
47. Donald Trump on Truth Social, November 25, 2024.
48. "Commutations Granted by President Donald J. Trump (2017–2021)," Office of the Pardon Attorney, U.S. Department of Justice.
49. *Fox & Friends*, Fox News, October 11, 2018.
50. FIRST STEP Act of 2018, Public Law 115-391.
51. Jared Kushner, "Fifteen Lessons I Learned From Criminal-Justice Reform," *Time*, April 24, 2019; Gabby Orr and Daniel Lippman, "Trump Snubs Jared Kushner's Signature Accomplishment," *Politico*, September 24, 2019.
52. "President Donald J. Trump's State of the Union Address," National Archives, February 5, 2019; Trump campaign Super Bowl ad, February 2, 2020; Republican National Convention, Night 4, August 27, 2020.
53. Donald Trump on Twitter, May 27, 2019; Trump campaign video, May 24, 2020.
54. "Trump Campaign Statement on Crooked Joe Biden's History of Racist Remarks," May 23, 2024.
55. Maggie Haberman and Jonathan Swan, "DeSantis Burnishes Tough-on-Crime Image to Run in '24 and Take on Trump," *The New York Times*, March 29, 2023, p. A13.
56. Donald Trump on Truth Social, January 21, 2025.
57. Oliver Holmes, "Rodrigo Duterte Vows to Kill 3 Million Drug Addicts and Likens Himself to Hitler," *The Guardian*, September 30, 2016; "Philippines President Rodrigo Duterte Urges People to Kill Drug Addicts," *The Guardian*, June 30, 2016.
58. Julie Hirschfeld Davis, "Trump Lauds 'Great Relationship' With Duterte in Manila," *The New York Times*, November 13, 2017, p. A4; David Nakamura and Barton Gellman, "Trump Calls Kim Jong Un a 'Madman With Nuclear Weapons,' According to Transcript of Duterte Call," *The Washington Post*, May 23, 2017.
59. Jonathan Swan, "Trump Privately Talks Up Executing All Big Drug Dealers," *Axios*, February 25, 2018; Sarah Karlin-Smith and Brianna Ehley, "Trump Suggests Death Penalty to Stop Opioid Epidemic," *Politico*, March 1, 2018; "Remarks by President Trump on Combatting the Opioid Crisis," National Archives, March 19, 2018; "President and First Lady Deliver Remarks at Drug Abuse Summit," C-SPAN, April 24, 2019; "War on the Drug Cartels," Trump 2024 campaign website.
60. *Special Report With Bret Baier*, Fox News, June 20, 2023.
61. Firearm Owners' Protection Act of 1986, Public Law 99-308.
62. *Congressional Record*, July 9, 1985, 131:13, p. 18229.
63. Alex Seitz-Wald, "Biden Voted With the NRA When the Senate, and the Nation, Were Very Different," NBC News, April 24, 2019.
64. Brady Handgun Violence Prevention Act of 1993, Public Law 103-159; Violent Crime Control and Law Enforcement Act of 1994, Public Law 103–322.

Notes (Introduction)

65. "President Biden's State of the Union Address," White House, March 1, 2022; "The Biden Plan to End Our Gun Violence Epidemic," Joe Biden 2020 campaign website.
66. *2024 Democratic Party Platform*, pp. 39–40.
67. Donald Trump, *The America We Deserve*, Renaissance Books, 2000, p. 102.
68. Donald Trump, remarks at the Conservative Political Action Conference, February 10, 2011.
69. Lisa Desjardins and Nathalie Boyd, "What Does Donald Trump Believe?," *PBS NewsHour*, July 16, 2015.
70. Donald Trump, *Great Again: How to Fix Our Crippled America*, Threshold Editions, 2015, pp. 108–9.
71. Benjamin Bell, "Donald Trump: Don't Blame Gun Laws for Oregon School Shooting," ABC News, October 2, 2015; *This Week*, ABC News, October 4, 2015; *Face the Nation*, CBS News, October 11, 2015.
72. Sixth Republican Presidential Candidate Debate, Fox Business, January 14, 2016.
73. First Presidential Debate, Hofstra University, September 26, 2016; Lauren Dezenski, "Trump Backs 'Red Flag' Laws," CNN, August 5, 2019.
74. Elizabeth Landers, "Trump to Lawmakers: 'Take the Gun First, Go Through Due Process Second' in Some Cases," CNN, February 28, 2018.
75. Michael D. Shear, "Trump Stuns Lawmakers With Seeming Embrace of Comprehensive Gun Control," *The New York Times*, February 28, 2018, p. A1.
76. Interpretive rule, Bureau of Alcohol, Tobacco, Firearms, and Explosives, 83 FR 66514, December 26, 2018; Dianne Feinstein, "Feinstein Statement on Regulation to Ban Bump Stocks," March 23, 2018; *Cargill v. Garland*, 57 F.4th 447 (5th Circuit 2023).
77. *Garland v. Cargill*, 22-976 (2024).
78. Jessica Chasmar, "Donald Trump Changed Political Parties at Least Five Times: Report," *The Washington Times*, June 16, 2015.
79. Ronald Reagan, "Remarks at the Annual Members Banquet of the National Rifle Association in Phoenix, Arizona," American Presidency Project, May 6, 1983.
80. 18 USC 922(g)(1) and (g)(3).
81. Tom Cotton 2012 congressional campaign website; NRA position ratings, 2020.
82. Tom Cotton, "Lame-Duck Congress' Rush for Criminal Justice Reform Plan Will Hurt, Not Help," *USA Today*, November 15, 2018.
83. OpenSecrets.org spreadsheet, October 26, 2023.
84. Benjamin Wood, "Romney and Wilson Split on Utah's Medical Marijuana Initiative, Medicaid Expansion, and the Future of U.S. Health Care," *The Salt Lake Tribune*, September 24, 2018; Mitt Romney, *No Apology: The Case for American Greatness*, St. Martin's Press, 2010, pp. 260–61.
85. Interview with Univision Noticias, September 19, 2012.
86. Democratic presidential debate, CNN, July 31, 2019.
87. Matt Stevens, "Cory Booker's Gun Control Plan Calls for National Licensing Program," *The New York Times*, May 6, 2019, p. A13.
88. Jaeger (November 2024).
89. Danny Franklin, "Overwhelming Majority Say War on Drugs Has Failed, Support New Approach," Bully Pulpit Interactive, July 9, 2021.

Notes (Introduction–Chapter 1)

90. Jeffrey M. Jones, "Majority in U.S. Continues to Favor Stricter Gun Laws," Gallup, October 31, 2023.
91. Texas Health and Safety Code, 481.121.
92. California Health and Safety Code, 11362.1.
93. Texas Firearm Carry Act of 2021, H.B. 1927.
94. *New York State Rifle & Pistol Association v. Bruen*, 20-843 (2022); California S.B. 2 (2023).
95. "California Gun Laws," Giffords Law Center to Prevent Gun Violence.
96. William Tonso, "Gun Control: White Men's Law," *Reason*, December 1985, pp. 22–25.
97. Clayton E. Cramer, "The Racist Roots of Gun Control," *Kansas Journal of Law & Public Policy*, Winter 1995, 42:2, pp. 17–25.
98. See, e.g. Maia Szalavitz, *Undoing Drugs: How Harm Reduction Is Changing the Future of Drugs and Addiction*, Hachette Go, 2021, and Sheila P. Vakharia, *The Harm Reduction Gap: Helping Individuals Left Behind by Conventional Drug Prevention and Abstinence-Only Addiction Treatment*, Routledge, 2024.
99. National Shooting Sports Foundation, "NSSF Releases Most Recent Firearm Production Figures," January 15, 2025; William English, "2021 National Firearms Survey: Updated Analysis Including Types of Firearms Owned," Georgetown McDonough School of Business Research Paper No. 4109494, May 13, 2022; Jennifer Mascia and Chip Brownlee, "How Many Guns Are Circulating in the U.S.?," *The Trace*, March 6, 2023; FBI Crime Data Explorer (about 260,000 violent crimes committed with firearms in 2022, including murder, rape, robbery, and aggravated assault); John Gramlich, "What the Data Says About Gun Deaths in the U.S.," Pew Research Center, April 26, 2023.

Chapter 1: The Racist Roots of Drug Laws

1. "The First Opium Raid," *The San Francisco Examiner*, December 6, 1875, p. 3.
2. "The Opium Dens," *San Francisco Chronicle*, November 16, 1875, p. 3.
3. "American Incomes ca. 1650–1870," Global Price and Income History Group, University of California, Davis, July 11, 2013.
4. "Police Matters," *San Francisco Chronicle*, December 7, 1875, p. 1.
5. "The Opium Dens."
6. Daniel Okrent, *Last Call: The Rise and Fall of Prohibition*, Scribner, 2010, pp. 11–12.
7. David F. Musto, *The American Disease: Origins of Narcotic Control*, Oxford University Press, 1987 edition, p. 244.
8. George Fisher, *Beware Euphoria: The Moral Roots and Racial Myths of America's War on Drugs*, Oxford University Press, 2024.
9. *Chinese Immigration: Its Social, Moral, and Political Effect*, Report to the California State Senate of Its Special Committee on Chinese Immigration, 1878, p. 114.
10. Ibid., p. 217.
11. "Chinese Immigration," *The San Francisco Examiner*, February 12, 1887, p. 5.
12. Diana L. Ahmad, *The Opium Debate and Chinese Exclusion Laws in the Nineteenth-Century American West*, University of Nevada Press, 2007, pp. 36–50.
13. "Chinese in New-York," *The New York Times*, December 26, 1873, p. 3.

14. "Ever on the Increase," *The San Francisco Examiner*, March 3, 1889, p. 3.
15. "Fifty Days in Jail," *The San Francisco Examiner*, May 22, 1894, p. 3.
16. Jacob A. Riis, *How the Other Half Lives: Studies Among the Tenements of New York*, Charles Scribner's Sons, 1914 edition, p. 96.
17. American Federation of Labor, *Some Reasons for Chinese Exclusion*, 1902, p. 29.
18. Report to the California State Senate, p. 35.
19. Ibid., p. 110.
20. Mikelis Beitiks, "'Devilishly Uncomfortable: *In the Matter of Sic*—The California Supreme Court Strikes a Balance Between Race, Drugs and Government in 1880s California," *California Legal History*, 2011, p. 230.
21. "San Francisco and California Pass Anti-Chinese Laws, 1858-1913," American Social History Project, City University of New York; Gregory Yee Mark, "Racial, Economic and Political Factors in the Development of America's First Drug Laws," *Issues in Criminology*, Spring 1975, pp. 49–72; Patricia A. Morgan, "The Legislation of Drug Law: Economic Crisis and Social Control," *Journal of Drug Issues*, 1978, 8:1, pp. 53–62.
22. Patrick McCaffrey, "Drug War Origins: How American Opium Politics Led to the Establishment of International Narcotics Prohibition," master's thesis, Harvard Extension School, 2019.
23. Jean Pfaelzer, *Driven Out: The Forgotten War Against Chinese Americans*, Random House, 2007, pp. 11–22.
24. Ibid., p. 20; "American Incomes ca. 1650–1870," Global Price and Income History Group, University of California, Davis, May 18, 2013.
25. 1858 Cal. Stat. 295.
26. 1862 Cal. Stat. 295; *Sing v. Washburn*, 20 Cal. 534 (1862).
27. Morgan, p. 3.
28. "The Chinese," *San Francisco Chronicle*, April 2, 1876, p. 1.
29. Bryan Denham, "Oriental Irritants and Occidental Aspirants: Immigrant Portrayals in Hearst Magazines, 1905–1945," *Journalism & Communication Monographs*, 2022, 24:1, pp. 4–64.
30. Scott Zesch, *The Chinatown War: Chinese Los Angeles and the Massacre of 1871*, Oxford University Press, 2012.
31. 8 USC 7.
32. Jeff Elliott, "The Year of the Anti-Chinese League," *Santa Rosa History*, June 6, 2018.
33. Mark, p. 67; Joshua S. Yang, "The Anti-Chinese Cubic Air Ordinance," *American Journal of Public Health*, March 2009, 99:3, p. 440.
34. *In re Yick Wo*, 68 Cal. 284 (1885); *Yick Wo v. Hopkins*, 118 US 356 (1886).
35. *Ex parte Yung Jon*, 28 F. 308 (1886).
36. *In re Sic*, 73 Cal. 142 (1887).
37. Mark, p. 62; Sarah Brady Siff, "A History of Early Drug Sentences in California: Racism, Rightism, Repeat," Ohio State Legal Studies Research Paper No. 644, 2021, p. 2.
38. Smoking Opium Exclusion Act of 1909, Public Law 60-221.
39. J. Worth Estes, "The Pharmacology of Nineteenth-Century Patent Medicines," *Pharmacy in History*, 1988, 30:1, pp. 3–18.

Notes (Chapter 1)

40. Pure Food and Drug Act of 1906, Public Law 59-384.
41. District of Columbia Pharmacy Act, H.R. 8097, 1906.
42. *Congressional Record*, January 26, 1909, 43:2, p. 1398.
43. *Congressional Record*, February 1, 1909, 43:2, p. 1681.
44. Ibid., p. 1683.
45. Ibid., pp. 1682–83.
46. Ibid., p. 1682.
47. Doris Marie Provine, *Unequal Under Law: Race in the War on Drugs*, University of Chicago Press, 2007, p. 74.
48. Harrison Narcotics Tax Act of 1914, Public Law 63-223.
49. Andrzej Grzybowski, "The History of Cocaine in Medicine and Its Importance to the Discovery of the Different Forms of Anaesthesia," *Klinika Oczna*, 2007, 109:1-3, pp. 101–5.
50. Estes, p. 12.
51. Lester Grinspoon and James B. Bakalar, *Cocaine: A Drug and Its Social Evolution*, Basic Books, 1976.
52. Ibid., p. 39.
53. Edward Huntington Williams, "Negro Cocaine 'Fiends' Are a New Southern Menace," *The New York Times*, February 2, 1914, p. 12.
54. Grinspoon and Bakalar, p. 40.
55. Catherine Carstairs, "'The Most Dangerous Drug': Images of African-Americans and Cocaine Use in the Progressive Era," *Left History*, March 2000, 7:1, pp. 46–61.
56. Ibid.
57. Ernest K. Coulter, "The Drug Bondage," in *Thirty-Seventh Annual Report of the New England Watch and Ward Society for the Year 1914–1915*, p. 35.
58. Musto, p. 7.
59. Carstairs, p. 46.
60. Fisher (2024), pp. 306, 314–16.
61. Carstairs, p. 46.
62. General Medical Convention et al., *The Pharmacopoeia of the United States of America*, 1851, p. 50; The *Antique Cannabis Book*, Chapter 15, http://antiquecannabisbook.com/chap15/Quack.htm.
63. "Mexican Immigration to the United States," *Oxford Research Encyclopedias*, July 29, 2019.
64. "Ordinance," *El Paso Herald*, June 12, 1915, p. 15.
65. George Fisher, "Racial Myths of the Cannabis War," *Boston University Law Review*, May 2021, 101:3, pp. 933–77.
66. "Maniac Kills a Patrolman," *El Paso Times*, January 2, 1913, p. 1; "Crazed by Weed, a Man Murders," *El Paso Herald*, January 2, 1913, p. 1.
67. "Policeman Lassoes a Drug Crazed Mexican," *El Paso Herald*, January 28, 1914, p. 4.
68. "Poisonous Weeds of Mexico Cause Death," *El Paso Herald*, May 9–10, 1914, p. 32.
69. "Not Unlawful to Sell Mari Juana," *El Paso Times*, May 13, 1915, p. 3.

70. "Declares American Diplomacy Is Laughing Stock of the World," *El Paso Herald*, May 14, 1914, p. 16.
71. "Law Against Marihuana," *El Paso Times*, May 15, 2015, p. 8.
72. "City School Bond Form Approved," *El Paso Times*, June 4, 1915, p. 16.
73. "New Anti-Marihuana Ordinance Very Stringent," *El Paso Herald*, June 7, 1915, p. 9.
74. "City School Bond Form Approved."
75. Fisher (2021), pp. 933, 944–45.
76. Isaac Campos, *Home Grown: Marijuana and the Origins of Mexico's War on Drugs*, University or North Carolina Press, 2012.
77. Campos, "Cannabis Effects," https://www.thedrugpage.org/cannabis-effects.
78. Adam Rathge, *Cannabis Cures: American Medicine, Mexican Marijuana, and the Origins of the War on Weed, 1840-1937*, Boston College Ph.D. dissertation, May 2017.
79. Dale Gieringer, "The Forgotten Origins of Cannabis Prohibition in California," *Contemporary Drug Problems*, June 1999, 26:2, pp. 1–36.
80. Ibid.
81. Ibid.
82. "War on Loco Weed," *Oakland Tribune*, December 9, 1911, p. 8.
83. Gieringer.
84. Texas Penal Code, 1920, p. 103.
85. Texas Penal Code, 1925, pp. 152–53.
86. Supplement to the 1928 Complete Texas Statutes, 1931, pp. 632–33.
87. "Cant Even Get an Imitation Jag Now," *Austin American-Statesman*, June 16, 1919, p. 8.
88. "New Smoke Has Strange Effect Says Officer," *Austin American-Statesman*, March 19, 1919, p. 2.
89. "Marihuana Weed Smoker Runs Amuck on Train," *The Austin American*, July 26, 1923, p. 2.
90. "Officers Locate Regular Marihuana 'Dive'; Intoxicating Mexican Weed Found Growing in Profusion in Austin," *Austin American-Statesman*, September 9, 1923, p. 6.
91. "Haskin: Questions and Answers," *The Austin American*, May 25, 1931, p. 4; "Marihuana Addict Sets New Record for Glee Spree," *Austin American-Statesman*, February 28, 1930, p. 14.
92. "First Term Given on Such Charge by Jury Here," *Austin American-Statesman*, April 14, 1932, p. 9.
93. "Se Prohibe la Venta de Narcoticos en Albuquerque," *El Nuevo Mexicano*, September 13, 1917, p. 1.
94. "Hashish Drug Used by 100 Members of the State Regiment," *Santa Fe New Mexican*, September 7, 1917, p. 3.
95. "Punish Grower of the Deadly Marijuana Weed," *Albuquerque Morning Journal*, July 30, 1917, p. 7.
96. "Military Police Start War Against Mariahuana Users," *The Evening Herald*, September 16, 2017, p. 3.

97. "Child Welfare Bureau to Get Public Hearing," *San Fe New Mexican*, January 31, 1923, p. 2.
98. "The Truth About Hollywood—Behind the Scenes," *Albuquerque Journal*, April 2, 1922, p. 17.
99. "Officers Make a Record Haul of Marihuana," *Albuquerque Journal*, February 18, 1923, p. 1.
100. "Marihuana May Not Be Grown in the City," *Arizona Republican*, May 12, 1917, p. 7.
101. "Ordinance No. 139," *Williams News*, July 6, 1928, p. 8.
102. "Vetoes Marihuana Bill," *Tombstone Weekly Epitaph*, February 20, 1921, p. 7.
103. "Marihuana Catch Made by Officers," *Arizona Daily Star*, December 13, 1931, p. 8.
104. "Marihuana Blamed for Neighborhood Fight, So Loco Weed Is Destroyed," *Arizona Daily Star*, July 25, 1917, p. 4.
105. See, e.g., "Whiskey Mixed With Marihuana; 5 Killed," *The Tucson Citizen*, February 3, 1918, p. 6; "A Marihuana Maniac," *The Daily Morning Oasis*, February 3, 1918, p. 1; "Marihuana [S]moker for Four Years, Young Man Held for Deportation," *Arizona Daily Star*, January 18, 1919, p. 3; "Too Much Marihuana; Mexican Lands in Jail," *The Daily Morning Oasis*, December 23, 1920, p. 1; "Find Marihuana Growing in Yard; Owner Arrested," *Arizona Republican*, July 10, 1923, p. 3; "Man Crazed With Marihuana Cuts Tucson Woodsman," *Arizona Daily Star*, December 19, 1923, p. 2; "Marihuana Fiend Is Crazed, Kills Six," *Arizona Daily Star*, February 21, 1925, p. 1; "Marihuana Smoker Shoots Mayor Dead," *Arizona Republican*, October 14, 1925, p. 13; "Marihuana Fiend Stabs Three to Death With Dirk," *Arizona Republican*, March 1, 1927, p. 9; "Williams Man Dead After Few Weeks Imprisonment," *Williams News*, November 25, 1927, p. 1.
106. "Murder Drug That Gives Gunmen Courage to Kill," *Tucson Daily Citizen*, August 22, 1931, p. 27.
107. Jacob Sullum, *Saying Yes: In Defense of Drug Use*, Jeremy P. Tarcher/Putnam, 2003, pp. 100–35.
108. R.F. Smith, *Report of Investigation in the State of Texas*, April 13, 1917, U.S. Department of Agriculture, pp. 33–37.
109. Ibid., pp. 6, 9, 85.
110. Ibid., p. 86.
111. Ibid., p. 13.
112. "Government Will Ask States to Ban Growing of Marijuana," *The New York Times*, September 16, 1931, p. B37.
113. "Dope Ring Specialized in Mexican Marijuana," *The New York Times*, December 3, 1933, p. E6.
114. "Use of Marijuana Spreading in West," *The New York Times*, September 16, 1934, p. E6.
115. Richard J. Bonnie and Charles H. Whitebread II, *The Marijuana Conviction: A History of Marijuana Prohibition in the United States*, University Press of Virginia, 1974, p. 109.

116. David F. Musto, "The Marihuana Tax Act of 1937," *Archives of General Psychiatry*, February 1972, 26:2, pp. 101–8.
117. Harry J. Anslinger with Courtney Ryley Cooper, "Marijuana: Assassin of Youth," *The American Magazine*, July 1937, pp. 18–19, 150–53.
118. Ibid., pp. 19, 150, 151.
119. Hearings on H.R. 6385 before the House Ways and Means Committee, 75th Congress, First Session, May 4, 1937, p. 123.
120. Bonnie and Whitebread, pp. 146–49.
121. House Ways and Means Committee hearings, April 27, 1937, p. 31.
122. Hearing on H.R. 6906 before a subcommittee of the Senate Finance Committee, 75th Congress, First Session, July 12, 1937, p. 11.
123. Larry Sloman, *Reefer Madness*, St. Martin's Griffin, 1979, illustration insert, p. 2.
124. "Nurse Attacked, Slain in Hospital," *The New York Times*, August 22, 1937, p. 22.
125. Fisher (2021), p. 944.
126. "Mexican Held for Selling Dope to School Children," *The Austin American*, July 31, 1930, p. 3.
127. "Marihuana Cigarets Sold School Youths," *Austin American-Statesman*, March 26, 1932, p. 1; "Marihuana Sale Laid to Mexican," *Austin American-Statesman*, April 8, 1932, p. 12; "First Term Given on Such Charge Here," *Austin American-Statesman*, April 14, 1932, p. 9.
128. "Fine Alleged Drug Offender," *Arizona Republican*, October 11, 1922, p. 6; "Mexican Jailed in Sale of Dope to Several Boys," *The Winslow Mail*, October 8, 1926, p. 10.
129. Richard J. Bonnie and Charles H. Whitebread II, "The Forbidden Fruit and the Tree of Knowledge," *Virginia Law Review*, 1970, 56:6, pp. 971–1203.
130. Hearings before the House Ways and Means Committee, 75th Congress, First Session, April 27, 1937, p. 33.
131. Hearings before the House Ways and Means Committee, pp. 18, 22, 27, 32, 33, 36, 38, 44.
132. *Congressional Record*, June 14, 1937, 81:5, pp. 5689–90.
133. Ibid.
134. Campos, "Cannabis Effects."

Chapter 2: The Racist Roots of Gun Laws

1. David W. Blight, *Frederick Douglass: Prophet of Freedom*, Simon & Schuster, 2018.
2. "The True Remedy for the Fugitive Slave Bill," *Frederick Douglass' Paper*, June 9, 1854, p. 2.
3. Don E. Fehrenbacher, *The Dred Scott Case: Its Significance in American Law and Politics*, Oxford University Press, 1978.
4. *Dred Scott v. Sandford*, 60 U.S. 393 (1857).
5. William Tonso, "Gun Control: White Men's Law," *Reason*, December 1985, pp. 22–25.
6. Nicholas Johnson, *Negroes and the Gun: The Black Tradition of Arms*, Prometheus Books, 2014.
7. Thomas L. Purvis, *Colonial America to 1763*, Facts on File, 1999, p. 128.

8. William Waller Hening, ed., *The Statutes at Large: Being a Collection of All Laws of Virginia, From the First Session of the Legislature, in the Year 1619*, R. & W. & G. Bartow, 1823, pp. 481–82.

9. Brief for Amicus Curiae National African American Gun Association in Support of Petitioners, *New York State Rifle & Pistol Association v. Bruen*, 20-843, July 16, 2021, p. 20.

10. Robert J. Cottrol and Raymond T. Diamond, "The Second Amendment: Toward an Afro-Americanist Reconsideration," *The Georgetown Law Journal*, December 1991, 80:2, pp. 309–61.

11. Ibid., pp. 336–38; Stephen P. Halbrook, "The Right to Bear Arms in the Virginia Constitution and the Second Amendment: Historical Development and Precedent in Virginia and the Fourth Circuit," *Liberty University Law Review*, October 2014, 8:3, pp. 619–47.

12. Patrick E. Bryan, *The Haitian Revolution and Its Effects*, Heinemann Educational Publishers, 1984.

13. Stephen B. Oates, *The Fires of Jubilee: Nat Turner's Fierce Rebellion*, Harper & Row, 1975, pp. 16–17.

14. Daniel Rasmussen, *American Uprising: The Untold Story of America's Largest Slave Revolt*, Harper, 2011.

15. James O'Neil Spady, "Power and Confession: On the Credibility of the Earliest Reports of the Denmark Vesey Slave Conspiracy," *William & Mary Quarterly*, April 2011, 68:2, pp. 287–304.

16. Oates; Charles P. Poland Jr., *America's Good Terrorist: John Brown and the Harpers Ferry Raid*, Casemate, 2020.

17. *Acts Passed at a General Assembly of the Commonwealth of Virginia*, 1832, pp. 20–22.

18. Glenn Harlan Reynolds, "The Right to Keep and Bear Arms Under the Tennessee Constitution: A Case Study in Civic Republican Thought," *Tennessee Law Review*, Winter 1994, 61:2, pp. 647–73.

19. 1836 Arkansas Constitution; 1838 Florida Constitution.

20. NAAGA brief, p. 9; *Cooper v. Savannah*, 4 Ga. 72 (1848); *State v. Allmond*, 7 Del. 612 (1856).

21. NAAGA brief, pp. 9-10; *State v. Huntley*, 25 N.C. 418 (1843); *State v. Newsom*, 27 N.C. 250 (1844).

22. Stephen P. Halbrook, *Freedmen, the Fourteenth Amendment, and the Right to Bear Arms, 1866–1875*, Praeger, 1998, pp. 2, 29–30, 35, 37, 89–90, 172.

23. Ibid., pp. 2–3, 8–9, 11–12, 22–23, 30–32, 74, 119–20, 128, 145–49.

24. Ibid., pp. 32, 34–35, 40–44, 62, 64, 67, 110, 193–95.

25. Ibid., pp. 1–44.

26. Ibid., pp. 1–44, 107–14.

27. Ibid., p. 42.

28. Ibid., p. 19.

29. Ibid., p. 126.

30. Ibid., pp. 145–148.

31. "The Modern Palladium of Liberty," *New Orleans Republican*, June 21, 1874, p. 4.

32. Halbrook (1998), pp. 159–61.
33. Ibid., p. 166.
34. *United States v. Cruikshank*, 92 U.S. 542 (1876).
35. Ida B. Wells, *Southern Horrors: Lynch Law in All Its Phases*, 1893, in Mia Bay, ed., *The Light of Truth: Writings of an Anti-Lynching Crusader*, Penguin Classics, 2014, pp. 57–82.
36. Ibid., p. 80.
37. W.E.B. Du Bois, *The Autobiography of W.E.B. Du Bois*, Diasporic Africa Press, 2013, p. 327
38. Johnson, pp. 209–12.
39. Ibid., pp. 193–208.
40. Robert F. Williams, *Negroes With Guns*, Marzai & Munsell, 1962, pp. 39–40, 45–46, 57; Johnson, p. 22.
41. Johnson, p. 26; UPI, "N.A.A.C.P. Leader Urges 'Violence,'" *The New York Times*, May 7, 1959, p. 22.
42. Williams., p. 40.
43. Charles E. Cobb Jr., *This Nonviolent Stuff'll Get You Killed: How Guns Made the Civil Rights Movement Possible*, Duke University Press, 2016, pp. 201–13, 225–26.
44. Roy Reed, "Armed Negro Unit Spreads in South," *The New York Times*, June 6, 1965, p. 1.
45. Ibid.
46. Cobb, pp. 7, 10.
47. Williams, pp. 12–13.
48. Johnson, pp. 262–63.
49. "Negro Leader Fails to Get Pistol Permit," *The Montgomery Advertiser*, February 4, 1956, p. 11; Donald T. Ferron, Notes on MIA Executive Board Meeting, February 2, 1956.
50. *New York State Rifle & Pistol Association v. Bruen*, 20-843 (2022).
51. Johnson, pp. 215–21.
52. Ibid.
53. Josselyn P. Huerta, *Control of Violence, Control of Fear: The Progression of Gun Control in San Francisco, 1847-1923*, Central Washington University master's thesis, Spring 2015, p. 30; "Disarming the Chinese," *San Francisco Chronicle*, December 27, 1875, p. 3.
54. Ibid.
55. Ibid.
56. Ibid.
57. "A Search for Knives," *Buffalo Courier*, March 5, 1888, p. 4.
58. Brief for Italo-American Jurists and Attorneys in Support of Petitioners, *New York State Rifle & Pistol Association v. Bruen*, 20-843, July 15, 2021, p. 2.
59. Ibid., pp. 25–26.
60. "First Conviction Under Weapon Law," *The New York Times*, September 28, 1911, p. 5; "The Rossi Pistol Case," *The New York Times*, September 29, 1911, p. 8.
61. Adam Winkler, *Gunfight: The Battle Over the Right to Bear Arms in America*, W.W. Norton & Co., 2011, pp. 239, 245.

62. Martin Smith, "Capitol Gun-Toters Draw Solons' Fury," *The Sacramento Bee*, May 3, 1967, p. 1; California Constitution, Article IV, Section 8.
63. Smith.
64. Ronald Reagan, "Remarks at the Annual Members Banquet of the National Rifle Association in Phoenix, Arizona," American Presidency Project, May 6, 1983; Winkler, p. 245.
65. Letter from Don Mulford to Lloyd E. Stahl, June 15, 1967; letter from Don Mulford to Paul F. Perati, June 15, 1967.
66. Smith.
67. Winkler, pp. 244–45.
68. Timothy P. Fong and Ann Lage, "Oral History Interview with David Donald Mulford," California State Archives, conducted April 11, 1988, and June 26 and 28, 1989.
69. David B. Kopel and Joseph G.S. Greenlee, "The History of Bans on Types of Arms Before 1900," *Journal of Legislation*, 2024, 50:2, pp. 223–386.
70. *Dabbs v. State*, 39 Ark. 353 (1882).
71. Kopel and Greenlee, p. 72.
72. Don B. Kates, ed., *Restricting Handguns: The Liberal Skeptics Speak Out*, North River Press, 1979, p. 15.
73. *Watson v. Stone*, 148 Fla. 516 (1941).
74. Robert Sherrill, *The Saturday Night Special*, Charterhouse, 1973, pp. 280, 283.
75. Barry Bruce-Briggs, "The Great America Gun War," *The Public Interest*, No. 45, Fall 1976, pp. 37–62; Johnson, p. 293.
76. Jennifer L. Behrens and Joseph Blocher, "A Great American Gun Myth: Race and the Naming of the 'Saturday Night Special,'" *Minnesota Law Review Headnotes*, Fall 2024, 108, pp. 293–313.

Chapter 3: The Drug War in Black and White

1. Stuart Taylor Jr., "Ten Years for Two Ounces: Congress Is Packing Prisons With Bit Players in Small-Time Drug Deals," *The American Lawyer*, March 16, 1990.
2. Ibid.; "New Drug Law Leaves No Room for Mercy," *Chicago Tribune*, October 5, 1989.
3. *Congressional Record*, June 20, 1991, 137:11, p. 15706.
4. Ibid., p. 15707.
5. George H.W. Bush, "Presidential Address on National Drug Policy," C-SPAN, September 5, 1989.
6. Joe Biden, "Democratic Response to Drug Policy Address," C-SPAN, September 5, 1989.
7. Anti-Drug Abuse Act of 1988, Public Law 100-690; *Congressional Record*, June 20, 1991, 137:11, p. 15707.
8. Elise Viebeck, "How an Early Biden Crime Bill Created the Sentencing Disparity for Crack and Cocaine Trafficking," *The Washington Post*, July 28, 2019.
9. Anti-Drug Abuse Act of 1986, Public Law 99-570.
10. *Congressional Record*, June 20, 1991, 137:11, p. 15706.
11. Ibid., p. 15726.

12. Tracy Thompson, "Cracking Down, Reluctantly, on Low-Level Drug Offenders," *The Washington Post*, August 28, 1989.

13. Arlette Saenz, "Biden: 'I Haven't Always Been Right' on Criminal Justice," CNN, January 21, 2019.

14. Drug Sentencing Reform and Cocaine Kingpin Trafficking Act of 2007, S. 1711, June 27, 2007.

15. Isaac Stanley-Becker, "'We Got Things Done': Biden Recalls 'Civility' With Segregationist Senators," *The Washington Post*, June 19, 2019; Ed Gilgore, "On Crime Policy, Biden Worked Closely With His Segregationist Friends," *Intelligencer*, June 26, 2019.

16. National Association for the Advancement of Colored People, "Eliminate Racial Sentencing Disparities," 2018; Emily Donaldson, "NAACP Panel: Reforming Marijuana Laws Is a Social Justice Issue," *San Antonio Report*, July 17, 2018.

17. Richard Nixon, "Remarks About an Intensified Program for Drug Abuse Prevention and Control," American Presidency Project, June 17, 1971.

18. Richard Nixon, "Special Message to the Congress on Drug Abuse Prevention and Control," American Presidency Project, June 17, 1971; Biden (1989).

19. Fred Gardner, "The Shafer Commission Report (1972)," *O'Shaughnessy's Online*, 2017.

20. Adam Nagourney, "In Tapes, Nixon Rails About Jews and Blacks," *The New York Times*, December 11, 2010, p. A13; "Nixon Tapes Reveal Anti-Semitic, Racist Comments," *The Daily Beast*, August 21, 2013.

21. Dan Baum, "Legalize It All," *Harper's Magazine*, April 2016, pp. 22–32.

22. Craig Reinarman and Harry G. Levine, eds., *Crack in America: Demon Drugs and Social Justice*, University of California Press, 1997, p. 2.

23. Tom Morgenthau, "Kids and Cocaine," *Newsweek*, March 17, 1986, p. 16.

24. Peter Kerr, "Extra-Potent Cocaine: Use Rising Sharply Among Teen-Agers," *The New York Times*, March 20, 1986, p. B1.

25. Tessa Melvin, "Hearing Called to Explore Use of 'Crack' by Teen-Agers," *The New York Times*, April 27, 1986, p. WC11.

26. Peter Kerr, "Crack Addiction Spreads Among the Middle Class," *The New York Times*, June 8, 1986, p. A1.

27. Shelly Feuer Domash, "Use of the Drug 'Crack' Growing on L.I.," *The New York Times*, June 8, 1986, p. LI11.

28. Richard M. Smith, "The Plague Among Us: The Drug Crisis," *Newsweek*, June 16, 1986, p. 15; Larry Martz, "Trying to Say 'No,'" *Newsweek*, August 11, 1986, p. 14.

29. John S. Lang, "America on Drugs," *U.S. News & World Report*, July 28, 1986, p. 48.

30. Reinarman and Levine, p. 4.

31. Larry Martz, "A Dirty Drug Secret," *Newsweek*, February 19, 1990, p. 74.

32. Lisa W. Foderaro, "Drinking Keeps Its Grip on Suburban Teenagers," *The New York Times*, October 7, 1989, p. A25.

33. Substance Abuse and Mental Health Services Administration, *National Household Survey on Drug Abuse: Main Findings 1998*, March 2000, pp. 26–27.

34. Substance Abuse and Mental Health Services Administration, *Results From the 2023 National Survey on Drug Use and Health: Detailed Tables*, July 2024, Table 1.1B.

Notes (Chapter 3)

35. Smith.
36. Paul J. Goldstein et al., "Crack and Homicide in New York City, 1988: A Conceptually Based Event Analysis," *Contemporary Drug Problems*, 16:4, Winter 1989, pp. 651–87.
37. Arnold S. Trebach, *The Great Drug War*, MacMillan, 1987, pp. 5–8.
38. Associated Press, "Examiner Confirms Cocaine Killed Bias," *The New York Times*, June 25, 1986, p. D25.
39. Ira Berkow, "After the Shock, It's Back to the Pipe or Pills," *The Des Moines Register*, June 29, 1986, p. 33; Jimmy Breslin, "The Crack Business Booms on New York's Streets," *The Evening Sun*, June 30, 1986, p. 10.
40. Lena Williams, "U.S. Drive on Drugs Urged," *The New York Times*, June 26, 1986, p. B9.
41. Ibid.
42. Associated Press, "Cocaine Killed Rogers, Tests Indicate," *The New York Times*, June 30, 1986, p. C5.
43. Lynn Norment, "The Front-Line General in the War on Drugs," *Ebony*, March 1989, pp. 128–34.
44. "Jackson Calls Himself 'General' in Drug War," *Chicago Tribune*, May 23, 1988.
45. Jesse Jackson, "It's Time to End Dismally Failed 'War on Drugs,'" *Los Angeles Sentinel*, June 9, 2011.
46. Crack-Cocaine Equitable Sentencing Act of 1999, H.R. 939, March 2, 1999.
47. Charles B. Rangel, "Bush and GOP Presidential Wannabes Show Compassion for Powerful Friends," *Huffington Post*, November 8, 2007.
48. *Crack: Cocaine, Corruption & Conspiracy*, Netflix, 2022.
49. *State v. Russell*, 477 N.W.2d 886 (1991).
50. U.S. Sentencing Commission, *Mandatory Minimum Penalties in the Federal Criminal Justice System*, 1991, pp. H17–H20.
51. U.S. Sentencing Commission, *Cocaine and Federal Sentencing Policy*, 1995, p. i.
52. Ibid., pp. v, viii–ix, 94–102.
53. Ibid., p. 156.
54. Ibid., pp. xi–xii.
55. Ibid.
56. U.S. Sentencing Commission, *Cocaine and Federal Sentencing Policy*, 1997, Concurring Opinion of Vice Chairman Michael S. Gelacak, p. 1.
57. U.S. Sentencing Commission, *Cocaine and Federal Sentencing Policy*, 2002, p. 63; U.S. Sentencing Commission, *Mandatory Minimum Penalties in the Federal Criminal Justice System*, 2011, p. 192.
58. USSC (1991), p. E5.
59. USSC (2011), pp. 154, 159.
60. Ibid., p. 192.
61. Ibid., pp. 181–82, 196–98.
62. Fair Sentencing Act of 2010, Public Law 111-220.
63. FIRST STEP Act of 2018, Public Law 115-391.

64. U.S. Sentencing Commission, *Impact of the Fair Sentencing Act of 2010*, August 2015, pp. 12, 26; U.S. Sentencing Commission, "First Step Act of 2018 Resentencing Provisions: Retroactivity Data Report," August 2022, Tables 1 and 4.

65. Michael Isikoff, "Drug Buy Set Up for Bush Speech," *The Washington Post*, September 22, 1989, p. A1.

66. Tracy Thompson, "D.C. Student Is Given 10 Years in Drug Case," *The Washington Post*, November 1, 1990; David Hoffman, "Bush Defends Luring Drug Suspect," *The Washington Post*, September 23, 1989.

67. David A. Harris, "Car Wars: The Fourth Amendment's Death on the Highway," *George Washington Law Review*, March 1998, 66:3, pp. 556–91; David A. Harris, "Driving While Black and All Other Traffic Offenses: The Supreme Court and Pretextual Traffic Stops," *The Journal of Law and Criminology*, 1997, 87:2, pp. 544–82.

68. *Whren v. United States*, 517 U.S. 806 (1996).

69. Jacob Sullum, "10 Ways a Roadside Police Stop Can Go Wrong," *Reason*, June 2020, pp. 40–48.

70. Frank R. Baumgartner et al., "Targeting Young Men of Color for Search and Arrest During Traffic Stops: Evidence From North Carolina, 2002–2013," *Politics, Groups, and Identities*, 2016, pp. 1–25.

71. Charles R. Epp, Steven Maynard-Moody, and Donald P. Haider-Markel, *Pulled Over: How Police Stops Define Race and Citizenship*, University of Chicago Press, 2014.

72. Ibid., p. 157.

73. Daniel Simmons-Ritchie and Angela Couloumbis, "The Pa. State Police Was Warned About Possible Racial Bias in Car Searches. The Agency's Answer? End the Research," *The Philadelphia Inquirer*, January 23, 2020.

74. Portland Police Bureau, *Stops Data Collection: 2022 Annual Report*, July 10, 2023, p. 18.

75. New York Civil Liberties Union, "Stop-and-Frisk Data," 2023.

76. Drug Policy Alliance and the Marijuana Arrest Research Project, "Unjust and Unconstitutional," July 2017, p. 22.

77. Ray Kelly, "Charging Standards for Possession of Marihuana in Public View," NYPD Operations Order No. 49, September 19, 2011.

78. Harry G. Levine, "New York City's Marijuana Arrest Crusade Continues," September 2009, p. 10.

79. Andy Newman, "Marijuana Arrests Rose in 2011, Despite Police Directive," *The New York Times*, February 1, 2012.

80. New York City Mayor's Office of Criminal Justice, "Marijuana Possession Arrests," 2023.

81. Ibid. and Drug Policy Alliance (2017); Jennifer Steinhauer, "Bloomberg Says He Regrets Marijuana Remarks," *The New York Times*, April 10, 2022, p. B7.

82. Steinhauer.

83. American Civil Liberties Union, *The War on Marijuana in Black and White*, June 2013, p. 4.

84. Ibid.

85. American Civil Liberties Union, *A Tale of Two Countries: Racially Targeted Arrests in the Era of Marijuana Reform*, 2020, p. 5.
86. Ibid., p. 35.
87. Ibid., p. 12.
88. FBI Crime Data Explorer.
89. Jamie Fellner, "Race, Drugs, and Law Enforcement in the United States," *Stanford Law & Policy Review*, 2009, 20:2, pp. 257–91.
90. FBI Crime Data Explorer.
91. 2023 NSDUH results, Tables 1.24B and 1.25B.
92. Fellner, p. 268.
93. "Estimated Number of Arrests by Type of Drug Law Violation, 1982–2007," Bureau of Justice Statistics, June 2, 2021.
94. Bureau of Justice Statistics, *Drugs and Crime Facts, 1994*, June 1995, p. 19.
95. Diane Whitmore Schanzenbach et al., *Twelve Facts About Incarceration and Prisoner Reentry*, The Hamilton Project, Brookings Institution, 2016, p. 7.
96. U.S. Sentencing Commission, *Demographic Differences in Federal Sentencing*, November 2023, pp. 27–28.
97. Michelle Alexander, *The New Jim Crow: Mass Incarceration in the Age of Colorblindness*, The New Press, 2010.
98. John F. Pfaff, "Escaping From the Standard Story: Why the Conventional Wisdom on Prison Growth Is Wrong," *Federal Sentencing Reporter*, 2014, 26:4, pp. 265–70.
99. Federal Bureau of Prisons, "Offenses," https://www.bop.gov/about/statistics/statistics_inmate_offenses.jsp.
100. E. Ann Carson and Rich Kluckow, *Prisoners in 2022—Statistical Tables*, Bureau of Justice Statistics, November 2023, Table 16.
101. Wendy Sawyer and Peter Wagner, "Mass Incarceration: The Whole Pie 2024," Prison Policy Initiative, March 14, 2024.
102. Jonathan Rothwell, "Drug Offenders in American Prisons: The Critical Distinction Between Stock and Flow," Brookings Institution, November 25, 2015.
103. Emma Pierson et al., "A Large-Scale Analysis of Racial Disparities in Police Stops Across the United States," *Nature Human Behaviour*, July 2020, pp. 736–45.
104. Cody Tuttle, "Racial Disparities in Federal Sentencing: Evidence From Mandatory Minimums," job market paper, October 19, 2019.

Chapter 4: Gun Control in Black and White

1. Brian Doherty, *Gun Control on Trial: Inside the Supreme Court Battle Over the Second Amendment*, Cato Institute, 2008, p. 29.
2. Ibid.; Nina Totenberg, "High Court Starts Case Challenging D.C. Gun Ban," March 18, 2008.
3. *Parker v. District of Columbia* complaint, U.S. District Court for the District of Columbia, March 2004.
4. Totenberg.
5. *Parker v. District of Columbia*, 311 F. Supp. 2d 103 (2004).
6. *Parker v. District of Columbia*, 478 F.3d 370 (2007).

7. *District of Columbia v. Heller*, 554 U.S. 570 (2008).
8. Brief for State Firearm Associations in Support of Petitioners, *McDonald v. Chicago*, 08-1521, November 23, 2009.
9. Caroline Connors, "Otis McDonald, Took Gun Case to Supreme Court," *The Beverly Review*, April 8, 2014.
10. *McDonald v. Chicago*, 561 U.S. 742 (2010).
11. Brief for the NAACP Legal Defense & Educational Fund in Support of Petitioners, *District of Columbia v. Heller*, 07-290, January 11, 2008, pp. 1–2.
12. *Parker v. District of Columbia* (2007).
13. *District of Columbia v. Heller* (2008).
14. LDF brief (2008), p. 1.
15. Ibid., p. 25.
16. Ibid., pp. 29–31.
17. Brief for the NAACP Legal Defense & Educational Fund in Support of Neither Party, *McDonald v. Chicago*, 08-1521, November 23, 2009.
18. Brief for the NAACP Legal Defense & Educational Fund in Support of Respondents, *New York State Rifle & Pistol Association v. Bruen*, 20-843, September 21, 2021.
19. Ibid., pp. 1, 10–14.
20. Brief for the National African American Gun Association in Support of Petitioners, *New York State Rifle & Pistol Association v. Bruen*, 20-843, July 16, 2021, pp. 4, 18.
21. Brief for Black Guns Matter et al. in Support of Petitioners, *New York State Rifle & Pistol Association v. Bruen*, 20-843, July 20, 2021, pp. 1, 5, 11.
22. Ibid., pp. 12–13.
23. Brief for the Black Attorneys of Legal Aid et al. in Support of Petitioners, *New York State Rifle & Pistol Association v. Bruen*, 20-843, July 20, 2021, p. 5.
24. Ibid.
25. Ibid., pp. 20–22.
26. Ibid., pp. 22–25.
27. Alvin Bragg, "A Real Plan to Stop Gun Violence in Manhattan," www.alvinbragg.com/gun-safety (archived website), March 17, 2021.
28. Emily G. Fitzsimmons and Ashley Southall, "Adams Unveils Plan to Quell Gun Violence," *The New York Times*, January 24, 2022, p. A1; *100 Shooting Review Committee Report*, City of Philadelphia, pp. 30, 42.
29. Interview with Maj Toure, August 26, 2024.
30. *New York State Rifle & Pistol Association v. Bruen*, 20-843 (2022).
31. Nicholas Johnson, *Negroes and the Gun: The Black Tradition of Arms*, Prometheus Books, 2014.
32. Ibid., p. 286.
33. William Glaberson, "Gun Makers Repel Lawsuit by N.A.A.C.P.," *The New York Times*, July 22, 2003, p. B1.
34. Emily Graves Fitzsimmons, "Police Arrest Jackson, Pfleger at Gun Protest," *Chicago Tribune*, June 24, 2007.
35. Sabika Sheikh Firearm Licensing and Registration Act, H.R. 127, January 4, 2021.

36. Kyle Jaeger, "House Approves Federal Marijuana Legalization Bill in Historic Vote," *Marijuana Moment*, December 4, 2020.

37. "Congresswoman Sheila Jackson Lee Introduces Major Bipartisan Sentencing Reform Legislation," press release, October 9, 2015.

38. Jesse J. Smith, "Massive Noncompliance With SAFE Act," *Hudson Valley 1*, April 1, 2019; J.D. Tuccille, "Popular Defiance Will Kneecap Gun Laws in New Mexico," *Reason*, March 4, 2019; Alvaro Castillo-Carniglia et al., "Comprehensive Background Check Policy and Firearm Background Checks in Three US States," *Injury Prevention*, November 2018, 24:6, pp. 431–36.

39. New York Civil Liberties Union, "New NYCLU Report Finds NYPD Stop-and-Frisk Practices Ineffective, Reveals Depth of Racial Disparities," May 9, 2012.

40. Jacob Sullum, "Bloomberg Likens the NYPD's 'Stop and Frisk' Program to Random DUI Checkpoints," *Reason*, May 11, 2012.

41. *Terry v. Ohio*, 392 U.S. 1 (1968).

42. Rachel Elise Barkow, *Justice Abandoned: How the Supreme Court Ignored the Constitution and Enabled Mass Incarceration*, Harvard University Press, 2025, pp. 163–98; *Mapp v. Ohio*, 367 U.S. 643 (1961); *Miranda v. Arizona*, 384 U.S. 436 (1966).

43. *Terry v. Ohio*.

44. NYCLU (2012).

45. *Floyd v. City of New York*, U.S. District Court for the Southern District of New York, original complaint, January 31, 2007.

46. Ibid., pp. 5–6.

47. Matt Sledge, "David Floyd, Lead Stop and Frisk Plaintiff, Takes Stand in First Day of Trial," *Huffpost*, March 18, 2013.

48. *Floyd v. City of New York*, U.S. District Court for the Southern District of New York, first amended complaint, April 15, 2008, pp. 13–14.

49. Sledge.

50. NYCLU (2012).

51. *Floyd v. City of New York*, U.S. District Court for the Southern District of New York, opinion and order, August 12, 2013.

52. Ibid., pp. 6, 9.

53. Ibid., pp. 10–11.

54. Ibid., pp. 11–12.

55. Ibid., p. 12.

56. Ed Krayewski, "Mayor Bloomberg: We Don't Stop and Frisk Enough Minorities," *Reason*, June 29, 2013.

57. *Floyd* opinion and order, pp. 8–11.

58. Ibid., p. 17.

59. Michael Bloomberg, "Frisks Save Lives," *New York Post*, August 13, 2013.

60. Aziz Z. Huq, "The Consequences of Disparate Policing: Evaluating Stop and Frisk As a Modality of Urban Policing," *Minnesota Law Review*, 2017, 101, pp. 2397–480.

61. *Floyd* opinion and order, p. 5.

62. *Floyd v. New York*, order modifying remedial order, July 30, 2014.

63. New York Civil Liberties Union, "Stop-and-Frisk Data," 2023.

64. Michael Bloomberg, speech at the Christian Cultural Center, November 17, 2019.
65. Gallup, "Guns," https://news.gallup.com/poll/1645/guns.aspx; Morning Consult, "National Tracking Poll," May 25, 2022.
66. Nate Cohn, "Voters Say They Want Gun Control. Their Votes Say Something Different," *The New York Times*, June 3, 2022, p. A12.
67. 18 USC 922.
68. Adam Winkler, "Scrutinizing the Second Amendment," *Michigan Law Review*, February 2007, 105:4, pp. 683–733.
69. 18 USC 922.
70. Sarah S.K. Shannon et al., "The Growth, Scope, and Spatial Distribution of People With Felony Records in the United States, 1948–2010," *Demography*, September 2017, 54:5, pp. 1795–818.
71. Substance Abuse and Mental Health Services Administration, *Results From the 2023 National Survey on Drug Use and Health: Detailed Tables*, July 2024, Tables 1.24B and 1.25B; Diane Whitmore Schanzenbach et al., *Twelve Facts About Incarceration and Prisoner Reentry*, The Hamilton Project, Brookings Institution, 2016, p. 7.
72. FBI Crime Data Explorer.
73. E. Ann Carson and Rich Kluckow, *Prisoners in 2022—Statistical Tables*, Bureau of Justice Statistics, November 2023, Table 17.
74. U.S. Sentencing Commission, *What Do Federal Firearms Offenses Really Look Like?*, July 2022, p. 10. The analysis excluded people sentenced as "career criminals" or solely for using a gun in connection with a violent or drug trafficking crime.
75. Ibid., pp. 24–25.
76. Ibid., p. 26.
77. Ibid., pp. 19–20, 24.
78. U.S. Sentencing Commission, *The Effects of Aging on Recidivism of Federal Offenders*, December 2017.
79. Humera Lodhi, "There's a Large Racial Disparity in Federal Gun Prosecutions in Missouri, Data Shows," *The Kansas City Star*, May 23, 2022.
80. Ibid.
81. 18 USC 922(g), 18 USC 922(a)(6), 18 USC 924(a)(1)(4), 18 USC 933.
82. Shannon et al.
83. Substance Abuse and Mental Health Services Administration, *Results From the 2010 National Survey on Drug Use and Health: Detailed Tables*, September 2014, Table 1.1A, and 2023 NSDUH results, Table 1.1A.
84. William English, "2021 National Firearms Survey: Updated Analysis Including Types of Firearms Owned," Georgetown McDonough School of Business Research Paper No. 4109494, September 28, 2022; Lydia Saad, "What Percentage of Americans Own Guns?," Gallup, November 13, 2020; Kim Parker et al., "America's Complex Relationship With Guns," Pew Research Center, June 22, 2017.
85. FBI Crime Data Explorer.
86. U.S. Sentencing Commission, *Overview of Federal Criminal Cases, Fiscal Year 2021*, April 2022, p. 5.

87. TRAC Reports, "Federal Weapons Prosecutions Rise for Third Consecutive Year," November 29, 2017.
88. U.S. Sentencing Commission, *Demographic Differences in Federal Sentencing*, November 2023, p. 29.
89. Jill Farrell, "Mandatory Minimum Firearm Penalties: A Source of Sentencing Disparity?," *Justice Research and Policy*, June 2003, 5:1, pp. 95–115.
90. D.C. Code, Section 22-4503.
91. U.S. Sentencing Commission, "Quick Facts: Felon in Possession of a Firearm," FY 2021.
92. Spencer S. Hsu and Keith L. Alexander, "D.C. Crackdown on Gun Crime Targeted Black Wards, Was Not Enforced Citywide As Announced," *The Washington Post*, September 3, 2020.
93. *100 Shooting Review Committee Report*, p. 43.
94. Lodhi.
95. Bonita R. Gardner, "Separate and Unequal: Federal Tough-on-Guns Program Targets Minority Communities for Selective Enforcement," *Michigan Journal of Race and Law*, Spring 2007, 12:2, pp. 305–49.
96. Ibid.
97. Gary Fields, "Going After Crimes—and Guns," *The Wall Street Journal*, August 5, 2008.
98. Interview with Toure.

Chapter 5: Drugs, Guns, and the Constitution

1. Timothy Leary, *Flashbacks: An Autobiography*, Tarcher/Putnam, 1983, pp. 234–43; *Leary v. United States*, 39 U.S. 6 (1969).
2. Ibid.
3. Ibid.
4. Associated Press, "Former Professor Given 30 Years in Marijuana Case," *San Antonio Express/News*, March 12, 1966, p. 4-B.
5. *Leary v. United States*.
6. Controlled Substances Act of 1970, Public Law 91-513.
7. National Firearms Act of 1934, Public Law 73–474.
8. David Pozen, *The Constitution of the War on Drugs*, Oxford University Press, 2024, pp. 21–24.
9. *Congressional Record*, January 26, 1909, 43:2, pp. 1397–1398.
10. Isaac Campos, "What We Know and What We Don't Know," www.thedrugpage.org/what-we-do-and-dont-know.
11. *Champion v. Ames*, 188 U.S. 321 (1903).
12. *Hoke v. United States*, 227 U.S. 308 (1913).
13. Associated Press, "Government Will Ask States to Ban Growing of Marijuana," *The New York Times*, September 16, 1931, p. B37.
14. *Nigro v. United States*, 276 U.S. 332 (1928).
15. A. Christopher Bryant, "Nigro v. United States: The Most Disingenuous Supreme Court Opinion, Ever," *Nevada Law Journal*, Summer 2012, 12:2, pp. 650–58.

16. *Wickard v. Filburn*, 317 U.S. 111 (1942).
17. *National Labor Relations Board v. Johns & Laughlin Steel Corp.*, 301 U.S. 1 (1937).
18. *Wickard v. Filburn*.
19. Controlled Substances Act.
20. Ibid.
21. *Gonzales v. Raich*, 545 U.S. 1 (2005).
22. Ibid.
23. Ibid.
24. Ibid.
25. National Firearms Act of 1934.
26. Hearing Before the House Ways and Means Committee on H.R. 9066, April 16, 1934, p. 8.
27. Ibid., p. 19.
28. Federal Firearms Act of 1938, Public Law 75-785.
29. An Act to Strengthen the Federal Firearms Act, 1961, Public Law 87-342; Gun Control Act of 1968, Public Law 90-618; Firearm Owners' Protection Act of 1986, Public Law 99-308; Domestic Violence Offender Gun Ban, 1996, Public Law 104–208.
30. Firearm Owners' Protection Act.
31. *United States v. Lopez*, 514 U.S. 549 (1995).
32. Seth J. Safra, "The Amended Gun-Free School Zones Act: Doubt As to Its Constitutionality Remains," *Duke Law Journal*, November 2000, 50:2, pp. 637–62.
33. *United States v. Danks*, 221 F.3d 1037 (8th Circuit 1999); *United States v. Dorsey*, 418 F.3d 1038 (9th Circuit 2005).
34. *Printz v. United States*, 521 U.S. 898 (1997).
35. *New York State Rifle & Pistol Association v. Bruen*, 20-843 (2022).
36. *Antonyuk v. Hochul*, 1:22-CV-00986 (N.D. N.Y. 2022); *Christian v. Nigrelli*, 1:22-CV-00695 (W.D. N.Y. 2022); *Antonyuk v. Chiumento*, 22-2908 (2nd Circuit 2023); *Koons v. Platkin*, 1:22-CV-07464 (D. N.J. 2023); *Kipke v. Moore*, 1:23-CV-01293 (D. Md. 2023); *Wolford v. Lopez*, 1:23-cv-00265 (D. Hawaii 2023); *May v. Bonta*, 8:23-CV-01696 (C.D. Calif. 2023); *Wolford v. Lopez*, 23-16164 (9th Circuit 2024).
37. *United States v. Metcalf*, 24-4818 (9th Circuit); "State Concealed Carry Permit Requirements," U.S. Concealed Carry Association.
38. Federal Firearms Act.
39. 18 USC 922(g)(1).
40. *Range v. Attorney General*, 21-2835 (3rd Circuit 2023).
41. *United States v. Duarte*, 22-50048 (9th Circuit 2024).
42. *Kanter v. Barr*, 919 F.3d 437 (7th Circuit 2019).
43. 18 USC 922(g)(8).
44. Brief for the Cato Institute and the Goldwater Institute in Support of Respondent, *United States v. Rahimi*, 22–915, October 3, 2023; Brief for Professors of Second Amendment Law et al. in Support of Respondent, *United States v. Rahimi*, 22–915, October 4, 2023.
45. *United States v. Rahimi*, 21-11001 (5th Circuit 2023).
46. *United States v. Rahimi*, 22-1915 (2024).

NOTES (CHAPTER 5)

47. Substance Abuse and Mental Health Services Administration, *Results From the 2023 National Survey on Drug Use and Health: Detailed Tables*, July 2024, Table 1.1A.
48. 18 USC 922(g)(3).
49. *United States v. Harrison*, 5:22-CR-00328 (W.D. Okla. 2023).
50. Senate Report No. 90-1097, April 29, 1968.
51. *Congressional Record*, 114:10, May 15, 1968, p. 13344.
52. Gun Control Act of 1968.
53. Joe Biden, "Statement From President Biden on Marijuana Reform," White House, October 6, 2022.
54. Bipartisan Safer Communities Act of 2022, Public Law 117-159.
55. *United States v. Harrison*; *United States v. Connelly*, 3:22-CR-00229 (W.D. Texas 2023); *United States v. Alston*, 5:23-CR-00021 (E.D. N.C. 2023).
56. *United States v. Daniels*, 22-60596 (5th Circuit 2023). The decision was vacated following *United States v. Rahimi* but reaffirmed in *United States v. Daniels*, 22-60596 (5th Circuit 2025). Also see *United States v. Connelly*, 23-50312 (5th Circuit 2024).
57. *United States v. Daniels* (5th Circuit 2023).
58. Indictment in *United States v. Biden*, 1:23-CR-00061 (D. Del.), September 14, 2023.
59. Motion to Dismiss, *United States v. Biden*, 1:23-CR-00061 (D. Del.), December 11, 2023.
60. *United States v. Biden*, 1:23-CR-00061 (D. Del. 2024); *United States v. Veasley*, 23-1114 (8th Circuit 2024).
61. Myah Ward and Betsy Woodruff Swan, "Biden's Son Stirs Discomfort for Gun Control Advocates," *Politico*, June 12, 2024; "Statement From President Joe Biden," White House, December 1, 2024.
62. *Duncan v. Bonta*, 3:17-CV-010117 (S.D. Calif. 2023).
63. *Miller v. Bonta*, 3:19-CV-01537 (S.D. Calif. 2023).
64. William English, "2021 National Firearms Survey: Updated Analysis Including Types of Firearms Owned," Georgetown McDonough School of Business Research Paper No. 4109494, September 28, 2022.
65. See, e.g., *Association of New Jersey Rifle & Pistol Clubs v. Platkin*, 1:22-CV-04360 (D. N.J. 2024) and *Barnett v. Raoul*, 3:23-CV-00141 (S.D. Ill. 2024).
66. Oral arguments in *United States v. Rahimi*, 22-915, November 7, 2023.
67. *Range v. Attorney General*.
68. Opening Brief of the United States in *United States v. Alston*, 23-4705 (4th Circuit), March 7, 2024.
69. Douglas N. Husak, "Guns and Drugs: Case Studies on the Principled Limits of the Criminal Sanction," *Law and Philosophy*, September 2004, 23:5, pp. 437–93.
70. Pozen, pp. 25–42; *Ravin v. State*, 537 P.2d 494 (1975).
71. Leary, p. 241.
72. "Specious Marijuana Defense," *The New York Times*, March 18, 1966, p. 38.
73. American Indian Religious Freedom Act of 1978, Public Law 95-341.
74. *Employment Division v. Smith*, 494 U.S. 872 (1990).
75. Religious Freedom Restoration Act of 1993, Public Law 103-141.

76. *City of Boerne v. Flores*, 521 U.S. 507 (1997).
77. *Gonzales v. O Centro Espírita Beneficente União do Vegetal*, 546 U.S. 418 (2006).
78. Jacob Sullum, "Spiritual Highs and Legal Blows," *Reason*, June 2007, pp. 42–54.
79. *Conant v. Walters*, 309 F.3d 629 (9th Circuit 2002).
80. Section 608 of the PROTECT Act of 2003, Public Law 108-21; Justin Monticello, "Joe Biden's 'Bold' Thinking Shredded Civil Liberties and Destroyed Lives," Reason TV, May 22, 2020.
81. "DEA Uses RAVE Act Threats to Block Montana NORML/SSDP Benefit," *Drug War Chronicle*, June 6, 2003; Jacob Sullum, "The Chill Is On: Fighting Raves, Squelching Speech," *Reason*, July 18, 2003.
82. *Wren v. United States*, 517 U.S. 806 (1996); *United States v. Sharpe*, 470 U.S. 675 (1985); *United States v. Knotts*, 460 U.S. 276 (1983); *United States v. Ross*, 456 U.S. 798 (1982); *Wyoming v. Houghton*, 526 U.S. 295 (1999); *California v. Carney*, 471 U.S. 386 (1985); *Oliver v. United States*, 460 U.S. 170 (1984); *United States v. Dunn*, 480 U.S. 294 (1987); *United States v. Leon*, 468 U.S. 897 (1984); *California v. Greenwood*, 486 U.S. 35 (1988); *Florida v. Riley*, 488 U.S. 445 (1989); *Vernonia School District v. Acton*, 515 U.S. 646 (1995); *Board of Education v. Earls*, 536 U.S. 822 (2002); *New Jersey v. T.L.O.*, 469 U.S. 325 (1985); *Illinois v. Gates*, 462 U.S. 213 (1983); *Florida v. Harris*, 568 U.S. 237 (2013); *United States v. Montoya de Hernandez*, 473 U.S. 531 (1985).
83. Steven Wisotsky, "Crackdown: The Emerging Drug Exception to the Bill of Rights," *Hastings Law Journal*, July 1987, 38:5, pp. 889–926.
84. *Carroll v. United States*, 267 U.S. 132 (1925).
85. *Wren v. United States*.
86. David A. Harris, "Car Wars: The Fourth Amendment's Death on the Highway," *George Washington Law Review*, March 1998, 66:3, pp. 556–91.
87. Harris, p. 571.
88. *Ohio v. Robinette*, 519 U.S. 33 (1996).
89. *Shaw v. Jones*, 6:19-CV-01343 (D. Kansas 2023).
90. *United States v. Place*, 462 U.S. 696 (1983).
91. *Illinois v. Caballes*, 543 U.S. 405 (2005); *Rodriguez v. United States*, 575 U.S. 348 (2015).
92. *Florida v. Harris*; Jacob Sullum, "This Dog Can Send You to Jail," *Reason*, March 2013, pp. 36–45.
93. Grant Rodgers, "Gamblers Say Cash Seizure Was Illegal," *Des Moines Register*, September 30, 2014.
94. Class action complaint in *Brown v. TSA*, 2:20-CV-00064 (W.D. Pa.), January 15, 2020.
95. Jason Clayworth, "Iowa Disbands Forfeiture Team, OKs $60,000 Settlement," *Iowa City Press-Citizen*, December 5, 2016.
96. Lisa Knepper et al., *Policing for Profit: The Abuse of Civil Asset Forfeiture, 3rd Edition*, Institute for Justice, December 2020.
97. *Culley v. Attorney General*, 21-13805 (11th Circuit 2022).
98. Ibid.
99. Oral arguments in *Culley v. Marshall*, 22-585, October 30, 2023.

100. *Culley v. Marshall*, 22-585 (2024).
101. Brittany Hunter, "A History of Civil Asset Forfeiture in America," Foundation for Economic Education, April 9, 2019.
102. Knepper.
103. *Calero-Toledo v. Pearson Yacht Leasing Co.*, 416 U.S. 663 (1974).
104. *Bennis v. Michigan*, 516 U.S. 442 (1996).
105. *United States v. Ursery*, 518 U.S. 267 (1996).
106. *Austin v. United States*, 509 U.S. 602 (1993).
107. *Timbs v. Indiana*, 586 U.S. 146 (2019).
108. *State v. Timbs*, 20S-MI-289 (Indiana Supreme Court 2021).
109. *Lockyer v. Andrade*, 538 U.S. 63 (2003).
110. *Harmelin v. Michigan*, 501 U.S. 957 (1991).
111. 18 USC 924(c).
112. Nick Madigan, "Judge Questions Long Sentence in Drug Case," *The New York Times*, November 17, 2004, p. A16; memorandum opinion and order, *United States v. Angelos*, 345 F. Supp. 2d 1227 (D. Utah 2004).
113. Eva S. Nilsen, "Indecent Standards: The Case of *U.S. versus Weldon Angelos*," *Roger Williams University Law Review*, Winter 2006, 11:2, pp. 537–63.
114. *United States v. Angelos*, 433 F.3d 738 (10th Circuit 2006).
115. *Muscarello v. United States*, 524 U.S. 125 (1998).
116. *Congressional Record*, July 19, 1968, 114:17, p. 22231.
117. *Smith v. United States*, 508 U.S. 223 (1993).
118. Greg Jaffe and Sari Horwitz, "Utah Man Whose Long Drug Sentence Stirred Controversy Is Released," *The Washington Post*, June 3, 2016; interview with Weldon Angelos, August 14, 2024.
119. FIRST STEP Act of 2018, Public Law 115-391.
120. Interview with Angelos.
121. Brian Doherty, "How Buying Drugs Online Became Safe, Easy, and Boring," *Reason*, December 2014, pp. 50–58; Brian Doherty, "Ross Ulbricht Gets Life Sentence for Silk Road Conviction," *Reason*, May 29, 2015.
122. Donald Trump on Truth Social, January 21, 2025; "Widespread Support for Ross Ulbricht's Clemency," freeross.org.
123. *United States v. Ulbricht*, 15-815 (2nd Circuit 2017).

Chapter 6: Drug-Related Violence

1. Tina Chen, "Baby in Coma After Police 'Grenade' Dropped in Crib During Drug Raid," ABC News, May 30, 2014.
2. *Phonesavanh v. Long* complaint, 2:15-CV-0024 (N.D. Ga.), February 3, 2015.
3. Ibid.
4. Ibid.
5. Rob Moore, "Child Burned by Distraction Device During Raid," AccessNorthGa.com, May 29, 2014.
6. *Phonesavanh v. Long*.

Notes (Chapter 6)

7. Habersham County Grand Jury, "Presentment, Report, and Findings of the Habersham County Grand Jury Regarding the Events Leading to the Serious Injury of Bounkham Phonesevanh" [*sic*], October 6, 2014.

8. U.S. Attorney's Office for the Northern District of Georgia, "Former Habersham County Deputy Sheriff Charged for Her Role in Flash Bang Grenade Incident," July 22, 2015.

9. Finch McCrainie, "Final Settlement Reached in Baby Bou Bou Flashbang Case for 3.614 Million Dollars," June 30, 2020.

10. Habersham County Grand Jury report.

11. Criminal Indictment of Nikki Autry, 215-CR-028 (N.D. Ga.), July 21, 2015; 18 USC 242.

12. Autry indictment.

13. Ibid.

14. Christian Boone, "Jury Begins Deliberations in Baby Bou Bou Case," *The Atlanta Journal-Constitution*, December 11, 2015.

15. Christian Boone, "Former Habersham County Deputy Acquitted in Flash-Bang Case," *The Atlanta Journal-Constitution*, December 11, 2015.

16. Ibid.

17. FBI, *Crime in the United States*, "Persons Arrested," 1995–2019; FBI Crime Data Explorer.

18. Substance Abuse and Mental Health Services Administration, *National Household Survey on Drug Abuse: Main Findings 1995*, March 1997, p. 25; Substance Abuse and Mental Health Services Administration, *Results From the 2023 National Survey on Drug Use and Health: Detailed Tables*, July 2024, Table 1.1B.

19. Centers for Disease Control and Prevention, Compressed Mortality, 1979–1998 Results, Accidental Drug Overdose Deaths, CDC WONDER database; Matthew F. Garnett and Arialdi M. Miniño, "Drug Overdose Deaths in the United States, 2003–2023," National Center for Health Statistics, NCHS Data Brief 522, December 2024.

20. David Boyum and Peter Reuter, *An Analytic Assessment of U.S. Drug Policy*, American Enterprise Institute, 2005.

21. Office of National Drug Control Policy, *National Drug Control Strategy Data Supplement*, 2015, pp. 88–90.

22. Drug Enforcement Administration, *2020 Drug Threat Assessment*, March 2021.

23. Radley Balko, *Rise of the Warrior Cop: The Militarization of America's Police Force*, Public Affairs, 2013.

24. American Civil Liberties Union, *War Comes Home: The Excessive Militarization of American Policing*, June 2014.

25. Peter Kraska, "Militarization and Policing: Its Relevance to 21st Century Police," *Policing*, December 2007, 1:4, pp. 1–13.

26. Joshua Jaynes, search warrant affidavit, Jefferson County Circuit Court, 20-1371, March 12, 2020; transcript of interview with Detective Joshua Jaynes by Sergeant Jason Vance, May 19, 2020, p. 18; Jason Riley et al., "Louisville Postal Inspector: No 'Packages of Interest' at Slain EMT Breonna Taylor's Home," WDRB, May 16, 2020; Radley Balko, "The No-Knock Warrant for Breonna Taylor Was Illegal," *The Washington Post*, June 3, 2020.

27. *Richards v. Wisconsin*, 520 U.S. 385 (1997).

28. Rukmini Callimachi, "Breonna Taylor's Life Was Changing. Then the Police Came to Her Door," *The New York Times*, August 30, 2020, p. A1.

29. Daniel Cameron, "Attorney General Announces Completion of Investigation in Death of Ms. Breonna Taylor," September 23, 2020.

30. Dylan Lovan, "Grand Jury Audio Details Moments Before Breonna Taylor Died," *The Detroit News*, October 2, 2020.

31. Michael Levenson, "Prosecutors to Drop Charges Against Boyfriend of Breonna Taylor," *The New York Times*, May 22, 2020, p. A22.

32. Daniel Cameron press conference, September 23, 2020.

33. Termination letter from Acting Police Chief Robert Schroeder to Detective Brett Hankison, June 19, 2020.

34. Steve Almasy et al., "Ex-Officer Brett Hankison Was Found Not Guilty of Endangering Breonna Taylor's Neighbors in a Botched Raid," CNN, March 4, 2022.

35. Andrew Wolfson et al., "Louisville Agrees to $12 Million Settlement, Police Reforms in Breonna Taylor Lawsuit," *Louisville Courier Journal*, September 15, 2020.

36. Termination letter from Interim Police Chief Yvette Gentry to Detective Myles Cosgrove, December 29, 2020.

37. Termination letter from Interim Police Chief Yvette Gentry to Detective Joshua Jaynes, December 29, 2020.

38. "Current and Former Louisville, Kentucky, Police Officers Charged With Federal Crimes Related to Death of Breonna Taylor," U.S. Department of Justice, August 4, 2022.

39. Ibid.

40. Amanda Musa and Michelle Watson, "Former Louisville Detective Pleads Guilty to Federal Charges in Breonna Taylor Case," CNN, August 23, 2022.

41. Rachel Smith, "Ex-Louisville Cop Brett Hankison's Federal Trial Ends in Mistrial," *Louisville Courier Journal*, November 16, 2023.

42. "Former Louisville, Kentucky, Metro Police Officer Found Guilty of Federal Civil Rights Crimes Related to the Breonna Taylor Case," U.S. Department of Justice, November 1, 2024; 18 USC 242.

43. Memorandum opinion and order in *United States v. Meany*, 3:22-CR-00085 (W.D. Kentucky), August 22, 2024.

44. Art Acevedo press conference, January 29, 2019; St. John Barned-Smith and Keri Blakinger, "DA Reviewing 800 Cases of Second Officer Involved in Deadly Pecan Park Drug Raid," *The Houston Chronicle*, March 5, 2019; petition by John Nicholas and Jo Ann Nicholas, Harris County Probate Court, July 25, 2019.

45. Acevedo press conference.

46. Ibid.

47. Adam Bennett and Marcelino Benito, "Neighbors Shocked 'Easygoing' Couple Accused of Shooting HPD Officers," KHOU, January 29, 2019.

48. Gerald Goines, affidavit for search and arrest warrant, Houston Municipal Court, January 28, 2019; warrant inventory, January 28, 2019.

49. Art Acevedo press conference, February 15, 2019; "District Attorney Charges Two Officers in Harding Street Raid," Harris County District Attorney's Office, August 23, 2019; *United States v. Goines* indictment (S.D. Texas), November 14, 2019.

50. "DA Ogg Announces Review of 1,400 Cases," Harris County District Attorney's Office, February 20, 2019; Barned-Smith and Blakinger.

51. St. John Barned-Smith, "Harris County DA Calls Houston Man's Conviction a 'Disaster' After Drug Setup by HPD's Gerald Goines," *The Houston Chronicle*, July 21, 2022.

52. St. John Barned-Smith, "HPD Records Show Misconduct in Narcotics Division Beyond Cops at Center of Botched Raid," *The Houston Chronicle*, November 21, 2019.

53. Nicole Hensley, "Disgraced Houston Cop Gerald Goines Found Guilty of Felony Murder in Harding Street Raid Deaths," *The Houston Chronicle*, September 25, 2024; Miya Shay and Chaz Miller, "Murder Trial Begins for Disgraced HPD Officer Gerald Goines in 2019 Harding Street Raid," KTRK, September 9, 2024; Nicole Hensley, "Gerald Goines, Ex-Houston Police Officer, Sentenced to 60 Years in Prison for Harding Street Raid Killings," *The Houston Chronicle*, October 8, 2024.

54. "District Attorney Charges Two Officers in Harding Street Raid," Harris County District Attorney's Office, August 23, 2019; Art Acevedo press conference, August 23, 2019; Mario Diaz, "Harding Street Investigation and Questions Surrounding 'Probable Cause,'" KPRC, August 30, 2019.

55. Goines federal indictment; St. John Barned-Smith, "Former Houston Police Officer Steven Bryant Pleads Guilty in Federal Court for Role in Harding Street Debacle," *The Houston Chronicle*, June 8, 2021; "Woman Sentenced for Making False 911 Report That Led to Deadly HPD Raid," KTRK, June 8, 2021.

56. Acevedo press conferences, August 23, 2019, and November 20, 2019.

57. "Harding Street Supervisors Charged in Probe of Houston Narcotics Division," Harris County District Attorney's Office, July 1, 2020.

58. *Narcotics Division Review and Revision of Relevant SOPs*, Houston Police Department, 2019; St. John Barned-Smith, "'An Operation Completely Out of Control': Damning HPD Narcotics Audit Reveals Hundreds of Errors," *The Houston Chronicle*, July 2, 2020.

59. *Nicholas v. Houston* complaint, 4:21-CV-272 (S.D. Texas 2021).

60. See, e.g., "Former NYPD Police Officer Sentenced to 97 Months' Imprisonment for Bribery and Drug Trafficking," U.S. Attorney's Office for the Eastern District of New York, April 20, 2022; "New Report Sheds Light on BPD's Disgraced Gun Trace Task Force," WJZ News, January 13, 2022; "Philadelphia Police: A History of Corruption," Philly Power Research, February 10, 2022; Grace Hauck, "A Corrupt Chicago Cop Destroyed Hundreds of Lives," *USA Today*, February 5, 2023; "Rampart Scandal Timeline," *Frontline*, PBS, June 17, 2001; "Video Tapes Contradict Embroiled San Francisco Police Unit Reports," *San Francisco Examiner*, March 8, 2011; and Mark Joseph Stern, "The Police Lie. All the Time. Can Anything Stop Them?," *Slate*, August 4, 2020.

61. Peter Keane, "Why Cops Lie," *San Francisco Chronicle*, March 15, 2011.

62. General Accounting Office, "Information on Drug-Related Police Corruption," May 1998.

NOTES (CHAPTER 6)

63. "Mexico's Long War: Drugs, Crime, and the Cartels," Council on Foreign Relations, September 7, 2022; Emilia Ziosi, "Enablers of Cocaine Trafficking," London School of Economics, February 13, 2023; "Juan Orlando Hernandez, Former President of Honduras, Extradited to the United States on Drug-Trafficking and Firearms Charges," U.S. Attorney's Office for the Southern District of New York, April 21, 2022.

64. "Former DEA Special Agent Sentenced to Prison for Money Laundering and Fraud Scheme," U.S. Department of Justice, December 9, 2021.

65. Jim Mustian and Joshua Goodman, "DEA's Most Corrupt Agent: Parties, Sex Amid 'Unwinnable War,'" Associated Press, December 1, 2022; Office of the Inspector General, *The Handling of Sexual Harassment and Misconduct Allegations by the Department's Law Enforcement Components*, U.S Department of Justice, March 2015.

66. Ibid.

67. Jim Mustian and Joshua Goodman, "'Greed and Corruption': Federal Jury Convicts Veteran DEA Agents in Bribery Conspiracy," Associated Press, November 8, 2023; "Drug Enforcement Administration Special Agent Convicted of Perjury, Obstruction of Justice and Falsification of Government Records," U.S. Department of Justice, August 28, 2019; "Former Border Patrol Agent Sentenced to More Than Nine Years in Prison for Accepting Bribes to Facilitate the Trafficking of Illegal Drugs," U.S. Department of Justice, March 8, 2019.

68. See, e.g., Josiah Bates, "The True Story Behind HBO's *We Own This City* and the Rogue Gun Task Force That Terrorized Baltimore," *Time*, April 25, 2022; Joel Rubin and Maya Lau, "L.A. County Sheriff's Deputy Is Charged With Selling Drugs and Offering to Hire Other Cops to Protect Dealers," *Los Angeles Times*, January 16, 2018; Mira Wassef, "NYPD Officer, Boyfriend Accused of Trying to Peddle Fentanyl, Heroin in Yonkers," WPIX, October 22, 2023; and Jeremy Roebuck, "Former Philly Officer Sentenced to 9 Years for Selling Drugs Stolen by Corrupt Baltimore Police Squad," *The Philadelphia Inquirer*, April 29, 2019.

69. See, e.g., "Corrections Officer, Inmate, and Alleged Supplier Charged With Bribery and Other Offenses," U.S. Attorney's Office for the District of Columbia, September 26, 2022; Emily Rose Grassi, "Correctional Officer Accused of Smuggling Drugs to Inmates in Chester Co. Prison," WCAU, October 10, 2023; and Emma Misiaszek, "Cayuga Correctional Officer Arrested for Alleged Smuggling of Drugs and Phone," WHAM, January 8, 2024.

70. National Commission on Law Observance and Enforcement, *Report on the Enforcement of the Prohibition Laws of the United States*, January 7, 1931.

71. John O'Brien, "The St. Valentine's Day Massacre," *Chicago Tribune*, February 14, 2014; Jonathan Eig, "The St. Valentine's Day Massacre and Al Capone," *Chicago*, April 30, 2010.

72. Milton Friedman, "The War We Are Losing," in Melvyn B. Krauss and Edward P. Lazear, eds., *Searching for Alternatives: Drug Control Policy in the United States*, Hoover Institution Press, 1991, pp. 53–67.

73. Peter Andreas and Joel Wallman, "Illicit Markets and Violence: What Is the Relationship?," *Crime, Law and Social Change*, September 2009, 52:3, pp. 225–29.

74. David Shirk and Joel Wallman, "Understanding Mexico's Drug Violence," *The Journal of Conflict Resolution*, December 2015, 59:8, pp. 1348–76.

75. Paul J. Goldstein et al., "Crack and Homicide in New York City, 1988: A Conceptually Based Event Analysis," *Contemporary Drug Problems*, Winter 1989, 16:4, pp. 651–87.

76. Richard Rosenfeld et al., "Homicide and the Opioid Epidemic: A Longitudinal Analysis," *Homicide Studies*, August 2023, 27:3, pp. 321–37.

77. Jonathan P. Caulkins and Mark A.R. Kleiman, "How Much Crime Is Drug-Related?: History, Limitations, and Potential Improvements of Estimation Methods," report to the U.S. Department of Justice, April 2014.

78. Jeffrey A. Miron, "The Effect of Drug Prohibition on Drug Prices: Evidence From the Markets for Cocaine and Heroin," *The Review of Economics and Statistics*, August 2003, 85:3, pp. 522–30.

79. Geoffrey Lawrence, *The Impact of California Cannabis Taxes on Participation Within the Legal Market*, Reason Foundation, May 2022.

80. Robin Goldstein and Daniel Sumner, "How Big Will Legal Weed Get?," *USA Today*, July 26, 2022.

81. Robin Goldstein and Daniel Sumner, *Can Legal Weed Win?: The Blunt Realities of Cannabis Economics*, University of California Press, 2022, p. 91.

82. Goldstein and Sumner in *USA Today*.

83. Vikram P. Krishnasamy et al., "Update: Characteristics of a Nationwide Outbreak of E-cigarette, or Vaping, Product Use–Associated Lung Injury—United States, August 2019–January 2020," *Morbidity and Mortality Weekly Report*, January 24, 2020, 69:3, pp. 90–94.

84. Deborah Blum, "The Chemist's War," *Slate*, February 19, 2020.

85. "Government to Double Alcohol Poison Content and Also Add Benzene," *The New York Times*, December 30, 1926, p. 1.

86. Ibid.

87. "Nationwide Public Health Alert Issued Concerning Life-Threatening Risk Posed by Cocaine Laced with Veterinary Anti-Parasite Drug," Substance Abuse and Mental Health Services Administration, September 21, 2009; Joseph J. Palamar et al., "Detection of 'Bath Salts' and Other Novel Psychoactive Substances in Hair Samples of Ecstasy/MDMA/'Molly' Users," *Drug and Alcohol Dependence*, April 2016, 161, pp. 200–05; "DEA Reports Widespread Threat of Fentanyl Mixed With Xylazine," Drug Enforcement Administration, March 20, 2023; Paul F. Ehlers et al., "Seizures, Hyperthermia, and Myocardial Injury in Three Young Adults Who Consumed Bromazolam Disguised as Alprazolam—Chicago, Illinois, February 2023," *Morbidity and Mortality Weekly Report*, January 5, 2024, 72:52–53, pp. 1392–93.

88. American Medical Association, *Overdose Epidemic Report*, November 2024.

89. Jacob Sullum, "America's War on Pain Pills Is Killing Addicts and Leaving Patients in Agony," *Reason*, April 2018, pp. 18–29.

90. Merianne R. Spencer et al., "Drug Overdose Deaths in the United States, 2002–2022," National Center for Health Statistics, NCHS Data Brief 491, March 2024.

91. Daniel Ciccarone et al., "Heroin Uncertainties: Exploring Users' Perceptions of Fentanyl-Adulterated and Substituted 'Heroin,'" *International Journal of Drug Policy*, August 2017, 46, pp. 146–55.

92. Noah Weiland and Margot Sanger-Katz, "Overdose Deaths Continue Rising, With Fentanyl and Meth Key Culprits," *The New York Times*, May 11, 2022, p. A1; "DEA Laboratory Testing Reveals That 6 out of 10 Fentanyl-Laced Fake Prescription Pills Now Contain a Potentially Lethal Dose of Fentanyl," Drug Enforcement Administration public safety alert, November 2, 2022.

93. David Powell and Rosalie Liccardo Pacula, "The Evolving Consequences of OxyContin Reformulation on Drug Overdoses," *American Journal of Health Economics*, Winter 2021, 7:1, pp. 41–67.

94. Joshua Vaughn, "2016 Crime Review: Heroin Deaths Rise As Prescription Policies Go Into Effect," *The Sentinel*, June 7, 2017.

95. Bryce Pardo et al., *The Future of Fentanyl and Other Synthetic Opioids*, RAND Corporation, 2019; "Counterfeit Prescription Pills Containing Fentanyls: A Global Threat," Drug Enforcement Administration intelligence brief, July 2016.

96. Roger Bate, "Fentanyl and Fatal Overdoses: From Chemical Production in China to Users in Pennsylvania," American Enterprise Institute, December 2018.

97. Mark Thornton, "Alcohol Prohibition Was a Failure," Cato Institute, Policy Analysis No. 157, July 17, 1991; Richard Cowan, "How the Narcs Created Crack," *National Review*, December 5, 1986, pp. 30–31.

98. Julie O'Donnell et al., "Opioid-Involved Overdose Deaths With Fentanyl or Fentanyl Analogs Detected—28 States and the District of Columbia, July 2016–December 2018," *Morbidity and Mortality Weekly Report*, March 13, 2020, 69:10, pp. 271–73.

99. Alex Wodak and Leah McLeod, "The Role of Harm Reduction in Controlling HIV Among Injecting Drug Users," *AIDS*, August 2008, 22 (Supp. 2), pp. 81–92; Erik S. Anderson et al., "High Prevalence of Injection Drug Use and Blood-Borne Viral Infections Among Patients in an Urban Emergency Department," *PLoS One*, June 4, 2020, 15:6.

100. Lindsay LaSalle, *An Overdose Is Not Murder: Why Drug-Induced Homicide Laws Are Counterproductive and Inhumane*, Drug Policy Alliance, November 2017.

101. Sasha Mital et al., "The Relationship Between Incarceration History and Overdose in North America: A Scoping Review of the Evidence," *Drug and Alcohol Dependence*, August 1, 2020, 213, Article 108088; Daniel M. Hartung et al., "Fatal and Nonfatal Opioid Overdose Risk Following Release From Prison: A Retrospective Cohort Study Using Linked Administrative Data," *Journal of Substance Use and Addiction Treatment*, April 2023, 147, Article 208971.

102. Bradley Ray et al., "Spatiotemporal Analysis Exploring the Effect of Law Enforcement Drug Market Disruptions on Overdose, Indianapolis, Indiana, 2020–2021," *American Journal of Public Health*, July 2023, 113:7, pp. 750–58.

103. Douglas N. Husak, *Drugs and Rights*, Cambridge University Press, 1992.

104. Kenneth D. Rose, *American Women and the Repeal of Prohibition*, New York University Press, 1996.

105. "Volstead Act," *Encyclopedia Britannica*, 2019.

106. National Conference of State Legislatures, "State Medical Cannabis Laws," November 2023.
107. Lydia Saad, "Grassroots Support for Legalizing Marijuana Hits Record 70%," Gallup, November 8, 2023.

Chapter 7: The False Promise of Gun Control

1. Jessica Gresko, "20 Years Later, San Ysidro McDonald's Massacre Remembered," Associated Press, July 18, 2004; Timothy Harper, "Quick-Thinking 11-Year-Old Lived Because He Played Dead," Associated Press, July 22, 1984; *Mass Murderers*, Time-Life Books, 1993, pp. 112–39.
2. Ibid.
3. Carl Ingram, "Restricting of Assault-Type Guns OKd by Assembly Unit," *Los Angeles Times*, April 9, 1985.
4. "Feinstein Calls for Hearing on Assault Weapons Ban," Senate Judiciary Committee, February 22, 2018.
5. Barack Obama, "Remarks by the President at a DCCC Event—San Francisco, CA," April 4, 2013 (describing a semi-automatic rifle as "fully automatic"); Hillary Clinton, Democratic presidential debate, April 16, 2008 (calling for "sensible regulations" to keep "machine guns" away from "folks who shouldn't have them"); Firearm Owners' Protection Act of 1986, Public Law 99-308.
6. John Gramlich, "What the Data Says About Gun Deaths in the U.S.," Pew Research Center, April 26, 2023.
7. "Weapon Types Used in Mass Shootings in the United States Between 1982 and December 2023," Statista, January 8, 2024.
8. Josh Sugarmann, "Assault Weapons and Accessories in America," Violence Policy Center, 1988.
9. William English, "2021 National Firearms Survey: Updated Analysis Including Types of Firearms Owned," Georgetown McDonough School of Business Research Paper No. 4109494, May 13, 2022.
10. "Guns," Gallup, undated.
11. "The May 2022 AP-NORC Center Poll," May 27, 2022; "National Trends (Registered Voters)," Quinnipiac University Poll, November 2, 2023.
12. Paula McMahon and Skyler Swisher, "Nikolas Cruz Passed Background Check, Including Mental Health Questions, to Get AR-15 Rifle," *South Florida Sun-Sentinel*, February 16, 2018.
13. Roberti–Roos Assault Weapons Control Act of 1989, Section 30605 of the California Penal Code.
14. Jay Mathews, "Gunman Said He Resented Enterprising Immigrants," *The Washington Post*, January 19, 1989.
15. Connecticut General Statutes, Section 53-202; Delaware Code, Title 11, Section 1466; Illinois Public Act 102-1116; Maryland Criminal Law Code, Title 4, Subtitle 3; Massachusetts General Laws, Chapter 140, Section 131M; New Jersey Revised Statutes, Sections 2C:39-1w, 2C:39-5, 2C:58-5, 2C:58-12, and 2C:58-13; New York Penal Law,

Sections 265.00(22), 265.02(7), 265.10, 400.00(16-a); Washington H.B. 1240, April 25, 2023.

16. Violent Crime Control and Law Enforcement Act of 1994, Public Law 103-322, Title XI.

17. National Shooting Sports Foundation, "NSSF Releases Most Recent Firearm Production Figures," January 15, 2025; Jennifer Mascia and Chip Brownlee, "How Many Guns Are Circulating in the U.S.?," *The Trace*, March 6, 2023; English; *District of Columbia v. Heller*, 554 U.S. 570 (2008); *McDonald v. Chicago*, 561 U.S. 742 (2010); *New York State Rifle & Pistol Association v. Bruen*, 20-843 (2022).

18. Gramlich.

19. "Public Mass Shootings: Database Amasses Details of a Half Century of U.S. Mass Shootings with Firearms, Generating Psychosocial Histories," National Institute of Justice, February 3, 2022.

20. Joe Biden, "Banning Assault Weapons Works," *The New York Times*, August 11, 2019, p. A23.

21. Assault Weapons Ban of 2023, S. 25, introduced January 23, 2023.

22. 26 USC 5841–5845.

23. *Miller v. Bonta*, 542 F. Supp. 3d 1009 (S.D. Calif. 2021).

24. Douglas N. Husak, "Guns and Drugs: Case Studies on the Principled Limits of the Criminal Sanction," *Law and Philosophy*, September 2004, 23:5, pp. 437–93.

25. Adam Winkler, *Gunfight: The Battle Over the Right to Bear Arms in America*, W. W. Norton & Company, 2013, p. 39.

26. *Heller v. District of Columbia*, 670 F.3d 1244 (D.C. Circuit 2011).

27. *Miller v. Bonta*.

28. FBI, *Crime in the United States 2019*, Expanded Homicide Table 8, September 2020.

29. English; NSSF.

30. *District of Columbia v. Heller*, 554 U.S. 570 (2008); Brett Kavanaugh Supreme Court confirmation hearing, Senate Judiciary Committee, Day 2, September 5, 2018.

31. *Association of New Jersey Rifle & Pistol Clubs v. Platkin*, 1:22-CV-04360 (D. of N.J. 2024).

32. Christopher S. Koper, *An Updated Assessment of the Federal Assault Weapons Ban: Impacts on Gun Markets and Gun Violence, 1994-2003*, report to the National Institute of Justice, June 2004.

33. "Effects of Assault Weapon and High-Capacity Magazine Bans on Mass Shootings," RAND Corporation, July 16, 2024.

34. Tanya Somanader, "President Obama on the Shooting in San Bernardino," White House blog post, December 5, 2015.

35. "Public Mass Shootings."

36. *100 Shooting Review Committee Report*, City of Philadelphia, January 2022.

37. Mariel Alper and Lauren Glaze, "Source and Use of Firearms Involved in Crimes: Survey of Prison Inmates, 2016," Bureau of Justice Statistics, January 2019.

38. See, e.g., Gallup Poll, June 2022, and Fox News Poll, April 2023.

39. Alvaro Castillo-Carniglia et al., "Comprehensive Background Check Policy and Firearm Background Checks in Three US States," *Injury Prevention*, November 2018, 24:6, pp. 431–36.

40. Michael Siegel et al., "The Impact of State Firearm Laws on Homicide and Suicide Deaths in the USA,1991–2016: A Panel Study," *Journal of General Internal Medicine*, March 2019, 34:10, pp. 2021–28.

41. Alvaro Castillo-Carniglia et al., "California's Comprehensive Background Check and Misdemeanor Violence Prohibition Policies and Firearm Mortality," *Annals of Epidemiology*, February 2019, 30, pp. 50–56.

42. "Effects of Background Checks on Violent Crime," RAND Corporation, July 16, 2024.

43. Adam Winkler, "Scrutinizing the Second Amendment," *Michigan Law Review*, 2007, 105:4, pp. 683–733.

44. Associated Press, "Trump Can Still Vote After Sentencing, but Can't Own a Gun and Will Have to Turn Over DNA Sample," January 10, 2025.

45. FBI, "National Instant Criminal Background Check System 2022 Operational Report," November 2023.

46. 18 USC 922(a)(6), 18 USC 924(a)(2), and 18 USC 924(a)(1)(A).

47. "Federal Weapon Prosecutions Rise for Third Consecutive Year," TRAC Reports, November 29, 2017.

48. Government Accountability Office, *Few Individuals Denied Firearms Purchases Are Prosecuted and ATF Should Assess Use of Warning Notices in Lieu of Prosecutions*, September 2018.

49. Office of the Inspector General, *Review of the Bureau of Alcohol, Tobacco, Firearms and Explosives' Enforcement of Brady Act Violations Identified Through the National Instant Criminal Background Check System*, Report No. I-2004-006, U.S. Department of Justice, July 2004.

50. "Cotton, Colleagues Introduce Legislation to Reduce Gun Violence," Cotton press release, June 9, 2022; Cotton House campaign website, November 6, 2012.

51. Alex Mann, "'You're Not Taking That!' Family Turmoil Preceded Fatal Police Shooting in Maryland's Only Red Flag Death," *The Baltimore Sun*, January 23, 2020.

52. "Maryland's 'Red Flag' Law Turns Deadly: Officer Kills Man Who Refused to Turn in Gun," WJZ/CBS News, November 5, 2018.

53. Phil Davis, "Anne Arundel Police Chief: Shooting Was Evidence That Month-Old 'Red Flag' Law Is Needed," *Capital Gazette*, November 6, 2018.

54. WBFF reporter Joy Lepola Stewart on Twitter, November 5, 2018.

55. Colin Campbell, "Anne Arundel Police Say Officers Fatally Shot Armed Man While Serving Protective Order to Remove Guns," *The Baltimore Sun*, March 24, 2020.

56. "Extreme Risk Protection Orders," Giffords Law Center, undated.

57. Dakin Andone, "The Warning Signs Almost Everyone Missed," CNN, February 26, 2018.

58. "Remarks by President Trump on the Mass Shootings in Texas and Ohio," White House, August 5, 2019.

59. Bipartisan Safer Communities Act of 2022, Public Law 117-159; "Statement From President Biden on Five Years Since Parkland," White House, February 14, 2023.

60. April M. Zeoli et al., "Extreme Risk Protection Orders in the United States: A Systematic Review of the Research," *Annual Review of Criminology*, September 18, 2024, 12:2, pp. 10.1–10.20.

61. Ana Radalat and Kelan Lyons, "CT's 'Red Flag' Law—an Early, but Narrow, Effort to Take Guns," *CT Mirror*, August 13, 2019.

62. Maryland Public Safety Code, Title 5, Subtitle 6.

63. Zeoli et al. (2024).

64. "Extreme Risk Protection Order (ERPO) Activity Report," District Court of Maryland, 2023.

65. "Risk Protection Orders by County, March 2018 Through June 2022," Florida Summary Reporting System.

66. Zeoli et al. (2024).

67. New York State Unified Court System, Division of Technology & Court Research, Extreme Risk Protection Orders Dashboard.

68. Consolidated Laws of New York, Chapter 8, Article 63-A.

69. New York State Unified Court System.

70. Giffords Law Center.

71. Ibid.

72. Colorado Revised Statutes, Sections 13-14.5-103(6)(g) and 13-14.5-104(1)(a).

73. Bianca Padró Ocasio, "Orlando Man Who Police Say Wanted to Commit Mass Shooting Barred From Having Weapons Under New Law," *Orlando Sentinel*, March 21, 2018.

74. Police interview with Christian Velasquez, March 16, 2018.

75. Interview with Kendra Parris, April 4, 2018; Florida Statutes, Title XXIX, Chapter 394, Part I.

76. Matthew Ochiuzzo, petition for risk protection order, *City of Orlando v. Christian Velasquez*, Ninth Judicial Circuit Court, March 16, 2018.

77. Temporary ex parte risk protection order, *City of Orlando v. Christian Velasquez*, Ninth Judicial Circuit Court, March 16, 2018.

78. Final order denying petition for risk protection order, *City of Orlando v. Christian Velasquez*, Ninth Judicial Circuit Court, April 4, 2018.

79. Interview with Kendra Parris.

80. Florida Statutes, Title XLVI, Chapter 790, Section 401.

81. Interview with Kendra Parris, May 13, 2019.

82. Ibid.

83. Interview with Oliver Hoyte, May 15, 2019.

84. Petition by Joanie Morgan for domestic violence injunction, Fifth Judicial Circuit Court, August 24, 2018; affidavit by Detective Rachel Ann Montgomery, Citrus County Sheriff's Office, in support of a petition for a risk protection order against Kevin Morgan, Fifth Judicial Circuit Court, September 18, 2018.

85. Joanie Morgan petition; ex parte order for involuntary examination, Fifth Judicial Circuit Court, September 13, 2018; order granting temporary ex parte risk protection,

Notes (Chapter 7)

Fifth Judicial Circuit Court, September 18, 2018; interview with Kevin Morgan, November 21, 2019; interview with Mike Blackstone, December 17, 2019.

86. Discharge report, The Centers, Ocala, Florida, September 14, 2018.

87. Brief behavioral status exam report, The Centers, Ocala, Florida, September 20, 2018.

88. Kevin Morgan hearing, Fifth Judicial Circuit Court, September 28, 2018; order denying petition for risk protection order against Kevin Morgan, Fifth Judicial Circuit Court, September 28, 2018.

89. Interview with Blackstone.

90. Interview with Kendra Parris (2019).

91. Jacob Sullum, "Why Didn't California's 'Red Flag' Law Stop the San Jose Shooter?," *Reason*, May 27, 2021; Jacob Sullum, "The Indianapolis Shooting Highlights the Shortcomings of 'Red Flag' Laws," *Reason*, April 19, 2021; Jacob Sullum, "Does California's Latest Mass Shooting Show the Country's Strictest Gun Laws Are Not Strict Enough?," *Reason*, April 6, 2022; Jacob Sullum, "The Buffalo Massacre Illustrates the Inherent Limitations of 'Red Flag' Laws," *Reason*, May 18, 2022; Jacob Sullum, "Why Didn't a 'Red Flag' Law Prevent the Illinois Mass Shooting, and Would New Federal Rules Have Mattered?," *Reason*, July 6, 2022.

92. Garen J. Wintemute et al., "Extreme Risk Protection Orders Intended to Prevent Mass Shootings," *Annals of Internal Medicine*, November 5, 2019, 171:9, pp. 655–58.

93. April M. Zeoli et al., "Extreme Risk Protection Orders in Response to Threats of Multiple Victim/Mass Shootings in Six U.S. States: A Descriptive Study," *Preventive Medicine*, December 2022, 165A, Article 107304.

94. "Suicide Data and Statistics," Centers for Disease Control and Prevention, November 29, 2023.

95. Zeoli et al. (2022).

96. Volusia County Sheriff's Office, risk protection order database, 2019–2023.

97. Andrew Kenney, "ERPO in 8 Charts: What We Learned From Reading Hundreds of 'Red Flag' Cases in Colorado," Colorado Public Radio, January 30, 2023.

98. Shauna Rakshe et al., "Five Years of Extreme Risk Protection Orders in Oregon: A Descriptive Analysis," *Psychological Reports*, April 26, 2024.

99. Zeoli et al. (2024).

100. Aaron J. Kivisto and Peter Lee Phalen, "Effects of Risk-Based Firearm Seizure Laws in Connecticut on Suicide Rates, 1981–2015," *Psychiatric Services*, August 2018, 69:8, pp. 855–62.

101. Jeffrey Swanson et al., "Implementation and Effectiveness of Connecticut's Risk-Based Gun Removal Law: Does It Prevent Suicides?," *Law and Contemporary Problems*, 2017, 80:2, pp. 179–208. Also see David Kopel's March 19, 2019, testimony before the U.S. Senate Judiciary Committee, which faults Swanson et al. for estimating the fatality rates for suicide attempts using various methods by "treating every instance of self-inflicted injury as if it were a suicide attempt."

102. Jeffrey W. Swanson et al., "Criminal Justice and Suicide Outcomes With Indiana's Risk-Based Gun Seizure Law," *The Journal of the American Academy of Psychiatry and the Law*, June 2019, 47:2, pp. 188–97.

103. Email from Jeffrey Swanson, June 4, 2019.
104. "Effects of Extreme Risk Protection Orders on Suicide," RAND Corporation, July 16, 2024.
105. "Effects of Extreme Risk Protection Orders on Violent Crime," RAND Corporation, July 16, 2024.
106. Richard A. Friedman, "Why Mass Murderers May Not Be Very Different From You or Me," *The New York Times*, August 8, 2019, p. A23.
107. Alexander W. Scherr, "Daubert & Danger: The 'Fit' of Expert Predictions in Civil Commitments," *Hastings Law Journal*, November 2003, 55:1, pp. 1–90.
108. Rosanna Smart and Terry L. Schell, "Mass Shootings in the United States," RAND Corporation, April 15, 2021.
109. Defense Science Board, *Predicting Violent Behavior*, U.S. Department of Defense, August 2012, pp. 79–83.
110. Original complaint in *Texas et al. v. ATF*, 6:23-CV-00013 (S.D. Texas), March 6, 2023, pp. 9–10.
111. "Gun Policy Research Review," RAND Corporation, undated; "Effects of Child-Access Prevention Laws on Suicide," RAND Corporation, July 16, 2024; "Effects of Child-Access Prevention Laws on Unintentional Injuries and Deaths," RAND Corporation, July 16, 2024; "Effects of Child-Access Prevention Violent Crime," RAND Corporation, July 16, 2024.
112. Rosanna Smart et al., *The Science of Gun Policy: A Critical Synthesis of Research Evidence on the Effects of Gun Policies in the United States*, RAND Corporation, 2020; Aaron Brown and Justin Monticello, "Do Studies Show Gun Control Works?," *Reason*, March 31, 2022.

Chapter 8: Hope for Help

1. Serge F. Kovaleski, "Federal Law Requires a Choice: Marijuana or a Gun?," *The New York Times*, November 29, 2023, p. A1.
2. ATF Form 4473.
3. Original complaint in *Fried v. Garland*, 4:22-CV-00164 (N.D. Fla.), April 20, 2022.
4. Statement from the governor's office, April 20, 2022.
5. Ben Adlin, "DeSantis on Federal Gun Ban for Marijuana Users: 'I Don't Think That's Constitutional, to Be Honest With You,'" *Marijuana Moment*, January 20, 2024.
6. Second Amendment Protection Act, H.R. 363, January 13, 2023.
7. Email from Amy Cooper, November 29, 2022.
8. FPC post on X, August 11, 2023; "FPC Maintains Offer to Hunter Biden in Challenge to Federal Gun Control Scheme," FPC press release, June 11, 2024.
9. See, e.g., Kyle Jaeger, "Florida Official Sues Biden Administration Over Gun Rights for Medical Marijuana Patients on 4/20," *Marijuana Moment*, April 20, 2022; Kyle Jaeger, "Hunter Biden's Lawyers Cite Marijuana and Gun Ruling to Deter Charges on Alleged Federal Form Lying, Reports Say," *Marijuana Moment*, June 2, 2023; and Kyle Jaeger, "Another Federal Court Rules That Banning Marijuana Consumers From Possessing Guns Is Unconstitutional," *Marijuana Moment*, April 10, 2023.

10. See, e.g., Kyle Jaeger, "Federal Court Strikes Down Gun Ban for People Who Use Marijuana, Calling Government's Justification 'Concerning,'" *Marijuana Moment*, February 6, 2023, and Kyle Jaeger, "Justice Department Makes 'Startling and Dangerous' Claim to Defend Medical Marijuana Patient Gun Ban," *Marijuana Moment*, April 11, 2023.

11. See, e.g., Kyle Jaeger, "Biden DOJ Says Medical Marijuana Patients Are Too 'Dangerous to Trust' in Motion to Dismiss Lawsuit Over Gun Rights," *Marijuana Moment*, August 8, 2022; Kyle Jaeger, "Biden's Justice Department Says Marijuana Consumers Are 'Unlikely' to Store Guns Properly in Latest Defense of Federal Ban," *Marijuana Moment*, November 16, 2023; and Kyle Jaeger, "DOJ Doubles Down on Claim That Medical Marijuana Patients 'Endanger Public Safety' If They Own Guns," *Marijuana Moment*, July 17, 2024.

12. Supplemental brief for appellees, *Cooper v. Attorney General*, 22-13893 (11th Circuit), July 12, 2024.

13. Dustin Blitchok, "Feds Say Nope to Guns and Dope," *Benzinga*, April 20, 2022; Kyle Jaeger, "Florida Ag Commissioner Blasts 'Insulting' Biden DOJ Response to Medical Marijuana Patients' Gun Rights Lawsuit," *Marijuana Moment*, August 9, 2022.

14. Douglas N. Husak, "Guns and Drugs: Case Studies on the Principled Limits of the Criminal Sanction," *Law and Philosophy*, September 2004, 23:5, pp. 437–93.

15. John Stuart Mill, *On Liberty, Utilitarianism & Other Essays*, Moncreiffe Press, 2022, p. 30.

16. See, e.g., Robert Nozick, *Anarchy, State, and Utopia*, Basic Books, 1974; David Boaz, *Libertarianism: A Primer*, Free Press, 1997; Charles Murray, *What It Means to Be a Libertarian: A Personal Interpretation*, Broadway Books, 1997; and Jeffrey A. Miron, *Libertarianism, From A to Z*, Basic Books, 2010.

17. Kevin Miller, "LePage Vetoes Bill Aimed at Increasing Access to Overdose Antidote," *Portland Press Herald*, April 20, 2016.

18. "Lawmakers Override Vetoes in Order to Fight Overdose Epidemic, Add Jail Funding," *Portland Press Herald*, April 29, 2016.

19. See, e.g. Maia Szalavitz, *Undoing Drugs: How Harm Reduction Is Changing the Future of Drugs and Addiction*, Hachette Go, 2021, and Sheila P. Vakharia, *The Harm Reduction Gap: Helping Individuals Left Behind by Conventional Drug Prevention and Abstinence-Only Addiction Treatment*, Routledge, 2024.

20. Kyle Jaeger, "NIDA Director Calls Abstinence-Only Approach 'Catastrophic' for OD Crisis," *Filter*, November 21, 2023.

21. Katherine McLean, "The Biopolitics of Needle Exchange in the United States," *Critical Public Health*, March 2011, 21:1, pp. 71–79.

22. Irvin Molotsky, "Programs to Fight AIDS Cleared by Senate, 87-4; House's Approval Is Seen," *The New York Times*, April 29, 1988, p. B4.

23. Matt Fisher, "A History of the Ban on Federal Funding for Syringe Exchange Programs," Center for Strategic and International Studies, February 7, 2012.

24. Consolidated Appropriations Act of 2016, Public Law 114-113.

25. "Public Support for Needle Exchange Programs, Safe Injection Sites Remain[s] Low in U.S.," Bloomberg School of Public Health, Johns Hopkins University, June 5, 2018.

26. "Safety and Effectiveness of Syringe Services Programs," Centers for Disease Control and Prevention, February 8, 2024.

27. "FDA Approves Narcan Nasal Spray," *Journal of Emergency Medical Services*, November 19, 2015.

28. "FDA Approves First Generic Naloxone Nasal Spray to Treat Opioid Overdose," Food and Drug Administration, April 19, 2019; Sam Breen, "Addressing Opioid Overdoses Through Statewide Standing Orders for Naloxone Distribution," The Network for Public Health Law, July 30, 2019.

29. "FDA Approves First Over-the-Counter Naloxone Nasal Spray," Food and Drug Administration, March 29, 2023

30. Merianne R. Spencer et al., "Drug Overdose Deaths in the United States, 2002–2022," National Center for Health Statistics, NCHS Data Brief 491, March 2024.

31. 21 USC 856.

32. Complaint for declaratory judgment, *U.S. v. Safehouse*, 2:19-CV-00519 (E.D. Pa. 2019).

33. Memorandum and order, *U.S. v. Safehouse*, 2:19-CV-00519 (E.D. Pa. 2020); Nina Feldman, "In Philadelphia, Judges Rule Against Opening 'Supervised' Site to Inject Opioids," WHYY, January 14, 2021; *Safehouse v. U.S. Department of Justice*, 20-1422 (3rd Circuit 2021).

34. Associated Press, "Justice Department Signals It May Allow Safe Injection Sites," February 7, 2022.

35. Michael Casey, "Providence Approves First State-Sanctioned Safe Injection Site in Rhode Island," Associated Press, February 2, 2024.

36. Callan Gray, "Minnesota Legislature Passes Law Opening Door to Creation of Safe Injection Spaces," KSTP, July 6, 2023; Susan Du, "Drug Use Resource Hub Opens in North Minneapolis After State Legalizes Safe Injection Sites," *Star Tribune*, April 3, 2024.

37. Calvin Cutler, "Vermont Lawmakers Override 6 of Governor's 7 Vetoes," WCAX, June 17, 2024; Katharine Huntley, "Burlington Officials, Health Dept. to Begin Work on Safe Injection Site," WCAX, June 18, 2024.

38. OnPoint numbers reported to the New York City Mayor's Office and the New York City Department of Health and Mental Hygiene.

39. Jorge Finke and Jie Chan, "The Case for Supervised Injection Sites in the United States," *American Family Physician*, May 2022, 105:5, pp. 454–55.

40. Indhu Rammohan et al., "Overdose Mortality Incidence and Supervised Consumption Services in Toronto, Canada: An Ecological Study and Spatial Analysis," *The Lancet*, February 2024, 9:2, pp. E79–E87.

41. Alex H. Kral and Peter J. Davidson, "Addressing the Nation's Opioid Epidemic: Lessons From an Unsanctioned Supervised Injection Site in the U.S.," *American Journal of Preventive Medicine*, 2017, 53:6, pp. 919–22.

42. "Car Crash Deaths and Rates," National Safety Council, 2024.

43. Jacob Sullum, *Saying Yes: In Defense of Drug Use*, Tarcher/Putnam, 2003; Carl L. Hart, *Drug Use for Grown-Ups: Chasing Liberty in the Land of Fear*, Penguin Press, 2021.

Notes (Chapter 8)

44. "The Relative Risks of Tobacco Products," Food and Drug Administration, July 18, 2024; *The Public Health Consequences of E-Cigarettes*, National Academies of Sciences, Engineering, and Medicine, 2018.

45. Kate Bryan, "Cannabis Overview," National Conference of State Legislatures, June 20, 2024.

46. *Ballotpedia*; Drug Addiction Treatment and Recovery Act, Measure 110, 2020.

47. Jamie Parfitt and Colten Weekley, "A Majority of Oregonians Want to See Measure 110 Tossed Aside, Poll Finds," KGW, August 29, 2023; Associated Press, "Oregon Lawmakers Pass Bill to Recriminalize Drug Possession," March 2, 2024.

48. Alex H. Kral, "Impact of Fentanyl on Overdose Mortality in Oregon Before and After Measure 110," presentation at Oregon Measure 110 Research Symposium, January 22, 2024; Michael J. Zoorob et al. "Drug Decriminalization, Fentanyl, and Fatal Overdoses in Oregon," *JAMA Network Open*, September 5, 2024, 7:9, Article 2431612.

49. See, e.g., "Oregon Set to Recriminalize Drugs, Return to Failed Approach of Arresting, Jailing People for Possession," Drug Policy Alliance, March 1, 2024.

50. Michelle Mancher and Alan I. Leshner, eds., *Medications for Opioid Use Disorder Save Lives*, National Academies Press, 2019.

51. Christine Timko et al., "Retention in Medication-Assisted Treatment for Opiate Dependence: A Systematic Review," *Journal of Addictive Diseases*, May 30, 2016, 35:1, pp. 22–35.

52. William M. Compton and Nora D. Volkow, "Extended-Release Buprenorphine and Its Evaluation With Patient-Reported Outcomes," *Jama Network Open*, May 10, 2021, 4:5, Article 219708.

53. Spencer et al.

54. Substance Abuse and Mental Health Services Administration, *Results From the 2023 National Survey on Drug Use and Health: Detailed Tables*, July 2024, Table 1.1A.

55. Mill, p. 31.

56. Don Kates et al., "Public Health Pot Shots," *Reason*, April 1997, pp. 24–29.

57. Nicholas Kristof, "A Smarter Way to Reduce Gun Deaths," *The New York Times*, January 24, 2023.

58. Humera Lodhi, "There's a Large Racial Disparity in Federal Gun Prosecutions in Missouri, Data Shows," *The Kansas City Star*, May 23, 2022.

59. John Pfaff, "What an Analysis of 2,000 Shootings Tells Us About How to End Gun Violence," *Slate*, February 14, 2022.

60. John Gramlich, "What the Data Says About Crime in the United States," Pew Research Center, April 24, 2024; Ames Grawert, "FBI Data Confirms Drop in Most Crimes in 2023, Especially Murders," Brennan Center for Justice, September 26, 2024.

61. Jeff Asher, "Murder Fell at the Fastest Pace Ever Recorded in 2023," *Jeff-alytics*, September 23, 2024.

62. Ernesto Lopez and Bobby Boxerman, "Crime Trends in U.S. Cities: Year-End 2024 Update," Council on Criminal Justice, January 2025; "YTD Murder Comparison," AH Datalytics; quarterly reports, FBI Crime Explorer.

63. Donald Trump, remarks at the 2024 Republican National Convention, July 19, 2024; "Homicides Are Skyrocketing in American Cities Under Kamala Harris," Trump campaign press release, August 12, 2024.
64. Steven D. Levitt, "Understanding Why Crime Fell in the 1990s: Four Factors That Explain the Decline and Six That Do Not," *Journal of Economic Perspectives*, Winter 2004, 18:1, pp. 163–90.
65. John J. Donohue and Steven D. Levitt, "The Impact of Legalized Abortion on Crime," *The Quarterly Journal of Economics*, May 2001, 116:2, pp. 379–420.
66. Oliver Roeder et al., *What Caused the Crime Decline?*, Brennan Center for Justice, 2015.
67. Danielle Kaeble and Lauren Glaze, "Correctional Populations in the United States, 2015," Bureau of Justice Statistics, December 2016.
68. Wendy Sawyer and Peter Wagner, "Mass Incarceration: The Whole Pie 2024," Prison Policy Initiative, March 14, 2024.
69. Neil Gorsuch and Janie Nitze, *Over Ruled: The Human Toll of Too Much Law*, HarperCollins, 2024, p. 110.
70. "A New Approach to Reducing Incarceration While Maintaining Low Rates of Crime," The Hamilton Project, Policy Brief 2014-03, May 2014.
71. Zach Weissmueller, "Long Prison Terms Are Wasteful Government Spending," interview with Mark Kleiman, *Reason*, July 2011, pp. 71–74.
72. "Case for Reform," Right on Crime website.
73. Christopher Hooks, "Who Killed Criminal Justice Reform in Texas?," *Texas Monthly*, October 2021; Michelle Russell, "5 Years in, 5 Things to Know About Louisiana's Justice System," Pew Charitable Trusts, November 1, 2022.
74. Jennifer Mascia and Chip Brownlee, "How Many Guns Are Circulating in the U.S.?," *The Trace*, March 6, 2023.
75. Maria Mercedes Ponce de Leon and Luca Rizzotti, "The Effect of Police Management on Crime and Officers' Behavior: Evidence from Compstat," SSRN paper, April 18, 2024.
76. "Community Violence Prevention," Center for Gun Violence Solutions.
77. Anthony A. Braga et al., "Focused Deterrence Strategies and Crime Control: An Updated Systematic Review and Meta-Analysis of the Empirical Evidence," *Criminology & Public Policy*, February 2018, 17:1, pp. 205–50.
78. Daniel W. Webster et al., "Estimating the Effects of Safe Streets Baltimore on Gun Violence, 2007–2022," Center for Gun Violence Solutions, Bloomberg School of Public Health, March 2023.
79. "Community Violence Prevention."
80. *100 Shooting Review Committee Report*, City of Philadelphia, January 1, 2022, pp. 83–84.
81. Pew Research Center.
82. "Suicide," National Institute of Mental Health, February 2024.
83. See, e.g., Kathryn R. Fingar et al., "Two Decades of Suicide Prevention Laws: Lessons From National Leaders in Gun Safety Policy," Everytown for Gun Safety, September 29, 2023.

NOTES (CHAPTER 8)

84. Guy Smith, *Guns and Control*, Skyhorse Publishing, 2020, pp. 39–55

85. Centers for Disease Control and Prevention, "Suicide Data and Statistics," November 29, 2023.

86. Gonzalo Martinez-Ales et al., "Why Are Suicide Rates Increasing in the United States?," in Enrique Baca-Garcia, ed., *Behavioral Neurobiology of Suicide and Self Harm*, Current Topics in Behavioral Neurosciences, 2020, 46, pp. 1–23.

87. Matthew F. Garnett and Sally C. Curtin, "Suicide Mortality in the United States, 2002–2022," National Center for Health Statistics, NCHS Data Brief 509, September 2024.

88. John Elflein, "Deaths by Suicide per 100,000 Resident Population in the U.S. From 1950 to 2021," Statista, March 6, 2024; "Gun Ownership in America: 1973 to 2021," Violence Policy Center, November 2022.

89. Emma Hofstra et al., "Effectiveness of Suicide Prevention Interventions: A Systematic Review and Meta-Analysis," *General Hospital Psychiatry*, March-April 2020, 63, pp. 127–40.

90. FBI Crime Data Explorer; John Gramlich, "What We Know About the Increase in U.S. Murders in 2020," Pew Research Center, October 27, 2021.

91. Spencer et al.

92. FBI Crime Explorer, Council on Criminal Justice, AH Datalytics.

93. "U.S. Overdose Deaths Decrease in 2023, First Time Since 2018," National Center for Health Statistics, May 15, 2024.

94. "Provisional Drug Overdose Death Counts," Centers for Disease Control and Prevention, February 2, 2025.

95. Mohammad Fazel-Zarandi and Arnold Barnett, "Why Did US Urban Homicide Spike in 2020? A Cross-Sectional Data Analysis for the Largest American Cities," *Risk Analysis*, July 2024, 44:7, pp. 1616–29.

96. Scott Alexander, "What Caused the 2020 Homicide Spike?," *Astral Codex Ten*, June 29, 2022.

97. Rohit Acharya and Rhett Morris, "Why Did U.S. Homicides Spike in 2020 and Then Decline Rapidly in 2023 and 2024?," Brookings Institution, December 16, 2024.

98. Mbabazi Kariisa et al., "Drug Overdose Deaths, by Selected Sociodemographic and Social Determinants of Health Characteristics—25 States and the District of Columbia, 2019–2020," *Morbidity and Mortality Weekly Report*, July 22, 2022, 71:29, pp. 940–47.

99. Abby Goodnough, "Overdose Deaths Have Surged During the Pandemic, C.D.C. Data Shows," *The New York Times*, April 14, 2021, p. A8.

100. Kristin E. Schneider et al., "Volatile Drug Use and Overdose During the First Year of the COVID-19 Pandemic in the United States," *International Journal of Drug Policy*, April 2024, 126, Article 104371.

101. Douglas A. Wolf et al., "State COVID-19 Policies and Drug Overdose Mortality Among Working-Age Adults in the United States, 2020," *American Journal of Public Health*, July 2024, 114:7, pp. 714–22.

102. Nabarun Dasgupta et al., "Are Overdoses Down and Why?," Opioid Data Lab, September 18, 2024.

Notes (Chapter 8)

103. See, e.g., Stanton Peele and Archie Brodsky, *Love and Addiction*, Taplinger, 1975; Stanton Peele, *The Meaning of Addiction: An Unconventional View*, Heath, 1985; Stanton Peele and Archie Brodsky, *The Truth About Addiction and Recovery*, Touchstone, 2014; and Stanton Peele, *A Scientific Life on the Edge: My Lonely Quest to Change How We See Addiction*, Broadrow Publications, 2021.

104. Joint Economic Committee, "Long-Term Trends in Deaths of Despair," Social Capital Project Report 4-19, September 5, 2019.

105. Second Republican presidential debate, September 27, 2023.

106. See, e.g., Michael R. Gottfredson and Travis Hirschi, *A General Theory of Crime*, Stanford University Press, 1990; Delbert S. Elliott, "Environmental Factors Contribute to Juvenile Crime and Violence," in Amy E. Sadler, ed., *Juvenile Crime: Opposing Viewpoints*, 1997, Greenhaven Press, pp. 83–89; and Stephen Katembu et al., "Childhood Trauma and Violent Behavior in Adolescents Are Differentially Related to Cognitive-Emotional Deficits," *Frontiers in Public Health*, April 3, 2023.

107. See, e.g., George M. Zimmerman, *Impulsivity, Offending, and the Neighborhood: Investigating the Person-Context Nexus*, doctoral dissertation, State University of New York School of Criminal Justice, 2009.

108. Interview with Weldon Angelos, August 14, 2024.

109. "Perlmutter Statement on Safe Banking," press release from Rep. Ed Perlmutter (D–Colo.), December 7, 2021.

110. 18 USC 924(c).

111. "After Acquittal on State Charges, Defendant Pleads Guilty to Federal Gun Offense," press release from the U.S. Attorney's Office for the Western District of Virginia, July 15, 2022.

112. "Employee Shoots, Kills Suspect During Attempted Pot Shop Robbery in Covington," KING, March 17, 2022.

113. Jennifer Dowling, "'Absolutely a Hero': Security Employee at Covington Pot Shop Shoots, Kills Would-Be Robber," KCPQ, March 18, 2022.

114. 18 USC 924(c)(1)(A), 18 USC 924(j).

115. Donald J. Trump, "Executive Grant of Clemency," December 22, 2020.

116. Interview with Angelos.

Index

Abernathy, Ralph, 68
Acevedo, Art, 169, 171–72
Adams, Eric, 118
addiction, 19, 141, 213, 218, 219, 224, 238–39; alcohol and, 179, 223; cocaine and, 36; crack cocaine and, 82–84, 86, 88; marijuana and, 39, 40, 42, 45, 48, 51; opioids and, 35, 180; opium and, 24, 27, 33
African Americans, 4, 9–10, 15, 17–18, 20, 34–38, 50, 52, 53–76, 77–100, 80, 81–82, 85, 90, 92, 93, 96, 97–100, 103, 101–26
Agnos, Art, 185–87
Agricultural Adjustment Act, 132–33
Alabama, 48, 59, 64, 66, 67, 73, 152
Alameda County, California, 70–71
Alaska Supreme Court, 145
Albuquerque, 44–45
Albuquerque Journal, 45
Albuquerque Morning Journal, 44
alcohol, 28, 31, 223, 224, 226–27
alcohol prohibition, 19, 22, 35, 58, 131, 148, 174–76, 178–79, 181, 182–83, 218, 224
Alexander, Michelle, 98, 125
Allen, Charles, 124
Altomare, Timothy, 197
The America We Deserve, 12
American Civil Liberties Union, 16, 96–97, 165
American Conservative Union Foundation, 231

American Family Physician, 222
American Federation of Labor, 25
American Indian Religious Freedom Act, 145
American Magazine, 48, 50
American Revolution, 53, 57
Anderson, Charles, 21
Anderson, Richard, 77, 79, 80
Angelos, Weldon, 1–3, 10, 154–156, 239–241
Angell, Tom, 215
Anne Arundel County Police Department, 197
Anslinger, Harry J., 47–51, 132, 141
anti-Chinese agitation, 21–34, 68–69
Anti-Drug Abuse Act of 1986, 79, 85–86, 221
Anti-Drug Abuse Act of 1988, 78
Anti-Saloon League, 178
anti-Semitism, 81
"assault weapon" bans. *See* gun control.
AR-15 rifle, 186, 187, 191–92, 204, 227
Arizona, 45–46, 50, 113
Arizona Daily Star, 46
Arizona Republican, 45
Arkansas, 58, 66, 73
Associated Press, 174, 187
Atlanta, 64
Auerbach, Red, 85
Auld, Thomas, 53, 54
Austin, Texas, 43
Austin American, 43
Austin American-Statesman, 43, 44, 50

Index

Autry, Nikki, 160–63
Avila, Refugia, 45
ayahuasca, 146

Baier, Bret, 11
background checks. *See* gun control.
Bailey, Joseph W., 130–32
Bakalar, James B., 35, 36
Baltimore, 53, 172, 174, 233
Baltimore Sun, 198
Barcelona, 222
Barkow, Rachel, 113
Barnett, Arnold, 236
Barrett, Amy Coney, 140
Baskette, Floyd K., 49
Bate, Roger, 181
Baum, Dan, 82
Baumgartner, Frank, 91–92
Bee, Carlos, 71
Behrens, Jennifer, 75
Benitez, Roger, 143–44, 190
Berkow, Ira, 84–85
Bernhardt, Sarah, 34
Bias, Len, 84–85, 86
Biden, Hunter, 143, 215
Biden, Joe: and "assault weapons," 12, 188–191; and drug policy, 4–8, 10, 15, 78–81, 81, 90, 146–147, 164, 221; and gun control, 11–12, 141–143, 188–191, 198, 215–216, 228
Big Brothers of America, 37
Bingham, John, 60
Birmingham, Alabama, 48, 67, 106
black codes, 59–60
Black Attorneys of Legal Aid, 107
Black, Galen, 145
Black Guns Matter, 4, 106–107, 109
Black Lives Matter, 168
black markets: and corruption, 19, 86, 173–75, 182–83; drug hazards and, 178–82, 225–26; and guns, 193, 232; prices in, 164, 176–78; profits from, 8–9, 174–76; and violence, 19, 84, 88, 175–76, 226

Black Panthers, 71–72, 110
Blackstone, Mike, 205
Blocher, Joseph, 75
Bloomberg, Michael, 94–96, 112–14, 116–19
Boden, F.C., 42
Booker, Cory, 15
Boston, 84, 85, 233
Bowser, Muriel, 124
Brady Handgun Violence Prevention Act, 12, 120, 138
Bragg, Alvin, 108–09
Brennan Center for Justice, 229–30, 232
Breslin, Jimmy, 85
Briar, J.A., 68
Bronx, New York, 94, 114
Brookings Institution, 98–99, 231, 236
Brooklyn, New York, 82, 94, 119
Broward County, Florida, 204
Brown, Aaron, 211
Brown, John, 58
Brown, Willie, 72
Bruce-Briggs, Barry, 75
Bryant, A. Christopher, 132
Bryant, Steven, 170–71
Buck, Frank, 51
Budd, James, 25–26
Buford, Rivers H., 73–74
Buffalo, New York, 69, 200
Buffalo Courier, 69
buprenorphine, 225, 237
Bureau of Alcohol, Tobacco, Firearms, and Explosives, 195–96
Bureau of Internal Revenue, 136
Bureau of Justice Statistics, 121, 193
Bush, George H.W., 78, 90–91
Bush, George W., 3
Butler, Mac Sim, 68
Butterworth, James, 162

Calhoun, John C., 55
California, 14, 16, 21, 23, 25–27, 29–31, 41–42, 50, 70–72, 120, 134–35, 139, 140, 143–44, 146, 177, 183, 185–87,

Index

192, 194, 200, 206, 208, 209, 230, 231, 239, 240
California Assembly, 70–72, 185–87
California Senate, 23, 25, 71
California Supreme Court, 26–27, 30–31
Cameron, Daniel, 167
Campbell, Thomas E., 45
Campos, Isaac, 41, 51–52, 131
Canada, 9, 222
Capital Gazette (Annapolis), 197
Capone, Al, 175
Carroll, George, 148
Carroll v. United States, 148
carry permits. *See* gun control.
Carstairs, Catherine, 37
Cassell, Paul, 3, 154, 155
Center for Constitutional Rights, 114
Center for Gun Violence Solutions, 233,
Chan, Jie, 222
Chaney, James, 66
Charleston, South Carolina, 58
Chicago, 50, 102–03, 110, 136, 172, 175,
Chilton, Richard, 113
China, 26, 32
Chinatown, 24, 25, 29, 34, 43, 69
Chinese Exclusion Act, 29
Citrus County, Florida, 205
civil asset forfeiture, 91, 151–54
Civil Rights Act of 1866, 59–60
civil rights movement, 55, 64–68, 110
Civil War, 55, 59, 106
Cleveland, 85, 113
clemency, 3, 6–7, 10, 142, 143, 155, 156, 241
Clinton, Bill, 146
Clinton, Hillary, 9
Coca-Cola, 34
cocaine, 5, 6, 9, 17, 22, 31, 34–38, 40, 41, 43, 46, 52, 77, 79, 80, 82, 84–85, 87–88, 90, 154, 164, 169, 177, 179, 180, 190, 221; and insanity, 35–36; and superhuman strength, 35–36; and violence, 17, 35–38. *See also* crack cocaine.

Colfax, Louisiana, 62
Colfax massacre, 62–63
Colombia, 174
Colorado, 9, 48, 49, 51, 150, 177, 183, 193–94, 201, 208, 239
Congressional Black Caucus, 86
CompStat, 232–33
Connally, Ben, 128
Connecticut, 187, 198, 200, 207–09
Congress of Racial Equality, 66–67
constitutional law: Commerce Clause, 27, 130–38; cruel and unusual punishment, 154–56; double jeopardy, 153; due process, 13, 62, 105, 128–29, 151, 153, 198, 200–04, 209–10, 231; enumerated powers, 18, 129, 130–135, 137; equal protection, 30, 55, 62, 87–88, 105, 114, 116–18, 126; excessive fines, 153–54; federalism, 18, 131, 138, 214; freedom of speech, 146–47; Ninth Amendment, 104, 145; police power, 29–30, 33, 58, 129, 130–32, 136; privileges and immunities, 54–55, 60–61, 105, 145; religious freedom, 145–46, 183, 217; right to arms, 4, 7, 13, 14, 15, 19, 60–61, 63, 68, 73, 101–110, 120, 121, 125, 138–145, 147, 188, 191–192, 194–196, 197, 201, 204, 213–216, 239–241; search and seizure, 3, 19, 91–96, 99–100, 104, 112–19, 147–51, 160–62, 165–72; self-incrimination, 128–29; tax power, 34, 128–32, 134, 135–36
Controlled Substances Act, 6–7, 129, 133–135
Cooper, Vera, 213–15
Cornelia, Georgia, 159
corruption. *See* black markets.
Cosgrove, Myles, 166–67
Cotton, Tom, 14–15, 196–197
Cottrol, Robert, 57
Coulter, Ernest K., 37

COVID-19 pandemic, 235–38
Covington, Washington, 240
crack cocaine, 5, 6, 9, 18, 77–80, 81, 82–91, 100, 143, 146, 176, 215, 221, 229, 232. *See also* addiction, cocaine, drug control, mandatory minimum sentences, and violence.
crack house statute, 146–47, 221
Cramer, Clayton, 17
crime trends, 229–32, 235–36, 239
Crystal River, Florida, 205
The Crisis, 64
Cruikshank, William J., 62
Cruz, Nikolas, 186, 202
Culley, Halima, 152
Cummings, Homer S., 136

Darrow, Clarence, 65
Dasgupta, Nabarun, 237–38
Davis, James J., 49
Davis, William, 151
Dayton, Ohio, 198
Deacons for Defense and Justice, 66–67
Deady, Matthew, 30
death penalty, 10–11, 240
deaths of despair, 238
De Blasio, Bill, 118
Delaware, 5, 58, 187, 193, 221
Delaware Court of General Sessions, 58
DeLone, Carrie, 180
Dennison, James, 21
Denver, 47
DeSantis, Ron, 214
Detroit, 64, 109, 148
Diamond, Raymond, 57
Dillinger, John, 136
dimethyltryptamine, 146
District of Columbia, 31, 101–03, 104, 190, 191, 201, 220
District of Columbia v. Heller, 101–05, 191–92
Donohue, John J., 229
Douglass, Frederick, 17, 53–55, 64, 103
Douglass, William, 21, 23, 68–69

Dred Scott v. Sandford, 54–55
Driesell, Lefty, 85
drug control: arrests, 1–3, 18, 21, 50, 78, 82, 91, 92–99, 112, 121, 123, 149-50, 152–53, 160, 163, 172, 173, 176, 177, 182, 238; interdiction, 8, 151–52, 181–82, 163–64, 237; penalties, 1–3, 5–6, 9–11, 14, 21, 38, 44, 77–80, 86–91, 98, 100, 128, 154–157, 170, 239–240; raids, 21, 23, 24, 69, 82, 159–63, 165–72, 179. *See also* black markets, constitutional law, mandatory minimum sentences, racial disparities, and racism.
drug deaths, 164, 178–82, 218–26, 235–38
drug decriminalization, 6, 94, 95–96, 213, 224–26
Drug Enforcement Administration, 147, 164, 173–74
drug interdiction. *See* drug control.
drug legalization, 5, 6, 8–9, 14, 15, 16, 81, 95, 97, 120, 141, 146, 177–78, 183, 213–14, 225–27, 239–40
drug penalties. *See* drug control.
drug-sniffing dogs, 147–48, 151, 152
drug treatment, 81, 220, 224–25
Drug Policy Alliance, 15–16
drug use rates, 83–84, 97, 98, 164, 226
Duarte, Steven, 140
Du Bois, W.E.B., 55, 64
Duffield, George W., 23, 27
Duterte, Rodrigo, 10

Eastland, James, 80
Edison, Thomas, 34
Edwards, Edward I., 178–79
Ehrlichman, John, 81–82
Eighteenth Amendment, 179, 183, 224
Eighth Amendment. *See* constitutional law.
El Paso, 38–40, 43, 44, 46–48, 198
El Paso Herald, 38–40
El Paso Times, 38–40
Emerson, John, 54

Index

Employment Division v. Smith, 145–46
Epp, Charles, 92–93
Evening Herald (Albuquerque), 44–45
Enforcement Act of 1870, 62
Evers, Medgar, 66
Everytown for Gun Safety, 119
Evans, Lindsey, 240

Farrell, Jill, 124
Fastow, Andrew, 195
Fazel-Zarandi, Mohammad, 236
FBI, 120, 121, 123, 138, 174, 190–91, 195–96
Federal Bureau of Narcotics, 47–49, 51
Federal Firearms Act, 136
Feinstein, Dianne, 12, 186–191
fentanyl, 7, 9, 164, 179–182, 218, 221, 223, 225, 226, 237
Fifth Amendment. *See* constitutional law.
Filburn, Roscoe, 132–33
Finger, Henry J., 41–42
Finke, Jorge, 222
Firearm Owners' Protection Act, 11–12
Firearms Policy Coalition, 214–15
First Amendment. *See* constitutional law.
FIRST STEP Act, 9–10, 14, 90, 156
Fisher, George, 23, 37–38, 41, 50
Florida, 9, 57–59, 73–74, 186, 199–200, 201–05, 208, 213–15
Florida Mental Health Act, 205
Florida Supreme Court, 73–74
Floyd, David, 114–16
Floyd, George, 107, 236
Floyd v. City of New York, 114–18
Food and Drug Administration, 220
Foster, Warren, 70
Fourteenth Amendment. *See* constitutional law.
Fourth Amendment. *See* constitutional law.
Fox News, 9, 11
Franklin, Neill, 215
Freedmen's Bureau, 61, 105
Freedmen's Bureau Act, 59–60

French Revolution, 57
Fried, Nikki, 213–14
Friedman, Richard, 209
Friedman, Milton, 175–76
Freud, Sigmund, 34
Fugitive Slave Act, 53

Gaines, Joseph H., 32–33
Gallup, 15–16, 183, 187
Gambling, John, 113
Garcia, Patricia Ann, 171
Gardner, Bonita, 125
Garland, Merrick, 6
Gelacak, Michael, 89, 100
Gentry, Yvette, 167
Georgia, 36, 58, 60, 61, 159, 161
Georgia Supreme Court, 58
Gieringer, Dale, 41–42
Giuliani, Rudy, 94
Glen Burnie, Maryland, 197
Glover, Jamarcus, 165
Goines, Gerald, 169–73
Gold Rush, 27
Goldstein, Robin, 177–78
Gonzales v. O Centro Espírita Beneficente União do Vegetal, 146
Gonzales v. Raich, 134–35
Good, Stanley, 39–40, 47
Goodlett, Kelly, 168
Goodman, Andrew, 66
Gorsuch, Neil, 230
Government Accountability Office, 195–96
Gordonsville, Virginia, 64
Grand Rapids, Michigan, 148
Great Again, 13
Greene, Bill, 71
Greenlee, Joseph G.S., 72–73
Greenville, South Carolina, 68
Grinspoon, Lester, 34–36
gun control: arrests, 14, 68, 70, 103, 107–09, 112–14, 121–23; "assault weapon" bans, 12–13, 15, 16, 19, 119, 143–44, 185–92, 210;

Index

background checks, 12, 13, 19, 111, 119–21, 138, 188, 192–97, 210, 227, 228; bump stock ban, 13; carry permits, 2, 16, 56–59, 68–74, 105–10, 112, 138–39, 214, 227; handgun bans, 72–75, 101–05, 110, 187, 188, 190, 191, 211; magazine limits, 12, 16, 143–44, 192, 227; ownership licensing, 56–59, 73–74, 110–12, 136; penalties, 2–3, 68, 70, 102, 106, 108, 110, 121, 122–125, 142–143, 154–156, 195, 196, 228, 239–240; prohibited persons, 4, 120–123, 137, 139–145, 196, 213–216; red flag laws, 12, 13, 19, 119, 188, 197–210, 227, 234; registration, 11–12, 14, 16, 101–02, 110–12, 129, 135–36. *See also* constitutional law, racial disparities, and racism.
Gun Control Act, 74, 137, 141, 155
Gun-Free School Zones Act, 137–39
gun licensing. *See* gun control.
gun penalties. *See* gun control.
gun registration. *See* gun control.

Habersham County Board of Supervisors, 161
Habersham County, Georgia, 159, 160, 161, 163, 165
Habersham County Grand Jury, 160–65
Haitian Revolution, 57
Halbrook, Stephen P., 60, 61
Haley, Richard, 66–67
Hall, L.L., 46
Hankison, Brett, 166–68
handgun bans. *See* gun control.
handguns, 2, 14, 16, 58, 64, 65, 67, 68, 69, 70, 72–73, 74–75, 101–12, 113, 155, 166, 170, 185, 186–87, 188, 190, 191, 192, 204, 206, 211, 213–14
Hansell, Nicole, 215
Hargraves, Darrell, 122, 125, 228
harm reduction, 4, 16, 19–20, 218–28, 232–35, 238–39

Harpers Ferry, Virginia, 58
Harris, David A., 149
Harris, Kamala, 6, 8, 10, 12, 15, 191
Harris, Stanley, 79
Harris County District Attorney's Office, 170–71
Harrison Narcotics Tax Act, 34, 36–38, 47, 81, 129, 132
Hawaii, 139
Heller, Dick, 102
Helms, Jesse, 219
heroin, 7, 31, 82, 154, 164, 169–70, 177, 180, 181, 218–19, 221, 225, 226, 237
Ho, James C., 140
Honduras, 173
Horn, John, 160–61
Houston, 168–72
Houston Chronicle, 170, 171
Houston Police Department, 169, 171
Howard, Jacob, 60
Howard, T.R.M., 56, 68
How the Other Half Lives, 25
Hoyte, Oliver, 204
Hubbard, H.H., 68
Huberty, James, 185
Husak, Douglas, 4, 145, 182, 190, 216–217, 228
hydrocodone, 120, 179

Illicit Drug Anti-Proliferation Act, 146–47
Illinois, 54, 151, 187, 206
inchoate offenses, 216–17
Indiana, 154
Indiana Supreme Court, 154, 206, 207–09
Institute for Justice, 152
Internal Revenue Service, 128
International Opium Commission, 32, 33, 131
Iowa, 151
Irizarry, José, 173–74
Italians, 68–70

Index

Jackson, Jesse, 85–86, 110
Jackson, Keith, 90–91
Jackson, Robert H., 133
Jackson Lee, Sheila, 110–12
Jacksonville, Florida, 63
Jaeger, Kyle, 215
Jaynes, Joshua, 165–68
Jeffery, Frederick, 170
Jenkins, Sylvia, 79
Jim Crow, 55, 63, 73, 98, 125–26
Johnson, Alice Marie, 9–11
Johnson, Andrew, 60
Johnson, Nicholas, 67–68, 74–75, 110
Joint Economic Committee, 238
Joliet, Illinois, 151
Juárez, 38–39, 47

Kansas, 150
Kansas City, 92, 122, 125
Kansas City Star, 122
Kansas Highway Patrol, 150
Kanter v. Barr, 140
Kates, Don, 73
Kavanaugh, Brett, 190, 191
Kavanaugh, Christopher, 240
Keane, Peter, 172
Katz, Carl, 113
Kelly, Ray, 118, 94–95
Kentucky, 56–57, 161, 167
King, Martin Luther Jr., 17, 56, 67–68, 80, 103, 106
Kiro, John, 148
Kleiman, Mark, 231
Koch, Christopher, 36
Kopel, David, 73
Koper, Christopher, 192
Kraska, Peter, 165
Krasner, Larry, 109, 124–25
Kristof, Nicholas, 227–28
Ku Klux Klan, 59, 61, 62, 65, 66, 67, 68, 73
Kushner, Jared, 10

LaPierre, Wayne, 125
Laredo, 127–28
Las Vegas, 13, 186, 201
Latinos, 38–52, 94, 95, 99, 112, 114, 117–19
Leary, Timothy, 127–29, 132, 145
Leary v. United States, 128–29
LeBlanc, Bob, 203
Lee, George, 66
LePage, Paul, 218–20
Lenahan, John, 23–24
Levine, Harry G., 83, 94–95
Levitt, Steven, 229–32
Lewis, Edward J., 25
life sentences, 1, 9, 10, 15, 154, 156, 168, 230
Little, Sam, 108
Lodge, Henry Cabot, 32, 131
Long, Charles, 159, 162
Long Depression, 27
Long Island, New York, 83
Los Angeles, 29, 71, 82, 109, 172, 174
Los Angeles Times, 42
Louisiana, 59, 62, 66, 231
Louisville, Kentucky, 161, 165, 166, 167
Loyal Georgian, 60–61, 105
Lucero, Michael, 77
Lund, Robert, 155–56
Lyerly, John, 35–36
Lynch, Gerald, 156–57
lynching, 37, 61–64, 65

magazine limits. *See* gun control.
Maine, 120, 218–19
Manhattan, New York, 94, 108
Mann Act, 132
Mann, James, 33
mandatory minimum sentences, 1–3, 5–6, 9–10, 14, 77–79, 86–91, 100, 110, 124, 154–156, 196, 231, 240
Mapp v. Ohio, 113
Marihuana Tax Act, 50, 51, 128–129

Index

marijuana, 1–2, 6–9, 14–17, 22, 38–52, 81–82, 93–97, 110–111, 112, 127–129, 132, 134–135, 141–142, 145, 146, 147, 150, 152–155, 169–170, 177–178, 183, 213–215, 224, 237, 239–241; and banking, 9, 240; decriminalization of, 6, 94, 95–96, 224; early local and state bans on, 38–46; federal prohibition of, 6–7, 47–52, 128–129, 134–135, 240; and insanity, 39–40, 42, 44–46, 48, 51; legalization of, 6, 8, 9, 14, 15–16, 81, 95, 97, 100, 110-111, 120, 141, 146, 177–178, 183, 213, 214, 224, 239–240; medical use of, 6–8, 14, 38, 39, 40, 43, 44, 45, 120, 134–135, 141, 146, 152, 183, 213–214, 215, 239; Mexicans and, 17, 38–52; rescheduling of, 6–7, 9; and superhuman strength, 46–48; and violence, 38–41, 43–52, 141, 215
Marijuana Moment, 215
Marjory Stoneman Douglas High School, 186
Martinez, Cora, 21
Martinez, Enrique, 44
Martinez-Ales, Gonzalo, 234–35
Maryland, 55, 57, 59, 84, 85, 124, 139, 187, 197–200
Massachusetts, 38, 187
mass shootings, 13, 185–193, 197–203, 206–210, 233–234
Mattingly, Jonathan, 166–67
Maynard, Horace, 61
McDonald, Otis, 102–03, 110
McDonald v. Chicago, 102–03, 105, 110
McFadden, Martin, 113–14
McKinnon, Bill, 162
McNamara, Joseph, 186
McSwain, William, 221
Meany, Kyle, 167–68
Measure 110, 224–25
Medical Record, 36

methadone, 225, 237
methamphetamine, 152, 160, 162, 164, 170, 180, 237
Metzenbaum, Howard, 79
Mexicans, 38–52
Mexico, 9, 14–15, 38, 39, 41, 46, 47, 49, 127–28, 173, 176, 237
Miami, 8, 82, 173
Michigan, 148, 230
Mill, John Stuart, 217–18, 226
Millbrook, New York, 127
Milton, Florida, 213
Minneapolis, 236
Minnesota, 87, 88, 221
Minnesota Supreme Court, 87, 88
Miranda v. Arizona, 113
Miron, Jeffrey, 176–77
miscegenation, 24–25, 33–34, 49, 50, 63
Mississippi, 57, 59, 66, 67
Missouri, 54, 122, 125, 150
Monroe, James, 57
Monson, Diane, 134–35
Montana, 147
Montgomery, Alabama, 68
Montgomery County, Ohio, 159
Moran, George, 175
Morgan, Kevin, 204–05
Mulford Act, 70–72
Mulford, Don, 70–72
Musto, David F., 22–23, 37

NAACP Legal Defense & Educational Fund, 103–06, 109–10
naloxone, 218–20, 222, 223, 225, 237
National African American Gun Association, 106, 109
National Association for the Advancement of Colored People, 64–65, 68, 110
National Firearms Act, 129, 135–36, 189, 211
National Instant Criminal Background Check System, 120, 138
National Institute on Drug Abuse, 219

Index

National Institute of Justice, 193
National Labor Relations Act, 133
National Organization for the Reform of Marijuana Laws, 95, 147
National Rifle Association, 11, 12, 14, 72, 74, 125, 214
Native American Church, 145
Native Americans, 56–57, 145
Nealon, Joseph M., 40
needle exchange, 219–20, 223
Nevada, 120
New England Watch and Ward Society, 37
New Hampshire, 214
New Haven, Connecticut, 70
New Jersey, 49, 82, 139, 187, 191–92, 200, 230
The New Jim Crow, 95, 125–26
Newmerzhycky, John, 151–52
New Mexico, 44–45
New Orleans, 50–51, 58
New Orleans Republican, 61–62, 64
New Orleans Times Democrat, 36
Newsweek, 82–84
New York, 69, 70, 94, 95, 105, 106–09, 127, 128, 138–39, 187, 200, 206, 221, 230
New York (magazine), 95
New York City, 8, 24, 25, 70, 78, 82, 84, 85, 93–96, 99, 107, 108, 109, 112–19, 125, 221, 232
New York Civil Liberties Union, 115–16
New York Police Department, 93–96, 112–19
New York State Rifle & Pistol Association v. Bruen, 105–09, 112, 138–45
New York Times, 10, 24, 35, 47–48, 50, 66, 70, 82–83, 85, 119–20, 132, 145, 189, 209, 227, 236–38
New York Tribune, 36
Newsome, Roger, 150
Newton, Huey P., 71–72
Nicholas, Rhogena, 169–72
nicotine, 178, 223, 227

Ninth Amendment. *See* constitutional law.
Nixon, Richard, 81–82, 175
Noreika, Maryellen, 143
North Carolina, 35, 58–59, 61, 65, 91–92, 142
North Carolina Supreme Court, 59
NPR, 101–02

Oakland, California, 71–72, 77
Oakland Tribune, 42
Obama, Barack, 6, 13, 90, 192–193
Ochiuzzo, Matthew, 202–03
Ogg, Kim, 171
Ohio, 132, 150
Ohio v. Robinette, 150
Oklahoma, 142
On Liberty, 217–18
OnPoint NYC, 221–22
Operation Ceasefire, 233
opium, 17, 21–34, 38, 42, 43, 47, 49, 52, 130–132, 181
Oregon, 30, 93, 145, 177, 200, 208, 224–25
Orlando, 202
oxycodone, 179, 180
OxyContin, 180

Pacific Railroad, 27
Pacula, Rosalie Liccardo, 180
Paddock, Stephen, 201–02
Paducah, Kentucky, 63
pain medication, 31, 120, 179–82, 205, 213, 226, 238
Panter, Jeffrey, 202–03
Parker, Shelly, 101–03
Parkland, Florida, 186, 187, 198, 199, 202
Parris, Kendra, 203–05
patent medicines, 17, 22, 31, 34
Paterson, Van, 30
Payne, Sereno E., 32–33
Peele, Stanton, 238–39
Pennsylvania, 36, 93, 140, 180, 221
peyote, 145
Pfaff, John, 228

297

Philadelphia, 53, 109, 124–25, 172, 174, 193, 221, 233
Phoenix, 45
Phonesavanh, Alecia, 159, 161
Phonesavanh, Bou Bou, 159–63
Phonesavanh, Bounkham, 159, 161
plea bargaining, 2, 143, 240
police abuse, 50–61, 68–69, 91–96, 99–100, 112–19, 147–53, 159–63, 165–75
Pope Leo XIII, 34
Portland, Oregon, 93
Powell, David, 180
Printz v. United States, 138
Prison Fellowship, 231
prohibited persons. *See* gun control.
Project Exile, 125
Project Safe Neighborhoods, 125
Prosser, Benjamin, 107–08
Prosser, Gabriel, 57
Providence, Rhode Island, 221
public health, 3, 30, 34, 38, 104, 178, 209, 223, 227
public opinion: on drug policy, 8, 15–16, 183, 224; on gun control, 16, 119–120, 187, 193
Purdy, Patrick, 187
Pure Food and Drug Act, 31

Quinnipiac University, 187

racial disparities: in gun control, 3, 18, 53–75, 101–126; in the war on drugs, 3, 6, 18, 9–10, 15, 17–18, 77–100
racism: and drug control, 17, 21–52, 80–82, 85, 87–89, 96–97, 98–100, 168–169; and gun control, 17, 53–75, 105, 112, 117–118, 123–126
Raich, Angel, 134–35
Ramaswamy, Vivek, 238–39
RAND Corporation, 192, 194, 209, 210, 211
Range, Bryan, 139–40, 144

Range v. Attorney General, 139–40, 144
Rangel, Charles, 85–87, 99
Rathge, Adam, 41
Ravin v. State, 145
Reagan, Ronald, 14, 71–72, 79, 85, 86
Reconstruction, 55, 59, 63
red flag laws. *See* gun control.
Reed, Daniel, 51
Rehnquist, William, 137
Reinarman, Caig, 83
Religious Freedom Restoration Act, 146
Rhode Island, 221
Richmond, 57, 125
rifles, 11, 13, 59, 63–64, 65, 67, 73–74, 101–02, 135, 143–44, 185–92, 204, 211
Right on Crime, 231
Riis, Jacob, 25
Roanoke, Virginia, 240
Roberts, John, 141
Robinette, Robert, 150
Rogers, Don, 85
Rogers, James R., 23–24
Rogers, William P., 81
Romney, Mitt, 14–15
Roosevelt, Frankin, 50
Rossi, Marino, 70, 108
Rothwell, Jonathan, 98–99
Russo, Bill, 12
Rustin, Bayard, 67

Sacramento, 50
Safehouse, 221
Safe Streets, 233
Salt Lake City, 1, 24
San Bernardino, California, 186, 192
San Diego, 185, 209
San Francisco, 21–31, 43, 69, 72, 172, 185
San Francisco Board of Supervisors, 21–22, 23, 28, 69
San Francisco Chronicle, 27–29, 69
San Francisco Examiner, 21, 24
The Saturday Night Special, 74
Saturday night specials, 74–75, 190

Index

Scalia, Antonin, 104
Scheindlin, Shira, 116–18
Schell, Terry, 210
Scherr, Alexander, 209–10
Schwarzer, William, 77–78, 87
Schwerner, Michael, 66
Scott, Dred, 54–55
Scott, Phil, 221
Seattle, 240
Second Amendment. *See* constitutional law.
Second Amendment Protection Act, 214
sentencing reform, 9–10, 14, 80, 86, 90, 111, 156, 224
sex education, 222
Shanghai, 32, 33, 131
Sheridan, Peter, 191–92
Sherrill, Robert, 74
short-barreled rifles and shotguns, 135, 211
shotguns, 11, 61–62, 64, 67, 101–02, 102, 135, 169, 185, 211
Simmons, Justin, 151–52
Simpson, Charles R. III, 168
slave revolts, 17, 54–58
slavery, 53–60, 63
Smart, Rosanna, 210
Smiley, Glenn, 67–68
Smith, Alfred, 145
Smith, Jerry E., 142–43
Smith, Reginald F., 46–47
Smoking Opium Exclusion Act, 31–33, 130–32
South Carolina, 58, 59, 68, 73
Spain, 222
Stevens, John Paul, 134–35
Stewart, Martha, 195
Stockton, California, 25–26, 30–31, 187
stop and frisk, 18, 93–96, 99, 107, 108, 112–19, 125
Stowe, J.E., 46–47
Students for Sensible Drug Policy, 147
St. Valentine's Day Massacre, 175–76

substance abuse, 19, 165, 184, 212, 216, 235
Sugarmann, Josh, 186–87
suicide, 19–20, 48, 75, 178, 182, 198, 207–09, 211, 234–35
Sullivan Law, 70, 106, 108
Sumner, Daniel, 177–78
supervised drug consumption sites, 220–223, 225
Sutherland Springs, Texas, 186
Sutton, Lena, 152–53
Swanson, Jeffrey, 208–09
SWAT raids, 159–63, 165
Sweet, Henry, 65
Sweet, Ossian, 64–65

Taft, William Howard, 148
Tandy, Karen, 147
Taney, Roger, 54–55
Taylor, Breonna, 161, 165–68, 173
Temple, Jackson, 30
Terry, John, 113
Terry v. Ohio, 113–14
Tennessee, 58, 72, 73
Terrell, Joey, 160–61
Texas, 16, 38, 42–44, 45, 46, 50, 73, 127, 142, 210, 230, 231
Texas Public Policy Foundation, 231
Thirteenth Amendment, 55
Thomas, Clarence, 135, 109, 138–39
Thomas, Earnest, 66–67
Thonetheva, Amanda, 159, 161
Thonetheva, Wanis, 160, 163
Thornburgh, Richard, 78
Thurmond, Strom, 79, 80
Timbs, Tyson, 154
Timbs v. Indiana, 154
Tonso, William, 17
Toronto, 222
Toure, Maj, 4, 109, 125–126
traffic safety, 223
traffic stops, 91–93, 99–100, 147–53
Trost, Michael, 162

Trump, Donald, 4–5, 8–11, 12–13, 14, 90, 156, 164, 188, 195, 198, 214, 229, 241; and drug policy, 8–11, 156, 198; and gun control, 12–13, 198
Tucson Daily Citizen, 46
Turnbow, Hartman, 67
Turner, Nat, 58
Tuttle, Cody, 100
Tuttle, Dennis, 169–72
Tydings, Joseph, 141

Ulbricht, Ross, 10, 156–157
United States v. Cruikshank, 62–63
United States v. Daniels, 142–43
United States v. Duarte, 140
United States v. Lopez, 137–38
United States v. Rahimi, 140–41
University of Central Florida, 201
University of Chicago, 102
University of Minnesota, 49
U.S. Centers for Disease Control and Prevention, 178, 179, 180, 207, 220, 226, 234, 236
U.S. Congress, 5, 9, 11, 12, 14, 29, 31–33, 36–37, 47, 48, 53, 59–61, 63, 74, 79, 85–86, 87–88, 89, 90, 100, 110, 122, 127, 129, 130, 131–39, 141, 142, 145–46, 155–56, 187, 188, 214, 219
U.S. Court of Appeals for the D.C. Circuit, 104, 190
U.S. Court of Appeals for the 2nd Circuit, 118, 156
U.S. Court of Appeals for the 3rd Circuit, 140, 144
U.S. Court of Appeals for the 5th Circuit, 140, 142–43
U.S. Court of Appeals for the 8th Circuit, 137–38, 143
U.S. Court of Appeals for the 9th Circuit, 138, 140, 146
U.S. Court of Appeals for the 10th Circuit, 154–55
U.S. Customs and Border Protection, 174
U.S. Department of Agriculture, 46

U.S. Department of Defense, 210
U.S. Department of Justice, 7, 78, 112, 123, 125, 141–44, 154, 167, 192, 196, 215, 221, 240, 241
U.S. Office of National Drug Control Policy, 8
U.S. House of Representatives, 32, 51, 86, 90, 136
U.S. House Select Committee on Narcotics Abuse and Control, 85
U.S. House Ways and Means Committee, 49, 51
U.S. News & World Report, 83
U.S. Senate, 14, 32, 37, 49, 60, 78, 86, 90, 141
U.S. Senate Judiciary Committee, 79
U.S. Sentencing Commission, 87–90, 98, 121–22, 123
U.S. Supreme Court, 13, 16, 19, 30, 54–55, 62–63, 68, 70, 91, 102–110, 112, 113–114, 117, 129, 131–135, 137–141, 146–155, 166, 188, 191, 239
Utah, 14, 154, 156, 240

Vancouver, 222
vaping, 178, 223
Veracruz, 39
Velasquez, Chris, 201–03
Vermont, 221
Vesey, Denmark, 58
Vin Mariani, 34
violence: alcohol prohibition and, 175; drug prohibition and, 19, 84, 88, 175–76, 226; drug raids and, 159–63, 165–72; prediction of, 188, 197–207, 209–10, 233–34. *Also see* black markets, cocaine, crack cocaine, crime trends, and marijuana.
Violence Policy Center
Violent Crime Control and Law Enforcement Act, 5, 10, 12, 188
Virginia, 56, 57, 58, 64, 125, 240

Virginia Assembly, 56
Volkow, Nora, 219
Volstead Act, 183, 224
Volusia County, Florida, 208
Vratil, Kathryn, 150

Wales, William and Cora, 64
Walker, Kenneth, 166–67
Walker, Sam, 171
Wall Street Journal, 125
Warren, Earl, 113
Washington (state), 120, 177, 183, 187, 193–94, 239
Washington Post, 42
Watson, C. J., 36
Wells, Ida B., 55, 63–64, 67
Westchester County, New York, 82
Wheeler, Wayne B., 178–79, 182
White House, 81–82, 85, 90–91
Whitmore, Fannie, 21
Whren v. United States, 91, 147, 148–49
Wickard v. Filburn, 132–33

Wickersham Commission, 174–75, 182–83
Wilkins, Roy, 56, 64
Williams, Arizona, 45
Williams, Edward Huntington, 35–36, 46, 84
Williams, Robert F., 65–66, 67, 71
Willis, Gary, 197–98
Willis, Michele, 198
Wilson, Cory T., 140
Winchester rifle, 63–64
Winchester shotgun, 64, 185
Winkler, Adam, 190, 194–95
Wisconsin, 54, 159
Woodruff, Rosemary, 127
Workingmen's Party, 27
Wright, Hamilton, 33–34, 36–37, 42

xylazine, 179, 237

Zabriskie, B.J., 47
Zeoli, April, 199, 200, 207
Zola, Emile, 34